THE PEACE PALACE

The production of this book has been
partly made possible by the kind donations of
the following sponsors:

STICHTING ALGEMENE LOTERIJ NEDERLAND, THE HAGUE
SHELL INTERNATIONALE PETROLEUMMAATSCHAPPIJ B.V., THE HAGUE
M.A.O.C. GRAVIN VAN BYLANDT STICHTING, THE HAGUE
VAN DEN BERCH VAN HEEMSTEDE STICHTING, THE HAGUE
DE NATIONALE INVESTERINGSBANK N.V., THE HAGUE

THE PEACE PALACE

Residence for Justice – Domicile of Learning

by Arthur Eyffinger

THE
PEACE PALACE
1913-1988

The Peace Palace, Residence for Justice, Domicile of Learning
is a publication of the Carnegie Foundation in The Hague
and Inmerc BV in Wormer.

© 1988 Carnegie Foundation The Hague / Inmerc BV, Wormer

Photography: Jan den Hengst, Aarlanderveen
Besides the Carnegie Foundation, the International Court of
Justice, the Permanent Court of Arbitration and the Hague
Academy of International Law the following persons and
institutions supplied visual materials: Algemeen Rijksarchief,
The Hague (p. 52 below, 53, 132); T. M. C. Asser Instituut,
The Hague (p. 184); Andrew Carnegie Birthplace Museum,
Dunfermline (p. 37–48, 50); J. van Dongen, Koninklijke
Bibliotheek, The Hague (p. 179 middle); Chr. van Etten, Delft
(p. 90); Documentatiecentrum Bouwkunst, Amsterdam
(p. 59 above; back right); Gemeentearchief 's-Gravenhage,
The Hague (p. 54, 58 above, 82, 85); Max Koot, The Hague
(p. 126, 160); R. S. B. van Megen, The Hague (p. 144, 161 below);
Stichting Nederlands Foto- en Grafisch Centrum, Haarlem
(p. 93, 116 above, 122 above); Nederlands Letterkundig
Musuem, The Hague (p. 186); Nieuwe Kerk, Delft (p. 127);
Rijksvoorlichtingsdienst, The Hague (p. 19, 23, 25, 57 below,
58 below, 79, 91); Stedelijk Museum, Amsterdam (p. 109);
H. J. Stuvel, Leidschendam (p. 124 above); Vereniging voor de
Effectenhandel, Amsterdam (p. 74).

Cover: Aerial photo of the Peace Palace, 1984, Delta-phot.

Front endpaper: Cordonnier's final design for the Peace
Palace, here assimilated with the design for the layout of the
park, 1908, Thomas H. Mawson.

Back endpaper: The original design for the Peace Palace,
1906, Louis Cordonnier.

Lay out: Joop de Nijs gvn (Inmerc BV)
Art direction and cover design: Loek de Leeuw (Inmerc BV)
Type setting: Fotozetterij Steenbergen BV, Groningen
Lithography: Rommerts' en van Santen BV, Utrecht
Printing: BV Kunstdrukkerij Mercurius-Wormerveer
Binding: Binderij Callenbach BV, Nijkerk
Production: Inmerc BV, Wormer

ISBN 90 6611 331 6
NUGI 641

CIP-GEGEVENS KONINKLIJKE BIBLIOTHEEK, DEN HAAG
Eyffinger, Arthur
The Peace Palace: residence for justice, domicile of learning/
Arthur Eyffinger; [photogr. Jan den Hengst]. – The Hague;
Carnegie Foundation; Wormer: Inmerc. – Ill., foto's
Uitg. ter gelegenheid van het 75-jarig bestaan van het
Vredespaleis. – Met bibliogr., reg.
ISBN 90 6611 331 6 geb.
SISO 398 UDC 341.645.2 + 725.15 (492 × 2500)(091)
Trefw.: Vredespaleis; geschiedenis

Preface

The problems of peace and disarmament have puzzled man over the centuries. They have posed as much of an intellectual challenge as they have evoked political dispute. They have been the persistent battleground of idealists and realists, and have occasioned endless speculation.

There have been times – and not so long ago indeed – when the name of The Hague had a similar ring to that which Geneva has today and when, with a mixture of hope and scepticism, mankind looked to The Hague for a halt to the arms race. Twice, in 1899 and 1907, the worlds of diplomacy, learning and politics met around the Hague Woods and the Binnenhof in what was then called "The Parliament of Man", in conferences that may be deemed the first meetings ever of the civilized world for the specific ends of general disarmament and the peaceful settlement of dispute.

Ever since, the flame has been kept alive and up to the present day the reputation of The Hague abroad is often linked to the "World Court", which is

generally considered the most prominent remaining result of the Peace Conferences. Nevertheless, illustrious though it may be, the *International Court of Justice* is only one aspect of the legendary "Oeuvre de La Haye", as it was called at the time. There is indeed much more to it: the Permanent Court of Arbitration, the Pride of the early twentieth century; the Hague Academy, the breeding ground of internationalists; and the Carnegie Library, still one of the great collections in the field of international law. And all of this centres around that charming *fin-de-siècle* building, both hub and symbol of peace studies, the Peace Palace, administered by the trustees of Carnegie's extraordinary gift, the Dutch *Carnegie Stichting*.

Now, seventy-five years after the gates were first opened to the public, the present Board of Directors feels it appropriate to have the history of the Palace presented in a comprehensive study from the early days of the Peace Conferences, through the building years of the "Temple", to the actual functioning of the various institutions that are housed in the grounds. In a book that may serve as a well-deserved homage to peace-makers and as a reference work to modern man, recording the story of idealism and disillusionment, of expectations wrenched from failure – in short, of man's struggle for progress. The book tells the story of an epoch, highlighting the ideals of artists as reflected in wall-pannellings, mosaics and the charms of the park. It is meant as a tribute to the fact that the "Oeuvre de La Haye" is still very much alive and Holland is still as eager as it was almost a century ago in trying to contribute to the furtherance of peace and world order.

Finally, I would like to express my sincerest thanks to the author, Dr. Arthur Eyffinger, without whose efforts this project would have been impossible.

MAX VAN DER STOEL, PRESIDENT

Contents

Nicholas II (1868–1918), the last Russian Czar (1894–1917). The portrait by Sophie Hirschmann (1871–1937) hangs in the Small Court Room of the Palace.

The Czar's Rescript

On Wednesday, 24 August 1898, at their weekly reception at the Foreign Office in St. Petersburg, the ambassadors and ministers of the nations accredited to the Russian Court stood gaping at each other in blank amazement. In their hands they found a written statement in the name of Czar Nicholas II presented to them by his Foreign Minister, Count Muraviev, to be forwarded to their respective governments. The past twenty years, the circular letter stated, had seen the steady increase all over Europe of ever-more sophisticated armament. The financially excessive burdens that went along with it had put an intolerable check to the upward march of humanity and the social and intellectual development of the nations. Indeed, armament had grown into a never-ending threat to the very ideals towards which all man's efforts should be directed, namely the maintenance of general peace. The Czar now wished to emphasize the desirability of putting a definite check to this alarming process. Swords had to be beaten into ploughshares and spears into pruninghooks, or rather quick-firing artillery into locomotives and bridges. To meet these ends he actually proposed the assembled nations should send representatives to an international conference which should occupy itself exclusively with these grave problems of world peace and disarmament.

The message went around to Berlin, Paris, London and Washington – and prompted a mixture of disbelief, scepticism and joy. Scepticism prevailed though. How noble and magnanimous were the motives really that prompted this absolute despot and monarch of the world's largest military power, who never for a moment felt the pressure from constitution or parliament, to call for peace? *Realpolitiker* all over the world were quick in detecting what they saw as the reasons proper that gave birth to this spontaneous peace crusade. The very repute of Count Muraviev, they held, spoke against all too lofty notions. And as for Nicholas himself, he was, according to Andrew White, the American Ambassador in Berlin: "a kindly man, wishing in a languid way the good of his country … but the indifference to everything about him evident in all his actions, his lack of force even in the simplest efforts for the improvement of his people, and, above all, his yielding to the worst elements in his treatment of the Baltic provinces and Finland, did not encourage me to believe that he would lead a movement against the enormous power of the military party in his vast empire".

Then, who really was the author and what was behind all this: the theories of the publicist de Bloch, the common sense of the diplomat de Martens, the unscrupulous Muraviev himself or, as White suggests in his autobiography, that grand old man of Russian politics, the aged Pobedonostzev?

Whatever may have been the case, the reservations were understandable, to say the least. Even nowadays, it is not easy to disentangle the blending of self-interest and purely humanitarian objectives which prompted the call at the time. Many suggestions have been made in the course of decades. It is true that the financial burdens of the armaments race did exhaust the Russian treasury. Indeed, during those very weeks the Commander-in-Chief

Count Michail Nikolajewitsch Muraviev (1845–1900). He became Russian Foreign Secretary in 1897.

Kuropatkin and Finance Minister Witte had discussed with Czar Nicholas and Count Muraviev the replacement of their somewhat antiquated artillery by more sophisticated but highly expensive material. This alone may easily have prompted a debate of a more philosophical nature, such as whence came this necessity for the replacement of the old equipment? The answer then must be that it came about from sheer fear; from anxiety regarding that highly impressive war machine that was steadily building up along Russia's western borders. We refer to the unification of the German nation in the *Reich* by that formidable politician and man of genius, *Kanzler* Otto von Bismarck.

In Bismarck we come upon the unchallenged master of European politics in the second half of the century. Not since Napoleon in the opening years of the century had Europe known so potent a force. In less than thirty years Bismarck had succeeded in rallying the former petty kingdoms, which only the other day had seemed but haphazardly thrown together, into a most formidable unity. Not only had the fierce Prussian spirit of reckless opportunism taken hold of the military, it had also completely won over German science. It had bent seemingly inexhaustible reservoirs of energy and ambition into the unequivocal support of an awakening patriotism. It had resulted in the rise of a military, naval, cultural and colonial power of the first order.

In recent years, moreover, the Russian outlook had turned for the worse as another potent force had come to manifest itself in Germany in no less a person than Emperor Wilhelm II himself. Eager to make a foreign policy of his own, Wilhelm, in 1890, had forced Bismarck to resign. Since then, Muraviev felt, the equilibrium of international politics was no longer to be relied upon. With Bismarck discarded, the checking of Emperor Wilhelm's apparent ambitions and of his insistence on *Welt-*

macht could no longer be taken for granted. Once the impulsive *Kaiser* was given room to upset the unstable balance and the ingenious network of treaties neatly woven by his Foreign Minister in past decades, even the Holy Alliance of the Habsburgs, Romanovs and Hohenzollerns which formally held Europe's absolute empires of Austria, Russia and Germany together, would soon prove a mere scrap of paper. Now, on 30 July 1898, Bismarck had died. His death was generally felt to be the end of an era and Muraviev did not fail to appreciate its impact. Russia, Muraviev knew, was in no position to withstand a German onslaught.

This latter consideration, however, was appreciated on both sides of the border, by Muraviev and his German counterpart, von Bülow, alike. The first remonstrance to the Russian circular letter, interestingly enough, came from Berlin, protesting that no armament could be called excessive which would guarantee peace and that no German felt its burden. The bare statistics of armament production of the day enable us to evaluate the national efforts involved.

1898	National Revenue*	Army	Navy	Education
Russia	230	43	11	4
Germany	70.5	30	6	12
Great Britain	106.5	19	21	11.5
France	136.5	25.5	11.5	8.5
Austria/Hungary	101.5	15	1.5	3.5

* in pounds (millions)

Undoubtedly, these figures played a role in the Russian considerations. Yet these were certainly not the only reasons which prompted Nicholas' initiative. Ethical reflections also played a role. If the step were deemed uncharacteristic of the Czar by observers from the West, it still came within the tradition of Romanov politics. It was Alexander I, who in 1804, in the midst of the Napoleonic turmoil had made the suggestion that after the general war

Left: Otto von Bismarck (1815–1898), the "Iron Chancellor" (Chancellor of Prussia, 1862–1890, "Reichskanzler", 1871–1890). He was the epitome of the reactionary, the unificator of the German "Reich" and the personification of its power politics in the late 19th-century.

Bernhard von Bülow (1849–1929), the German under-secretary for Foreign Affairs and later "Reichskanzler" (1900–1909). A man of eloquence and tact, though unable to put a halt to Emperor Wilhelm's ambitions.

Wilhelm II (1859–1941), the whimsical German Emperor. In the photo he is flanked by the Austrian Emperor Franz Joseph I (1830–1916), a level-headed, somewhat narrow-minded man, who was never too successful in his foreign policy throughout his long reign of almost seventy years.

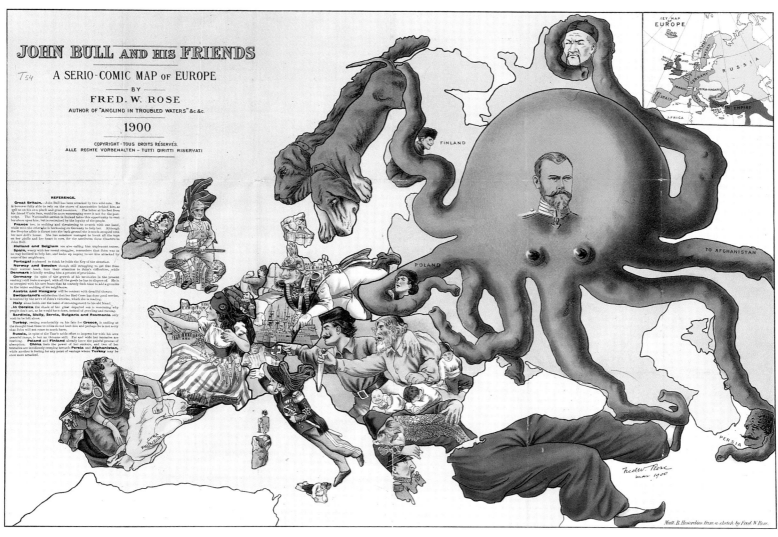

A rather cynical portrayal of European politics around the turn of the century.

and Napoleon's downfall the nations of Europe should unite in a treaty which would determine "the positive rights of nations ... (and) assert the obligation of never beginning war until all resources which the mediation of a third party could offer have been exhausted". On such principles, he maintained, one could proceed to a general pacification, and give birth to a league of which the stipulation would form, "a new code of the law of nations ..."

It is true that no pressure whatever from public opinion made itself felt in the austerity of Nicholas' palace. Still, one of the most eloquent and best documented assaults on the current system of international politics of recent years had come precisely from Russia. It was Count de Bloch, banker and pacifist, who in 1892 published an impressive and widely read six-volume work on future war, in which he protested against the barbarity of modern warfare and the utter self-destruction to which armament *à l'outrance* would ultimately lead man. The Czar was rumoured to have been strongly influenced by de Bloch's works – through summaries presumably, for they were extremely voluminous.

Nor was Russia totally isolated from the trends of public opinion which manifested themselves in the Western World. The Czar himself had a perfect command of French and English and kept in touch with events through the modern media. One of his cabinet ministers, de Basily, had recently attended the 1896 Budapest Conference of the Inter-parliamentary Union, the influential assembly made up by delegates from most European and American parliaments. He had become very impressed by the call for disarmament. Therefore a genuine stroke of goodwill also played its role.

The Replies

Though admittedly scepticism prevailed, not all nations, to be sure, answered the call in the averse or reserved German manner. The replies that came in from Western democracies at least showed more courtesy and nuance. The first to put in an official answer was the United States, by means of an oral acceptance in the most cordial terms from its Ambassador. The event actually constitutes a landmark in America's foreign policy, for it was on this occasion that the United States first abandoned its policy of splendid isolation. Admittedly, the armaments and navy built up by the former colony were not yet of any real impact on world politics. Still, the increasing capitalism and rapidly expanding international trade had opened the eyes of United States politicians and captains of industry to the world markets and had already resulted in the conflict with the Spanish over Cuba and the Philippines. The young triumphant republic, as Carnegie preferably

called it, was on the brink of entering the concert of nations and colonizing powers; it was soon to become a power to be reckoned with.

In an immediate response to the Russian idea from Britain, Balfour, First Lord of the Treasury and leader of the House of Commons, expressed his "warm sympathy with and approval of the pacific and economic objects in view", but it was only on 24 October that Prime Minister Lord Salisbury ventured to reply officially. The extreme costliness of modern warfare and the horrible carnage which ensued, he stated, had long served as a serious deterrent to war, but along with it the burdens imposed thereby upon the nations had produced feelings of unrest and discontent. He therefore promised Britain's full co-operation to a conference intent on discussing "the most effective methods of securing the *continuance* of general peace and of putting *some* limit on the constant increase of armaments". The words italicized by us clearly show the prudence exercised by their author.

There was indeed cause for circumspection, since from the very beginning critics in the leading European journals showed that the circular letter left ample room for misinterpretation. Accordingly, as early as 4 September, the *Journal de Pétersbourg* published an official communication to the extent that what the Czar had in view was not so much a general and instantaneous disarmament, as had been suggested in the western press and to which, as was generally felt, there were insurmountable problems, but rather a united effort finally to bring about some downward tendency, at least in the yearly increase in expenditure on weapons. Nevertheless, even at St. Petersburg, most members of the Diplomatic Corps deemed the proposal "visionary and Utopian, if not partaking of Quixotism", as it was put in a despatch from the American Ambassador dated 9 November. The armaments problem was generally

felt to contain two aspects: first the strictly *economic* issue of the absorption of men and resources for purely military purposes to the detriment of national wealth and prosperity; second the *humanitarian* aspect, looking toward a future universal peace. The latter, however, was generally considered the dream of philanthropists rather than the attainable ends of State policies. It was only to be hoped, one could hear in circles of politicians, that undue enthusiasm for the humanitarian cause would not obscure the gravity of the economic problem. These were no idle apprehensions, as soon became evident, for – ironically enough – if anything helped to obscure the perspective of the Czar's initiative in high political circles it was the unequivocal adoption of the idea by large parts of the world peace movement.

In this introductory chapter we must draw attention to the incentives of this movement, which truly was a mainstream of public thought in the years under consideration.

Peace Ideals

Man's views on the issues of war and peace fairly reflect his state of sophistication in the long process of intellectual growth towards political consciousness. In early classical times war was considered the natural state of man. Peace, if defined at all, constituted the sparse intervals between inevitable outbursts of violence. In the ideology of the Homeric era military accomplishments indeed were felt to be the sublimation of man's virtues, granting him fame – if not downright immortality. Interstate relations were long taken to be necessarily hostile. The first glimmerings of diplomacy in the Greek commonwealth, the *proxenia*, took a long time to arrive and in their turn by centuries outdate the *amphictyones*, being the first known formal interrelations of States on terms of peaceful coexistence. The same holds good, incidentally, for notions of arbitration and mediation as a means of non-military settlement of disputes. In due time, how-

Left: Lord Salisbury (1830–1903), for more than twenty years the undisputed leader of the Conservative party and the great antagonist of the liberal Gladstone. Prime Minister and Foreign Secretary from 1895.

"The Scarecrows of World Peace", featuring Uncle Sam and John Bull and the minor characters Turkey and Italy.

De vogelverschrikkers van den wereldvrede

ever, formal agreements as to the submitting of differences to third parties became the integral part of peace treaties. From then on, gradually, humanitarian aspects came to the fore. Thus the appointment of champions to represent the State was just another means of limiting conflict – and consequently bloodshed. These considerations prevailed the more as the grim effects of increasingly sophisticated armaments made themselves felt. The Erasmian adage *bellum dulce inexpertis,* war is sweet to him who has never experienced it, ultimately dates back to the lyrics of Pindar. Similarly, Thucydides was the first to point out the generally brutalizing and debasing impact of war. Reason, morals, the very preservation of orderly life called for peace. Yet even to Plato war was but the predictable outcome of the natural growing process of States. Likewise, Aristotle characterized warfare as just another means of acquisition in the same category as hunting and fishing, but he also insisted that it should aim for peace.

Interstate relations received a new impetus from the Alexandrian campaigns: apart from widening the horizons they resulted in the formation of leagues of States of a multiplicity and intensity never experienced before. Meanwhile, influential philosophic schools like the Cynics, Stoics and Epicureans advertized the uselessness of weapons. But at this juncture Rome took over.

For all its military glory, Rome did not do much to further the cause of peace of its own accord. Grotius for one, in his "Prolegomena" to *De Jure Belli ac Pacis,* quotes authors such as Cicero, Sallustius, Tacitus and Seneca embracing ideas of peace, arbitration and that order, but everyday reality was quite different. Preconditioned, in Virgil's words, to rule mankind by sheer power and grimly set on conquering the world, Rome saw the doors of Janus' Temple closed only twice in half a millennium. To the strict Roman, as to the Spartan before, growth and expansion were imperative to survival. The *Pax Romana* of later centuries provided for political stability, administrative orderliness and social rest to an extent virtually unparalleled, but it did not really alter theory. As late as the fourth century the expert author on military matters, Vegetius, jotted down the adage: *qui desiderat pacem, praeparet bellum.*

All this changed with the coming of Christianity – that is, in theory, and then initially. Christ preached the abolition of all violence and his early followers lived up to the standard. But soon they were in their turn led to victory *in hoc signo.* As the Roman Empire collapsed it was the Church that set out to preserve the values of classical tradition amidst the barbaric onslaught. Pursuant to political pressure, idealism must needs give in somewhat: issues were restated, views modified. Obviously, lasting peace was unattainable, as war would always claim its place: hence the theory of the *just war.* As St. Augustine put it: war was the price to be paid for peace – and this goal its very justification. For many centuries to come, Christian warriors were thus ordered to fight for the dawning of peace in the long, long term ...

With the breakdown of central authority and the increase in feudal strife, new means were found to limit the grim effects of war. Warfare was "humanized" in restricting its most abasing atrocities. To protect agriculture and trade whole categories of men were exempted from war in the "Peace of God". Similarly, in the "Truce of God" violence was forbidden on certain days. And at the edge of all this, "radical heretics" such as the Cathars and Hussites fought their embittered rear-guard actions, insisting on the stricter observance of humanitarian principles. Mostly in vain, of course, for man has always been more resourceful in checking the impact of his shortcomings than in anticipating them.

It was during this period that the first attempt at a proper world organization as a means of warranting peace was made. It was the Paris jurist Pierre Dubois who, as far back as 1305, formulated regulations for a United Europe. United, admittedly, under the French king, and mainly to fight better the Mussulmen. Still, fresh ground was broken and in subsequent decades we meet similar ideas in such varying works as Dante's *De Monarchia,* the *Arbre de Bataille* of Honoré Bonor and Paduan Marcilius' *Defensor Pacis.* In due time even kings adhered to the idea, such as George Podiebrad of Bohemia and – best-known of all – Henry IV of France who, around 1600, had his minister de Sully work out a *Grand Dessein* ("Great Design") for a truly Christian republic covering most of the then known monarchies and republics (with the notable exception of the Austrian Emperor!) and provided with an army and navy to which all contributed and with a council of sixty empowered to decide all disputes. A similar idea, though distinctly more idealistic and less strictly aimed at political revenue, is found twenty-five years later in Crucé's *Le Nouveau Cynée* of 1623, that seriously projected the ending of all warfare through arbitration by an assembly, and had Venice in mind as the capital of a true league of nations. Curiously enough, the greatest authority of the period in the field of international affairs does not quite fit into this picture. Hugo Grotius, for all his pleas for arbitration and international conferences to settle disputes – which for that matter have probably most affected the practice of international law in subsequent ages – presumably never seriously considered the idea of an international league.

Still, the idea had become firmly rooted and in the course of subsequent centuries spread among scholars, politicians and military men alike. Among numerous projects by scholars such as Campanella, Zouche, Comenius and the Quaker William Penn, whose *General Diet* was a judicial body mainly, undoubtedly the most interesting was the *Projet de Paix perpétuelle* (1712–1716) of the Abbé de Saint-Pierre, who influenced profoundly Rousseau and was backed by Voltaire, Swift and Hume, to name only some of his adherents. His project in fact sought to perpetuate the settlement effected by the 1713 Treaty of Utrecht and to settle controversies between nations by pacific means. It projected a perpetual alliance of some nineteen sovereign States for their mutual security against both foreign and civil war, provided for a permanent seat in Utrecht and incidentally also covered the field of private law so as to further international trade.

The closure of the 18th century saw two more projects developed by prominent thinkers. The first originated with the British jurist Jeremy Bentham; it was devised in 1789 but only published posthumously in 1849. Its most typical aspect is seeking to avoid the scourge of war by means of a permanent congress that should sit as an international court of justice and to which all nations should send two delegates. Public opinion, Bentham maintained, would enforce obedience and eventual non-compliance would be punished by simply banning the refractory State from the congress.

The second plan came from no less a man than Immanuel Kant who, in 1795, published his *Zum ewigen Frieden*. A first condition in his scheme was that all members of his league of nations should have a republican constitution. Kant's feeling was that if the citizens are themselves made responsible for any burdens and calamities that come over them from war, they will less easily rush into it. Republican, incidentally, is here not to be confounded with democratic: by it Kant meant any form of government limited by a popular representation. The second condition he made was that the public law of Europe should be founded upon a "Confederation of Free States". Two years later, in his *Metaphysik der Sitten* he coined the term "General Congress of Nations" for this conference. In this, for the rest, he did not have in mind an indissoluble union along the American model, but a formal league only, of which both meeting and duration depended entirely on the sovereign wills of the league members.

At the opening of the 19th century, therefore, there were several feasible models at hand for the unification of Europe and the final dismissal of war.

Either the Anglo-Saxon judicial schemes, Penn's diet and Bentham's court, or the continental more politically oriented designs of de Sully, Saint-Pierre and Kant would do in their own way, always provided the presence of political willpower. It was precisely the absence of the latter, which as centuries passed by had made political observers grow pessimistic as to its feasibility, and for that matter of the intellectual progress of man in general. Accordingly, though similar schemes, and indeed more detailed ones were submitted from different angles in the decades preceding the Hague Conferences, they did not really affect everyday politics. Neither William Ladd's *Congress of Nations* (1840) on the American model, nor Bluntschli's *Federation* (1878) along the lines of the German unification into the *Reich*, or for that matter Lorimer's scheme for an *International Government* in Geneva, for all their merits, invited any serious debate. Pressure, so much was for certain, had to be brought in from other angles. Interestingly enough, this is exactly what happened, and the very way in which it was brought to bear upon the matter may be deemed typical of the period.

The 19th Century Peace Movement

In the previous survey, however succinct and incomplete, we have met most of the arguments put forward through the ages to stop wars and put a check to the armaments spiral: strictly religious ones next to socio-economic ones, those prompted by opportunism along with others from sheer conviction. Ideologies and strategies changed with time and were dependent on the issues at stake, be they either the short-term goals of ending an ongoing war or preventing an impending one, or the long-term objective aiming at the betterment of the world order. One thing is for certain though: all these efforts are found strikingly intensified in the century leading up to the Hague Conferences, not surprisingly to reach their apogee in those culminating years of the armaments race that would finally discharge in the "Guns of August" 1914.

If anything, it was the carnage of the Napoleonic war that gave rise to the simultaneous outburst of peace societies to be signalled in Britain, the Continent and the United States alike from 1815 onwards. In the Anglo-Saxon world it was, traditionally, the Quaker and Memnonite sects that were organized in "friends for peace societies" – just as they were active in the antislavery campaigns. On the Continent pacifists, as a rule, steered a more practical course and mainly criticized the deleterious effects of war on the economy and human intellectual development.

Whatever it was that occasioned pacifism though, the movement soon outgrew its original impulses. Indeed, its expansion marks a major social phenomenon of the period. In 1829 the Genevan reformer J. J. Sellon was the first in Europe to organize a *Société de la Paix*. Seventy years later inter-

Immanuel Kant (1724–1804), the author of a short treatise "Zum ewigen Frieden" (1795), discussing world peace on the basis of a "Confederation of Free States".

national efforts had resulted in some hundred flourishing peace societies all over the world, registered at the *Bureau International de la Paix* in Bern, the movement's undisputed headquarters: the word "Pacifism" had been officially coined.

In this maturing process of the peace movement three phases are discernible. Interestingly enough, they roughly parallel the systematic establishment of similar idealistic movements such as temperance activists, educational and language reformers and suffragettes. Predictably, the first phase, up to the middle of the century, is characterized by resistance to violence on principle, which often sprang from the profound abhorrence of war as essentially contradictory to Christian tenets. In due course the more practical, and mainly socio-economic motives increased. These resulted in the first international conferences, held in Brussels and Paris in 1848–1849.

In the second phase, covering the third quarter of the century, and with the absolute non-resistance movement undermined by incidents such as the Crimean War and the almost simultaneous struggles for unification in Italy, Germany and the United States, in which all had to choose sides one way or the other, economic and strictly philosophical issues came to the fore. Men like Richard Cobden, Victor Hugo, Alexis de Tocqueville and Guiseppe Garibaldi formed the opinion of this generation. The increase in international contacts also prompted the founding of major organizations. Thus, in 1867, the *Ligue Internationale et Permanente de la Paix* was founded in Paris by Frédéric Passy, duplicated the same year by the *Ligue Internationale de la Paix et de la Liberté* in Geneva. In the following year a separate women's league was set up.

A highly interesting issue in these decades is the relation of the peace movement to growing socialism, Marxism and the First International, and

to trade union activists. Liberal bourgeois thinking often clashed here with militant nihilism in matters of conscription and civil disobedience. With the entering of socialism into parliament though, the wide gulf as a rule soon shrank and out of decades of apparent cacophony there arose finally the positive intention of united action.

The third phase, broadly covering the period from the French-German War to the First World War, saw the further ramification of peace societies within nations not involved before, intensive campaigning, often coined as Peace Crusades, and the publishing of major theoretical treatises by some highly influential authors. Thus, Scandinavia and Italy were opened to pacifist ideals; Hodgon Pratt, initiator of the *English International Arbitration and Peace Association* established sister groups abroad and William Stead and G. H. Perris were to follow in his footsteps. Likewise, students in Paris reoriented French pacifism through their *La Paix par le Droit*. Among the authors were Germany's Bertha von Suttner (*Die Waffen Nieder*, 1889, translated into sixteen languages at the end of our period) and Alfred Fried (*Friedens-Katechismus*, 1895), Poland's Jean de Bloch (*Der Zukunftskrieg*, 1892), Britain's Norman Angell (*The Great Illusion*, 1910) and such widely differing Russians as Leo Tolstoy and Ivan Novikoff. The movement produced spell-binding literature, academic masterpieces and scientific analyses on military techniques and the likely outcome of modern warfare. Besides, new lines of argument were developed which also spoke of the growing political maturity of pacifism. No longer were total and instant disarmament its major goals, but rather the gradual outlining of a new system of international law which through a network of intergovernmental agreements would provide lasting international security by means of tribunals, neutrality treaties and – keyword of the period – the

settlement of dispute through arbitration. At least until this system prevailed, and men like Passy envisioned this would take seventy-five years or more, arms were accepted as instrumental and indeed necessary for peacekeeping.

An important step was made in 1889 with the creation, again at Bern, of the Interparliamentary Union, organizing periodic conferences for members of national electoral bodies. Here, Nobel Prize winners of later years such as Frederic Bajer of Denmark, Henri La Fontaine of Belgium and Albert Gobat of Switzerland co-ordinated international pacifism. Two years later the International Peace Bureau was set up here. Pursuant to the enormous coverage of von Suttner's, Fried's, Bloch's and Angell's bestsellers and all ensuing publicity, and due also to the less radical outlook and more coherent organization of the movement, many now crossed the borderline, joined the ranks and underwrote pacifist ideals. Among these were two undisputed champions of capitalism, Alfred Nobel and Andrew Carnegie. It was the former's Will of 1896 and the latter's many gifts, culminating in the Carnegie Endowment of 1911 which lent prestige and gave the badly needed funds to the movement. In their footsteps, Henry Ford was to launch a peace mission. Thus, around the turn of the century pacifism could no longer be ignored. In a way, therefore, Nicholas' initiative was carried on the wave of a changing tide. And whatever may be thought of the outcome of the two Hague Conferences, the very fact of their being launched is momentous, as it implied the final, formal acceptance in the high world of politics and diplomacy of the issues hammered out for decades in the numerous peace societies.

Still, the Conference of 1899 was an experiment. Though not quite unprecedented, it was unparalleled in many respects. To be sure, so-called Peace Conferences had been held throughout the centuries. As a matter of fact, they had determined the structure of European politics and the balance of power for ages. New pages of European history had been turned at Westphalia in 1648, Utrecht in 1713, Vienna in 1814 and, to a lesser degree, Paris and Berlin in 1856 and 1878 respectively. Still, each of these conferences owed their very existence to a

The Congress of Berlin (1878), dominated by Otto von Bismarck, solved an international crisis by satisfying the British naval and Austrian territorial interests. In the picture one recognizes Bismarck and Disraeli among others.

Alfred Nobel (1833–1896), the inventor and producer of all sorts of explosives. In his will he left his wealth to found the Nobel Institute. The Peace Prize was instigated by Bertha von Suttner.

specific war, and merely aimed at the conclusion of a given controversy. For all alliances made, any device for establishing lasting peace, any notion for creating such a thing as a permanent representative body surveying international law and its impact on inter-governmental relations had been virtually absent up till then, that is with the possible exception of the Conference of Paris in 1856.

Keen observers had spotted the dawn of a new era though and the first glimmerings of a true international order in a new type of conference held in Geneva in 1864, St. Petersburg 1868 and Brussels 1874, and discussing war customs. These gatherings did not meet at the start or in the wake of war, but actually dealt with the problems of warfare on a more philosophical level, no matter how restricted their programme.

Optimists did not fail also to point out a third type of conference recently brought to life in Berlin and Washington respectively. These concerned the Congo and Pan-American conferences which were actually convened to prevent war, dissolve conflicts through peaceful settlement – preferably arbitration – and systematically regulate international relations for many years to come. In other words, as many held at the time, the world was indeed growing ripe for something like "The Hague". It was at this juncture that the Czar's initiative constituted the price-less precedent of a meeting at the time of profound peace to discuss durable means of settling conflicts by resort to – be this good offices, mediation or arbitration – anything but arms!

The Second Circular Letter

Having in the end received a positive reply from all the nations addressed, Count Muraviev, on 11 January 1899, despatched a second circular letter. In this communication melancholic reference was made to the new outbursts of violence which had clouded the political horizon since the issuing of the first circular letter. France and England had been on the brink of war over the Fashoda incident in Africa, there was the Khalifa in revolt, and so much more. In view of these recent setbacks the exchange of ideas was deemed of the utmost urgency. The objectives of the proposed conference were generally considered to be twofold: first to set a limit to the progressive increase of armaments and second to discuss the possibilities of preventing armed conflicts by the pacific means at the disposal of international diplomacy such as mediation and arbitration.

It was suggested therefore that the programme of the Conference would take into consideration the following eight issues:

1 the freezing of the present military effectiveness and budgets for a fixed period and the examination as to the future reduction of both;
2 the immediate prohibition of any new fire-arms and explosives more powerful than the ones actually in use;
3 the restriction in war-time of the existing explosives and the prohibition of projectiles dropped from balloons or other aircraft;
4 the prohibition of submarine torpedo-boats and ram-equipped vessels;
5 the extension of the stipulations of the 1864 Geneva Convention to the area of naval warfare;
6 the neutral status of ships employed in rescue operations during or after an engagement;
7 the revision of the still unratified Declaration of the 1874 Brussels Conference on the laws and customs of war;
8 the acceptance of the principles of mediation and facultative arbitration as a means of preventing or settling international disputes, and the establishment of a mode and uniform practice in these respects.

In order to restrict and to better direct the debate, a proviso was made to the extent that questions which were felt to have no direct bearing on this programme were to be formally excluded from discussion.

On this occasion, too, a suggestion was made as to the place of the Conference. It was thought advisable by its authors that the Conference should not sit in St. Petersburg or for that matter any other capital of a great power. Even the slightest partiality might impede the progress of work in which all the countries of the world were equally interested. It seems that at the time Count Muraviev had no particular capital in view. Only four weeks later though he made known to the world at large that the young Queen of the Netherlands, Wilhelmina, had formally accepted his suggestion of The Hague as the seat of the Conference.

The decisive motives for this choice are not altogether clear. It is a fact that Brussels was taken into consideration, too. Actually, the Belgian King Leopold II went out of his way to point out to the Russians the advantages of his capital. In retrospect, Switzerland would have been a plausible option as well. But, as Andrew White claims in his memoires: "the number of anarchists and nihilists who had taken refuge there, and the murder of the Empress of Austria by one of them shortly before, at Geneva, in broad daylight, had thrown discredit over the ability of the Swiss Government to guarantee safety to the conference".

As regards The Hague several reflections may have been taken into consideration. It has been suggested that it was because Holland was neutral at the time and for this reason alone well suited to the idea. Other arguments were, presumably, that The Hague was easily attainable by ship from all quarters of the world; that Holland was the native country of Grotius and Bynckershoek, had a firm parliamentary tradition and had been the scene of many former international conferences. The kinship of the Dutch royal family to the Czar may conceivably have been of influence. King William III (1849–1890) was the son of William II and Anna Paulovna, the daughter of Czar Paul I. De Martens also pleaded in

The First Hague Conference of Private International Law 1893, presided over by T. M. C. Asser. The Conference was initiated by the Netherlands Government and convened six more times since 1893, before, on 15 July 1955, a Statute entered into force which lent the Conference its present status of a permanent intergovernmental organisation. Since, regular sessions have been held every four years.
The Conference is instrumental in the drawing up of multi-lateral treaties in the field, which includes family law, commercial law, contracts and torts and international judicial and administrative cooperation. The activities of the Conference are organized by a Secretariat, which has its headquarters in The Hague and has an international staff.

favour of The Hague. He had attended the conferences of the Interparliamentary Union there in 1893 and 1894 and at the time had been very much pleased by the way the Dutch had organized the meetings. He was also on very friendly terms with the Dutch Professor Tobias Asser, who was the initiator of the Conference of Private International Law at The Hague.

Formal Invitations

On the following 7 April, the Dutch Minister for Foreign Affairs, W. H. de Beaufort, formally invited the nations involved. Significantly, the opening of the Conference was anticipated for 18 May, that being the birthday of Czar Nicholas. Very much delighted by the honour conferred upon her country, the eighteen-year old and only recently installed Queen Wilhelmina had placed at the disposal of the Conference one of the most charming historic sites in Holland, the summer residence of the royal family, the palace *Huis ten Bosch* (House in the Woods), not far from the city centre.

Admittedly, the pace of events since the appearance of the first circular letter only nine months before had been anything but tardy. However, the principle on which the invitations were issued was thought of by some as less than admirable. In order to prevent endless debate over the status of the younger States in the continents overseas, whose very legitimacy and independence were questionable, only the nations accredited to the Petersburg Court had been invited, that is with the addition of Luxembourg, Montenegro and Siam. Understandably, this policy did not meet with universal consent. Dutch public opinion, for instance, as deeply resented the exclusion of the young South African republics as the United States

did the absence of the Central and South American representatives, the authoritative international lawyer from Argentina, Carlos Calvo, among them. Along the lines so arranged, the American and Mexican delegates were to represent the whole of their hemisphere! Another noticeable absentee was the delegate from the Holy See. Italy obstinately declined to attend the Conference if the Papal representative were to be admitted. Prolonged intermediation on the part of the Dutch Foreign Minister, de Beaufort, did not help.

Most of the objections raised are perfectly understandable still, they do not in the least detract from the Russian policy in these matters, which all in all seems to have been sound, wise and just. It would have been hard to avoid conflicts of the kind anyway, no matter what course was steered. In fact the way the Russians handled the affair was probably the only way that lay open without risking a complete deadlock in negotiations. At least the Conference was saved this way: about mid-May, there were some one hundred delegates, representing twenty-six nations, registered in the more fashionable hotels of The Hague.

The American delegation heading for the Conference. Andrew D. White is shown carrying the pipe of peace, Seth Low the olive branch, Stanford Newel the caged dove of peace. Captain Crozier is presented in full array with sword and helmet, Captain Mahan is bearing a sophisticated gun and Frederic W. Holls is carrying piles of books and a cash-register.

THE HUIS TEN BOSCH

Through the ages the *Huis ten Bosch* has served many ends. It was mainly used either as a summer retreat or as a palace proper for the Orange family. Its history, therefore, is closely linked with that of the Dutch Royal House and numerous were the national highdays celebrated there. The tiny palace has all the characteristics and charms of the *villa urbana* of the Italian Renaissance. It was built in 1645, in the very heyday of the Dutch Republic, and by one of its leading architects. The house was to become the summer residence of Stadholder Prince Frederick Henry of Orange and his wife Amalia of Solms, a former lady-in-waiting of Elisabeth Stuart. It was the latter, the "Winterqueen" of Bohemia, who laid the foundation stone. The Prince himself, a brilliant general and great diplomat, was not destined to enjoy much of his *Sael van Oranje*, as the palace was named at the time; he died in 1647.

In the course of time, and with the changes in taste, the house and gardens underwent a number of renovations, by Daniel Marot among others. Amalia herself gave her court a splendour and grandeur unprecedented in the Netherlands. In 1686 a great ball was given at the house in honour of William and

Mary, spotlighted among others by the most colourful presence of the Ambassador from Morocco. It was here, too, in 1733 and 1752 respectively, that William IV and V of Orange were invested with the Knighthood of the Garter. Both Princes lived in the palace for many years and did much to embellish it and enrich the grounds, notably with a zoo! Among the celebrated artists featured at the theatre productions, operas, ballets and concerts were Mozart and Beethoven. This all came to an abrupt end in 1795, when William V had to flee the country because of the invading French armies. The palace then was turned over to the public, to open its doors in 1800 as a National Art Gallery at an entrance fee of threepence ... and with no trace left of the Oranges. In 1806–1807 it became the residence of King Louis Napoleon; but already in 1813 William Frederick, Prince of Orange, had returned. In July 1814 the old building again shone forth in all its splendour, well-prepared to receive Czar Alexander of Russia, who drove up to the gala ball through the brilliantly illuminated woods. Only two years later, then sovereign king of the Netherlands, William stood ready again on the terraces to receive the young

bride of his eldest son, the Russian Grand Princess Anna Paulovna. There was a Russian connection long before the late nineties therefore!

In the middle years of the century Queen Sophie lived here amid her magnificent collection of Chinese porcelain and Delft pottery and received prominent scientific and political figures such as the historian Ranke and Lord Clarendon. At her invitation J. L. Motley lived in the grounds for some time, preparing his *Rise of the Dutch Republic*. On the arrival of the delegates in 1899, it still stood as on the first day, invariably surrounded by the wood known as the *Haagse Bos*, and still to be reached by the same carriage-ways. Despite some damage done afterwards in the Second World War it has kept its outer appearance up till the present day. For over three centuries visitors have found themselves enchanted by the simple elegance of the building, the beauty of its proportions and the spell of the site.

It was only recently that, after careful restoration, the palace began upon a new phase in its glorious history: since 1981 it serves as the Royal Palace for the present Queen Beatrix and her family.

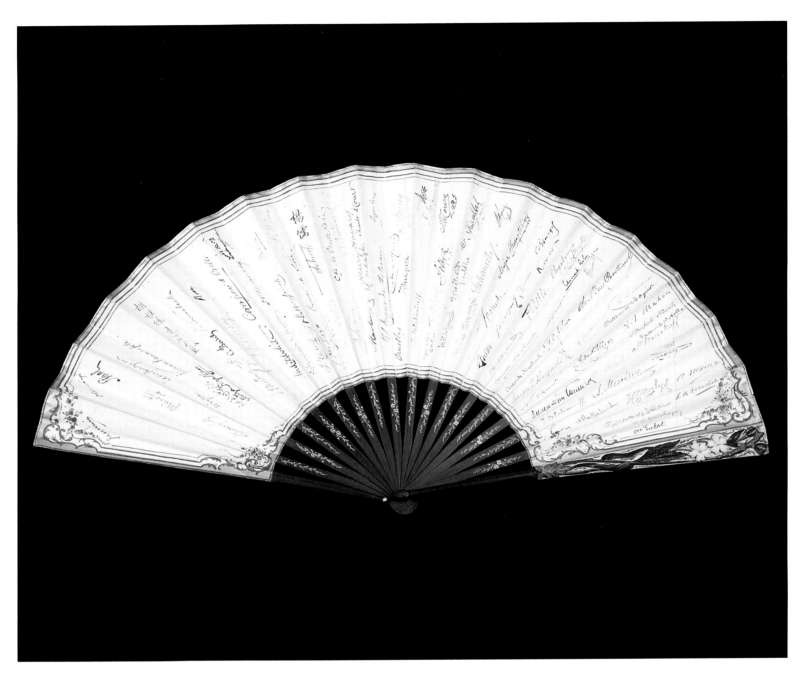

The fan with the names of all the delegates. One of the treasures of the Peace Palace archives. It is also shown in the photograph of the First Commission on page 30 in the hands of one of the delegates.

Right: A pseudo-allegorical presentation of the Conference by Charles Touché. In the centre is the cupola of the Huis ten Bosch. On the left, on a pedestal, Hugo Grotius. To the right, Czar Nicholas and a medallion showing Queen Wilhelmina. At the front feature allegorical groups representing Peace (left) and War (right). In the centre Mercury hurries away to bring the good tidings. Three American Presidents, Lincoln, Washington and Theodore Roosevelt feature in the upper centre of the ornamental border along with, to the left, from above: Alfred Nobel, Edward VII, Randal Cremer and to the right, from above: Count Albert Apponyi, the Hungarian delegate, Emile Loubet the French president, and Jean de Bloch. Below left: Andrew Carnegie, right: Frédéric Passy.

The 1899 Peace Conference

The opening of the International Peace Conference on 18 May was welcomed by a perfect spring day; The Hague presented a stirring and picturesque spectacle. The flags of many nations were flying in the wind from public buildings, hotels and embassies and from many private houses. At 10 a.m. the members of the Russian delegation, in full uniform and with a splendid escort, attended mass in the tiny Orthodox Chapel near Scheveningen to pray in honour of the Czar's birthday. Interestingly enough, this chapel was situated on the very spot where, eight years afterwards, the founding stone of the Peace Palace was to be laid.

The opening ceremony of the Conference was set for 2 p.m. From noon onwards, shining varnished open carriages drawn by four in hands could be seen traversing the two miles from the city centre. They passed by the drill field of the Malieveld, then through the woods, skirting the ponds, up to the simple, but striking beauty of the tiny summer palace. The brilliant caparisons of the horses and the colourful ceremonial dress of the delegates were a sight to see in the beaming sun.

Through the ages the charms of the Hague Woods have inspired poets and statesmen alike. The humanist scholars Hugo Grotius and Constantine Huygens both wrote poems of considerable length in an eulogy of the park. On 15 July, G. H. Perris, publicist and attender at the Peace Conference, jotted down the following lines in his notebook: "Between the Hague and the palace is the Bosch – a splendid park nearly two miles long, divided lengthwise by a series of lakes embowered by magnificent trees, in whose shade one may walk, or rest, and think. All around reigns, not indeed dead silence – for unseen birds are fluting ceaselessly in their leafy heights, and a rumble of human life is faintly audible from the nearest boulevard – but perfect tranquillity. The face of the long water, a brown mirror except where it is covered with a cream of weed, is hardly disturbed by a ripple in these burning days; the swans, lazily majestical, alone break the picture of over-arching branches. Brave old beeches and towering elms shake themselves gently in the sun, and the limes throw out the last wealth of their intoxicating perfume. A fairy network of leaves against the azure sky is repeated in shadow on the grass and soil. A place in which to forget old passions and prejudices and the grosser forms of selfishness; a place for good consideration, courtesy, patience, and the philosophic mind. Yes, decidedly, it was an inspiration to hold here the first parliament of peace; and the Hague has its appropriate reward, for has not this tiny capital become the juridical metropolis of the world? What capital can boast a prouder title?"

Of the Palace itself he said: "... this is a mere shooting box compared with the palaces at Moscow and Petersburg, and yet it is already one of the

world's historical buildings, and the cradle of an idea that might, if anything could, reconcile us to that singular institution, the Russian Tsardom".

The Opening Ceremony

The hundred representatives filled the *Oranjezaal* to capacity. The seats had been arranged along four rows of concentric semi-circular tables, covered with green baize. In this way all the delegates enjoyed a clear view of the President's chair in the bay window and of the adjoining tables of secretaries and attachés. Seats had been allotted in alphabetical order of States, only minor adjustments of protocol had been made in a stealthy way. Thus, seats of honour for the American delegates had been provided for by arranging them under the heading A of Amérique, next to Allemagne. On this the veteran diplomat Count Münster, head of the German delegation, in jest inquired of his American neighbours, with a reference to their Spanish war, whether this arrangement formed part of their new imperialistic policy. On their protesting their innocence he remarked: "Surely innocence has always been your drawing card in diplomacy." Münster, indeed, was a character. White felt "he was saturated with the ideas of fifty years ago". He thought telegraphs and telephones a curse and at a reception spoke of bacteria and microbes as "all a modern humbug".

No space whatever was reserved, or for that matter could be spared, for spectators or journalists. The delegates agreed that the character of the negotiations did not call for open discussion. Only a handful of invited guests were admitted to attend the ceremony from the narrow gallery in the cupola; apart from them, all outsiders were strictly excluded from the Conference. In this way the privacy of deliberations was duly guaranteed – only it meant war with the press, who insisted on being informed of the proceedings daily and in detail. No Conference of the sort had ever been held before, so no one exactly knew how to handle this problem. At the second meeting of the Conference, on 20 May, the delegates agreed upon the maintenance of secrecy for the full duration of the deliberations. The President and the bureau alone were authorized to communicate to the members of the press a summary of the proceedings of each committee. Embittered journalists and representatives of all sorts of peace organizations who had crowded into the premises, spat venom on this pretended secrecy of the proceedings. Although strict regulations were somewhat relaxed afterwards, no satisfactory solution was found. In the end, this would very much hamper the general acceptance abroad of the results of the sessions. In view of the widely spread misunderstandings as regards the goal of the Conference and the ensuing scepticism and mistrust, the scenario decided upon did not testify as to the tactical genius of the organizing committee.

A plenary session of the Conference in the "Oranjezaal". In the centre, at the rear, is President de Staal.

The *Huis ten Bosch* contains some eight state rooms. Among these are a blue and green salon, a white dining room, a ballroom and a Japanese and a Chinese room decorated with silk tapestries and exquisite furniture, and, as White observes, "the most perfect specimens of … bronzes, ivory carvings, lacquer work, and the like". The central piece of interest, however, is the central hall, the so-called *Oranjezaal* or Mausoleum. The building of this hall, designed on the Prince's orders to show off the portraits of the ruling European monarchs, had not even been begun when, on 14 March 1647, Frederick Henry died. Amalia then decided to dedicate the hall to the memory of her husband.
The foremost architect, Jacob van Campen, was commissioned and assisted by the Prince's secretary Sir Constantine Huygens set himself to design a symbolic portrayal of the life and deeds of Frederick Henry. The result was one of the greatest cultural monuments in the Netherlands. The cross-shaped hall with its elegant cupola and walls eight metres high is

covered all over with paintings on canvas and wood. The theme of the paintings was suggested by the Peace of Munster, which was concluded in 1648. "Munster" virtually meant the recognition of the Republic of the United Provinces as a sovereign State by the leading European nations. It was widely acknowledged that Frederick Henry, by his military successes against the Spanish, had been the actual founder of this nation and therefore the initiator of this Golden Age to come. It was indeed these ideals the artists set themselves to represent in the entwining of factual history and classical myth, alive with the allegory and symbolicisms that were so typical of the classicist taste of the time. The canvasses, illustrating successively the birth, education, marriage and feats of arms of the general, culminate in a true apotheosis of Frederick Henry, represented as the Prince of Peace. If anything, the series resembles Rubens' portrayal of the life of Maria de Medici in the *Palais du Luxembourg* in Paris (1621) or his paintings in the *Banqueting Hall* in

London depicting the life of James I (1629). They also have the spatial effect known from the frescoes in the Palladian manner in the villas of the Italian *Cinquecento*.
Small wonder this is so, though, for the prominent painter engaged for the project by Amalia was Jacob Jordaens, who was a pupil of Peter Paul Rubens. It was he who in 1652 completed the nine central canvasses representing the *Thriumph of Frederick Henry*. Jordaens was helped, however, by a team of specialists from both the Southern and Northern provinces, including Pieter Soutman, Jan Lievens and Gerard van Honthorst. All in all fifty paintings and pieces of sculpture were produced covering all the walls, doors and ceilings with lofty themes as Venus in the smithy of Vulcan, brandishing the arms of the Prince; the young Hercules strangling the snakes; the Dutch maiden offering the Prince the supreme command; Frederick Henry as lord of the seas; his ascension into heaven, and putti closing the doors of the Temple of Janus.

The American delegate Frederic W. Holls, who in 1914 edited a very capable survey of the proceedings, vividly remembered the opening ceremony. At two o'clock sharp, he noted, "an impressive silence came over the assembly, in which every member doubtless realized that a great and solemn historical moment had arrived". In this atmosphere the Dutch Minister for Foreign Affairs rose to call the meeting to order. Standing in front of the huge allegorical panels by Jordaens commemorating the *Peace of Westphalia* of 1648 and representing among others the entrance into the room of the Goddess of Peace about to close the Temple of Janus, de Beaufort gave a welcoming address. In it he referred to the lofty initiative of Czar Nicholas, but also called to memory Nicholas' predecessor Alexander and the latter's desire to see "all sovereigns and all the nations of Europe united for the purpose of living as brethren, aiding each other according to their reciprocal needs". He read the text of a congratulatory telegram which he proposed to despatch to the Czar and amidst unanimous applause conferred the presidency of the Conference on the Russian Ambassador, Mr. de Staal. In his address this veteran diplomat promised the assembly to employ all the efforts which "the sad privilege and feeble auxiliary" of his advanced age offered to justify the confidence placed in him. He then recalled the historic importance of The Hague and for that matter the Netherlands in the development of international law and proposed to send a telegram to its young Queen Wilhelmina, their hostess Queen. He then proceeded to the appointment of the honorary and vice-presidents, Mr. de Beaufort and the "clear-headed and straightforward" (White) van Karnebeek, the Foreign Minister and first delegate of the host country respectively, and to the election of the secretariat. The assembly passed a resolution declaring all meetings of the Conference and of its Committees to be absolutely secret and was then adjourned to Saturday, 20 May.

The Second Plenary Session

At this second meeting congratulatory telegrams from the Russian Czar and the Dutch Queen were read, whereupon President de Staal set out to summarize the objects and general tendencies of the Conference. In the name *Peace Conference*, instinctively given to this assembly by the common man, the President held that the essential object of the proposed work was accurately indicated. The Conference, according to the Czar's edict, was to go in search of "the most efficacious means to assure to all peoples the blessings of a real and durable peace". In this it must not fail! The more so, de Staal argued, as the very field of diplomacy, of old, concerned with the softening of rivalries, the conciliation of interests and the substitution of harmony for discord, had come at the juncture where it was rapidly becoming a true science. International relations, and conflicts in particular, had to be submitted to a set of fixed

The Russian delegation, showing de Staal in the middle of the front row with de Martens at his right and de Basily on his left.

rules. It was a hopeful omen, therefore, that the delegates attending included not only eminent career diplomats, but likewise expert representatives of the military and navy, scholars of fame in the field of international law and excellent veteran statesmen. They had not come to conceive miracles and were not asked to enter the domain of Utopia. Together, not following abstractions but taking account of the possible, they had to lay the solid foundations for the durable prevention of armed conflict by pacific means. The urgency for such a construction became imminent with the steady growth of the human family into an organic entity from which no nation could remain isolated. In modern days the consequences of any conflict would have their repercussions all over the globe and no outsider could be allowed to remain indifferent. These truths were not new, he argued; indeed, they had been appreciated by statesmen and philosophers throughout the ages; but its proclamation in front of an assembly such as the one gathered formed a true landmark in the history of humanity. Yet another truth went along with it. Till the day that conflict was banished forever, man was set to mitigate the horrors of war. International agreements opened the way to this goal and it was a major task of the Conference therefore to lay down new principles in this area. One last thing was up to the wisdom of the governments represented, de Staal continued, and that was whether the very welfare of their peoples did not demand a limitation of progressive armaments. Mr. de Staal asked the assembly to consider this issue along with the other ones in a lofty and conciliatory spirit. Thus, he felt assured, they would earn the thanks of future generations.

It will be observed that in this opening speech no reference was made to "disarmament". Neither will the word be found in any of the official documents relating to the Conference. It is only the public at large which from the very beginning almost unconsciously seized upon the name "Disarmament Conference" and then, as stubbornly, resisted dropping the term. Indeed, it is this very misconception which accounts for the widely spread feeling of "failure" which emanated when the final results of the Conference became known to the public. This went over the head of some far-reaching and momentous results which had been agreed upon to the full satisfaction of all and to the positive amazement of some of the delegates. As far as the members themselves were concerned, it was perfectly permissible to call it a "Disarmament" or a "Peace" Conference, as these ends were to be the ultimate goals of this sort of international meeting. But at the same time, they maintained, one must keep trying to see things in the right perspective: world peace must remain a utopian idea for the time being: at The Hague there were at least a hundred men who were fully aware of that truth.

Having outlined the programme of the Conference, Mr. de Staal then proceeded to the actual division of work on the basis of the second Muraviev circular letter. Three commissions were proposed. The first commission was to consider Articles 1, 2, 3 and 4 of the second circular letter, including the limitations of armaments, the humanizing of war, expanding bullets and methods of naval warfare. The second commission was to discuss Articles 5, 6 and 7 of the circular letter, including the adaptation of the principles of the 1864 Geneva convention to maritime warfare and the laws and customs of war. The third commission was to come to terms with Article 8 of the circular letter, including the maintenance of general peace, good offices and mediation, international commissions of inquiry and international arbitration. Each commission had the power to subdivide itself into subcommittees, which they did as we shall presently see. Another principle to which we referred in the foregoing was once more reaffirmed, namely that the Conference declared itself incompetent on any other issue which was brought up for discussion.

So after two plenary sessions the Conference came to grips with the work in hand. Most of this work was done within the committees. No definite time schedule had been drawn up beforehand,

The Japanese room in the Huis ten Bosch after the recent restoration.

which, incidentally, gave rise to all sorts of speculation in the media with regard to a possible immediate failure and quick dispersal of the assembly. Nothing of the sort happened or was ever for a moment imminent. For over two months the delegates worked in zealous harmony and conscientious labour, and in the best of spirits. This at least soon became apparent: here were gathered a hundred men all of whom were very conscious of the numerous resentments and grudges that were alive or kept smouldering between the nations they represented.

There were more apparent disadvantages with which they had to cope, for that matter. They were led, a true parliament of peace, by a president who at home had never experienced anything like a parliamentary tradition. They entered the Conference room with very varying instructions indeed. And yet, from the very beginning, a keen sense of determination and enthusiasm pervaded the ranks. Whatever the issue at hand, as high as the debate might run and as hard the solution to find, never an embittered word was heard. Meetings were usually held from 10 till 12 a.m and from 2 till 6 p.m. Most delegates attended some four or five meetings a week, but some, like the experts of the first and second committees were kept extremely busy from day to day.

Members were seen definitely surpassing themselves in willpower and resourcefulness; as time went by former animosities gave way to friendships. It may simply have been the personal affront they took of the scepticism, the disavowal and the patronizing condescension with which many outside observers met the Conference that prompted them to close their ranks and made them determined to succeed. As a journalist stated: "The delegates are here, settling down to business, everyone prepared to say: J'y suis, et j'y reste!" At all events they proved that in their eyes at least the ideas at stake here were worth fighting for. Sir John Fisher, the British chief delegate once remarked: "Are you not surprised to see me here, me, a regular fighting man? At first everybody seemed to think, what a bore it is to have to come to this place. What's the use? It will all end up in smoke. Now that's all changed. I'm an optimist, you know, and I believe we're going to do great things."

Social Entourage

If circumstance and outside conditions may be of some help to the success of enterprises of the kind, they certainly contributed on this occasion. Several of the delegates jotted down their impressions in afterthought and they all declared themselves under the spell of the surroundings. As the American commissioner Seth Low remarked during a meeting: "Both Peace and Hospitality appear to us to have laid aside their sandals at The Hague, as if there they had found their permanent abiding-place."

We have already dwelt on the charms of the House in the Woods with its lovely vistas and its ancient park with colourful flowerbeds under the ramification of noble elms. Weather conditions favoured the Conference most of the time. It was even exceptionally warm at times, which also had its disadvantages according to some observers: "All day The Hague had been as hot as a bakehouse, and it would be a straining of courtesy to pretend that the canals are as pleasant to the nose as to the eye."

Officials and private persons at The Hague vied with each other in entertaining the delegates. As Frederick W. Holls, the American delegate, wrote: "The Conference was eminently a businesslike body, without ostentation or display of any kind. On two occasions only did the members appear in full uniform." Yet, the informal gatherings were numerous and helped by creating an atmosphere of style without affectation. A sumptuous luncheon was served daily at the House by courtesy of the Dutch Government in the dining room upstairs and occasioned unrestrained personal contact. After two months, in this simple way, all the delegates had got to know each other. On the evening of 24 May the Queen and Queen Mother gave a grand soiree in honour of the Conference at the Royal Palace in the Noordeinde in The Hague. On 6 July they ordered a special train to take the members to a state dinner at the Royal Palace on the Dam in Amsterdam. The streets were crowded: "We were indeed a brave show" all dressed in "gorgeous uniforms with no end of ribbons, stars, and insignia of various offices and orders". On this occasion the young Queen impressed the delegates by her perfect command of French, English and German.

On 27 May the Burgomaster of The Hague invited the delegates to a gala concert in the *Gebouw van Kunsten en Wetenschappen*, with music by Tschaikovsky, Grieg and Wagner which White deemed rather "noisy and tending nowhither"; but in between they had pieces by Mozart and Beethoven "which gave a delightful relief". On 17 June the Dutch Government presented them with a musical and artistic festival in which the master violinist Johannes Wolff featured and dancers in historical costumes created *tableaux vivants* representing famous pictures in the Dutch galleries like Rembrandt's *Night Watch* and Jan Steen's *Peasant Wedding*. On 4 June the Conference attended a great floral parade and equestrian competition in Haarlem "for which I cared nothing" (White again) and, last but not least, on 12 June the *Société des Bains de Mer de Schéveningue* offered a grand concert and ball at the Kurhaus.

Likewise, the official society and the diplomatic corps in The Hague were profuse in their social attentions. On 30 May and 9 June the delegates were splendidly received at the British Legation, which White called "an example of John Bull's good sense in providing for his representatives abroad … a social influence … which rapidly becomes a political influence", and on 7 June they were received by the French.

Again, on Saturday 3 July Mr. Stead was invited to the party given by the President, de Staal: "On Wednesday I am fifty years old, and on Saturday evening I was at my first ball! I was brought up in an austere circle, where cards, balls, and theatres were as so many snares of the devil. Cards were his prayer-book; balls were the carnival of the world, the flesh, and the devil; the theatre was the ante-chamber of Hell. No sound of distant cannon has broken upon Madame de Staal's … party in the Vieux Doelen. Yet, after all, it is my first ball, and I think it will be my last."

Stead, incidentally, was one of the few outsiders who was really accepted by the delegates. His reports of the sessions in the *Manchester Guardian* and his "Chronique" in the *Dagblad van Zuid-Holland en 's-Gravenhage* (a sternly conservative journal which was discontinued soon afterwards) were much appreciated by all of them, we are told. Said a fellow reporter: "The delegates could not help reading it and, reading, feeling the eyes of King Demos upon them and his voice in their ears, could not help being influenced. This capture of the leading paper

H.M. Queen Wilhelmina of the Netherlands at eighteen. Portrait by J. ten Kate, Sr. (1850–1929).

The tomb of Hugo Grotius in the "Nieuwe Kerk" of Delft, where the ceremony took place on 4 July, 1899.

THE HUGO GROTIUS CELEBRATION

It was on the occasion of Independence Day that under the auspices of the American delegation a Grotius celebration took place at the tomb of the famous lawyer in the apse of the *Nieuwe Kerk* in Delft, next to the tomb of the *pater patriae* William of Orange, called "the Silent". Here a silver wreath with an inscription was unveiled. A very stimulating speech was delivered by Andrew D. White. He referred to Grotius' work *De jure belli ac pacis*, which "of all works not claiming divine inspiration ... has proved the greatest blessing to humanity. More than any other it has prevented unmerited suffering, misery, and sorrow; more than any other, it has ennobled the military profession; more than any other, it has promoted the blessings of peace and diminished the horrors of war." The date and place, he concluded, were most fit for this commemoration, which was held on Independence Day near the harbour which saw the departure of the *Mayflower*, the very ship which brought to the New World the Pilgrim Fathers and with them the germs of toleration of which Grotius was the apostle. From that day on to the present day and *pace* Macchiavelli, White continued, "the progress of reason in theory, and of mercy in practice, has been constant on both sides of the Atlantic" to result in this "first Conference of the entire world ever held". In his *peroratio* White summoned the Conference to go on with its work despite all the setbacks that would materialize: "Pseudo-philosophers will prophesy malignantly against you; pessimists will laugh you to scorn; cynics will sneer at you; zealots will abuse you for what you have *not* done; sublimely unpractical thinkers will revile you for what you have done; ephemeral critics will ridicule you as dupes; enthusiasts, blind to the difficulties in your path and to everything outside their little circumscribed fields, will denounce you as traitors to humanity. Heed them not; go on with your work ... of strengthening peace and humanizing war; give greater scope and strength to provisions which will make war less cruel; perfect those laws of war which diminish the unmerited sufferings of populations; and, above all, give to the world at least a beginning of an effective, practicable scheme of arbitration."
White adored Grotius. Next day, 5 July, he visited M. Cornets de Groot, the descendant of the prodigy, at Ryswyck. Here he perused a fine collection of relics, "sundry poems" and a multitude of portraits and engravings. Professor T. M. C. Asser, the Dutch delegate and President of the *Institut de Droit International*, whose members were also attending the meeting, spoke after White. Asser gave an outline of the twenty-five years of research at the Institute, ever since its first scholarly meeting in Geneva in 1874: its work on codification in the field of private international law under its former President, Mancini, and the diplomatic conference held at The Hague in the early nineties.
The celebration was concluded by a luncheon in the ancient Town Hall on the market place of Delft, opposite the huge bronze statue of Grotius. At night a gala concert featuring American national airs was held at Scheveningen.

of the little city was at once the simplest and the most far-reaching of all it's author's propagandist efforts. By the force of its novelty, boldness, resource, and eloquence it dominated the situation; and we shall never know how much of the result we owe to Mr. Stead."

Another welcome guest, indeed a centre of attraction at the receptions was Baroness von Suttner, authoress of *Die Waffen Nieder,* which had passed through thirty editions in Germany. She was besieged by reporters throughout the Conference and proved the best propagandist of peace: "Clear and logical in argument, graceful and dignified in manner, her soft musical voice is so persuasive that the most hardened sinner is not proof against it.

Ridiculed and caricatured as she has been for the last ten years, she now finds herself sought out by the mighty of the land."

There was yet one other famous observer: Monsieur de Bloch, the wealthy Russian banker who devoted eight years of his life to his book on the horror of war, a work ... "of 4,000 pages and weighing about twelve pounds which so directly influenced the Tsar and which fortunately for his friends, he is ever disposed to summarize for their benefit."

One or two sad events occurred: the railway accident near Flushing which caused the death of the daughter of the Swiss delegate Roth, in July, and the death of the heir apparent, Grand Duke George of Russia, on 10 July.

The most interesting social and scholarly event took place on 4 July at Delft, when amid severe rain-storms and most inclement weather the American delegates availed themselves of their national Independence Day to lay a wreath on the tomb of Hugo Grotius, the "father of international law", whose memory has always been kept alive in the United States.

General Outline of the Conference

The Conference held ten plenary sessions in all. The first and second session, as described above, were filled with regulations and matters of agenda. At the third session, on 23 May, the various committees were announced. Then for nearly a month work was done in the committees and subcommittees. Only on 20 June was a fourth plenary session arranged to appoint a committee to draw up the Final Act and to discuss the first report brought up, on the Extension of the Geneva Rules to naval warfare, handed over by the second committee. At the fifth session, on 5 July, another report submitted by the second committee was discussed, on the laws and customs of war. A fortnight afterwards, at the sixth session on 21 July, the report of the first committee on disarmament and on the employment of certain instruments of warfare was agreed to. Four days later, on 25 July this was followed by the report of the third committee on the peaceful adjustment of international differences. The eighth and ninth sessions, on 27 and 28 July, were devoted to the discussion of the Final Act and various formal declarations. The concluding tenth session on 29 July was reserved for the signing of the various conventions and declarations agreed upon.

The Conference went into recess from 7 to 17 July, which enabled the delegates to consult their governments in matters of the arbitration treaty particularly, before final decisions were to be taken. These latter negotiations, incidentally, were carried through with painstaking care, but to some seemed to linger on endlessly. It provoked from the Chinese delegate, Yang-Yü, the sad remark: "Too much talkee-talkee, too little doee-doee."

During the ten weeks the meeting lasted, the secretariat of the Conference was confronted with an overwhelming mass of communications, addresses, petitions and similar things from all over the world: "wise and unwise, thoughtful and crankish, shrewd and childish", as White observes. Among these, a category of its own was formed by the various pamphlets and books submitted by scores of peace societies: "The number of people with plans, schemes, notions, nostrums, whimsies of all sorts, who press upon us and try to take our time is enormous; and when to this is added the pest of interviewers and photographers, life becomes serious indeed."

The plans contained for the better part wholly impracticable or even absurd schemes for disarmament or arbitration, yet some of them did further the Conference substantially. This held good for instance for a book on *International Tribunals* by W.

Complimentary address to Czar Nicholas II from the "Comité général néerlandais pour la manifestation pacifique", issued on the eve of the Conference. On the left a satirical response to the address printed in a Dutch periodical, showing Nicholas temporarily laying aside the whip he used to lash the Jews, Finns and Lithuanians among others.

Evans Darby, secretary to the London Peace Society. Delegations from oppressed nations gravitated to The Hague to insist on immediate action: the Conference was faced with young Turks, Poles, Finns, Armenians and Macedonians. The first gave rise to some hilarity among delegates, when after they had been granted an informal hearing, "the main object being to get rid of them" (White), they appeared in full evening dress and announced very impressively: "Your Excellencies, ve are ze Young Turkeys." Peace required justice, they argued, and the latter was conditioned by the satisfying of their own political aspirations. They threatened to embarrass the Conference with revolutionary outbreaks and so set its members on a study of political pathology. Many were the demonstrators who demanded and confidently expected from the hundred delegates in The Hague the virtual solution to each particular racial and political problem.

The First Commission

THE ARMAMENT QUESTION

This commission's main concern, as already mentioned, was the armament question and the humanizing of war. The commission held eight plenary reunions between 23 May and 20 July. Unfortunately, the commission did not reach any concrete arrangements on the first main issue. It was unanimously felt that the realization of a limitation of armaments was at present premature. But the practical discussion of the question by representatives of powers with conflicting or even hostile interests, proved in itself of value. The main participants in the debate were the Russian Colonel Gilinsky and his German opponent, General von Schwarzhoff. The former made himself known as a realist, though at the same time a fervent partisan if not of limitation, at least of fixation of the armaments budgets. To this end he formulated two proposals from which he wished the colonies to be excluded:

As to armies:
1 an international agreement on the non-augmentation of troops for a term of five years
2 the determination of the number of troops in time of peace by all the powers
3 the maintenance of the military budget for a term of five years.

As to navies:
The fixing of the naval budget for three years and the obligation to publish the present tonnage of men-of-war, the number of officers and crews and costs on fortifications.

The views Gilinsky had in mind were both humanitarian and economic, he argued. To this General von Schwarzhoff replied, arguing that no one in Germany felt the economic burden of the armaments race. Far from facing ruin, the nation was

more prosperous than ever before in its history. Moreover, he noticed some inconsistency in the argument that, on the one hand, excessive armaments would lead humanity to the brink of general war, whereas on the other the exhaustion of national wealth was said to make war impossible. Besides, the technical obstacles to the proposals, he felt, were insurmountable, as for instance the number of divisions required depended totally on things like population statistics and geographical circumstances. To this Gilinsky replied that he congratulated his colleague on Germany's economic welfare, but still maintained that money spent on armament would be better and more humanely applied to serve social, cultural and intellectual ends. Von Schwarzhoff agreed with this, but then fell back on the impossibility of inspection of troops and the eventual disturbance of the present military equilibrium which, he held, would really endanger peace.

William Stead, keen as always, did not fail to notice the gist of the debate: "There is something mysterious about Col. Schwarzhoff's speech against the arrest of armaments proposals ... the declaration was full of audacity and good humour, and blended the eloquence of the orator with the boldness of the soldier ... but it has destroyed the illusion created by the Kaiser's words [at Wiesbaden, on the very day of the meeting of the Peace Conference] and has plunged the subject into black mystery, for it was a repudiation of the very basis of the Russian Rescript. Progress is impossible amid these constant variations of a capricious policy."

In this deadlock Vice-President van Karnebeek warned that if nothing were done it was only the forces of unrest and anarchy that would profit from the failure of the Conference to agree upon some limitation. It was then decided to make a final effort and refer Gilinsky's proposals to two subcommittees on military and naval affairs respectively. The first subcommittee held six meetings from 26 May to 26 June, the second met seven times between 26 May and 30 June.

The first subcommittee could only report that with the exception of Colonel Gilinsky it had unanimously decided against the proposals, to which enactment it saw all sorts of, for the better part technical, problems. A more profound study of the issue was recommended to the respective governments in the months to come. The second subcommittee, it proved, had agreed upon the same meagre conclusions. It appeared that even the most peace-loving men, from self-evident fear and acquainted as they were with the phantom of war lurking around the corner, were not prepared to face such an imminent crisis less than fully equipped. It was felt that only the experience of some successful cases of arbitration in occurring conflicts could produce a radical change in this universal way of thinking. To this understandable conclusion, but rather poor show, due protest was raised by the Swedish-Norwegian delegate Bildt (author of an authoritative study of Queen Christina of Sweden and minister plenipotentiary at Rome) and the French delegate Bourgeois. Matters had to be considered in a less technical and a more philosophical way, they argued. It must be a matter of principle for the Conference to show the world its fair intentions. They proposed thereto a resolution to the intent that "a limitation of the military charges which now weigh upon the world is greatly to be desired in the interests of the material and moral welfare of humanity". This resolution was adopted unanimously. It must be said that, probably contrary to everyone's apprehensions, in the years to come the urgency of some limitation was to become generally felt. As a matter of fact the debate was bound to become a major issue during the second Hague Conference.

THE HUMANIZING OF WAR

As regards the second major issue of the first commission, the humanizing of war, somewhat the same procedure was followed. The subject-matter of Articles 2, 3 and 4 of Muraviev's circular letter was divided over two subcommittees for the military and navy respectively. The first subcommittee considered Articles 2 and 3, the problems involved with powders and explosives, field guns, balloons, muskets and bullets, whereas the second occupied itself with Article 4 and discussed submarines, torpedo boats and ram-armed warships.

The debate in both subcommittees descended into an often highly technical exposure by experts such as the American Captain Crozier. Numerous propositions were made, again, by Colonel Gilinsky, who reworked the Muraviev circular letter. Most of these propositions, however, were rejected; again it proved hard to attain unanimity. The first one adopted, though only after frequent emendation, concerned the dropping of missiles or explosives from balloons and other aircraft, which was banned in view of the unpredictable damage to civil life it caused through lack of accuracy. However, the prohibition was to cover a period of five years only ... for man's destructive genius could always be entrusted soon to improve in its efforts to harm! Captain Crozier maintained that his country abstained from this sort of proposition for "it did not consider limitation in regard to the use of military inventions to be conducive to the peace of the

The First Commission on the steps of the Huis ten Bosch. The commission was presided over by Beernaert, the Belgian Minister of State and first delegate.

world". The proposal to forbid all new military inventions to be expected from the rapid progress in the processes of electricity and chemistry went the same way.

More active, if not hot-tempered, debate arose over the expanding bullets, such as the so-called dum dum bullet, manufactured in India and generally considered to be unnecessarily cruel, but in current use by the British army in the colonies. The jacket of this bullet left a small part of the core uncovered, which resulted in a more pronounced force at the cost of effectiveness. The British protest upon its proposed prohibition was fierce: no cruelty was involved, they maintained. At Omdurman, it was argued by Lord Pauncefote, the Dervishes managed to flee even if hit five times by these bullets. Still, the objective of any bullet, as Captain Crozier pointed out in a strong plea, should be to put the enemy *hors de combat,* without unnecessary injuries. Even William Stead had to admit, if much against his will, that the dum dum bullet was indeed justly brought up for discussion: "15 July. I have hitherto defended the position of the British government in regard to the Dum Dum bullet. But I have now the painful duty of confessing that our government's action is indefensible. In the first place, reports from India show that the effects of the bullet are not of the innocent character they have been represented to be, but that they have inflicted terrible injuries. Secondly, after stating that they were only intended for 'savage' warfare, it appears that millions of rounds have been sent to South Africa for use, if need be, against the Boers. This is a very grave matter."

The final draft of the declaration which was adopted read: "The use of bullets which expand or flatten easily in the human body, such as jacketed bullets of which the jacket does not entirely cover the core, or has incisions in it, should be forbidden."

The imminent danger of all these too-specified propositions, incidentally, was that malevolence would always manage to escape the general principle of the proposition by a mere change of detail and specification. What to say in this context of yet another proposal by the Russians "to limit the calibre of guns to seventeen inches, the initial velocity to thirteen thousand feet a second, and the length of guns to forty-five calibres; further, that armour should be limited to fourteen inches of the latest Krupp pattern".

A last point worth mentioning was the discussion on projectiles spreading asphyxiating gases. A proposition regarding its prohibition was agreed upon with only the United States voting against it. Captain Alfred T. Mahan, its stout, eloquent and cynical representative, argued among other things "that it was illogical and not demonstrably humane, to be tender about asphyxiating men with gas, when all were prepared to admit that it was allowable to blow the bottom out of an iron-clad at midnight, throwing four or five hundred men into the sea to be choked by water, with scarcely the remotest chance of escape."

The widely differing views on these issues alone bear witness to the value of the discussion, which sadly but inevitably had to be limited to a first exchange of ideas, some recommendations and a few expressed desires.

The Second Commission

This commission was to discuss Articles 5 to 7 of Muraviev's circular letter which related to the adaptation of the 1864 Geneva Convention to naval warfare and the laws and customs of war.

THE GENEVA CONVENTION

This issue was recommended to a subcommittee presided over by the Dutch delegate Asser, which in its turn referred the question to a committee of experts, among whom were Professor Renault of France, Vice-Admiral Fisher of Britain, Captain Mahan of America and Captain Scheine of Russia. The commission decided to concentrate on general principles and not to enter into details of organization and regulations. Humanity, Renault argued, did not gain much from the adoption of rules which remained a dead letter; this would only enfeeble the respect for such engagements! It was therefore

Frederic Frommhold de Martens (1845–1909), a Russian diplomat and professor at St. Petersburg University. He was Vice-President of the Institute of International Law in 1885 and a member of the Permanent Court of Arbitration from 1902 to 1904.

The Second Commission, headed by Frederic de Martens.

Right: The British delegation, with Sir Julian Pauncefote third from the left in the first row and Sir John A. Fisher second from the left.

essential to avoid results inspired by generous sentiments, but likely to be disregarded by belligerents. For instance, the care for the wounded from sentiments of humanity was noble and welcome – as long as it did not unduly impair the freedom of action of the combatants. A treaty was outlined in fourteen articles, and regulations were suggested concerning hospital ships, their distinguishing marks and flags, their personnel, and the status of captured sick and wounded, and the shipwrecked. Furthermore, it was suggested to the Swiss Federal Council to convoke a special Conference in the near future in order to revise the Geneva convention.

LAWS AND CUSTOMS OF WAR

The second issue conferred on this commission and by the latter assigned to yet another subcommittee, was the revision of the 1874 Brussels declaration on the laws and customs of war on land which, incidentally, had never been ratified. This subcommission, headed by de Martens of Russia, set out to prepare a code. Along the line of argument it was proposed by Eyschen of Luxembourg to examine also the rights and duties of neutral States. This question, though, did not come under the Brussels declaration and was, in a unanimously adopted resolution, referred to a later Conference. The convention agreed upon was approved by all delegates except the Swiss and Chinese. In the first three articles it gave a definition of belligerents and determined that the laws, rights and duties of war also be applied to all militia and volunteer corps that were openly armed, were commanded by a responsible person, were equipped with a fixed and recognizable distinctive emblem and conducted their operations in accordance with the regular laws and customs of war. The same held good for civilians rising in defence of their frontiers and for non-combatant elements of regular armed forces.

Articles 4 to 20 provided for the humane treatment of prisoners of war, regulating their status, detention, labour, wages, food, quarters, clothing and discipline, matters concerning pay, postage, religious tolerance, wills, burials and repatriation, and prisoners' obligations such as to declare their name and rank and questions of parole. The status of cap-

tured journalists, the institution of a bureau of information as regards prisoners and the charity of relief societies were also bound by rules. Next came articles on the sick and wounded, on the restrictions put on the means of injuring the enemy, on bombardments and pillage, on the status of spies, on flags of truce and treachery involved, on capitulations and armistices and on military authority over hostile territory including conscription, taxation, allegiance and the confiscation of property. The concluding articles dealt with various matters such as railway plants from neutral territories, the trusteeship of occupied property and the detention and care of belligerents in neutral countries. All in all sixty articles of impressive impact on warfare were concluded. What was their worth?

"There have been severe critics who have characterized the labours of the Conference as 'threshing out Russian straw'", declared Professor Zorn in the *Deutsche Rundschau* of 1900: "this work alone [the two treaties agreed upon by the second commission] would suffice to give the lie to these ignorant and frivolous critics". This view was corroborated by Professor de Martens, who in the *North American Review* of November 1899 declared that these treaties were, as far as he was concerned, as notable as the treaty on arbitration agreed upon by the third commission. "Through it prisoners of war will be treated, not as enemies, but as disarmed and honorable adversaries, worthy of respect."

It must be said that the Hague Conference did reach more as regards the wounded and naval warfare than all the previous Red Cross Conferences taken together. Though disparaged by the peace societies, Holls observes, the humanizing of war serves the same ends as the peaceful adjustment of differences. Unbridled military licence, he argued, would only lead to the raising of the black flag and savagery and in no way serve, as is falsely understood, the deterrence of war.

The Third Commission

ORGANIZATION

If the work of the first and second commissions, which was all in all of a rather technical nature, could perhaps have been accomplished by a meeting of experts, like the Geneva and Brussels Conferences referred to above, the task of the third commission, the settlement of disputes through arbitration, was essentially of a diplomatic nature and most directly touching on the issue of the sovereignty of the specific States. It was generally felt that the discussions of this commission constituted the *pièce de résistance* of the Conference. As one journalist observed in the opening days: "Arbitration is the subject first in favour and Disarmament the last among delegates." Small wonder, therefore, that the nations chose their most expert delegates to represent them in this debate – with the notable exception of Germany which only nominated military and naval experts.

The presidency of the committee was conferred upon Léon Bourgeois, a former French Prime Minister, eminent both as statesman and orator and, again according to Holls, "a happy combination of idealist and opportunist". Honorary presidents were Count Nigra of Italy, an outstanding diplomat with long experience in Paris, London and Vienna, and Lord Pauncefote, a man of genius who had only recently distinguished himself in helping negotiate the eventually unratified arbitration treaty between the United States and Great Britain.

The full committee convened nine times between 23 May and 25 July. In its second session it was decided, on the suggestion of Mr. Bourgeois, that a Special Committee of Examination (*Comité d'Examen*) was to be installed, which then would report the text of the proposed treaty to the full committee. To this *Comité* were appointed Asser of Holland, Descamps of Belgium, d'Estournelles of France, Holls of the United States, Lammasch of Austria-Hungary, de Martens of Russia, Odier of Switzerland and Zorn of Germany. The president and honorary presidents usually attended its meetings.

This committee soon became the centre of interest of the whole Conference. "It was soon felt," as Holls put it in his reports "that the question of success or failure of the Conference as a whole depended almost entirely upon the chance of unbroken harmony in this Committee." As he saw it, these men eventually saved the Conference from failure. Their absorbing interest in the issue at stake and their common endeavour to accomplish the noble goals set, as difficult as these might seem at first, became in his opinion the most memorable feature of the entire Conference. Its members soon dropped all diplomatic reserve, and "sincere personal esteem as well as genuine good fellowship, appeased even the most serious differences of opinion". These latter, however, were not long in coming to the fore. One of the central issues of the debate concerned the establishment of a Court of Arbitration. The Germans firmly resisted the idea, the *Kaiser* having declared himself categorically opposed to any inter-

The Third Commission, headed by Léon Bourgeois, the French first delegate.

Léon Bourgeois (1851–1925), a very persuasive orator and author of a famous book, "Solidarité" (1897). He attended both Hague Conferences, was a member of the Court of Arbitration, Nobel Prize Laureate in 1920 and has been called the spiritual father of the League of Nations.

vention in his affairs of state. So the sessions were suspended halfway and in the midst of the debates Zorn, the German representative in the committee, and Holls left for Berlin to consult Count von Bülow, the German Minister for Foreign Affairs, so as to avert the imminent crisis. In this they succeeded, upon which the discussions were continued. All in all this *Comité d'Examen* held eighteen sessions, usually three times a week from two till six in the afternoon. The delegates first convened in the famous Chinese Room of the palace, but afterwards met in the *Salle de Trèves* at the Binnenhof in the centre of The Hague. Baron d'Estournelles admirably summarized the discussions, which were held in French mostly, in his *procès verbaux*.

The basis for all discussions was the eighth article of Count Muraviev's circular letter of 13 January and the project developed from it by the Russians. This provided for the *ad hoc* constitution, and the regulation, of arbitral tribunals, as was explained by Baron de Staal in the meeting of 26 May. The chief articles of the project concerned:

1 Good Offices and
   Mediation   Articles 1–6
2 Arbitration   Articles 7–12
3 The Tribunal   Articles 13 and 26,
                          Articles in appendix
4 Investigation   Articles 14–18

Under the first point, mediation was understood as the submitting of friendly counsel, in no way obligatory, by third parties – either at the instance of the parties in dispute or of neutral powers. The second point, arbitration, was generally considered the most efficacious and equitable means of settling disputes. The third point aimed at a code of arbitral procedure subject to arrangements at the option of the disputant parties. The fourth point provided for the creation of International Commissions of Inquiry, whose reports, again, would be purely advisory.

It proved upon enquiry by Bourgeois, that the basic ideas of this fourfold proposal were acceptable to all the attending delegations. This alone was considered a fair success at the moment. But then, to the utter surprise of all present, Lord Pauncefote rose and, gladly accepting the Russian scheme as far as it went, proposed to supplement it by the constitution of a Permanent International Tribunal. Stead, in his column in the *Manchester Guardian,* observed: "You could have heard a pin drop in the Conference. Members looked at one another for a moment in blank amazement, and not a few felt for the first time that they were face to face with serious business put forward by practical statesmen in grim earnest."

Then their surprise was once again heightened by the subsequent announcement of de Staal that the Russian Government would also submit a proposal to this purport and that the American delegates were likewise preparing such a scheme, whereas the Italians had some amendments to offer, too. So, oddly enough, in the first days of June the

Drafting Committee of the Arbitration Commission found itself overwhelmed by an *embarras du choix* of six proposals:

1 the Russian scheme, including the code of arbitral procedure;
2 the British scheme for a permanent tribunal;
3 the American scheme for a permanent tribunal;
4 an American project for special mediation;
5 an Italian amendment to the Russian scheme for mediation and arbitration;
6 the Russian supplementary scheme for a permanent tribunal.

The British and American proposals soon proved much the same in essence. The schemes provided for a permanent bureau which would summon the court whenever litigants so demanded. The court would be chosen by the litigants from a list to which each contracting power had contributed names, though in the English proposal the litigants might also choose one or more judges not listed. Decisions of the tribunal would go by majority. The Russian supplementary scheme provided for a court to be established at The Hague and made up of five arbitrators to be designated by as many powers and possibly two arbitrators appointed by the litigants themselves. The court had to be controlled by a secretariat equipped with an adequate staff that would render an annual account of its operations. The object of the Italian amendment, incidentally, aimed mainly at the restriction of the obligatory element in the Russian proposal.

THE WORK OF THE COMITÉ D'EXAMEN

In high spirits the *Comité* set to work. On 5 June the first point on the agenda, concerning good offices and mediation, was dealt with, resulting in the amalgamation of the suggestions made by the Russians, the Italians and the Americans.

On 7 and 9 June debate started within the committee on the matter of arbitration, leading to the acceptance of the British proposal as the basis for further discussion. It was at this juncture that Zorn interfered and pointed out the *Kaiser's* objections. Arbitration, Wilhelm held, was dangerous and derogatory to the monarch's sovereignty and the nation's independence. Reaction was firm and violent. Lord Pauncefote himself suavely replied that the view of statecraft exposed by the *Kaiser* was "perhaps not altogether modern". Nevertheless he consented in some modifications of the scheme in an utmost effort to induce the German Emperor to modify his attitude. Holls then took trouble to defend these along with the conciliative Zorn at Berlin. Meanwhile, on 21 June, the committee adopted, though in a somewhat modified form, the third issue at stake, the Russian articles dealing with International Commissions of Inquiry.

On 3 July, Pauncefote's arbitration scheme came up for discussion anew and some minor amendments were agreed upon concerning the

Heinrich Lammasch (1853–1920). An Austrian jurist, who was Prime Minister in the last months of the World War.

Left: Count Constantino Nigra of Italy (1828–1907). He was a diplomat and philologist who much impressed his colleagues at The Hague.

number of arbiters on the list and their diplomatic immunity. More interesting though, it became increasingly evident that an obligatory clause would never pass German opposition. On 4 July the *Comité* was definitely forced, on behalf of Germany mainly, to cut out this clause and adhere to the principle of optional arbitration. It was here, later critics would argue, that by far the best opportunity to achieve something really spectacular was missed.

On 7 July the final scheme drawn up by the *Comité d'Examen* was presented to the plenary session of the third commission; here it was only slightly modified. In his concluding remarks that day Descamps, who was the reporter of the *Comité*, called to mind that at least it had been established that the principle of arbitration had definitely penetrated into international practice, and could now be acclaimed with favour by all the members of the committee. Despite political differences and some legal uncertainties that had come up, the principle had "all the sympathies of the present and the richest promise for the future". The institution of a Permanent Court had been unanimously agreed to. The Court would be competent for all questions and its members have a mandate fixed at six years. The session then was adjourned till 17 July to leave the delegates time to refer the scheme to their respective governments or do as the Japanese delegation did, when they cabled the integral text of the treaty to Tokyo at enormous cost.

After new objections the deliberations of the third commission were brought to an end on 25 July, and a Convention comprising sixty-one articles brought before the full Conference. A farewell dinner that night at the *Hotel d'Orange* concluded the work of the *Comité d'Examen*. It had a fine piece of co-operation to show: regarding arbitration Britain's plan was adopted with amendments of phraseology and a few unimportant additions; the Inquiry Commissions were justly Russia's pride; the duty-clause was the boast of the French; the mediation plan on the analogy of the actions of "seconds" in duelling went to the credit of the Americans.

For our purposes the implications regarding the Permanent Court of Arbitration are the more relevant ones. They will be discussed in detail in Chapter XI.

The Final Session

On Saturday 29 July, a fair summer's day, at ten o'clock, the members assembled for the last time in the *Huis ten Bosch* for the signing of the Final Act and the various conventions and declarations. The beautifully engrossed documents, with the seals of the signing plenipotentiaries affixed to them, were spread out upon the large tables of the dining room. After the signing, which took up all morning, a farewell luncheon was served and final toasts were made. It was as the *Times* correspondent observed: "Two and a half months ago the atmosphere at the House in the Wood was one of frigid reserve, not to

A meeting of the "Comité d'examen", presided over by Léon Bourgeois, at the Binnenhof in the "Trèveszaal", so called after the Twelve Years Truce with Spain (1609–1621) that was concluded there. The room was redecorated in 1697 by Daniel Marot in the style of Louis XIV, featuring allegorical wall-panels.

say mutual mistrust; yesterday was like a breaking-up for holidays at school. Everybody was pleased with everybody in general, and with the president in particular."

At three o'clock the closing meeting, to which special guests and members of the press were invited into the little gallery of the cupola, was called to order. Jhr. van Karnebeek summed up the concrete results of the Conference laid down in the Final Act that was signed by all the powers represented. It consisted of three conventions (to be signed by the represented powers before the end of the year), three declarations, one resolution and six desideratums.

And so the Conference had come to its end; only formalities remained. Telegrams exchanged by Queen Wilhelmina and Pope Leo XIII were read, in which the Queen implored moral support for the Conference, and the Pope, whose delegates had been banned due to grim Italian protests, reminded her of the time-honoured role of the Supreme Pontiff as mediator of peace, whose authority embraced all nations and actually surpassed the special interests of the Heads of State. Speeches were delivered by President de Staal, Prince Münster, Baron d'Estournelles and Mr. de Beaufort, and the hope was expressed that the present Conference would meet again "within some years". Then at last, de Staal tapped on his desk with his hammer and said: "Messieurs, la séance est levée!"

Conclusions

"Any one who would have predicted, even as late as July 1898, that a Conference would meet and accomplish even a fraction of the results attained at The Hague, – that the subject of a federation of the civilized world for justice would even be discussed, not by enthusiasts and private individuals, but by leading diplomats of all civilized nations, called together for that purpose by the most powerful autocrat in the world, – would have been regarded as a dreamer, if not as demented."

The words are from Holls' report of the Conference. Interestingly enough, many of the attending delegates in their memoirs express their contentment with the results attained in The Hague. Public opinion on the whole has been less sympathetic, though. Indeed, many critics of later days have actually ridiculed the meagre outcome of the Conference. What were the results of the Conference really and how should they be evaluated? Or rather, what could have been expected anyway?

The first observation which must be made is that, in a way, the Hague Conference was a unique experiment. It was the first Conference of its sort ever attended by representatives of so many nations. To some, the Americans for instance, it marked their first entrance in international affairs at this level. But although the experimental aspect may count as its highest value, it also accounts for most of the shortcomings of the Conference. At the dinner table delegates, as likely as not, were to take their place next to the unknown world on their left and a traditional enemy on their right. This alone called for initial mistrust, suspicion and reservation. "Dense ignorance, insipid wit, and the silliest sarcasm" on the part of most members of the press, as Holls puts it in a weaker moment, only strengthened these feelings. And yet, ten weeks afterwards, all these delegates parted as good friends, that is if William Stead is to be believed. Already on 3 June, he noted in his diary: "A month of amicable discussion of the gravest problems has worked the happiest change in the spirit of the Conference. The fact is that the intrinsic absurdity and unreason of the existing international anarchy are such that honest men cannot seriously consider them without the conviction growing that a little good faith and sincere effort are alone wanting for a great step toward a happier future. In personal contact, too, old suspicions and prejudices have given way. The courage and enthusiasm of the British and American delegates have contributed to this change. So have the skill, lucidity, and good sense of the French representatives."

The delegates had come from all quarters of the earth; they covered more fields than any gathering of the sort before: they were both jurists and military men, both diplomats and scholars of international law. Men of action ranked next to masters of the word. This added up to something at least. Thus, what they found out together was that the former were no more bloodthirsty animals than the latter were quixotic dreamers. For instance, they all were

very much aware of the fact that no obligatory clause, without the sanction of armed force, could ever stop malicious intent. At the same time they realized that the public conscience which formed world opinion could well do without enforcement either. Indeed, the moral profit to be gained from a Conference like the present one, they held, could well overshadow its material results. No pressure on unanimity in decision-making should therefore be allowed to wreck negotiations or lure ultimate aspirations into a deadlock. The moral effect of any convention which was passed, maybe not with unanimity (and this might happen for all sorts of reasons), but still with an overwhelming majority by a true "Parliament of the World", was as binding to mankind, they felt, as enforcement could ever hope to be. In a way they proved right.

As they had anticipated, their united efforts concentrating on the idea of arbitration and the installation of a court rather than on disarmament, could not prevent war at all times – as little as the police can prevent all crime. Before long, Russia, the very initiator of the Conference, would come to grips with another participant, Japan and another prominent representative, Great Britain, in the meantime had gone to war with the Boers. But in 1904 the outbreak of war between Russia and Britain over the Dogger Bank Affair was indeed prevented by a Commission of Inquiry installed according to the third Article of the 1899 Convention on the pacific settlement of disputes. This was the more noteworthy, as in this conflict the "honour and vital interests" of both nations were concerned, which had expressly been excluded from the competence of such a commission in the convention. And only a few months afterwards President Theodore Roosevelt, with the help of the same article, initiated the negotiations which ended the Russo-Japanese conflict with the Treaty of Portsmouth of 1905. Likewise, within five years from its installation, the Permanent Court at The Hague had proved instrumental four times: in a conflict between the United States and Mexico (1902), in a case regarding European claims against Venezuela (1904), in the case of the Japanese leases (1902) and in the so-called Muscat Dhows case between Britain and France (1905). In the meantime, however, in the Boer War the convention on the laws of war on land was not exactly fulfilled to the letter.

Nothing utopian had been aimed at, nothing quixotic was worked out, nothing miraculous had been accomplished. At its best, a piece of solid workmanship in the field of international law had been produced. Dimly, on the far horizon, maybe the first glimmerings of an international code could be perceived. But the wheels of progress grind slowly, as statesmen are among the first to appreciate. In 1899, as at any other juncture of history, too many, often conflicting, forces had been at work in the domain of high politics to ask for more. Perhaps, considering this perspective, the Conference had indeed, as in Lord Pauncefote's opinion, "greatly surpassed the expectations of its most enthusiastic supporters".

The Dutch delegation, featuring from left to right: Tadema, den Beer Poortugael, van Karnebeek, Asser and Rahusen.

Andrew Carnegie: Life, Ideals

Opposite left: Andrew Carnegie (1835–1912), portrayed in 1913 by the Dutch painter B. J. Blommers (1845–1914). The panel was presented to the Board of the Carnegie Foundation by Carnegie's Dutch admirers.

In the summer of 1899 William T. Stead, the energetic British journalist and pacifist, paid a visit to Skibo Castle, the princely summer residence of Andrew Carnegie in the Scottish Highlands. Talk arose about what had at the time become Carnegie's prime concern and which was in a subsequent publication by Stead to be descibed as "Carnegie's Conundrum: £40 million – what shall I do with it?" It was not that Carnegie lacked counsellors on the issue, in fact he sometimes had as many as three hundred a day, he told Stead, but their suggestions didn't result in much. His general idea was to spend his fortune "in the interests of humanity", but he found that it was very easy to do harm when you wished to do good. Therefore, he selected friends for their practical knowledge and common sense to consult him on the matter. Besides, he confided to Stead, he had developed quite strong ideas of his own as to the distribution of his fortune.

It was typical of Stead that on his return he set out to solve Carnegie's problem by bringing matters up for public discussion, towards the end of the year, in the 1900 Annual of the *Review of Reviews*, of which he was the editor. In the course of preparing this publication and a sequel he interviewed many men of prominence. Among these, in December, he approached the Russian Counsellor of State and prominent delegate at the Hague Conference, Mr. Frederic de Martens. It was he, apparently, who first made the suggestion of having Carnegie create a fund for the building of a "headquarters" for the

recently established Hague Court of Arbitration, which might also serve as a home for future Peace Conferences. Nothing came of the idea; in fact it is uncertain whether the suggestion made to Stead ever reached Carnegie at all, as de Martens believed for certain at the time. Still, the idea was born and had stuck with de Martens himself. In June of the following year he arranged a meeting in Berlin with an old acquaintance from The Hague, Andrew D. White, the former head of the American delegation at the Peace Conference, who was then the United States Ambassador in Germany. On this occasion de Martens renewed his proposal and knowing White to be on very friendly terms with Carnegie (one of his "old shoes", as Carnegie would say), asked him to plead the idea with the multi-millionaire philanthropist. White promptly wrote a letter to Carnegie to this intent and received a formal reply within a week. In the years to come it would entail much laborious negotiation, running into complete deadlock several times and almost ending in total failure before the Palace was to be opened in 1913. Still, in short, this is how Andrew Carnegie first became involved with his major project in matters of peace.

Early Childhood

Andrew Carnegie was born in Dunfermline in 1835 "of poor but honest parents, of good kith and kin", as he himself states in the opening lines of a rather smug autobiography. Dunfermline was a centre of the damask trade and for generations the fortune of the Carnegie family had gone up and down with that of the linen industry. His father was a damask weaver, though an impoverished descendant in a long and proud line. It appears from Andrew's words that he was in every sense a nice man, though not too strong a character. Not much of an entrepreneur, he lacked a keen eye for business and did not anticipate the impending revolution from hand- to steam-loom weaving. It took the endeavours of "that power which never failed in any emergency", his mother, to add to the slender revenues, and thus keep the family at least respectable. Andrew's mother was a Morrison girl and she, if anyone, had been the dominating force in Andrew's life. After his father's untimely death he found her "all my own" and his first book was dedicated to her, his "favorite Heroine". He never considered marriage until after her death in 1886.

The house in Dunfermline where Carnegie was born. It is now a museum owned by the Carnegie Dunfermline Trust.

Young Andrew was of an optimistic nature. He believed that a sunny disposition is worth more than a fortune. "All his ducks are swans" his young playmates used to say and business companions of later years observed that trouble ran from his back like water from a duck's back. In his own view it was this ability to laugh his way through life that was the key to much of his success. "Thine own reproach alone do fear" ran his motto, taken from the Scottish poet Robert Burns, whose works meant much to him. He said it was the Dunfermline surroundings that accounted for "this potency of the romantic and poetic strain" that permeated him.

Andrew was fond of his birthplace, which was dominated by its 11th-century abbey and the imposing ruins of the great monastery and former royal palace. He felt privileged and "absorbed the romance of the scenery with the air he breathed". It also inspired another trait of character, though. The Dunfermline of the period ranked next to Paisley for its radicalism. Both the Morrison and Carnegie families were known as outspoken fanatics in political matters. Andrew, in his turn, had adopted the motto "death to privilege" before ever properly understanding its implications. The "borrowed plumes", the "accident of birth", soon became familiar notions with him and his hatred for the man whose "most fruitful part of his family, as with the potato, lies underground", was as naive as it was sincere. It was the Lairds of Pittencrieff Glen, the Dunfermline acropolis, who embodied all this: consequent to some riots they had banned all Morrisons from the Glen. Accordingly, no gift which Carnegie made in later years could in his eyes possibly approach his purchasing of this Dunfermline Glen for the benefit of the town population.

William Wallace and Robert the Bruce, predictably, were the youngster's heroes and Bannockburn his pride. It came as a severe shock, therefore, when in the spring of 1848 he was informed by his parents of their departure for America. Two million Scots would go that way in the "hungry forties", when hopes were down and life offered no prospects. They ran from famine and suppression to the land "where a man is a man even though he must toil". Yet, to the boy of thirteen it meant the loss of fairyland. The memory of the abbey contours, slowly fading out of view, remained alive for years with him and long after he would hear the drone of the curfew bell tolling, treasuring all the recollections of childhood. It also meant the end of schooling: he could read, write and do sums, and had some algebra and Latin.

First they joined relatives in Pittsburgh. Going by steamboat up the Ohio they finally settled in Allegheny City, residing with kinsmen in a shabby weaver's shop in Rebecca Street. Here Andrew's father resumed his trade, selling his hand-made table-cloths under the same extreme conditions and gaining the same meagre returns. And again the resourceful mother helped, earning four dollars a week by binding shoes and meanwhile reciting the gems of Scottish minstrelsy to her Andrew and Tom,

the latter boy being nine years the younger. Children of honest poverty they were – and they felt blessed beyond compare.

Andrew Carnegie's dominating mother, Margaret Morrison († 1886).

The Eager Apprentice

Here starts the tale of the American Dream, though not too splendid at first. The early years proved a bitter struggle. Andrew started in a cotton mill, for $1.20 per week, as a bobbin-boy, at the steam-engine and firing the boiler in the cellar. It was a hard life and not without peril. He took the first opportunity that offered itself to get out and to join the ranks of clerks. He soon proved good at figures and eagerly took up the novelty of double-entry bookkeeping. However, the real start in life came in 1850, when he seized the chance to wash off the coal dirt and start in Pittsburgh as a messenger-boy.

Pittsburgh at that time was rapidly expanding as a transfer station from river to canal, though the business life of the day was slowly recovering from the great fire of 1845 which had paralyzed all industry. Its valuable deposits of coal and ample stores of natural gas were not yet fully appreciated at this juncture. As a messenger boy for the Eastern Telegraph Line at a salary of $2.50 a week, Andrew

The old building at the corner of Third and Wood Streets in Pittsburgh where Carnegie started as a telegraph messenger in 1849.

managed to attract attention: he was keen, clever, prompt and resourceful and eager to learn. In the process he made the acquaintance of a certain Colonel Anderson who opened up his library to the boy. In this way he read Macaulay's essays and Lamb and developed a taste for literature. In later years Carnegie would found some 2,800 public libraries all over the world; it is to Colonel Anderson's 400 well-worn volumes that he ascribed this much satirized inclination of his. Here it was that he came under the spell of Shakespeare: messenger-boys delivering telegrams at the theatre were often allowed to slip upstairs and watch the plays being performed. Andrew therefore, adroitly, withheld the telegrams until showtime. During these years he also became

Andrew Carnegie and his brother Tom, nine years his junior, in about 1850.

interested in the mysteries of the Pittsburgh Swedenborg Society, in which some of his relatives were prominent. His taste for music was first aroused through its choir.

His ambition made him not too popular with his young colleagues, who also resented his meanness, as they so interpreted his refusal to spend his extra dimes in their company which he knew were needed badly at home. But as a rule his employers were content with him and picked him out for promotion. On his own initiative he learned the art of telegraphy and the morse code. "Knowledge is sure to prove useful in one way or another; it always tells", he held, and for him for once it did: before the year 1852 was over he found himself installed as an operator at $25 per month, which he then thought a fortune. It lent him the prestige to enter the local Webster Literary Society. His training from debating in these circles gave a clearness and fixity to his ideas and produced his famous self-possession in public speaking: "be your own self and talk, never 'orate' until you can't help it" read his motto.

A Railroad Man

It was as a clerk and operator that in 1853 he secured a position offered by Thomas A. Scott, then superintendent of a branch of the Pennsylvania Railroad. Both the man and the firm would prove of major importance throughout his life. Andrew would rise under the aegis of this management genius and along with the spectacular expansion of the company. From here on his career would go up by leaps and bounds. Thus, on the threshold of manhood, on his eighteenth birthday, he entered the railroad service, though he almost ruined his career when in the very first weeks through carelessness he managed to lose the first pay-rolls and cheque ever entrusted to him. It never broke his confidence, though. He steered with a firm hand: he became a strong partisan of the cause of the Union and the anti-slavery movement and actually was among the first, as he so states, to avail himself of the meticulousness of women in the telegraph office.

Again, in his new position, Andrew distinguished himself by bold initiative and self-assurance, when in a case of emergency in the absence of Scott he ran the line all by himself. "Scott's Andy" became a household word in the company: "the battle of life is already half won", he jotted down in his autobiography, "by the young man who is brought personally in contact with high officials; and the great aim of every boy should be to do something beyond the sphere of his duties – something which attracts the attention of those over him." Gradually he took over from Scott.

The year 1855 was marked by two incidents, his father's death in October and the "knocking of Fortunatus" some weeks afterwards, when Scott suggested to him a first investment of $500. This implied a loan, for which his mother proved prepared to pledge their house as a security. The ten shares of Adams Express provided him with the first pennies of revenue from capital. Another opportunity soon came when he met the celebrated T. T. Woodruff, the inventor of the sleeping-car. Carnegie saw its importance in a flash. He secured two cars for the Pennsylvania and an eighth interest for himself in the venture of the young enterprise. It was from this source that he made his first considerable sum.

Towards 1860 he succeeded Scott as superintendent of the Pittsburgh Division. The success was not appreciated by his inferiors. As he himself states, he rather overworked his men, judging the limits of human endurance by his own iron constitution. He never knew fatigue and needed only "snatches of sleep" at intervals during the night. He was fairly thin at the time, weighing not more than a hundred pounds at twenty-four years of age.

The first months of the Civil War saw him summoned to Washington in charge of the military railroads and telegraphs. It was a sad experience. Lack of organizing talent in the Union camp hampered the running of his department. Long years of peace had fossilized the service. He was not unhappy for it after all, for here it was that he learned to know Abraham Lincoln. Carnegie was much impressed by the President's marked features, his imposing personality and keen intellect. Lincoln's charm, he observed, lay in the total absence of mannerisms. Here was the perfect democrat, revealing in every word and act the equality of men.

Worn out, Carnegie, along the line, suffered sunstroke and broke down completely. He became seriously ill and afterwards never could stand heat, which accounts for his annual long stays in the Scottish Highlands in summertime in later years. He was granted leave and in June 1862 with his mother set sail for Scotland. The return to Dunfermline was a treat and his reception very hearty. Still, as mentioned above, it was disappointing in one sense:

"Everything there was in miniature...Here was a city of the Lilliputians." It all ended in sad tones for again he became seriously ill. The return ocean voyage strengthened him, though.

The Iron and Oil Industry

He now set off on a course of rapid expansion. Iron was the thing, he reckoned, and along with Scott he ventured upon iron bridge-building. In 1863 he founded the Keystone Bridge Company. Similarly, the ever rising prices of iron and the urgent requirement of rails on the part of the railroads led him in 1864 to organize a rail-making concern. Two years later the great demand for locomotives made him set up the highly prosperous Pittsburgh Locomotive Works, which "have always been my pet as being the parent of all the other works". In the meantime Carnegie quite naturally set eyes on that other promising source of income of the period, the great Pennsylvanian oil wells. His $40,000 investment in oil proved, for him, the best so far. The revenues enabled him to build a new iron mill in Pittsburgh. Profitable though they were, these numerous investments began to require ever more attention. It was at this juncture that he decided to leave the service of the Pennsylvania Railroad Company and concentrate on his own affairs. On 28 March 1865 he received the predictable gold watch from his former colleagues. From then on Andrew Carnegie never worked for a salary.

The year 1867 was to be a memorable one for quite different reasons. With some friends he made a most instructive tour of Europe and travelled extensively throughout Britain. It was there that he learned to appreciate the masterpieces of the arts and to develop a taste of his own which made him judge his former favourites by new standards.

Reconstruction of Carnegie's study in the Dunfermline Museum. On the wall the portrait of Carnegie's wife.

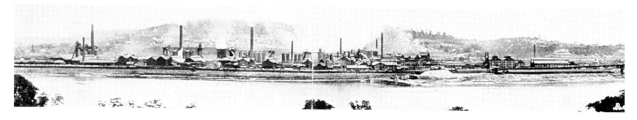

A panoramic view of the "Lucy Furnace", opened in 1873 and soon to become by far the most profitable branch of business.

Among other things, the Händel Anniversary celebrated that year at Crystal Palace made him appreciate the power and majesty of music. These visits served him well, too, in a commercial sense. To the energetic American everything on the Continent seemed almost at a standstill compared to the swirl and spin of his "Triumphant Republic".

Carnegie's commercial successes inevitably made him climb the social ladder. Expanding business persuaded him to move his headquarters to New York and there, in the Nineteenth Century Club and other salons, he tended to meet prominent people and undergo definite educational influences, which he enjoyed enormously. Among the long-standing relationships initiated there was that with the above-mentioned Andrew D. White, at the time President of Cornell University and some thirty years afterwards America's chief delegate to the Hague Conference of 1899. White was to become Carnegie's life-long friend and counsellor.

Indeed, New York laid open new horizons in many ways. One of these was, of course, speculation. It is interesting to note that Carnegie had always been very strict in those matters. "Speculation is a parasite feeding upon values, creating none", he held. With a single exception he never bought a share of stock speculatively in his life.

The Birth of a Steel Tycoon

He now rapidly learned to "think big". The enormous success of the sleeping car, a "positive necessity upon the American Continent", forced his Central Transportation Company to make ever deeper investments and face serious competition from a Mr. Pullman, that other example of the American dream, then opening business at the world's greatest railway centre of Chicago. Carnegie and Pullman, a former carpenter with a keen eye for the drift of things and "always to be found, so to speak, swimming in the main current", soon came to terms. The companies merged and placed the new one beyond all possible rivals. Two years later both men were to be found, along with Scott, on the board of the Union Pacific Railway Company. This led, incidentally, to one of the major disappointments of his life when some time later he found himself cheated by Scott, who, in his absence, had sold out for speculative purposes. "I saw that I was still young and had a good deal to learn. Many men can be trusted, but a few need watching."

Another lesson he was to learn from the failure of friends was to freely invest whatever of one's surplus money was available, but never to entrust one's name as endorser or member of a corporation with individual liability. A trifling investment could indeed possess deadly explosive power! To counteract this, however, were the delights he took in contracting business with reliable men such as Pierpoint Morgan, father and son. High standards of integrity and personal honour, Carnegie felt, marked these negotiations throughout and he appreciated this to the full.

However, another lesson was soon to come when in 1873 a stock-exchange crisis interfered with Carnegie's large scale business transactions. In September panic came upon him in the midst of negotiations and he was in for some of the most anxious moments of his business life. Firm after firm failed, largely because of the absence of a proper banking system, and a total paralysis of business was the result.

Nevertheless, Carnegie steered straight by making it his policy (contrary to the adage) "to put all good eggs in one basket and then watch that basket", in other words: to concentrate on the one business engaged in and not to invest in far away enterprises, "while the true gold lies right in your own factory". Iron was his business, and this branch he watched closely. Thus, once having heard rumours of the Bessemer process he was first to conceive that soon the Iron Age would pass away and the Steel Age take its place. He promptly anticipated these events, sending some of his most competent men to Britain to investigate the process and then went on in search of the proper raw material and took over mines that had long been neglected.

On 1 January 1873 his steel-rail company was organized and a newly opened plant, the Lucy Furnace, was soon to become by far the most profitable branch of business. The combination of perfect machinery, admirable plans laid out by most skilful engineers and great management, provided a success that was phenomenal.

Up to this time Carnegie's meagre background but rapid growth in business had made his reputation in circles of elder Pittsburgh businessmen as being merely one of those reckless youngsters venturing upon a career more brilliant than substantial. "If his brains will not carry him through, his luck will", it was heard. Andrew himself had always argued with them, specifically on this one point, namely the bold and fearless part. Though younger than most of his competitors he claimed that his supply of Scots caution never had been small. At least among bankers at home and abroad he seems to have enjoyed much credit throughout his career. And it must be said that he for one had been keenly aware always of both his talents and his possible shortcomings and had been seen persistently concentrating on the thing he was best fitted for while rarely blundering into something he couldn't perform.

Years of Travelling and Marriage

In 1878 Carnegie saw fit to fulfil a long-cherished purpose of going around the world with some friends. The new horizons opened before him quite changed his intellectual outlook. He saw China and India, travelled from Singapore to Lapland, read Confucius, Buddha and Zoroaster – and quietened down. Out of chaos sprang order and with it came mental peace. The former Swedenborg mystic saw some truth in the revelation of each religion and found them ethically akin, every race, he observed, having received the message best adapted to its own stage of development: "The Unknown Power had neglected none", he wrote. He kept a journal and some time later had the satisfying experience of reading his own words in printed form. The success of this book *Around the World* encouraged quite a series of publications from his hand, including several travel books.

In 1877 he had also entered seriously upon his career as a public speaker as a result of the first so-called "Freedom" conferred upon him by his native town. He ended up by collecting fifty-three similar honours bestowed upon him by as many cities. In this he beat his later good friend, Prime Minister Gladstone, by some thirty-five. Most of these honours were due to his offering free libraries. The first opening in this almost endless series, which

Carnegie's fêted entry into Dunfermline in 1881 to open his first public library.

would close near to 3,000, also occurred at Dunfermline in 1881. It was his mother who laid the foundation stone. Because of the lack of a proper coat of arms he had a rising sun carved over the entrance shedding its rays and with it ran the motto "Let there be light". The words were to be applied numerous times.

The year 1886 ended in deep gloom. In November, and within a few days of each other, his mother and younger brother passed away, while he took to bed with a severe attack of typhoid fever. This was to open a new beginning, though. Having recovered he started dating an old acquaintance, Louise Whitfield, in the Central Park. His advances at first met with indifferent success, the girl being many years his junior and feeling she could add little to his life of luxury. Eventually they were married in New York in April 1887 and went to the Isle of Wight for their honeymoon. He showed her his native town and they then went on to the Scottish capital Edinburgh to receive another Freedom (Lord Rosebery making the speech) and took a highland piper along with them to New York who remained in their service for many years. Louise loved the highlands and much preferred to spend the summer there, which they did almost yearly. The purchase of Skibo Castle, years afterwards, was the result. She was a peace-loving girl, not too easily impressed by rank, wealth or social position, as Carnegie puts it. The marriage was a happy one and was blessed, ten years later, in March 1897, with a daughter Margaret, named after Andrew's mother. Carnegie was sixty-two at the time.

Back at work he decided on new investments. And this not merely on the sound principle that a manufacturing concern that stops expanding begins to decay. Vital to his steel purposes he now needed dominance of the total line of production, that is from the raw material to the completed article. It would secure independence, specifically in matters of obtaining regular supplies which appeared to him then imperative for survival. This was realized in 1886 by new purchases and through the reorganiza-

Left: "Around the World" with Andrew White. The photograph was taken in Ceylon in 1878.

tion of all his firms. They now produced everything, from a wire nail up to a steel girder. But he did not rest there. He tested new ores in Virginia and secured for his enterprise the first line of ferro-manganese in the States. Speed was everything to him and his business model of partnership instead of a corporation proper proved a great advantage here. He had no worries over board consultations and the like and steered a course, all of his own. The success of his labours speaks from the progress made in the next decade: investments were doubled, iron and steel production trebled.

Halfway through this decade, in 1892, he suffered an everlasting dark spot on his reputation as the result of the well-known Homestead strike. Carnegie always boasted of his fair understanding of and warm sympathy with the working classes. However, when, at the major plant in Homestead, Carnegie Brothers ran into conflict with union leaders over new sliding scales that led to riot and strikes, the managing directors called in the help of the Pinkerton detective agency to preserve order and replace the culprits. A fight broke out and men were shot on both sides. Carnegie himself was on holiday in Scotland at the time ("very conveniently", it was rumoured) and though "Andy" had a way of getting on with the "boys" easily which did not hold for his partners, his correspondence over the period calls for serious doubts as to his proper attitude in the controversy. At all events, the result at the time was outright slander (which he much resented), though somewhat mitigated by the personal support he received from both William Gladstone and some of his Homestead workers afterwards. At a mass meeting in Pittsburgh on his return he solemnly declared that "capital, labour and employer were a three-legged stool, none before or after the others, all equally indispensable".

The Gospel of Wealth

The year 1900 marked a sharp transition in Carnegie's life. He finally took the step which he had announced so many years before: virtual retirement from business affairs. And this marked, in his eyes quite naturally, the transition to the second phase of his life. What he meant by this was laid down in the book that was published that very year and which contained the core of many previous publications, suitably headed as Carnegie's Gospel of Wealth. With King Steel firmly on his throne, all other metals being swept out, and with the ever-extending Carnegie Steel Company having reached an all time record profit on a yearly base of about 40 million dollars and with prospects even more dazzling, Carnegie decided "to stop accumulating and begin the infinitely more serious and difficult task of wise distribution". It has been said that conflicting views within the management and increasing competition, particularly on the part of Pierpoint Morgan's Federal Steel Company, helped accelerate this decision. Be this as it may, Carnegie's intention to sell out was suggested to Morgan informally and his price for the Company and all its holdings set at $480 million. This Morgan promptly accepted. The deal was made in no time and left Carnegie the richest man on earth. Having concluded the sale he left for Europe to think over the new task set, known in literature as "Mr. Carnegie's Conundrum", how to

Andrew Carnegie in about 1886.

Carnegie's wife, Louise Whitfield († 1946). Andrew and she were married in 1887. On her right Margaret, their only daughter (born 1897).

best discharge the stewardship of wealth in order to avoid final disgrace, true to his own motto: "the man who dies rich, dies in disgrace."

It must be said that he applied the same shrewdness, cunning and common sense to the distribution of his "surplus wealth" that had marked him in the process of accumulating it. His gifts, it is known, were many and of a widely varying nature. Hardly any, however, come in the sphere of pure charity. Carnegie certainly did not give his money away unconditionally. He was always extremely careful in examining the ultimate implications of his involvements and often had ample inquiries made, well aware of the fact that unconditional financial support could have very detrimental results. In later years he would receive hundreds of letters daily imploring his benevolence for all sorts of ends. Most of these he refused flatly. However, once being satisfied of the importance of a specific goal and a trust being established, he allotted the money very generously, making very sure though of the proper administration of the capital.

The Distribution of a Fortune

Though of widely diverging character, Carnegie's gifts come mainly under three headings: education, welfare and peace. In this they reflect his main interests in social affairs. A first major category is formed by the public libraries. Mention is made above of the mental profit Carnegie drew from Colonel Anderson's 400 well-worn books. He considered a free library the best gift to be given to a community and numerous towns profited from his benevolence in this way – always provided the community would accept the maintenance of the building and the upkeep of the collection: "I do not give, I make others give", he stated frequently. Often

"A taste for reading drives out lower tastes", one of Carnegie's numerous aphorisms, in the façade of St. Louis Public Library.

he would extend these projects to art galleries, museums, lecture- and music-halls, or even swimming-baths, the many facilities offered to his home-towns Dunfermline and Pittsburgh being exemplary in these respects. Noteworthy here are the thousands of organs he endowed to churches and public halls at home and abroad.

Another category was science and research, "to be applied to the improvement of mankind". The centres founded by Carnegie which afterwards merged into Carnegie-Mellon University are probably the best known, but have their counterparts all over the world. Worth mentioning are the Carnegie Trusts for the Universities of Scotland and the very similar Carnegie Institution of Washington, an independent scientific research centre at the service of university life and the academic world. The gifts were not always of this order: Carnegie had numerous minor colleges founded and special chairs installed.

In the field of education proper also came his Endowment for the Advancement of Teaching, originally meant to raise the standards of education by improving the social conditions of teachers through the provision of pensions, but in recent times concentrating on studies on education. Here is an example of an endowment made in a sphere and towards ends that were gradually taken over by governments and whose goal could and was therefore reformulated within the ample limits set by the foundation deed.

Left: Pittencrieff House in Dunfermline, the ancestral home of the Lairds which Carnegie had made into a public park. The park was designed by Mawson, who laid out the grounds of the Peace Palace.

Most of these efforts in educational spheres covered the first years of his retirement. Gradually, a shift of interest can be observed towards the field of the international peace movement. Carnegie had never been averse to the ideals of pacifism and certainly had proved himself an opponent of war before. His fierce opposition to the growing imperialism in the States which brought about the acquisition of the Philippines in 1898 led to one of his rare outspoken political stands. Indirectly, though, his views were well-known – and not in America only: at one stage he owned eighteen British newspapers, running them as profitably as any of the investments he made and all of them crying out his fairly radical views – on home rule for instance. His ideas were also promulgated by his rather successful books: from *Triumphant Democracy* (1886) to *The Empire of Business* (1903) to *Problems of To-day. Wealth-Labor-Socialism* (1908). Besides, he gave frequent public addresses at openings and ceremonies. Many of these speeches were afterwards published in pamphlets and several contained unequivocal pleas for international peace.

At times he did have some influence on high politics in his way. As years went by his name opened up all sorts of worlds for him. He was on very friendly terms with the writers Mark Twain and Matthew Arnold and had been positively influenced by his contacts with Herbert Spencer and Darwinism. Some of his ethical optimism at least may go back to these authorities: "All is well since all grows better" became his motto in later years. Many were his political friends on both the Continents. He counted leading English politicians as Gladstone, Chamberlain, Lord Rosebery and that other Dun-

fermline lad, Campbell-Bannerman among his correspondents and freely discussed hot issues such as free trade with them. The same held good for American politics. Through his friend Secretary of State Elihu Root he had access to the inner circles of Washington and in due time got to know Cleveland, Hay and McKinley, Harrison and Blaine, Roosevelt and Wilson personally. Several of these men featured on the board or as a trustee of one of his Foundations and Trusts. It was through them also that his one political appointment ever came about. In 1891 he was among the American delegates to the second Pan-American Congress.

The Peace Endowments

Carnegie's quest for peace led to the founding of a wide range of Funds and Trusts and within fifteen years (1904–1919) he had donated over $25 million to this end. His conversion to its august cause had been a reluctant one at first, though. For a long time he withstood the pressure from Stead and other activists to join the peace movement: "There is nothing that robs a righteous cause of its strength more than a millionaire's money", he once observed with his usual good sense. But he was definitely looking for a mission and finally found it in the pursuit of peace. "Peace at any price" one is tempted to say, for accustomed to the power of wealth he deemed peace a thing that might be purchased like anything else. His "pacifism" had a personal brand therefore which did not help to endear him to everyone, but to its cause he dedicated himself and his fortune unconditionally.

Carnegie was among the first to interest himself in the conditions of the American negro population. He was a friend of Booker T. Washington (who is seen here next to Carnegie, along with President Taft and Robert Ogden) and made many donations to black institutions.

OUR ANGEL OF PEACE

Board for its inertia, withdrew his support with the typical statement: "I have much better use for twenty-five thousand dollars a year".

By far his most significant endowment in this field though concerned the Carnegie Endowment for International Peace, which was founded in December 1910. The original endowment amounted to $10 million. Its professed aim as expressed in the Trust Deed was: "to hasten the abolition of international war, the foulest blot upon our civilization." The policy of the Endowment was to be directed towards the renunciation of war as an instrument of national policy, towards the peaceful settlement of international disputes, the increase of international understanding and the acceptance by all nations of international law as their guiding principle. It was his friend ex-Secretary of State Elihu Root who persuaded Carnegie, who was reluctant at first, to have the Trust established and who himself accepted its Presidency. The Endowment was started with high hopes, but a first setback was soon to present itself in the outbreak of the First World War. Still, its Board took a firm stand against the German oppressor and opted in favour of the American war policy, stating on 1 November 1917 that Germany's blind reliance on military power must be broken "before any other effective steps can be taken to secure international peace". It published numerous monographs on the social effects of the slaughter and a monumental 155 volume *Economic and Social History of the War*. Ten years later, through its second President Nicholas M.

Left: Carnegie's donations and ideas in matters of peace and education provoked satire all over the world: "Nothing injures a righteous cause more than a millionaire's money", Carnegie once said.

Libraries and organs were his favourite gifts. All in all, he donated 7,689 organs to churches and halls!

Carnegie's first move concerned the successive foundation of eleven Hero Funds for civilian heroes in America and throughout Europe, with the intention of honouring those who had risked their lives voluntarily in attempting to save other men's lives and were injured or killed in the attempt. To this end he endowed some $10 million between 1904 and 1911, awarding both grants and medals to the hero or the dependants. Over the years many thousands have benefited by this initiative.

His founding of The Simplified Spelling Board was a curious move, which emerged from his conviction that the uniting of the nations would emerge quite naturally from the undoing of the "babel of tongues". Spelling reforms were in vogue in those days and in 1907 Carnegie voted a substantial sum "gradually to substitute for our present chaotic spelling. which is neither consistent nor etimologic, a simpler and more regular spelling". Handbooks and quarterly journals were published and hundreds of scholars, writers and businessmen joined the advisory council, including Theodore Roosevelt who ordered the adoption of the new spelling in all White House documents. There was a time when this seemed indeed "the greatest and most enduring monument" which he had built. But Swinburne called it a monstrous absurdity, Mark Twain spoke of a capital crime, the British Trusts he had founded refused to adopt it and cynics heaped ridicule on the idea. The movement soon lost impetus, until at last Carnegie himself, disillusioned and blaming the

BUILDING A VERY SOLID TEMPLE OF FAME

The unveiling of Carnegie's statue in Dunfermline on Saturday, 27 June 1914.

from the Central American Peace Conference in Washington, held in December 1907. It was to provide a permanent court for the representatives of the five Central American Republics at Cartago in Costa Rica, but proved ill-fated. Destroyed by an earthquake shortly after its opening, it was rebuilt in San José but closed for ever in 1917 upon the expiration of the Convention. The third Temple and Carnegie's favourite, was the Peace Palace at The Hague. Its building history will be the subject of the next chapters.

Epilogue

On the foregoing pages we have presented Carnegie's life, works and ideals. The man who emerges from this outline was a remarkable personality. If anything, he was a man of strong character, indomitable energy and unwavering self-confidence. He rose from the depths of poverty to a world of unbounded wealth and privilege. His business career was marked by bold initiative and infallible instinct. As a competitor he was shrewd and adamant, merciless if need be, though fair and honest if he could be so. To his employees he was straightforward, but exigent. He was a man of his time in seizing the vast opportunities the new land offered. Still, in a way he stands apart from these other business tycoons of his day. Proud and condescending at times and self-satisfied as any of them, he lacked that detestable ostentatiousness, tempered as it seemed by his rather intellectual and cerebral approach. He was the self-made man of vast, though not too deep learning. Thus, he was the author of a monograph of some merit on *James Watt* (1905). He had a peculiar taste for the literary and musical, which few of his business colleagues shared. Unlike them, he was very sensitive to the idea of social justice and, by virtue of his background, earnestly and genuinely committed to the lower social group. This background even made him a fanatic and radical in matters of social reform, even if these came to clash with his genuine abhorrence of violence and deep hatred of war. Apparent contradictions of this order are found throughout his life. He was a pacifist, though not at all costs and certainly not naive. Thus, he protested fiercely against the Spanish war urged by American imperialism in the late nineties, but took up arms willingly to help end slavery in the early sixties. Very practical motives prompted his thinking.

Butler, the Endowment was instrumental in fashioning the Kellogg-Briand pact of 1928. It emerged from the Second World War with John Foster Dulles as chairman of the Board and in subsequent decades expanded rapidly towards New York and Geneva in order to keep in close touch with the respective United Nations Agencies. To date, three-quarters of a century later and back at its base in Washington, the Endowment under its President Thomas L. Hughes, also through its quarterly magazine *Foreign Policy* (founded in 1970, circulation 25,000), is one of the leading independent organizations in the fields of international relations and peace studies. Its professional staff of about twenty-five experts, recruited from the academic, governmental and operational fields at home and abroad, conducts a wide range of research and educational programmes and justly claims expertise in matters of global peace problems. It does not promote "research for the shelf, research without recommendations" but is aiming, very concretely, at topical issues and practical goals in the true Carnegian spirit.

Not unlike the former fund was the founding in 1914 of the Church Peace Union, aimed at the promotion of peace through the rallying of men of all religions and operating on a less academic level than the Peace Endowment. It was directed at the ordinary man in the street in an independent, nonsectarian way. Its prime concern was the ethics and values of the world's religions and their effects on political and economic decision-making. In 1961 the Union was renamed the Council on Religion and International Affairs. Its present headquarters are in New York.

The last gifts worth mentioning in Carnegie's peace-founding project are the three Temples of Peace he created. First of these was the Pan American Union Building, completed in 1907 with the hearty approval of President Roosevelt and functioning as an international home "for the union of all the republics of this hemisphere". The second one, prompted like the first by Elihu Root, was the Central American Court of Justice. The gift resulted

Indeed, Carnegie had many sides. He was strong-headed, wilful and stubborn, yet in private contacts he was as a rule most charming, kind and gentle, with a keen sense of humour and a disarming impishness. But above all, he was found very stimulating by all he met and very convincing in all his beliefs. And to this we owe the many institutions, trusts and funds bearing his name which are so very much alive still today.

Andrew Carnegie died aged eighty-three, on 11 August 1919 in Lenox, Massachusetts.

48

The Idea of a Peace Palace Takes Shape

Frederic W. Holls (1857–1903). He was a lawyer and publicist and gave an account of the 1899 Conference ("The Peace Conference at The Hague and its Bearings on International Law and Policy", 1900).

Right: Andrew Dickson White (1832–1918), American minister to Germany (1879–1881) and Russia (1892–1894), ambassador to Germany (1897–1902) and, the capstone of his career, first American delegate to the Hague Conference in 1899. He had a deep respect for German culture.

In the previous chapter we have described how Andrew Carnegie first became acquainted with the concept of a Peace Palace. On 18 June 1900 he received a letter suggesting the idea from his friend Andrew D. White following the latter's meeting with de Martens on 8 June. The prompt reply from Skibo Castle, received by White on 23 June, is another specimen of Carnegie's cunning and shrewdness. Applying what White called "the Socratic method", he raised all sorts of objections, as if testing the resolution and determination of his friend. Yet at the same time he invited him to come over and spend some days in the Highlands to discuss things. Unfortunately, White was in no position that year to pay a visit. Accordingly, matters lingered on in the regular exchange of letters from Alassio, White's winter residence, and Ithaca, New York, where Carnegie spent the better half of the year.

In February 1901 White, in his turn, invited Carnegie to Berlin, where he was stationed as American Ambassador. Carnegie had to decline for practical reasons, but did not fail to refresh his invitation to White for the summer months. This went on in two rejoinders till, predictably, on 14 May it was White who gave in, projecting a visit somewhere between mid-July and the first days of September. Then a tragic incident occurred. On 8 July White's only son died suddenly and, understandably, the father's summer plans were frustrated. Contact was made though during those months through another channel. On 3 August 1901 a mutual acquaintance and a man with whom we too have become familiar by now, Frederic W. Holls, signed the Skibo Castle visitors book. Holls came well informed: he had visited his friend White in Berlin in May and June previously, but apart from that he had in the meantime been appointed a member of the Permanent Court of Arbitration, on 2 March 1901 to be precise. Through this channel, too, his interest in the project was awakened.

On 10 April the Secretary-General of the Court, Baron Melvil van Lynden had dispatched a circular letter to the arbitrators on the Court's behalf as to their ideas on the launching of an International Law Library at The Hague. Holls was charmed with the idea of the library but did not share White's ardent enthusiasm for the Peace Palace, and presumably his lukewarm interest in the plan did not help to stimulate Carnegie very much. Be this as it may, from Holls' prompt letter to White on the outcome of his meeting with Carnegie, it can be learned that the latter had no intention whatever to have a "Temple of Peace" or for that matter any building erected in The Hague at his cost. In Carnegie's view the very idea was rather premature and presumptuous to a degree that could only hamper the authority of the Court itself. However, Holls continued, the idea of a "Standard Library of International Law" which Secretary-General Melvil van Lynden had advocated in his circular letter and which according to Holls' estimation could be provided for less than $250,000, Carnegie found very much worth considering. In a subsequent letter to White, Holls gives his friend timely warning of the canniness which Carnegie applied in negotiations of the sort and of his sporting with delegates as with trout in his highland lochs. Under no conditions, he stated explicitly, must White raise the point of his own accord.

A Library of International Law

Either disquietened or stimulated by these reports, White made up his mind to see Carnegie at Skibo on his way to the United States, about mid-September. On his arrival he found himself much impressed by the surroundings, the varying scenery,

"the piper in full tartan solemnly going his three rounds about the castle walls at dawn, and the music of the organ swelling, morning and evening, through the castle from the great hall …" White was absolutely fond of organ music. During his stay in Holland in 1899 he took his secretary along on visits to all the major churches, praising Gouda and Delft and loathing Haarlem, despite its organ's restoration since his first visit to the place years before. He enjoyed every minute of his stay at Skibo, was "arrayed in Scotch caps, cloaks and tippets", fished for trout in sundry lochs – catching none all day for that matter –, talked about universities and the like … and was quite satisfied to return none the wiser as regards the Hague library proposal, when at the end of the last banquet Carnegie addressed him as if stealthily and in a "still, small voice" – to unfold a panoramic view of the whole subject. It then proved that with Carnegie the original idea of a book collection had developed into something far grander, namely "the creation of a centre and symbol of a world's desire for peace and goodwill to men". Whatever this might mean in terms of money, back in New York White discussed these developments eagerly with his friend Holls over luncheon on 30 October. Consequently, in November a confidential communication from Mr. Holls came in to the office of the First Secretary of the Court, informing him that an American millionaire, who wished to remain unnamed, had asked him "to find out whether an offer from him to supply the Court with a first-class library of international law and diplomacy, and possibly too, with a building in which to house it, would or would not be received with favor".

On 17 March 1902 Holls received his answer: no government had raised objections on principle, though several did wish to know in advance whether this plan would imply any increase in expenditure on their behalf. There was one major problem, however, on the part of the Dutch Government, and this would have far-reaching consequences. Neither the Court of Arbitration, nor the Administrative Council or for that matter the International Bureau possessed the qualifications of corporations. Therefore, they could not acquire property under Dutch law. It was owing to this uncertainty, incidentally, that the tenancy contract of the Court's actual premises had at the time been effected by Baron Melvil van Lynden in his own name! The problem posed here could be overcome, however, by the constituting of a foundation embracing the library and the building and by the endowment of this foundation with capital from which expenses incurred for maintenance, surveillance and taxes could be met.

Carnegie, verified by Holls, reacted with circumspection. On 7 April he announced his wish to come over to The Hague incognito to discuss matters. This visit, eventually, did not materialize, but in his place and on behalf of Holls another British pacifist descended on The Hague, being no less a person than William Stead, the well-known author of *Mr. Carnegie's Conundrum.* In the summer of 1902

Skibo Castle, the fairy-like summer residence of Andrew Carnegie in the Scottish Highlands.

Stead attended the opening of the first arbitration case at The Hague (America v. Mexico over California, submitted to the Court by President Roosevelt) and paid a visit to the premises secured at the Prinsegracht 71. Humble headquarters they were and indeed in singular contrast to the lofty aims of the institution. It seems that on this occasion, sometime in July, Stead acted as a sort of intermediary in the matters of Carnegie's proposal, however, without much of a result.

Matters did gain pace though in August, when Holls paid a second visit to Skibo Castle and here secured the solemn promise from Carnegie that he provide an ample sum for the projected library (to be put at $250,000 provisionally), that is if the idea were acceptable to the Court and a proper site could be found. Holls was also empowered to refer to the generous donor by name. On 25 August, therefore, he wrote a lengthy letter to Jhr. Ruyssenaers, who had in the meantime succeeded Melvil van Lynden as Secretary-General of the Court, expanding on Carnegie's desires. The Scotsman, Holls argued, was prepared and willing to offer $100,000 for the land and the building, and $150,000 for the procurement of "the best obtainable library on international law and diplomacy". The building was meant to be elegant, comfortable and dignified, but not too elaborate and ostentatious. As to the site, he surmised that this could best be provided by the Dutch Government.

From a report by Stead, in the wake of a second visit he made to The Hague in September, it can be ascertained that not all parties were equally enthusiastic about the idea. The Dutch Government for instance showed its reserve. However, on 20 November 1902, Holls received word from The Hague that the Government had formally expressed its readiness to intervene. But then the news leaked out in The Hague and rumour had it that a formal offer by Carnegie had been officially rejected. On 28 January 1903 Melvil van Lynden, then Minister for Foreign Affairs, was questioned about the affair, but could both truthfully and circumspectly reply that no formal offer had so far been received. He was right – in fact no offer of the sort was destined ever to reach him, for once again events took a sudden turn.

A Temple of Peace

In the meantime a new thread had been woven by White himself. In one of his numerous letters to Carnegie, dated 5 August 1902, he saw fit once again to make a plea for the more extensive de Martens plan of a "temple of peace, of which the doors, unlike those of the Temple of Janus, shall be kept wide open in time of peace and closed in time of war … as a solemn and silent reminder to the nations that there is at last, after all these weary centuries, a Court for the peaceful settlement of international questions, open to all".

In his glowing rhetoric and bold allegory White outlined a true gallery of former heroes of international law, culminating in Grotius, his perennial idol. Endowed with a rich imagination he pictured artists from all over the world adorning the temple, thus testifying to the progress of mankind. It would be an "outward and visible sign", the tangible revenue of the 1899 Conference and a holy place for all to visit. White had great persuasive power and was a lover of architecture; his glowing appeal did not fail in its effect on Carnegie. White's letter arrived during the very days when Carnegie gave in to Holls' idea of the Library, but resulted in White's option being kept open as well. As a matter of fact, as weeks passed by, Carnegie became increasingly fascinated by the idea. It was either (and this is more feasible) on his request, or through White or Holls, that in September William Stead paid another visit to The Hague, to sound out some prominent characters as to their feelings on the larger project. Thus he met the American Stanford Newel, who volunteered that one thing was for sure: "the present building was much too small, and ridiculously out of the way, and would be hopelessly inadequate if there were two arbitrations going on at the same time".

Jhr. A. P. C. van Karnebeek, a prominent parliamentarian and former Minister for Foreign Affairs, confided to Stead that the original idea had been to rent a large four-storeyed house on the respectable Vijverberg; this idea was afterwards dropped mainly for financial reasons. He did feel, however, that the present offer from a private donor was somewhat *infra dignitatem* for the Court: really, the powers had to provide adequate accommodation for themselves! De Martens in his turn fell in with the idea of van Karnebeek that the present Court was utterly inadequate and badly situated, but he at least expressed himself positively delighted with Carnegie's idea and only pressed for prompt action. The Dutch Prime Minister Dr. Kuyper stated with clear foresight in an interview that once the Court had

come into proper use, a far more imposing building than the actual one would soon be required. The conclusion Stead drew from these interviews was that, if anything, the larger project had to be favoured and that consequently a free foundation should be created with full legal facilities.

On 21 October, White and Carnegie met at St. Andrews, where White was endowed with an honorary doctorate of laws, and Carnegie installed as Lord Rector. The issue must have come up quite naturally on that occasion. Again, on 19 January 1903, White, from Alassio, pressed the idea with Carnegie in New York. This time he bluntly asked for a million dollars to have the larger project launched, have Holls enrolled as advisor and have a simple, massive building set up as an everlasting tribute to International Law and its students.

On 26 January, in what must have been the last in quite a series of interviews, Carnegie talked the project over with Holls just once more. He now definitely showed himself prepared to consider the idea. Holls, in turn, promised to bring the proposal up at the first meeting of the Board of Administration at The Hague. One and a half million dollars (!), he thought, would be ample. On 6 February Holls had a productive interview with Baron Gevers, the Dutch Minister to Washington. In this he urged circumspection. Through the years Carnegie had become highly sensitive as to the impression his actions might make upon the world at large. Least of all he wanted it rumoured that he himself had pressed the idea on the Dutch Government and that he would be accused of presumptuous self-conceit …

On 5 March a very positive reply came in from The Hague. If only legal conditions were complied with, which could be done through a foundation, nothing stood in the way of the transfer of the money and the materializing of the projected building. The Dutch Government in its turn was fully prepared to co-operate in the purchase of the site and the drafting of the plans for the building.

On 6 April Carnegie and Gevers met in New York through the intermediary of Holls. Carnegie at the time much preferred to have the money placed at the disposal of the young Queen Wilhelmina and rather not of just another commission, whose lack of urgency had frustrated or postponed the materializing of so many of his projects. Gevers, however, convinced him of the need to have the money transferred to the board of a foundation. As to the building itself, Carnegie expressed his wish for an open and international competition resulting in a house that was to stand alone, preferably in the midst of a park, provided with spacious rooms, large enough to hold any meetings and provided with a great library equipped with all the modern technical devices. Gevers willingly agreed to all this. It was obvious now that the decisive step was soon to be made. So it was: around 22 April Carnegie instructed his Hoboken banker to "pay the draft of one and one-half million dollars drawn by the accredited officials of the Dutch Government, on account of the Temple of Peace at The Hague".

W. A. F. Gevers (1856–1927), who negotiated with Carnegie on behalf of the Foundation in matters of the Deed and the transfer of the donation.

From this it was understood that Carnegie did not wish to *make* a gift but, typically enough, simply and *passively* had made provisions that the money was to be transferred through a draft that would be duly honoured by the Hoboken banker. In Holland *De Nederlandsche Bank* was prepared to pass the draft without a charge for commission. Accordingly, on 9 May the bank presented a bill on sight to Baron Melvil van Lynden, Minister for Foreign Affairs, for his signature. This bill was received on 9 June. Its net proceeds, which were deposited in the Consignment Fund, amounted to Dfl. 3,712,008. On 11 June Queen Wilhelmina sent her heartfelt thanks to Carnegie, to which Carnegie replied in a most dignified manner, referring to her as "The Guardian Angel of Peace". This first phase ended in sad tones though, as on 23 July one of the initiators of the building, Frederic Holls, was called away by death in the midst of his active life.

The Carnegie Foundation

As said above, the realization of Carnegie's plan still faced a single formality, namely the founding of a so-called "Stichting" or foundation, and the constituting of a board of trustees, this being the only way to overcome the legal difficulties that arose from the present status of the Court and the Administrative Council. This step, incidentally, had some other practical consequences as well. Against the other way that lay open, namely of vesting the ownership in the Dutch Government – it had of course the disadvantage that it implied the transfer of taxes, but this was counterbalanced by the far greater advantage of freeing the Foundation from parliamentary debates and questions. So when in August 1903 the gift had been actually transferred, Baron Melvil van Lynden in his new capacity as Minister for Foreign Affairs was all set to launch the Foundation. It all seemed easy sailing until at the end of August fiscal difficulties arose. The transfer of the money to the Foundation would formally imply that a duty of 10 per cent, in fact over Dfl. 500,000 would be levied. Fortunately enough, this obstacle was eliminated by having the persons appearing in the notarial deed act on behalf of their American benefactor, who was not resident in Holland and therefore not liable to taxes.

In September the text of the Foundation Deed was drafted by Gevers and Melvil van Lynden with the help of the public notary Eikendal. All sorts of problems arose here. Cabinet questions arose as to "whether a foundation could really be set up without a Board being previously nominated". Besides, the legal status of Carnegie himself in the proposed construction proved somewhat irregular. On 2 October 1903, however, Baron Gevers set sail for Skibo Castle to have Carnegie sign the English Foundation Deed.

It would not prove a pleasure trip. In rather uncourteous terms Carnegie objected to the words "maintenance" and "maintaining" which occurred in

The banker's bill of exchange of 11 May 1903 signed by Baron Melvil van Lynden, the Dutch Minister for Foreign Affairs, for the transfer of 1,500,000 dollars from New York to The Hague.

the Foundation Deed with respect to the Court House and Library. His fear was that one or the other governments would herewith feel relieved from all financial obligations to the Court in the future. In the beginning Baron Gevers was optimistic, as Andrew Carnegie was well-known for his initial reluctance in everything he was confronted with, and for his inclination to have things wrenched from him rather than to simply hand them over. But despite all diplomacy and patience applied by Gevers, Carnegie remained adamant throughout and insisted on the rephrasing of the passages concerned and on the inclusion in the Deed of a postcript the final text of which read: "The words maintaining, maintenance, in this agreement are not to be construed as relieving the signatory Powers to the Treaty of July 29th 1899 from the financial obligations incurred and so far discharged in connection with the Permanent Court of Arbitration."

We shall have occasion to see that Carnegie was not altogether wrong in stipulating this. As a matter of fact, it is a pity that he was not himself involved in the further proceedings of the Foundation. Several of the problems to be faced by its Board in later years would never have occurred in his presence – or else have been dealt with radically.

On 7 October Carnegie and Gevers agreed on the final phrasing of the Deed, which then was duly signed by the Scotsman. Meanwhile, the minor corrections to the text required the copying of the official document, which was subsequently done at

The draft of the Deed discussed between Carnegie and Baron Gevers at Skibo Castle in the beginning of October 1903, including the former's correction of the text on the maintenance.

Jhr. Mr. A. P. C. van Karnebeek (1836–1925), a prominent Dutch politician around the turn of the century. Minister for Foreign Affairs in 1885–1888, Vice-President of the First Hague Peace Conference and Minister of State since 1909, he became the first President of the Carnegie Foundation in 1903.

The final version of the Deed agreed upon in Skibo Castle on 7 October 1903 and there-fore bearing that date, though officially signed in New York on 2 November following.

The Hague in a great hurry, as Gevers had to leave for the United States aboard the *S.S. Noordam* on 17 October. The final version of the official document was at last signed by Carnegie in New York on 2 November.

Pursuant to a Royal Decree of 30 May, the Foundation's Regulations were determined by notarial deed of 6 June 1904. In it the Carnegie Foundation was said to aim at the "erection and mainte-nance of a building and library for the use of the Permanent Court of Arbitration". The Foundation was to be administered by five directors under the control of a Supervisory Council. The directors, who had to be of Dutch nationality, were to be nominated for two years at a time: four of them by Her Majesty the Queen, the fifth by the Administrative Council of the Permanent Court. The nine members of the Supervisory Council included the Ministers of Justice, Finance, Public Works and Foreign Affairs (the last was to be chairman), the Lords President of the two Chambers of the States General, the Presi-dent and the Attorney-General of the Supreme Court of the Netherlands and the Vice-President of the Council of State.

The first Board was appointed by Royal Decree of 20 June 1904. The Board was made up of: Jhr. Dr. A. P. C. van Karnebeek, President, Jhr. Dr. A. F. de Savornin Lohman, Baron Dr. L. P. M. H. Michiels van Verduynen, Jhr. S. van Citters, Secretary-Treasurer and Mr. W. H. de Beaufort, on behalf of the Administrative Council of the Permanent Court.

Numerous things had yet to be regulated in 1904. Among these was a proper meeting place for the recently installed directors. As may be gathered, the Board had no proper home during these first years. Accordingly, meetings were held in several places, at a ministry or at the president's home, among others. Another regular meeting place was the villa Rustenburg, on the very spot where the Peace Palace was to be built later. At the beginning of 1905 rooms were hired at the Mercurius premises in the Noordeinde – and this then became the regular meeting place where over fifty meetings were held till, from the end of 1912 onwards, meetings could be held at the Peace Palace itself.

One of the first issues to be dealt with by the newly appointed Board was the verifying of the legal status of the Foundation. The opening session, on 22 July 1904, was dedicated mainly to this point. It was Professor Asser who first expressed his doubts as to whether subsequent to the present regulations the Foundation was entitled to the right to own property. The Dutch Government soon reassured the Board in these respects. What was also lacking so far, were proper instructions for the Board and provisions in the matter of investment and the custody of funds and liquid cash of the Foundation. All this was dealt with satisfactorily, however, by the Supervisory Council at its meeting of 24 September 1904. From then on the Board could focus on its main goal, the materializing of the projected Temple of Peace.

option No. 7). This again caused a serious clamour on the part of the military authorities. To meet this the Preparatory Commission on 9 May handed in yet another suggestion, namely the Belvédère, a strip of dunes in the area of the Scheveningen Woods, near the so-called Waterpartij ponds (option No. 8). In fact, on second thoughts, the commission thought this the best area possible. This, however, was the last suggestion ever to be heard from the commission, for with the constituting of the Board of the Carnegie Foundation on 20 June 1904 it was deemed proper to have the question left to the wisdom of its directors: consequently, the preparatory commission disappeared as suddenly as it had appeared! Fortunately enough, de Savornin Lohman constituted a sort of a personal union of the two committees.

Endless Negotiations

On the occasion of its first meeting, on 22 July 1904, the Board gave expression to its candid preference – neither for the Zorgvliet area, the choice of the preparatory commission, nor for the Malieveld, the option made by the Kuyper Government, but for two other sites. First of all the Koekamp area (No. 6 on our list), the very spot to which objections had been raised by the Minister of Public Works; second, the site which had been allotted the fourth place only by the former preparatory commission, namely the Benoordenhoutseweg area, opposite the entrance to the Hague Woods, at the other end of the Malieveld. With van Karnebeek's prompt resolution it was also decided to enter preliminary negotiations for the eventual purchase of the latter strip of land with representatives of the young Countess van Bylandt.

It was in these terms that the Board in August 1904 sent an urgent appeal to the Dutch Government to have matters settled for once and for all. It was time indeed! Over a year had elapsed since the transfer of the money by Carnegie. As no public announcement had been made in between, both in Holland and abroad sharp protests had been made as to the lack of resolution of the Board … The present address to the Government, however, which was soon circulated in the newspapers, in its turn evoked a storm of protest from the Hague community against the proposed site.

The most intriguing issue by far concerned the Koekamp area, the spot curiously preferred by the Board. It proved a soft and delicate spot indeed! The very idea of the sacrosanct Woods being violated caused great agitation among individuals and societies alike and instantly alarmed the public conscience of the true Hague residents. The issue was finally settled when on 19 September the Hague magistrate, hastening to the aid of its citizens, simply forbade the idea. To express its co-operation it declared itself prepared to hand over on acceptable conditions either St. Hubert dune (option No. 5), the Belvédère dune (option No. 8) or yet another option,

a newly proposed site between the lengthened Wagenaarweg and the Nieuwe Duinweg, the present Westbroekpark (option No. 9).

However, before the Board was able to conclude upon this dilemma two other things happened. First the Park Zorgvliet Company made the suggestion of a site located near the previously considered option No. 1, namely at the crossing of Stadhouderslaan and Oude Scheveningseweg (option No. 10). Second, Countess van Bylandt handed in a definite proposal with respect to option No. 4, the meadow between the Benoordenhoutscheweg and Wassenaarscheweg. Secretly the Board preferred the latter site which it thought might be bought by the Government and then presented to the Foundation. On 15 October the Board in its reply to the triple proposal on behalf of the Government from mid-September persisted in its preference for the van Bylandt option.

Oddly enough, the Government fell in with this idea and was actually prepared to purchase the land and hand it over to the Board. Within a few days full agreement was reached with the young Countess and on 15 November by Royal Decree a bill to this end was presented to the States General. Then it proved that the Second Chamber of the States General was not at all pleased with the idea. In fact its members thought it the worst place imaginable. Besides, a strong faction in parliament favoured the idea of the Malieveld (option No. 7).

The curtain fell when quite another authority raised his voice: Professor de Martens, who happened to be in The Hague for reasons regarding the 1899 convention on hospital ships. On 18 December he expressed his feelings on the choice in a lengthy address to Minister Melvil van Lynden at the Foreign Office. He referred to international opinion on the question, spoke of "a patriarch in contemporary diplomacy" who considered "the unfortunate fate of the Carnegie gift … the most distressing deception in the whole of his long public career", of another prominent politician who "expressed himself in terms I deem it better not to reproduce" and added his own distress that after a year and a half nothing yet had come of the gift. Indeed, the question was raised now, "via diplomatic channels, of transferring the Permanent Court of Arbitration to … Brussels, where certainly the best site in the City would be sacrificed for the Court of Arbitration". Matters were taking a grave turn indeed!

In this letter de Martens also came to speak of the proposed site: "Now, Mr. Minister, during the past few days I have visited that site on two occasions. The first time I thought I was mistaken, so struck was I by the gloomy and desolate aspect of the spot. On the second occasion, I took a guide with me; I now consider it my duty to tell Your Excellency quite frankly, that rather than have the Peace Palace erected on that swamp, it would perhaps be better to go on seeking for a further period of time … I am taking the liberty of requesting Your Excellency to do everything in the world to promote that this evil project shall not be carried out."

The Countess van Bylandt, who owned several meadows in the vicinity of The Hague and negotiated with the Carnegie Foundation in regarding the purchase of land for the site of the Peace Palace.

of Peace.

Numerous things had yet to be regulated in 1904. Among these was a proper meeting place for the recently installed directors. As may be gathered, the Board had no proper home during these first years. Accordingly, meetings were held in several places, at a ministry or at the president's home, among others. Another regular meeting place was the villa Rustenburg, on the very spot where the Peace Palace was to be built later. At the beginning of 1905 rooms were hired at the Mercurius premises in the Noordeinde – and this then became the regular meeting place where over fifty meetings were held till, from the end of 1912 onwards, meetings could be held at the Peace Palace itself.

One of the first issues to be dealt with by the newly appointed Board was the verifying of the legal status of the Foundation. The opening session, on 22 July 1904, was dedicated mainly to this point. It was Professor Asser who first expressed his doubts as to whether subsequent to the present regulations the Foundation was entitled to the right to own property. The Dutch Government soon reassured the Board in these respects. What was also lacking so far, were proper instructions for the Board and provisions in the matter of investment and the custody of funds and liquid cash of the Foundation. All this was dealt with satisfactorily, however, by the Supervisory Council at its meeting of 24 September 1904. From then on the Board could focus on its main goal, the materializing of the projected Temple of Peace.

Administrative Council of the Permanent Court.

The first Board was appointed by Royal Decree of 20 June 1904. The Board was made up of: Jhr. Dr. A. P. C. van Karnebeek, President, Jhr. Dr. A. F. de Savornin Lohman, Baron Dr. P. M. H. Michiels van Verduynen, Jhr. S. van Citters, Secretary-Treasurer and Mr. W. H. de Beaufort, on behalf of the Council of State.

Pursuant to a Royal Decree of 30 May, the Foundation's Regulations were determined by notarial deed of 6 June 1904. In it the Carnegie Foundation was said to aim at the "erection and maintenance of a building and library for the use of the Permanent Court of Arbitration". The Foundation was to be administered by five directors under the control of a Supervisory Council. The directors, who had to be of Dutch nationality, were to be nominated for two years at a time: four of them by Her Majesty the Queen, the fifth by the Administrative Council of the Permanent Court. The nine members of the Supervisory Council included the Ministers of Justice, Finance, Public Works and Foreign Affairs (the last was to be chairman), the Lords President of the two Chambers of the States General, the President and the Attorney-General of the Supreme Court of the Netherlands and the Vice-President of the Council of State.

The Hague in a great hurry, as Gevers had to leave for the United States aboard the S.S. *Noordam* on 17 October. The final version of the official document was at last signed by Carnegie in New York on 2 November.

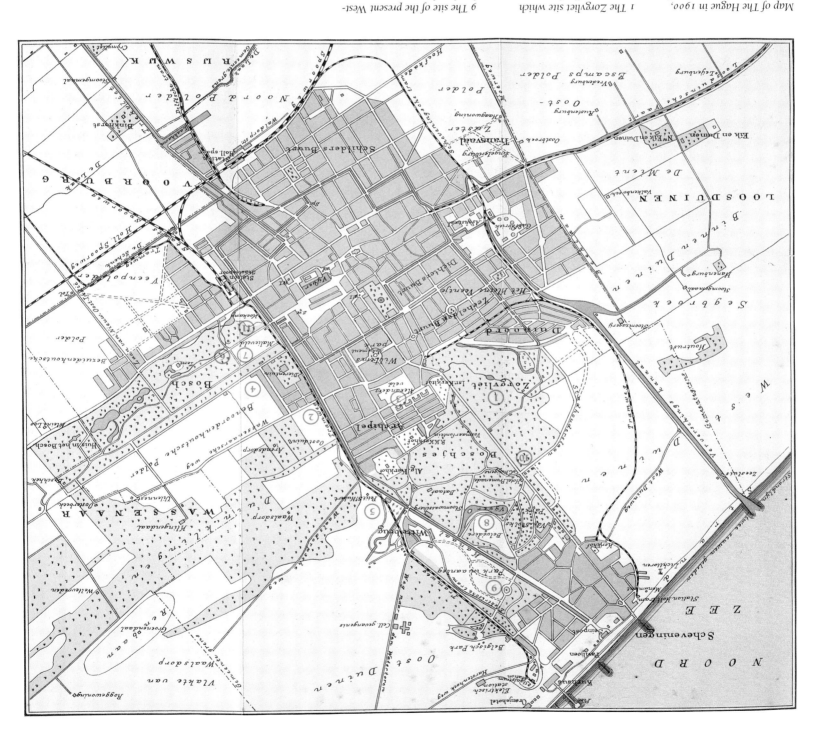

Map of The Hague in 1900,
showing the sites successively
considered by the Board of
the Carnegie Foundation for
the Peace Palace.

1 The Zorgvliet site which
was eventually chosen.
2 The strip along the Scheveningen Canal (Wassenaarseweg), belonging to the
Countess van Bylandt.
3 The Alexanderveld, where
the military barracks were
situated.
4 Another meadow belonging
to Countess van Bylandt
(Benoordenhoutseweg).
5 The St. Hubert Hill,
occupied by the rifle club.
6 The site in the fore section
of the Hague Woods, behind
the Malieveld, in the
Koekamp area.
7 The Malieveld, the time-
honoured drill-ground.
8 The Belvédère, near the
Waterpartij.

9 The site of the present Westbroekpark.
10 The site along the Scheveningseweg, opposite the
Promenade.
11 Another section of the
Koekamp.
These are the sites that were
seriously considered; many
others, several of which in the
dunes, were abandoned.

The Choice of the Site

Portrait of Jhr. A. F. de Savornin Lohman (1837–1924) by Jan Veth (1864–1925).

A rticle 22 of the treaty for the pacific settlement of international disputes, concluded on 29 July 1899, determined that the Permanent Court of Arbitration was to be established at The Hague. Carnegie's gift of 1903 was meant primarily for the erection of a court house and a library to serve its arbiters. There could be no argument, therefore, as to where this Temple of Peace was to be built: it should be at The Hague. But where in The Hague precisely was quite another thing. To bystanders it must remain a puzzle as to how on earth the Hague community could raise so many objections to the idea as it did in the two years it would take the Board to settle this argument. Before that day dawned upon them many were the delegates who sincerely regretted that they had not chosen Brussels or Geneva after all in 1899.

The Preparatory Commission

It was Carnegie himself who, when first considering a library of the court, and later on for the court house precisely, had expressly wished the Dutch Government to select the site. Actually both White and Holls had made suggestions to this end. Inspired no doubt by melancholy memories of the 1899 Peace Conference, they had opted for a site in "The Hague Woods, preferably at the end of that beautiful colonnade of trees running from the Voorhout in the direction of the Huis ten Bosch". White had not anticipated any problems in these respects. In fact, at the time he thought things could be settled in a single interview with the charming young Queen …

Delay was certainly not due to the Government of Dr. Kuyper. Challenged by Carnegie, the cabinet was quite prepared to be of assistance in any way it could. Matters were complicated though by the sheer fact that the Dutch State simply did not possess any suitable grounds in the area. Therefore, grounds had to be purchased. As early as 5 March 1903 Baron Gevers argued that the money needed to this end could easily be spared from Carnegie's lavish gift. Now from the first day this news spread to the general public through the debates on the issue in the States General, all kinds of suggestions and offers were put forward spontaneously from everywhere – for all too human reasons. They make interesting reading for socio-psychologists. It soon became evident that a preparatory commission was required here, made up mainly of experts. Such a committee was indeed appointed on 24 September 1903. It was headed by de Savornin Lohman with Jhr. Röell as secretary. Other members were Professor Asser, Jhr. Ruyssenaers and the architects Cuypers, Muysken, Salm, Peters and Knuttel, some of whom we shall meet again in the discussion on the building history.

On 10 February 1904 this commission proposed a list of suitable sites in order of preference:

1 part of the "Zorgvliet" estate, including the mansion "Buitenrust";
2 a strip along the Scheveningen canal belonging to Countess van Bylandt (Wassenaarseweg);
3 the Alexanderveld, where the military barracks were situated.
4 a meadow between Benoordenhoutseweg and Wassenaarseweg, also belonging to Countess van Bylandt;
5 another site alongside the Scheveningen canal (Waalsdorperweg-Kwekerijweg), at the time occupied by the St. Hubert rifle club.

Already a week later, de Savornin Lohman made an additional suggestion to Melvil van Lynden:

6 a strip in the fore section of the Hague Woods, behind the Malieveld, near the Park Ranger's Lodge on the Benoordenhoutscheweg (Koekamp).

Interestingly enough, it soon appeared that this latter strip of land, actually the one suggested by Holls and White, was in fact State property. Therefore, as Lohman suggested, the State could well make a gift of it to the Foundation. Melvil van Lynden soon expressed himself charmed with the specific site, if not with the idea of the gift. As for the other sites, all sorts of practical objections prevailed, especially concerning the Zorgvliet area, originally preferred by the commission.

On 11 March 1904, by the cabinet's decision, the Minister for Foreign Affairs handed the choice to his colleague of Public Works for further examination. It all appeared easy sailing so far. But then the latter Minister raised serious and indeed understandable objections to the felling of the sacrosanct Hague Woods for the purpose of the Palace. He proposed rather to select a part of the Malieveld, the time-honoured drill ground for the army (this made

option No. 7). This again caused a serious clamour on the part of the military authorities. To meet this the Preparatory Commission on 9 May handed in yet another suggestion, namely the Belvédère, a strip of dunes in the area of the Scheveningen Woods, near the so-called Waterpartij ponds (option No. 8). In fact, on second thoughts, the commission thought this the best area possible. This, however, was the last suggestion ever to be heard from the commission, for with the constituting of the Board of the Carnegie Foundation on 20 June 1904 it was deemed proper to have the question left to the wisdom of its directors: consequently, the preparatory commission had suddenly disappeared as it had appeared! Fortunately enough, de Savornin Lohman constituted a sort of a personal union of the two committees.

Endless Negotiations

On the occasion of its first meeting, on 22 July 1904, the Board gave expression to its candid preference – neither for the Zorgvliet area, the choice of the preparatory commission, nor for the Malieveld, the option made by the Kuyper Government, but for two other sites. First of all the Koekamp area (No. 6 on our list), the very spot to which objections had been raised by the Minister of Public Works; second, the site which had been allotted the fourth place only by the former preparatory commission, namely the Benoordenhoutseweg area, opposite the entrance to the Hague Woods, at the other end of the Malieveld. With van Karnebeek's prompt resolution it was also decided to enter preliminary negotiations for the eventual purchase of the latter strip of land with representatives of the young Countess van Bylandt.

It was in these terms that the Board in August 1904 sent an urgent appeal to the Dutch Government to have matters settled for once and for all. It was time indeed! Over a year had elapsed since the transfer of the money by Carnegie. As no public announcement had been made in between, both in Holland and abroad sharp protests had been made as to the lack of resolution of the Board ... The present address to the Government, however, which was soon circulated in the newspapers, in its turn evoked a storm of protest from the Hague community against the proposed site.

The most intriguing issue by far concerned the Koekamp area, the spot curiously preferred by the Board. It proved a soft and delicate spot indeed! The very idea of the sacrosanct Woods being violated caused great agitation among individuals and societies alike and instantly alarmed the public conscience of the true Hague residents. The issue was finally settled when on 19 September the Hague magistrate, hastening to the aid of its citizens, simply forbade the idea. To express its co-operation it declared itself prepared to hand over on acceptable conditions either St. Hubert dune (option No. 5), the Belvédère dune (option No. 8) or yet another option,

a newly proposed site between the lengthened Wagenaarweg and the Nieuwe Duinweg, the present Wagenaarweg and Westbroekpark (option No. 9).

However, before the Board was able to conclude upon this dilemma two other things happened. First the Park Zorgvliet Company made the suggestion of a site located near the previously considered option No. 1, namely at the crossing of Stadhouderslaan and Oude Scheveningseweg (option No. 10). Second, Countess van Bylandt handed in a definite proposal with respect to option No. 4, the meadow between the Benoordenhoutscheweg and Wassenaarscheweg. Secretly the Board preferred the latter site which it thought might be bought by the Government and then presented to the Foundation. On 15 October the Board in its reply to the triple proposal on behalf of the Government from mid-September persisted in its preference for the van Bylandt option.

Oddly enough, the Government fell in with this idea and was actually prepared to purchase the land and hand it over to the Board. Within a few days full agreement was reached with the young Countess and on 15 November by Royal Decree a bill to this end was presented to the States General. Then it proved that the Second Chamber of the States General was not at all pleased with the idea. In fact its members thought it the worst place imaginable. Besides, a strong faction in parliament favoured the idea of the Malieveld (option No. 7).

The curtain fell when quite another authority raised his voice: Professor de Martens, who happened to be in The Hague for reasons regarding the 1899 convention on hospital ships. On 18 December he expressed his feelings on the choice in a lengthy address to Minister Melvil van Lynden at the Foreign Office. He referred to international opinion on the question, spoke of "a patriarch in contemporary diplomacy" who considered "the unfortunate fate of the Carnegie gift ... the most distressing deception in the whole of his long public career", of another prominent politician who "expressed himself in terms I deem it better not to reproduce" and added his own distress that after a year and a half nothing yet had come of the gift. Indeed, the question was raised now, "via diplomatic channels, of transferring the Permanent Court of Arbitration to ... Brussels, where certainly the best site in the City would be sacrificed for the Court of Arbitration". Matters were taking a grave turn indeed!

In this letter de Martens also came to speak of the proposed site: "Now, Mr. Minister, during the past few days I have visited that site on two occasions. The first time I thought I was mistaken, so struck was I by the gloomy and desolate aspect of the spot. On the second occasion, I took a guide with me; I now consider it my duty to tell Your Excellency quite frankly, that rather than have the Peace Palace erected on that swamp, it would perhaps be better to go on seeking for a further period of time ... I am taking the liberty of requesting Your Excellency to do everything in the world to promote that this evil project shall not be carried out."

The Countess van Bylandt, who owned several meadows in the vicinity of The Hague and negotiated with the Carnegie Foundation in regarding the purchase of land for the site of the Peace Palace.

The customshouse which marked the borderline of the town at the head of the Scheveningseweg. It was the first road to run through the dunes to Scheveningen and the shore, hence ist name Zeestraat, as it was called by Sir Constantine Huygens, who designed both the highway and the ornamental gates at its entrance in the mid-17th century.

Anna Paulovna (1793–1865), daughter of Czar Paul I and sister of Czar Alexander I. In 1816 she was married to the later King William II of the Netherlands (1840–1849). They maintained a strict Romanov etiquette at court throughout. After William's death she devoted herself entirely to charitable work.

In a postscript he expressed himself categorically in favour of the Malieveld. As a result of all this the bill never came up even for public discussion ...

The Zorgvliet Option

The Government, cornered on all sides, now endeavoured to put pressure on the Hague municipal council to reconsider its former refusal in matters of the Malieveld. Military objections could be discarded, for another drill ground would be found somehow. The council, however, remained adamant. But then, presumably to show their goodwill, the burgomaster and aldermen came up with a quite extraordinary offer, suggesting ... a section of the Koekamp (option No. 6), the very spot that had been so much resented by the Hague population. Predictably, another storm of protest arose, cut short this time by the final and definite dismissal of both the Malieveld and Koekamp plans by the municipal council on 23 January 1905. As cool as a cucumber the Board of the Carnegie Foundation then managed to propose yet another section of the Koekamp (option No. 11). Quite understandably, this obstinacy served only to embitter the debate and rally all the public sympathy against the Foundation.

Fortunately enough, in this their darkest hour, dawn proved near. At the meeting of the Board on 24 January a communication was brought forward from the Park Zorgvliet Company, which was prepared to put another section of its territory, between Oude Scheveningseweg and Groot Hertoginnelaan, at the disposal of the Foundation. Another suggestion was made at the same time from a private side, namely to build the Palace on the Alexanderveld (option No. 3), haul down some houses in the Javastraat opposite to it, and so create an avenue towards the beautiful Plein 1813, which was then deemed to be the most respectable spot in town.

However, both for financial reasons and on account of the reports handed in by experts, concentration now gradually but definitely focussed on the Zorgvliet area. Around mid-February the Board had virtually decided on this site, which indeed offered advantages: it was already provided with a full-grown wood and was very favourably situated. The price of Dfl. 700,000 for the 5 hectares (12 acres) was considered reasonable, though admittedly higher than the Dfl. 440,000 of the van Bylandt option. But definite disadvantages also offered themselves here. Thus, at the last purchase in 1895, when the Zorgvliet Company took over from the Grand Duchess of Saxe-Weimar-Eisenach, it had been stipulated that no building activities were to take place on the grounds within a term of fifteen years, which therefore expired in 1910 only.

Another thing was that the chapel of the Russian community in The Hague, the same, incidentally, where mass was attended by the Russian delegates on that glorious opening day of the 1899 Conference, was situated in the Rustenburg mansion, the former residence of the Russian princess, Anna Paulovna. Could this chapel be demolished without offering a proper alternative to the Russian orthodox community? Both objections were overcome in the course of negotiations and on 23 March the Board thought it wise to inform the Government of its plans.

On 7 June, already, the *Staatscourant* published the Act containing the grant from the Treasury to the Carnegie Foundation for the purchase of the site, as a contribution to the expenses to be met for the erection of the Court House. The purchase itself was effected on 18 August 1905. Thus, after a long odyssey of exactly two years, the Board had arrived at the very starting-point of the preparatory commission, which, as will be remembered, had placed this spot precisely on top of its list. Harsh comments on the choice from laymen and experts alike were to be read in the papers. Carnegie, however, who had been furious over the delay, in a letter of 16 August expressed himself reassured by the news from his sister-in-law and nephews who had visited the site. Van der Steur, the Dutch architect, who was to play a prominent part in the building process, gave a favourable opinion on the choice.

Some of the objections raised against the location were nullified by the purchase, on 3 January 1908, of an additional adjacent strip of land of about a hectare along the Scheveningseweg for some Dfl. 100,000. Protests against the all too narrow premises were thus quenched. It would be the last extension of the grounds for a long time. Later opportunities, which offered themselves in 1914 and 1923 to purchase the station and grounds of the former steam-tram line which had run parallel to the premises, could, for reasons of economy, not be effected.

World Centre of Peace

Intricate as the previous account may have seemed, we have not yet given the whole story. There is one other option which we have not had occasion to discuss yet and which, though the idea never materialized, actually constitutes one of the most interesting, if not typical debates of the time. This concerns the conception of creating a true world peace centre at The Hague, in a capital which might rank next to the Vatican as a symbol of global unity in earthly matters. It was first heard of in Stead's *Dagblad* of 17 June 1899 and originating, it seems, from the debate within the *Comité d'Examen* of the Conference to constitute a *Haute Cour d'Appel* at The Hague. The *auctor intellectualis* of this court, was M. Hagerup, the Scandinavian delegate and president of the Swedish Nobel Peace Committee.

It seems that The Hague was chosen first to harbour the peace centre, though soon enough competing schemes were submitted favouring other cities, such as the one by Gaston Moch which aimed at Geneva or Strasbourg. From then on, publicists all over the world raised their voices in favour of some capital. Consequently, the original claim laid by The Hague had to be based on a solid foundation of facts and arguments. Needless to say, they were found by the dozen: they lay, it was argued, in the very fact of Czar Nicholas' choice, in Roosevelt's apparent preference of The Hague for purely sentimental reasons and in the city's location: situated far from the whirlpool of high politics, near to the oceans and therefore easily accessible, and yet not that far from London (the port to the United States!), Berlin, Paris or even St. Petersburg. They were found too in Holland's mild climate and the peaceful and phlegmatic, liberal and sedate character of its native population (which seemed altogether better than having to deal with the inflammable residents of Brussels or Paris!). Arguments were even drawn from the barrier of its obscure language which was said to be helpful in promoting the very welcome acceptance of *Esperanto* as the new "lingua franca". But best of all: the actual building site of the centre had already been outlined, in a 3,000 acres dune-basin called Mussenberg, not too far from the sea; even the designs had already been submitted to the Board of Initiators, the "Fondation pour l'Internationalisme" at Van Lennepweg 6.

But then other towns proclaimed their virtues as well. A call for Brussels, for instance, or rather for the Waterloo scenery, was brought up by La Fontaine in *l'Indépendence Belge,* with an outline drawn up by Paul Otlet. Brussels, it was argued here, was a railway centre with a modern seaport (Zeebrugge); the first Peace Conference was summoned here in 1848; it was a university town and harbouring the offices of forty-two out of the fifty-nine permanent international institutions. Life was cheaper, too, in Belgium, – and due to its cultural life, museums and healthy climate definitely more cheerful than in "un village de campagne endormi, infesté de malaria, loin de Paris – le centre des désirs du monde -, dépourvu de l'esprit internationaliste, la capitale d'une sorte de Sibérie marécageuse, où il serait cruel d'exiler l'élite de l'humanité ..."

Brussels in its turn though, was challenged by Bern, capital of a true "Federation", which in itself had much to speak for it, that is if the Swiss were to

be believed. Besides, here were the headquarters of the Interparliamentary Union and the International Peace Bureau, and it also harboured organizations such as the International Post and Railway Unions. Apart from being a centre of diplomacy, it was favoured by superb scenery. But the latter held good too for Geneva along the Lac Léman, seat of the Red Cross Society and a truly historic site. French, English and Italian were spoken fluently by its residents and the new Simplon tunnel was soon bound to make the area easily accessible from all quarters. Despite other claims by Paris (which would for that matter never have been tolerated by the German-speaking and Anglo-Saxon worlds) and even Strasbourg (mind you: in the very centre of international strife!) the general feeling was much in favour of either Brussels or The Hague.

As mentioned earlier, the Hague centre of propaganda in these respects was the bureau for internationalism, founded by P. H. Eykman and Paul Horrix. Eykman was a medical man and brother of Chr. Eykman, the 1929 Nobel laureate who earned world fame for his research on vitamines. P. H. Eykman was a theosophist, pacifist and idealist and, if anything, a man of theory. He was the director of a Physiathric Institution at the Van Stolkpark in The Hague. In 1905, for purely idealistic reasons, he founded the bureau for internationalism at the same address. It was a private enterprise, aiming at the betterment of understanding among men. He sought to materialize these lofty goals by the concentration of international offices in The Hague and the amassing of documentation on international organizations and peace movements, which made a gigantic bibliographical enterprise in itself and kept dozens of employees busy at the office in The Hague. In fact, Eykman's idea was just another branch of World Federalism.

Eykman's second man and secretary was Paul Horrix, a man of ample means, idealist *pur sang,* pacifist and (not unlike Felix Ortt and William Stead) a spiritualist. Horrix was not much of a theorist, but a man of extreme persuasive powers. Since Eykman

Paul Horrix was the co-founder of Eykman's "Hague Foundation for Internationalism". A most persuasive man and an enthusiastic pacific. In the end, he lost his considerable wealth in the project and died in poverty.

The "Rustenburg" villa, where Anna Paulovna who spent most of her later years at the Buitenrust palace nearby, had a Russian orthodox chapel installed. It was here the Russian delegation attended mass on the opening of the Peace Conference in 1899. It stood on the grounds of the present Peace Palace.

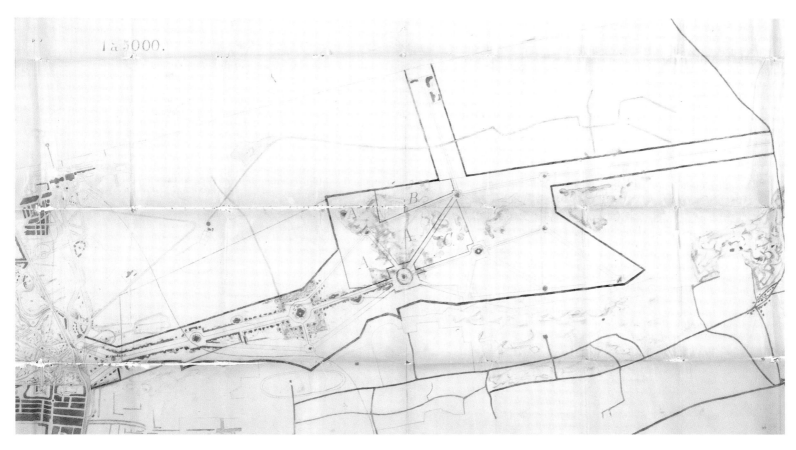

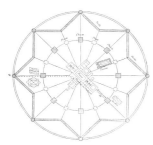

Above: a first draft by K. P. C. de Bazel (1869–1923) for the world peace centre at the Mussenberg area in the dunes near Wassenaar.

Below: "Sforzinda", a design for the "città ideale" made by Antonio Filarete (1410–1469) at the request of the Sforzas of Milan. The harmonious design of the octagonal plan was imitated by de Bazel and later copied by Berlage.

himself was a rather stern and tactless dogmatist and not precisely gifted with social charms or winning manners, Horrix was bound to be of great help to him in breaking the idea to the public. Between 1905 and 1912 the bureau was very active indeed, editing among others an authoritative periodical, the *Review of Internationalism,* which went through twelve issues in three years and featured prominent publicists such as Richard Barthold, President of the Interparliamentary Union, Alfred Fried of Vienna, William Stead and Bertha von Suttner. Its editorial policy was admittedly broad-minded and stimulating in its projection of all sorts of global institutions.

Observed with scepticism at first, the centre gradually gained momentum and influence. Its heydays were the very months of the second Hague Conference, in the summer of 1907, when its aims were finally supported by the Dutch pacifist society, *Vrede door Recht,* and even received some official support from leading Hague politicians. During the Conference it opened a highly successful *Cercle International* at Prinsessegracht 6a, which served as a most convenient and luxurious meeting centre for delegates and leading journalists. Daily lectures given here by politicians and publicists such as Richard Barthold and Baroness von Suttner stimulated the general debate on actual topics. These premises also were the editorial headquarters of Stead's *Courrier de la Conférence de la Paix,* the more or less official journal which did so much to spread the word of the 1907 Hague Conference to the public abroad. In short, the idea had everything in it to be successful, except for the lack of an internationally oriented Board and the strictly personal outlook of its director. In the end, in about 1912, it went down

along with the final shipwreck of Eykman's major and most daring initiative, the creating of a World Capital in The Hague.

It is precisely this initiative which is of major concern to us here, as the project, quite understandably, included the construction of a Peace Palace in the very heart of the projected capital. The idea in itself was not unprecedented. In fact, from the very drawings of its designer, the leading Dutch architect K. P. C. de Bazel, it can be ascertained that the founding fathers were well aware of the historical – in fact Renaissance backgrounds of this "utopian city", the *città ideale* as exemplified by Antonio Filarete's 15th-century design of *Sforzinda*. One of its leading characteristics was the idea of the central perspective. This lent a distinct orderliness and sense of unity to the design reflecting the all-commanding harmony which was embedded in the deeply theosophical conceptions that constituted a mainstream in the thinking of both de Bazel and Eykman. The same conception, incidentally, lay at the base of Hausmann's *Place de l'Etoile,* with its six traffic arteries emanating from the centre, and which had been propagated anew in 1898 by Ebenezer Howard in his conception of the garden-city.

Eykman first contacted de Bazel by a letter dated 31 January 1905. Ensuing discussions led to the architect's submitting a detailed outline at the end of that spring, actually in the very months that the Board of the Carnegie Foundation was negotiating with the Zorgvliet Company for the purchase of its grounds. De Bazel was very much impressed by the Memorial that Eykman submitted to him. The plans that were outlined there concerned the foundation of three separate international academies, to be led by scholars of world fame: one for anthropology, one for arts and one for pedagogics, hygiene and economics. The latter academy prevailed and covered a wide area indeed: its "pedagogical" aspect for instance had to include matters of education, simplified spelling, a universal shorthand language, and all sorts of social and teaching issues, to be tested by an educational institute in an "experimental garden" as it was called, which would provide science with useful data to be applied in the area of town-planning. The same held good with the other academies. They all aimed at practical research in the world capital which in the end would enable mankind to apply the findings of this micro-cosmos to the world at large.

The location of this world capital, also chosen at an early stage by Eykman, was situated in a 3,000-acre dunes area, stretching from The Hague and Scheveningen to Wassenaar, roughly speaking from the Wittebrug to Meijendel. The site of the Peace Palace was planned in the new city centre, at the Mussenberg, the commanding dune in the Waalsdorp area which offered a panoramic view of the grounds and seaside and would have the Palace stand out like a beacon ashore to the passing sailor.

De Bazel's design of the projected town has its distinct merits and, though never materialized, offers some points of interest. Its basic plan provided for an octangular town centre with eight broad avenues leading from all quarters to the central square featuring a park dedicated to the "Brother-hood of Man". Thus the idea of an eight-pointed star was conceived, its central axis, the so-called *Paradère* being directed to The Hague town centre. With its width of over 100 metres this *cardo* was due to create a boulevard which surpassed anything Hausmann had ever conceived! The overall view gave one the impression of a cross with unequal arms, symbolic – it was argued – of the peace won through strife. Along the avenues a Peace Hotel and Conference Centre, a Museum of Contemporary Arts and a residence for the World Government were planned, including Senate and Parliament buildings and the like. The electric railway line from Scheveningen to Rotterdam then under construction (and demolished about 1950) was to skirt the grounds and directly connect the centre with Brussels, Paris and London.

Comments from the media, fellow architects and politicians were, generally speaking, favourable. De Bazel's design, for one thing, lent itself very well to the dune area. At the same time it expressed by its very groundplan the idea that "lofty conceptions emanate from the world centre to all quarters of the earth". Thus, at least, de Bazel expressed his views in an article published in the 1906 issue of the authoritative German periodical *Der Städtebau*. William Stead, for one, was exultant about the idea and so were most of the Hague Conference delegates and members of the press who attended the inspection trip of the area organized for them by Eykman on 7 June 1907, shown by references to it as the "Athens of the Future, announcing a new era of Pericles".

And yet the idea never had a chance, really. First of all because, as mentioned above, Eykman never managed, or even intended, to get an international commission afoot to propagate the idea abroad. Second, because from the beginning the Board of the Carnegie Foundation showed itself averse to Eykman, if not to his plans. Third, because support in the Hague political circles was at the best lukewarm. Only when it appeared that the idea itself was at last gaining ground worldwide and that instantly Brussels, Bern and Geneva developed schemes of their own, reaction was heard of from the Binnenhof. This is not to say that Eykman and Horrix did not do their utmost to advance their project. At their own expense they travelled all over the world for years, gathering signatures from prominent men everywhere. Horrix particularly was very persuasive. Accordingly, their lists of adherents included numerous Nobel Prize winners and such varying celebrities as Grieg, Liebermann, Anders Zorn and Rodin.

As regards the financing of the idea Eykman, typically enough, had anticipated the free transfer of the grounds, which were State property, to his foundation. Though he never received any solid promise in these respects, he took this transfer for granted whenever discussing or publishing something on the idea. The actual costs were estimated at some fifty-two million guilders all included. The financing of this astronomical amount was left to the care of a private person who had to be found prepared to lend the money on a three to five year term. High revenues were expected from the purchase of parts of the area and adjacent grounds by commercial building societies and speculators – all taking it for granted that the Dutch Government would agree to such an undertaking.

As to the financing, Eykman and Horrix, predictably enough, had in mind to submit a request to Andrew Carnegie. To this end they went over to New York in April 1905. Carnegie, however, had got word, presumably from the Board of the Carnegie Foundation, as to their intentions. Therefore, when on their arrival they could not show any official mandate or high credentials, Carnegie bluntly refused to see them. Unrelentingly, Horrix managed to draw attention to the idea in the United States by getting some interviews published in the *New York Herald* of 9 and 16 April. In these he expanded on the plans in his typical optimistic argument, presenting it as an "international project, now favored by the diplomatists of the world ... With this vision of international Utopia reduced to dollars and cents, Messrs. Eykman and Horrix, with the backing of the Home Secretary and other Holland authorities, hope to show Mr. Carnegie the widest, most attractive road to immortality." This, at least, resulted in making Carnegie curious. Accordingly, he promised them an interview which ended up in the three of them travelling back to Europe together aboard the *S.S. Baltic*.

In the meantime, back in Holland, the Board of the Carnegie Foundation had decided to purchase the Zorgvliet area. Apart from this, however, it had

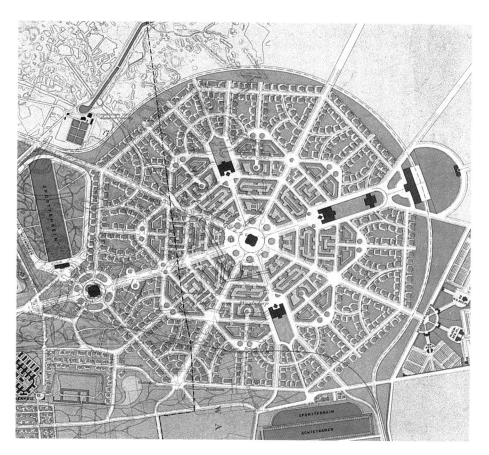

In 1908 H. P. Berlage (1856–1934) was commissioned to draw up the extension plans of The Hague. He incorporated de Bazel's plan for the peace centre as a tribute to his colleague.

judgment of the jury on the Peace Palace competition was assailed for good reasons. Architects all over the world felt ashamed and belittled by the choice and motivation of the jury – an issue we shall discuss in the following chapter. At the same time this petition praised the superior qualities of the Mussenberg location as compared to the Zorgvliet grounds and demanded the sale of the latter. Actually, during the second Hague Conference a list featuring the signatures of over 150 prominent Europeans, all of them members of the so-called Preliminary World Committee of the Foundation of Internationalism was circulated in support of the idea. Nevertheless, the issue was never brought up at the Conference.

Despite these setbacks it soon appeared that the backbone of the movement had not yet been broken. In 1908 Berlage was commissioned with the extension plans of The Hague. In his extensive project he included a modified version of de Bazel's ideas for the Mussenberg area. The groundplan was slightly altered and subjected to the rigid concentration on geometrical patterns that were so typical of Berlage's rather massive style. Friends and foes alike felt that Berlage's step was to be due hommage to de Bazel.

Oddly enough, at the same time sympathy with the idea of the bureau of internationalism was increasing as well in parliamentarian circles. To be sure, this was mainly due to the keen interest which was apparent now in Brussels, Bern and Geneva to lure international bureaux, but at least it resulted in lukewarm support of Eykman at home, if only from lack of alternatives. At the time, Eykman and Horrix were themselves kept busy in preparing a modified scheme of a part of the former plan, meant to house the projected Academy of International Law, a conference centre and a Wagnerian theatre. These halls were projected to be built along St. Hubert's dune, as becomes evident from detailed drawings by Scheltema and other architects, made as late as the autumn of 1911. But even this project was due to be frustrated by the Board of the Carnegie Foundation, which in the end went so far as to back the Brussels Bureau of Internationalism, if only to get rid of Eykman. This blow at last finished the Hague bureau, which was dissolved in the following year. Eykman died within two years; Horrix lived on till 1929, broken and bankrupt. When in 1923 T. M. C. Asser was honoured with the Nobel Prize for his advancement of peace, he gave part of the money to the impoverished Horrix. Eykman's plans, to be sure, were theoretical to the point of becoming quixotic; likewise the ideas for his movement were admittedly naive. Yet in a sense they were messianic and if anything bore a typical Dutch touch in their seeking the betterment of the world.

Eykman's drawings ridiculed in the Dutch papers. Protest arose about this unfortunate manoeuvre – on Horrix's initiative – from William Stead, who openly supported Eykman's conceptions in *The Westminster Gazette* of 15 May. Eykman and Horrix hurried back to Holland and soon afterwards, still in May 1905, addressed the States General and submitted a petition in which the conflicting ideas were amply discussed. It was in this arena however that they lost the battle for good. The purchase of Zorgvliet was pushed through by the Parliament and made law. From then on even the zealous support of William Stead was futile. By means of publication in his *Review of Reviews* for August of that year he once more tried to win over the Interparliamentary Union in Brussels to the idea, but this, too, was wrecked by the obstinate resistance of the Dutch delegation, for financial as much as other reasons, as was rumoured at the time.

At this crucial point Eykman had reached one thing, however, namely the rallying under his banner of all the adversaries of the Zorgvliet plans, for whatever reasons. Among these were prominent Dutch architects such as Berlage, Kromhout and Walenkamp, who had strongly resented the outcome of the competition for the building of the Peace Palace produced by the Carnegie Foundation and leading to the selection of a design by Cordonnier of Lille. Embittered polemics appeared in the leading magazine *Architectura et Amicitia* and international support for Berlage and his colleagues came in from the Royal Institute of British Architects.

As late as May 1907 this ever-growing group of malcontents, if only for matters of principle, submitted a petition to the Parliament, in which the

As regards the Mussenberg area: till the present day the dunes stretch untouched, a nature sanctuary, the calm beauty of its scenery being, as before, only rarely disturbed by the harsh commands and intermittent firing of exercising soldiers and royal hunting parties.

The Prize Competition

The prize-winning design of Louis Cordonnier with the separate Court House and Library (far right) and featuring the four towers and rich ornamentation.

As early as February 1904 the Preparatory Commission, which as we have seen had been constituted in September 1903, had submitted a full programme for the building competition. In drafting the plan it had been guided by the findings of its architect members who had visited modern library and court house projects both at home and abroad. However, before issuing the terms and constituting a jury, the commission felt that certainty had to be obtained as regards the site of the Palace. As we know by now, the final choice in this respect was only to be made in August 1905. In June 1904, however, when the Board of the Carnegie Foundation was nominated, the governmental preparatory commission was dissolved, its President, de Savornin Lohman being appointed on the Board of the new Foundation. In August 1905 the Board felt it had to make a clean start. To this end, expert guidance was obtained by the nomination of the State architect Knuttel as building adviser.

However, the first dilemma that appeared for the Board in opening the competition, was not so much of a technical nature as rather a question of principle. Was it to be an open and unlimited competition, free for all to enter, or a closed one and restricted by invitation from the Board only. And besides, must it be a national competition, on which the Society of Dutch Architects (BNA) insisted, or rather an international competition, as was the express wish of Carnegie among others. On both issues the Board resolved on the latter option. The idea itself of the Palace, it felt, was born at a world conference and the temple was to become the very symbol of global unity. All this suggested an international competition, to which the best architects should be invited. And as for the open or restricted competition, word had come from England that in case of an open competition literally the best architects were likely to withdraw: entrance therefore should be open by invitation only.

After lengthy discussion as to the proper criterion for invitation it was decided to have the governments of the nations signatory to the Final Act of the 1899 Hague Conference suggest two or three names of competent men or bureaux. As for the American competitors it was decided to leave the choice to Carnegie personally. However, when the Board informed the press of its intentions, vehement protests arose among architects. Indeed, as months went by, the call for an open competition grew louder. Formal requests to this end from Dutch

architects found general favour abroad and the Board was literally besieged with petitions submitted by societies from all over the world. Carnegie himself, incidentally, also made the suggestion at least to take into consideration plans submitted by architects who had won the first prize in previous competitions. In the end the Board gave in to the pressure, though not to the full.

The Programme

On 15 August 1905 the *Programme of the Competition for the Architectural Plan of the Peace Palace for the use of the Permanent Court of Arbitration with a Library* was sent out all over the world, specifying the terms. Sure enough, the competition was open to all. In its first article, though, the programme stipulated that the Board reserved the right to invite a number of prominent architects of its own accord and against remuneration. Actually, this is what the Board did: altogether some twenty-five architects were invited, of whom two or three withdrew for personal reasons, while some others refused to accept the terms. Not all of them were replaced and finally twenty-one were invited to participate against a remuneration of Dfl. 4,000. Though in all other respects terms were to be equal for all.

What then were the major terms of the competition as stated in the programme? First the costs were specified: they should not be higher than Dfl. 1,600,000. Then, as to the time schedule: competitors had to present their plans within seven months. These had to consist of a situation sketch, a full colour perspective view of the building and its surroundings, ground plans of floors, drawings of the façades, vertical sections featuring court rooms and library and more detailed drafts of the front façade, the interior of the large court of justice and the main staircase – in other words, very specific plans in which the lay-out of the building should be clearly shown, and the intended use of rooms stipulated in French. On top of this had to come a short explanatory note, again in French.

Entries had to be anonymous: to this end mottoes had to be added, and the same epigraph was to feature on drawings, notice and package alike. A sealed envelope should contain the architect's name, its outside bearing the motto and corresponding address. Rules were strict in other respects too: prize-winning projects automatically became the property of the Foundation, which also claimed for itself all rights as to whether or not any of the plans submitted should be carried out. Prizes to be awarded were Dfl. 12,000 for the winning design, Dfl. 9,000 for the second, Dfl. 7,000 for the third, Dfl. 5,000 for the fourth and two prizes of Dfl. 3,000 each for the fifth and sixth. An exhibition of the plans and the jury report was planned at The Hague in the month following the awards. The jury was to consist of Th. E. Collcutt (London), Dr. P. J. H. Cuypers (Roermond), Geh. Ober-Hof-Baurat von Ihne (Berlin), Professor K. König (Vienna), Paul Nénot (Paris), Professor W. R. Ware (Milton, Mass., USA).

The programme also offered a specified division of the Palace as projected by the Board. The court house had to consist of a *basement* storey (containing rooms for concierges, clerks and stenographers, store-rooms, "a place for the caloriferes with fuel store" and wardrobes and the sort), a *principal* storey (featuring the great hall and main staircase, a large and a small court room with galleries, council rooms, rooms for the parties and a chancery room), and an *upper* storey (featuring a room for the Conseil Administratif of the Permanent Court of Arbitration, rooms for the president, the secretary-general, studies and rooms for archives, for secretaries, clerks and messengers).

The library had to form a separate part of the Palace, its main entrance being accessible from the park, yet connected with the court house proper by an interior access. Its basement floor featured servants staircases, store-, packing- and book-binders rooms. On the principal floor was to be found the library itself, featuring 10,000 square metres of bookshelves over five floors, reading and

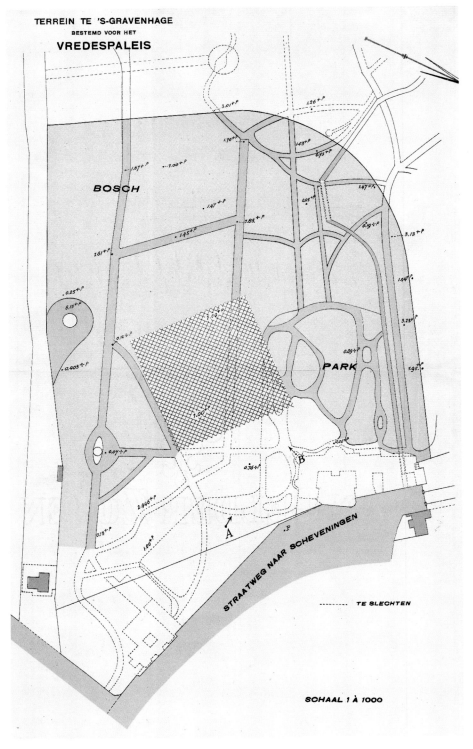

The plan of the site that provoked so many comments from architects.

cataloguing rooms, rooms for the librarian and sub-librarian, and for clerks, bibliographers, messengers and wardrobes. On the upper floor was situated a room for the Board of Directors of the Carnegie Foundation with a waiting room, a chancery room and various service rooms.

Specifications as to measurements were also submitted by Knuttel, who was the general editor of the programme and the one to whom the architects should send their enquiries. Finally, two photographs of the grounds and a plan of the site were annexed to the programme.

Precise and detailed though the programme seemed, numerous indeed were the enquiries made by scores of architects from all over the world who

Left: The programme of the 1905 prize competition.

had made up their minds to compete. They were an inventive lot and Knuttel was virtually overwhelmed by a variety of often surprizing questions like the one from Elder-Duncan in London as to whether "scale 1:500" referred to metres or inches and whether "20 m²" stood for 20 square metres or 20 metres square – "in other words: are the figures given in cubical measurement or in superficial floor area?" In the programme reference was made to a point marked *o*, but The Read Co. in New York could not find such a point on the plan. Albert R. Ross asked for a map of The Hague, Peabody & Sterns whether the lifts were to be passenger lifts, E. Godfrey Page for the number of judges on the courts, Watson of Edinburgh whether cloak rooms and lavatory accommodation in the library section were also to provide for females and indeed how many were the clerks. Again, Charles Bizot of Geneva reported that he found two parks indicated on the plan, one in front and one behind and wondered where the devil was this main entrance of the library to be put! Misunderstandings arose about labelling packages ("giving our own address is likely to do away with the desired concealment") and the same held good for the drawings; for instance, was the use of colours other than black allowed and what about shading, as Lange of Berlin asked. Another London

Four out of the dozens of requests from architects for more specific information as to measurements and so forth.

architect politely informed Knuttel that he had taken the liberty of anglicizing some of the more crucial phrases in the programme.

Obviously, they were not disheartened. On the contrary: at the express request of many architects from abroad the time-limit had to be prolonged by a month. On the closing day, 15 April 1906, no less than 216 plans had been submitted, covering a total of more than 3,000 drawings, while two other plans which arrived too late were refused. Even before the jury had ever convened, the Dutch *Maatschappij tot Bevordering der Bouwkunst* had already made a contract with the Carnegie Foundation for the publication of the plans in a lavishly illustrated book. Optimism ruled everywhere as to the quality of the plans; indeed, the world at large had great expectations with regard to the awards.

The Awards

Much has been said and written about the work of the Hague jury – and for good reasons. Prize competitions of that sort are very likely to arouse jealousy in some, disappointment in others, and protests from all sides. But rarely will the congregation of architects have reacted in such great agitation as it did when the outcome of the Peace Palace competition became known to the world at large – and not too often will a jury have given such ample reason for it. Laymen and architects alike queried the awards and the motivation. Indeed, it must be said that both the outcome of the competition and the argument over the report are open to serious debate, if not flat disapproval. Best proof of this: it was to take a full seven years before the Board of the Carnegie Foundation had finally overcome all lawsuits arising from it. This is the more remarkable as it appears from the records that the constitution of the jury had been a matter of the greatest concern to the Board and on which it had consulted the world's greatest experts in the field. In fact, the members of the jury were all men of standing and of repute in the field: Collcutt was the president elect of the Royal Institute of British Architects, Cuypers the designer of the *Rijksmuseum* at Amsterdam, von Ihne the German Emperor's private architect, König a professor of the Technische Hochschule at Vienna, Nénot the president of the society of French architects and Ware was emeritus professor of Architecture at Columbia University. They were admittedly on the conservative side, most of them, but then this had been anticipated in the papers and only reflected the views held by the Board of the Foundation itself. What went wrong then? Let us discuss things in their proper order.

The jury first convened on 3 May. The exhibition of the 3,000 drawings in itself had been a subject which had caused severe headaches to van Karnebeek and his colleagues. The Board had contacted several institutions (the artists centre *Pulchri Studio* along the Voorhout and its president, the painter H. W. Mesdag among others), before eagerly comply-

ing with the offer spontaneously made by Queen Wilhelmina herself to have the plans arranged for inspection in some of the major salons of the Kneuterdijk Palace.

In these lofty surroundings it was, then, where the jury met between 3 and 11 May to produce its report on 12 May. The short time taken to arrive at a decision was in itself alarming to some, but as the report stated, each member of the jury had taken ample time to inspect all two hundred and sixteen plans separately and in a series of examinations. They then had reassembled, examined the designs collectively and subsequently given their votes. Forty-four plans had obtained one or more votes and were consequently retained for further consideration.

After subsequent diligent inspection by each of the members separately, a vote by ballot was taken and a number of four votes deemed the minimum for further consideration. Sixteen remained (two of them incidentally bearing the same motto) to enter the decisive round. On 11 May final votes were taken, from which the verdict by majority followed. Unfortunately, unanimity was never reached. Indeed, in several cases, particularly as regards the second place, only the slightest majority was acquired. The actual outcome was:

1	No. 213	S'G
2	No. 194	Pax
3	No. 132	Concordia parvae res crescunt, discordia maximae dilabuntur
4	No. 17	l'Art de l'époque
5	No. 79	Q
6	No. 130	Eirene

On opening the sealed letters the jury found that it had allotted the first prize to L. Cordonnier of Lille, the second to A. Marcel of Paris, the third to F. Wendt of Charlottenburg, the fourth to O. Wagner of Vienna, the fifth to Greenley & Olin of New York and the sixth to F. Schwechten of Berlin. Four of these were in the group of architects who had been specially invited by the Board. In its report the jury declared that in its view the two hundred and sixteen plans submitted basically exhibited three types of plan:

1 separate buildings for Court House and Library connected by a corridor;
2 one building for both ends, "lighted from external courts, that are enclosed on only three sides";
3 one building for both ends, "lighted from internal courts, one or more in number, enclosed on all sides".

The second-prize winning design by A. Marcel of Paris. It very much resembles the "Petit Palais" which Marcel built at the 1900 World Exhibition in Paris.

The third-prize winning design by F. Wendt of Charlottenburg with the "impressed" dome. The jury considered the plan competent and dignified, though "somewhat stiff and monotonous".

As stated in the report, Collcutt, Cuypers, von Ihne, König, Nénot and Ware had seen fit to select the six designs required for the awards and needed by the committee as a base "from which to proceed in finally obtaining from the architect, whom they would employ, a design for execution". In doing so they had thought best to select those designs which "in their judgment, best embody these three different schemes".

By these very words the jury stated implicitly what afterwards became officially known, that not a single design out of the two hundred and sixteen was found suitable for consideration as the definite plan for the building. In fact, the jury was not altogether pleased with the plans which had hitherto been submitted. Indeed, a minority had pleaded for the renewal of the contest among the winning or an otherwise restricted number of architects. From the records of the Foundation it can be understood that this proposal by the jury was voted down within the Board for reasons of time alone.

Secondly, the allotment of prizes had evidently been conditioned by the expressed wish to have all three ground plans represented, if only for the benefit of the Board. As one will remember, it was the winning designs only which, following the rules of the contest, became the undisputed property of the

Carnegie Foundation. For obvious reasons, therefore, the jury wished to leave every option open to the Board.

The jury's lukewarm acclaim of the entries is also proved by the arguments. Cordonnier's design had been selected mainly for its "following the local traditions of xvi century architecture" in The Hague. Now, apart from the fact that this is obviously not the case, as was instantly and painfully pointed out by many Dutch critics, it certainly was not one of the requirements put forward by the programme. "Why on earth the 16th-century style?" one critic exclaimed: "Is it because Holland was engaged in war (with Spain) most of that period?" Cordonnier's design was of the first type, the jury report continued "but it has failed to give a sufficient unity of character to the two different portions of the structure" – and this was not precisely a recommendation either.

As for the design submitted by Marcel of Paris, here the general arrangement was approved of by the jury: it fell in with its position in the park, the well-lighted large rooms and the cloister structure of the library. What was criticized, however, was the lack of originality of treatment and its departure from the "noble simplicity, which should characterize a building devoted to the serious and dignified purposes of the Peace Palace".

The third prize winner, the jury argued, had submitted a simple and straightforward design "though an undesirable amount of space is given to vestibules and corridors. The exterior, though it exhibits a suitable dignity of character, is somewhat stiff and monotonous". Here it is seen that the jury, besides being highly critical in its judgments and very succinct in its argument – the total report amounts to some five pages, and this included the full list of plans – had not managed to escape some intrinsic controversy in wording as regards matters of the required "simple dignity".

The verdict of the fourth place was not less unfavourable: in fact the jury report here became somewhat condescending. In seeking for "novel methods of artistic treatment" as expressed in his written memorandum, its architect had – "though the plan has obvious defects" (!) – "fairly well" met the chief requirements of the programme. So much for the fame of Otto Wagner of Vienna!

Indeed the most favourable comment of all is bestowed on Greenley & Olin, who happened to end fifth all the same: "The exterior is greatly to be praised both for simplicity and for suitability of character. But the round ends of the principal façade injure this effect, and the room of the Administrative Council on one side and a series of smaller rooms on the other are lighted only from beneath colonnades. The plan is well studied and is distinguished from most of the others by a notable economy of space." With minor adjustments this plan could well have served its ends, one would argue!

Schwechten's design, which ended sixth, had not precisely impressed the members of the jury, it would seem, witness the report: "The exterior of this design is well composed, though not particularly interesting or dignified, and while the noticeably unsymmetrical plan shows some careful study, the small, narrow light-areas seem out of place in a building occupying an open site."

Understandably, not everybody felt pleased with this off-hand appraisal by a commission, which had taken hardly more than a week to ponder over and virtually dismiss the collected work produced by over two hundred of the world's best architects. But were they right and had world architecture indeed reached the abyss?

On 11 June 1906 the exhibition of the plans was officially opened, attended by the members of the Court, the *corps diplomatique*, both chambers of parliament and the Hague council. Admittedly, the survey of designs gave no cause for lyrical outpourings. One thing is certain, the Peace Palace competition, though enthusiastically entered upon by scores of private people and firms, had not produced the brand new idea and change in style which, for instance, the Paris 1889 world exhibition had produced and which this organizing committee as much as any other one had secretly hoped for. But neither had the Paris 1900 exhibition! All over the world able craftsmen had certainly done a good job, as the reporter for *Architectura et Amicitia* wrote one of those weeks, but true greatness was absent altogether.

The greater part of the five thousand people who in the five weeks following the awards visited the exhibition in the Kneuterdijk Palace fell in with this conclusion. The new idea of peace and arbitration had sadly enough not found expression in the new architectural order of its own which it deserved.

The fourth-prize winning design by Otto Wagner of Vienna, a daring imitation of the classical styles, illustrating – as the jury argued somewhat condescendingly – the architect's seeking for "novel methods of artistic treatment".

Below: Detail of Otto Wagner's design, showing the obelisk.

The fifth prize was won by Greenley & Olin of New York, whose design had class and dignity, as it was felt at the time. The jury criticized the round ends of the principal façade which it thought spoiled the total effect.

Some plans, true enough, were bizarre and out of the ordinary, but none of these spoke of genius. In fact, most of the schemes fell within the time-honoured patterns of temples, town halls, stations and museums. Most of them looked backwards, very few looked ahead. At least some of them evidently despaired both of the peace idea and future architecture! They were the classicist styles of the Pantheon and the White House on the one hand, and the gothic halls of the Anglo-Saxon colleges on the other that prevailed. Press comments agreed on this, but then, what was to be expected? The programme itself had little to stimulate modern-minded young architects. The preference felt by the Board of the Carnegie Foundation for limiting the competition to the arrivés, though not surprising of such a committee, was well understood, and the very names found in the jury could only corroborate this. Small wonder therefore that few modernists, those who fell in heartily with the *art nouveau*, had cared to submit a plan at all.

All the more surprising it was, therefore, that this same jury, after what it had sown, should criticize the harvest it reaped. In the allotment of prizes it had followed the course one had expected of it and had only thus virtually confirmed the impression one had gained of it in advance. Anything out of the ordinary had been discarded in the first round: convention prevailed. Cordonnier, whatever might be the merits of his style – and some indeed deemed it typical of the parvenu – had proved static in his ideas and uniform in their execution through the decades. His style had been acclaimed by many, indeed a design of his, though never executed, had been allotted first prize as far back as 1885, in the international

competition for the Exchange in Amsterdam. The plan he had submitted now was a replica of his Dunkirk townhall. The same held good for Marcel: his design too was predictable and generally felt to vary but little from the 1900 Petit Palais. As a critic remarked cynically: "from the World Exhibition to Universal Peace is but a single step for Marcel!" His drawings were superb though and, as reporters insinuated, the jury must have fallen for their majestic perspective. But apart from that, any French patrician could afford such a home, so why house Peace in it?

Wendt's third prize plan most resembled the church type, featuring ninety pillars towering above a somewhat "impressed" dome and was not precisely remarkable for its efficiency. In contrast, the plan submitted by Otto Wagner, that Viennese genius, at least revealed mastership and daring in its highly original imitation of the classical styles. One had to allow for the flat roofs of course and as to the marble slabs on the walls, these evidently did not suit the Dutch sea climate; but in most respects this was the best design available.

Much acclaim, too, met the Greenley & Olin fifth award design, actually the only American plan that was out of the very ordinary and indeed almost resembling the French style. It had class and dignity – if nothing else. Schwechten's contribution on the contrary missed all force and had nothing but tradition to speak up for it. This, however, held true for most architects representing the formerly leading nations in the field.

Most distressing to continental observers – and really astounding indeed – was the absolute failure of British architects to produce anything but

the obligatory *Palladio*-style. As little as, for that matter, German architects seemed prepared to budge as much as an inch from Wallot's *Reichstag*. And as for the Italians, they too proved true to tradition: they were artists rather than architects, with the possible exception of Mancini, whose design, though unpractical, spoke of ardour and genius. France, too, for that matter, confirmed the impression that "nothing good was to be expected from a republic".

As for the Dutch architects, it was felt by many that three of them had deserved better than the jury had conceded them. First of all John F. Groll of Delft, whose design was deemed somewhat akin to and in many respects preferred to Cordonnier's plan. But Berlage, too, had sent in a contribution worthy of his talent: a sober, but highly logical plan in sandstone, including a nice campanile, which in fact marks a transit from his Amsterdam Exchange plan of 1885 to his 1908 design of the Beethovenhuis. Though it just missed an award, it stands out as a highly interesting moment in his career. Kromhout, to conclude, had submitted an audacious plan of the first type, elaborated in a masterful series of aquarels. To be true, on second sight there were many noteworthy contributions, like those of the Romanian professor Töry of Bucharest, whose Doric design spoke of heroic power.

Most impressive by far though, and widely discussed in the magazines, was the simple but highly artistic plan called "l'homme" submitted by

No. 147, Saarinen of Finland. It was this plan precisely, which in subsequent weeks, came up in the discussions of the Board as to the further steps which had to be taken.

The Board's Dilemma

The practical advice the jury had given the Board was to enter into consultations with the prize winning architects as to the adjustments to their designs, and if no agreement could be reached to open a new competition. The Board fell in with the first proposal but unanimously refused even to take the latter into consideration. Obviously, this procedure would take much time and too many months

The sixth prize went to F. Schwechten of Berlin with another elaborate ground plan in the classical style.

One of the more bizarre designs to be submitted came from Emile Töry of Bucharest, who had won the prize-competition of the Memorial of Queen Elizabeth.

A design by the Dutch architect W. Kromhout Czn of Amsterdam.

Appreciating this point to the full, van Karnebeek and his colleagues then made a very singular move, which indeed caused a most awkward incident. Through the American Minister Newel at The Hague the Board contacted Carnegie with the request ... to have an additional endowment put at the disposal of the Foundation. In the covering letter van Karnebeek referred in great detail to the latest vicissitudes of the Board, praised the prize-winning design and pointed out that the 1903 gift would only just cover the expenses of the Court House, certainly not those of the projected Library. In putting it this way the Dutch diplomat no doubt hoped to touch Carnegie's weak spot. Carnegie's refusal through Hill on 18 June 1906 brought him back to earth, though: "One million Dollars was the sum suggested to me, but to make sure that there would be no deficiency I added one half more. ... The Library contemplated by the Baron [Gevers] is a new idea. It was never mentioned. ... A large showy building would I feel be incongruous. A moderate structure only is needed ... I feel that no more money could properly be spent upon the matter."

In mentioning the Library, Carnegie now stated that he had meant a collection of books, not the building. Actually, the jury's report, which referred to "The Library and Court of Arbitration" was "shocking" to him: "I am positively wounded", he wrote. To speak of "the Library and Court of Arbitration" was as if a bereaved husband were to ask plans for a sacred shrine to "my nephew and my

had been lost already. Accordingly, about mid-June, somewhat hasty consultations began with Cordonnier, in these same weeks, incidentally, that Otto Wagner offered to adapt his design to the wishes of the Board at a moderate price and have a Dutch architect execute the work.

Soon enough it appeared that time was not the only thing the Board had to spare: matters of finance became problematical as well. Though the capital had only increased from the accrual of interest over the three years since Carnegie's gift was transferred, it proved that most of the winning designs exceeded by far the sum stipulated in the programme. Consequently, large-scale alterations and simplifications had to be put through, if any of the plans were to be executed at all.

The design of H. P. Berlage (1856–1934), typical of his sober and sturdy style.

put it at this meeting: the central part of the façade was borrowed from Dunkirk, whereas the extension to the right lacked all harmony with this central part and the tower to the left was simply plump. It was at this juncture too that the architects first expressed their feelings that Cordonnier was in fact an artist, rather than an architect. With four votes against one it was nevertheless decided to continue. However, the Frenchman's new drawings, submitted on 15 January, were even worse.

At this point Knuttel and Muysken definitely insisted with the Board on the contracting of a Dutch architect to become associated with the Frenchman. To this end they suggested three names: van der Steur, Posthumus Meyjes and Limburg. At a further meeting on 30 January Cordonnier was bluntly given an ultimatum, ordering him either to become associated with a Dutch architect or to come to The Hague in person for some months. Cordonnier finally gave in to this, having first presented the Board with extravagant financial claims. His fee was finally settled at 5 per cent of the total building costs. But then again his proposal of an associé had to be rejected: the suggested Jozef Cuypers, Jr., was in fact the son of a jury member.

The second proposition of Cordonnier, concerning the architect van Dorsser had also to be disapproved, for practical reasons this time. Another ultimatum on the part of the Board on 26 March finally made Cordonnier give in and thus led to the appointment of van der Steur as associate to Cordonnier. On 27 March the contract was drawn up: another step was made on the long road to peace – that is, it appeared that way. For little did the Board expect at the time the wave of protest which was soon to overrun them and which would keep them occupied with the affair for another four years.

The Architects' Protest

Protests against the jury's report had been numerous, but this was only too natural. One might also foresee that they would ebb away in due time. At first, none of the Board members therefore was seriously disturbed by the rather vehement accusations brought up in magazines like the *Bouwkundig Weekblad* and *Architectura*. The more so as the writ of execution applied for by some hotheaded architects in the weeks following the jury's verdict ended satisfactorily for the Board.

In May 1907, however, events took a more serious turn when an increasing number of Dutch architects, headed by Berlage, de Bazel and Kromhout, addressed a petition to the Second Chamber of the States General in which all resentment which the course of events concerning Carnegie's gift had caused was assembled. These concerned, in fact, each and every step made up till then: the site chosen, the terms of the competition, the report of the jury and the plans adopted. The protesters actually claimed reconsideration of the site and restitution of

Cordonnier's design for the Amsterdam Exchange in 1885.

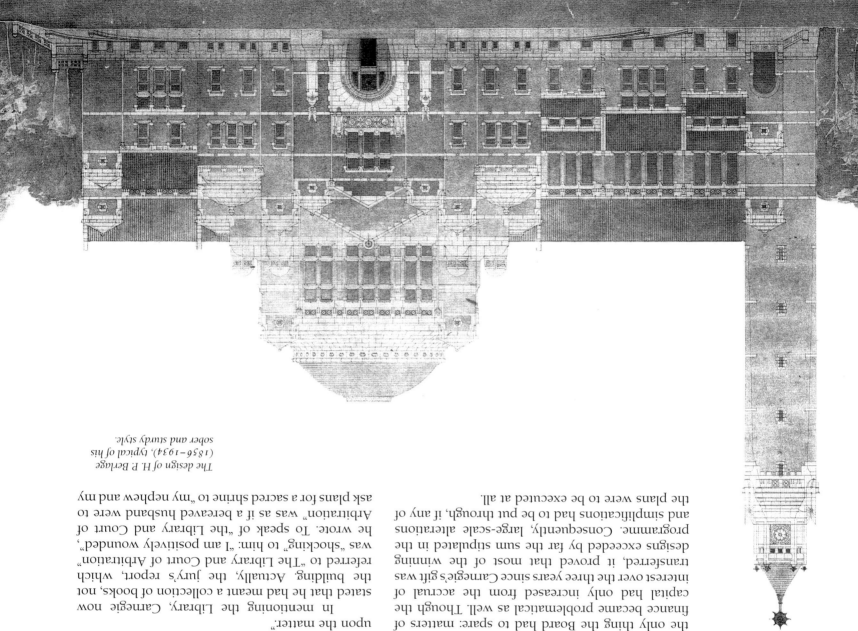

The design of H. P. Berlage (1856–1934), typical of his sober and sturdy style.

Appreciating this point to the full, van Karnebeek and his colleagues then made a very singular move, which indeed caused a most awkward incident. Through the American Minister Newel at The Hague the Board contacted Carnegie with the request ... to have an additional endowment put at the disposal of the Foundation. In the covering letter van Karnebeek referred in great detail to the latest vicissitudes of the Board, praised the prize-winning design and pointed out that the 1903 gift would only just cover the expenses of the Court House, certainly not those of the projected Library. In putting it this way the Dutch diplomat no doubt hoped to touch Carnegie's weak spot. Carnegie's refusal through Hill on 18 June 1906 brought him back to earth, though: "One million Dollars was the sum suggested to me, but to make sure that there would be no deficiency I added one half more. ... The Library contemplated by the Baron [Gevers] is a new idea. It was never mentioned. ... A large showy building would I feel be incongruous. A moderate structure only is needed ... I feel that no more money could properly be spent upon the matter."

In mentioning the Library, Carnegie now stated that he had meant a collection of books, not the building. Actually, the jury's report, which referred to "The Library and Court of Arbitration" was "shocking" to him: "I am positively wounded", he wrote. To speak of "the Library and Court of Arbitration" was as if a bereaved husband were to ask plans for a sacred shrine to "my nephew and my

the plans were to be executed at all.

Soon enough it appeared that time was not the only thing the Board had to spare: matters of finance became problematical as well. Though the capital had only increased from the accrual of interest over the three years since Carnegie's gift was transferred, it proved that most of the winning designs exceeded by far the sum stipulated in the programme. Consequently, large-scale alterations and simplifications had to be put through, if any of

A design by the Dutch architect W. Kromhout Czn of Amsterdam.

had been lost already. Accordingly, about mid-June, somewhat hasty consultations began with Cordonnier, in these same weeks, incidentally, that Otto Wagner offered to adapt his design to the wishes of the Board at a moderate price and have a Dutch architect execute the work.

"dear wife". Although van Karnebeek made clear with reference to the Foundation Deed of 1903 that Carnegie was wrong on this point, he could do little to clear up the atmosphere. After frequent exchanges of letters, he made up his mind to consult the American Scot at Skibo. In the interview which took place in the presence of Hill on 13 August, major obstacles were indeed smoothed away. It was agreed that should any surplus remain after the completion of the Court House and grounds, this should be spent on library affairs. Van Karnebeek felt relieved: from now on, he presumed, he could once again concentrate on Cordonnier's design.

This intention was soon frustrated, though. In order to get a better impression of Cordonnier's work the Board had decided, sometime in June, to pay a visit to the town hall of Dunkirk. This visit, which took place during the first days of July, proved disenchanting. The Board was very unfavourably impressed by what struck them as a complete lack of style and taste both as regards the inside and the outside. Apart from this it proved that the plan would be much too costly. The trip had a sobering effect on all of them. A majority was satisfied now that they would never come to business with Cordonnier. Consequently, two other plans were brought up.

First the Greenley & Olin design, which offered both practical and financial advantages and second the plan of Saarinen, which had caught the attention of the world of architects and was praised in the journals as a truly visionary design. As van Karnebeek pointed out, though, the nomination of Saarinen posed a secondary problem, it meant an affront to the jury. This, however, as Lohman argued, was exactly what the jury deserved. Whereupon it

was decided to have Professor Evers of the Delft Polytechnic evaluate the technical and financial aspects of the Saarinen plan. Should nothing be found amiss it was this plan which had to be executed – always provided the reports on Saarinen would be favourable.

But Professor Evers was not too impressed by the design and fairly pessimistic about the costs of the Saarinen plan. Despite vehement protests on the part of its secretary, van Citters, who argued that Evers was biased by the Cordonnier plan, and who pleaded strongly on Saarinen's behalf, the Board finally decided not to risk its neck for the Finn from Helsinki. Van Karnebeek now carried his views through with all the weight of his authority. He was right in stating that a decision had at last to be reached, that all the technical counsel received had led to nothing, and that the Board was right in not taking too great financial risks: matters were serious enough as they stood.

And this was how in its twenty-eighth meeting, on 28 August 1906, seven years to the day before the opening of the Palace, it was decided once again to open negotiations with Cordonnier. Little could the Board know that these discussions were once again bound to drag on for ages – to the point of becoming an agonizing trial for all concerned.

Negotiations with Cordonnier

Louis Marie Cordonnier was a French architect's son, born on 7 July 1854. Having completed his education at the *École des Beaux Arts* at Paris, he soon became the leading architect in the eclecticism

This design by the Finnish architect Saarinen of Helsinki in the modern style of the period, was much appraised by the scholarly journals of the day and by the public. It was only on the advice of Delft Polytechnic that the idea to materialize this plan was abandoned by the Board.

Louis Marie Cordonnier of Lille (1854–1938). A competent though not precisely innovative architect, who was the exponent of the late 19th-century revival of self-confidence in Northern France. Both his design for the Amsterdam Exchange in 1885 and the Peace Palace in The Hague in 1905 were awarded first prizes.

which from 1880 onwards came to the fore in Lille, the centre of Northern French culture. The gist of this "Neo-Flemish" movement was based on the style of the "Flemish Renaissance" and, it must be said, was perfectly in its place in this partly gothic, partly baroque entourage. For the same obvious reasons its propagation outside this area was less fortunate and in fact of no consequence. Accordingly, Cordonnier never had any of his designs executed other than in these parts of France.

Oddly enough though, Cordonnier's claim to posterity is mainly due to the two prize-winning designs he entered for Dutch competitions, the one for the Peace Palace and the other for the Amsterdam Exchange produced twenty years before. Both do, however, bear his signature in their major characteristics, to wit the *campanile* or belfry, the central hall and staircase, and the entwining of brick and stone. All these elements Cordonnier literally imitated from the Renaissance style. This accounts for the rather static impression one gains from his oeuvre. These classical echoes could only be expected to be consistently copied throughout his work. The more so since they actually served his political ends in accentuating the province's administrative independence from the Paris centralizing system – which in a way were the very ideals that many decades later led another Lille native, General Charles de Gaulle, to direct all highways to this "capital of the North".

Small wonder therefore that Cordonnier's designs are found scattered throughout the landscape. In their chronology, from Loos-lez-Lille (1883) through La Madeleine (1885) and Dunkirk (1896) to Armentières (1901) and the Exchange in Lille (1906–1910) Cordonnier's designs reflect nicely the evolution of, for instance, the belfry: from its central position in front of the building to, first, its incorporation into the façade and, later, its position in the corner. Still, despite these and other minor modifications, the basic concept of the ground plan remains unchanged throughout his career. One would almost deem his oeuvre a dull monotony and Cordonnier's talents narrow and limited but for the Louis XVI Theatre just opposite the Lille Exchange and actually built during those same years (1908–1914), which shows a totally different outlook.

Unfortunately, the Dunkirk town hall was burned down on 27 May 1940. If anything it was this project which, though not the architect's happiest conception by far, most resembled the Peace Palace design. In fact, on studying its façade the members of the Board must have felt at home – if not downright cheated by the plagiarism. The Hague was indeed a collage of former elements. The base was identical, the belfries were facsimiles, the balconies copies. As a matter of fact, the Board were wise to remain in Dunkirk in July, for in Lille they would have been stunned to find their own lovely library turret featuring on top of the Exchange – that is with the single addition of an element which keen eyes would have found inserted in the belfries at The Hague. The roof, including its mansards, was copied from Loos and Dunkirk – and was applied afterwards in Armentières, with the addition of the Hague central peak.

This is not simply to belittle Cordonnier's merits. Experienced from previous competitions and their hazardous outcomes, the French architect, like many others, presumably did not risk running into the very trouble which Berlage *cum suis* accused the Board of having imposed on those participants who did follow the programme to the letter and did care for lofty ideals. He probably never thought of having his initial design executed at all! Consequently, he submitted drawings on the ground plan that was requested, knowing very well that should the jury fall in with his style, subsequent deliberations would soon lead to a final proposal. This, at least, is what happened – and we will now follow the course taken by these deliberations.

On 6 September the Board first discussed seriously the project with Cordonnier, stipulating that negotiations were strictly conditioned by the latter's willingness to adjust his plan to the numerous objections the Board had to make, particularly as concerned the main façade. To this Cordonnier expressed himself prepared. The Board, on their part, were prepared to extend the financial means to a maximum of Dfl. 1,800,000, whereupon the Frenchman promised to hand in new drawings as soon as possible. The Board then decided to have a true Building Committee installed, made up mainly by the architects Knutel and Muysken.

On 15 October Cordonnier effectively submitted two new ground plans to the committee. These, however, had both to be rejected, along with the drawings of the façade which still resembled the baroque Dunkirk variant so loathed by the Board. New plans were to be sent in on a three weeks' term. These too failed, but at a subsequent meeting on 21 November the ground plan at least was agreed upon. New drawings of the façade were once again rejected by Knutel and Muysken on 21 December. As Citters

put it at this meeting: the central part of the façade was borrowed from Dunkirk, whereas the extension to the right lacked all harmony with this central part and the tower to the left was simply plump. It was at this juncture too that the architects first expressed their feelings that Cordonnier was in fact an artist, rather than an architect. With four votes against one it was nevertheless decided to continue. However, the Frenchman's new drawings, submitted on 15 January, were even worse.

At this point Knuttel and Muysken definitely insisted with the Board on the contracting of a Dutch architect to become associated with the Frenchman. To this end they suggested three names: van der Steur, Posthumus Meyjes and Limburg. At a further meeting on 30 January Cordonnier was bluntly given an ultimatum, ordering him either to become associated with a Dutch architect or to come to The Hague in person for some months. Cordonnier finally gave in to this, having first presented the Board with extravagant financial claims. His fee was finally settled at 5 per cent of the total building costs. But then again his proposal of an associé had to be rejected: the suggested Jozef Cuypers, Jr., was in fact the son of a jury member.

The second proposition of Cordonnier, concerning the architect van Dorsser had also to be disapproved, for practical reasons this time. Another ultimatum on the part of the Board on 26 March finally made Cordonnier give in and thus led to the appointment of van der Steur as associate to

Cordonnier. On 27 March the contract was drawn up: another step made on the long road to peace – that is, it appeared that way. For little did the Board expect at the time the wave of protest which was soon to overrun them and which would keep them occupied with the affair for another four years.

The Architects' Protest

Protests against the jury's report had been numerous, but this was only too natural. One might also foresee that they would ebb away in due time. At first, none of the Board members therefore was seriously disturbed by the rather vehement accusations brought up in magazines like the *Bouwkundig Weekblad* and *Architectura*. The more so as the writ of execution applied for by some hotheaded architects in the weeks following the jury's verdict ended satisfactorily for the Board.

In May 1907, however, events took a more serious turn when an increasing number of Dutch architects, headed by Berlage, de Bazel and Kromhout, addressed a petition to the Second Chamber of the States General in which all resentment which the course of events concerning Carnegie's gift had caused was assembled. These concerned, in fact, each and every step made up till then: the site chosen, the terms of the competition, the report of the jury and the plans adopted. The protesters actually claimed reconsideration of the site and restitution of

Cordonnier's design for the Amsterdam Exchange in 1885.

the damage done to the fifteen undersigned architects. Let us start by pointing out that most of these resentments were sincerely felt and that most of the arguments raised were sound and valid:

- As for the site, it was maintained that the selected spot was too small and lacked the monumental atmosphere which must be attached to a building of the stature aimed at here. The latter argument was corroborated by a display of historical parallels from all cultures. The Malieveld would have done nicely and so would have the Mussenberg, as had repeatedly been pointed out …
- As regards the prize competition, here the predilection of some architects over others was rejectable, and so was the allotting of sums in advance to the selected ones. To the serious loss of time already run into by previous blundering, costly months were added by the requirement of specified plans and detailed drawings; this at least could have been anticipated by the arrangement of a so-called *Ideeen-Wettbewerb* which was applied so often abroad. More serious still was the question of finances. The maximum prize was stipulated *disertis verbis* in the programme. Yet most of the plans that had been awarded prizes surpassed the given sum by far, as was clear for all to see. Again, the virtual lack of any circumstantial data as to The Hague surroundings had, at least to foreign competitors, made the requirement of adapting the scheme to the area a purely theoretical and academic one indeed. The programme, incidentally, had been published in The Hague only. Thus, architects from abroad had lost many weeks before ever getting hold of the text.

- As for the results of the jury, these too were commented on in no uncertain terms, which for that matter only voiced the echoes of the learned magazines and popular press at the time. The report, it was held, attested to either superficial knowledge or complete disinterest on the part of the jury: it was very succinct to say the least; it contained some curious discrepancies; in its awards it did not respect the self-imposed terms of competition; in its motivation of the first prize the jury was perfectly blundering as to style and moreover implicitly preferring one style to others, though no stipulations were made on this point precisely in the programme.
- As to Cordonnier's design, this was anything but distinct and noble. In fact, in its display of cupolas and towers it was typical of the vain pompousness which the very programme had tried to prevent. Finally, along with four others out of the six awarded plans, it effectively sinned against more technical specifications of the programme such as size and drawing techniques.

However justified, the petition missed its effect completely. From sheer frustration the architects then lodged a claim against the Carnegie Foundation – which through its president they held responsible for this failure – for the rescinding of contract and for damages suffered. This claim was disallowed by a judgment of the Hague Tribunal dated 11 May 1909. Thereupon the plaintiffs entered an appeal, which again was disallowed by the Hague Court of Appeal on 11 January 1911. It was here that this most regrettable episode in the early history of the Peace Palace ended.

One of many satirical comments on the prize-competition, taken from the "Nederlandsche Spectator" and featuring a cacophony of styles, with a pair of guns at the front entrance and Golden Calf idols all over the grounds so as to stress the idea of vainglorious pomp.

Supplément au No. 50.

NO. 50. DIMANCHE 11 AOÛT 1907

Courrier de la Conférence

DE LA PAIX

Rédigé par WILLIAM T. STEAD

Prix d'abonnement par semaine:
pour la Hollande fl. 0.65
„ l'Etranger fl. 0.75
Prix du numéro:
fl. 0.15

Collaborateurs:
Mme la Baronne BERTHA VON SUTTNER,
M. ALFRED H. FRIED,
M. FRÉD. PASSY,
M. FELIX MOSCHELES.

Publié sous les auspices de la FONDATION POUR L'INTERNATIONALISME à La Haye.

Directeurs-Editeurs: MAAS & VAN SUCHTELEN

BUREAUX: Princessegracht 6A, La Haye. — Téléphone No. 287. — Adr. Télégr. MAASSUCHTELEN.

LA HAYE, LA CAPITALE DES ÉTATS-UNIS DU MONDE.

L'empereur de Russie,
qui a convoqué la Conférence.

I.

Le 17 juin 1899, le Dagblad, le prédécesseur du Courrier de la Conférence, publiait un article intitulé „La Haye, Capitale du Monde". L'occasion de l'apparition de cette proclamation des destinées mondiales de La Haye était la décision prise par le Comité d'Examen de faire de La Haye le siège de la Haute Cour d'Appel. Cette décision fut prise à la suite d'une discussion qui n'est pas rapportée dans le compte-rendu officiel. Tout ce que l'on y trouve, c'est un paragraphe où il est dit que le Président donna lecture de l'Art. 2 du projet de Sir Julian Pauncefote, commençant par les mots: „Un Bureau central est établi à La Haye."

Art. 2. „Un Bureau central est établi à La Haye, par les soins et sous la haute surveillance du Gouvernement des Pays-Bas. Ce Bureau est placé sous la direction d'un Secrétaire Général résident. Il sert de greffe au tribunal arbitral. Il est l'intermédiaire des communications relatives à la réunion du tribunal. Il a la garde des archives et la gestion de toutes les affaires administratives."

Telle était la brièveté et le peu de détails d'une décision qui devait peut-être avoir pour résultat de fixer le centre de l'Etat mondial.

L'article du Dagblad était peut-être la première indication qu'il se trouvait quelqu'un pour apprécier la grande portée de la décision que venait de prendre la Conférence. Mais le Dagblad même insistait plutôt sur les avantages qu'en retirerait la Hollande au point de vue de sa sécurité, qui serait ainsi augmentée, et des garanties additionnelles qui seraient données à son indépendance, que sur les aspects de la question qui préoccupent maintenant l'attention publique. A cette époque, les autres nations acceptaient le choix de La Haye comme siège de la Haute Cour en le considérant comme le corollaire naturel du choix de La Haye

comme siège de la Conférence de la Paix.

On oublie généralement que la première pensée du comte Mouravieff, lorsqu'il fut pour la première fois question d'une Conférence en 1898, était de la tenir à Bruxelles. Ce n'est que plus tard qu'on pensa à La Haye; et l'on sera généralement d'accord que dans ce cas la seconde pensée de la Russie a été meilleure que la première. Quoiqu'il en soit, bon ou mauvais, ce choix fut fait, et les Délégués se réunirent à la Maison du Bois au lieu de se réunir au Palais de Justice de Bruxelles. On voit donc que la décision originale qui donna à La Haye sa position prééminente fut plutôt due, comme tant d'autres évènements dans l'Histoire, à un accident qu'à une intention arrêtée. Si le Roi Léopold avait répondu avec plus de cordialité aux ouvertures du Gouvernement russe en 1898, Bruxelles se serait vue conférer le prestige qui appartient maintenant à La Haye et qui semble devoir

plutôt augmenter que diminuer avec le temps.

Si le choix de La Haye comme siège de la première Conférence fut plutôt accidentel qu'intentionnel, on n'en pourrait dire autant de la seconde Conférence, qui s'y réunit sur le désir clairement exprimé du président Roosevelt. Le 30 Octobre 1904, le Président fit envoyer à tous les Ministres américains accrédités dans chacun des pays représentés à la Première Conférence, une note dans laquelle il n'invitait pas seulement les Puissances à se réunir de nouveau, mais à le faire à La Haye. Voici le dernier paragraphe de cette note: „Enfin vous exprimerez le désir et l'espoir du Président que les souvenirs immortels qui s'attachent à La Haye comme le berceau de l'oeuvre bienfaisante commencée en 1899 soient fortifiés par la réunion de la Deuxième Conférence de la Paix dans cette cité historique." L'Empereur de Russie approuva le choix fait par le Président, et la réunion de la Deuxième Conférence a augmenté les souvenirs immortels qui garantiront d'une façon encore plus certaine à La Haye la supériorité sur tous ses concurrents.

Dans quelques jours la Conférence prendra une décision grosse de conséquences d'établir la continuité de la réunion des Conférences Internationales, et par suite, de faire de la Conférence comme un élément permanent de l'organisation

Ridderzaal La Haye,
où la Conférence siège à présent.

du monde. Il est possible qu'elle recule devant toute résolution générale, et se borne à prévoir sa prochaine réunion; mais il importe peu que la Conférence décide en faveur d'un intervalle régulier de sept ans, ou qu'elle fixe seulement sa prochaine réunion à 1914. Le succès de la réunion de la Deuxième Conférence a rendu la Troisième inévitable, et quand il y aura eu trois réunions on pourra dire alors que la Conférence est sortie de l'enfance pour prendre place parmi les institutions reconnues du monde.

Il est peu probable que l'on discute sérieusement la question du lieu où se tiendra la prochaine Conférence. Les souvenirs immortels de La Haye, dont parlait le Président Roosevelt, ainsi qu'un salutaire respect des précédents établis, suffiront probablement à assurer une décision unanime en faveur de La Haye comme siège de la Troisième Conférence. Il y a toutefois une ou deux considérations

Le Président des Etats-Unis.

seule maîtresse. On peut prédire sans courir grand risque de se tromper que la Conférence actuelle n'osera pas prendre une initiative si courageuse, et que la proposition de créer en Europe un District de Colombie sera remise à une date ultérieure.

Il est pourtant bon de se rappeler que la création d'un centre neutralisé et internationalisé, ou d'une Cité Mondiale, était l'idée centrale de presque tous les projets des rêveurs des siècles passés et du siècle présent qui ont publié des projets de paix universelle. Ecartant donc pour le moment l'idée de la cession d'un territoire national au contrôle d'une Conférence Internationale, il faudrait au moins signer un accord, sinon une Convention positive, garantissant à la Troisième Conférence la certitude qu'elle sera bien accueillie à La Haye. Dans d'autres Associations et Bureaux internationaux, le Gouvernement du pays est chargé de prendre les mesures indispensables pour faciliter l'acquisition et la construction de l'installation nécessaire au Bureau, à l'Association ou à la Conférence. En vue du fait que, si la Troisième Conférence, se réunit à La Haye, toutes les Conférences suivantes s'y réuniront aussi, il est très désirable que tous ceux qu'intéresse la question sentent l'importance de la décision qui doit être prise avant la fin du mois. Le Gouvernement néerlandais a-t-il quelque proposition à faire à la Conférence? Et les autres Gouvernements qui désirent rivaliser avec la Hollande pour l'honneur de recevoir les Délégués de la 3me Con-

qui entrent en ligne de compte.

D'abord, tant à la première qu'à la deuxième Conférence, les Délégués se sont réunis sur l'invitation de Sa Majesté la Reine des Pays Bas, qui leur a fourni le local nécessaire à la Maison du Bois, puis la Salle des Chevaliers, et a mis à leur disposition plusieurs des Bureaux du Gouvernement. Mais il est bien différent de venir en Hollande comme invités de la Souveraine, ou de s'y inviter soi-même en qualité d'Assemblée autonome. La Conférence est une assemblée réunie sur l'invitation personnelle de cette Souveraine régnant; elle va se transformer en une assemblée décidant que dans l'intérêt supérieur du monde elle doit tenir ses assises à date fixe. La question se pose donc tout naturellement: Quelle sera l'attitude du Gouvernement hollandais vis-à-vis de la Troisième Conférence? Conseillera-t-on à Sa Majesté la Reine d'offrir aux Conférences futures une invitation perpétuelle, ou faut-il que la Conférence se présente chapeau bas devant Sa Majesté et sollicite respectueusement sa gracieuse permission de se réunir dans la capitale de son Royaume à l'avenir comme par le passé? Il faudra en passer par là vis-à-vis du tout souverain, qu'il s'agisse des Pays-Bas ou de tout autre Pays, à moins que la Conférence n'envisage courageusement l'alternative suggérée par M. Hayne Davis, et ne propose la création d'un „District de Colombie" international, où la Conférence elle-même serait

M. de Nélidoff,
Président de la Conférence.

M. de Beaufort,
Vice-Président de la Conférence.

The 1907 Peace Conference

The first Hague Peace Conference of 1899, as we have seen, established a system of good offices, mediation and arbitration to prevent the outbreak of conflicts. In some cases it did indeed, as we have already had occasion to point out. In matters of political aspirations though, and with ambitions in the field of foreign policy at stake, purely legal observations of equity and right as a rule do not prevail. Thus it happened that within five years of the Peace Conference Japan had extended its influence over the Kingdom of Korea, France and Germany were pushing forward in the Middle East, while Great Britain applied its energy and resources to control the future of South Africa at all costs. Nothing much had been changed, it seemed, by the Conference: despite all the solemn promises of a second meeting "within a reasonable time", friends of the 1899 Conference began to fear that The Hague would stand as an isolated experiment.

Their fears were idle: something had changed! Public opinion had been awakened, and it was the growing discontent, notably within peace organizations, which in 1903 found expression in a petition for an international congress, presented by the American Peace Society to the Massachusetts Legislature. This body, in its turn, passed a resolution requesting the Congress "to authorize the President of the United States to invite the governments of the world to join in establishing … a regular international congress to meet at stated periods to deliberate upon the various questions of common interest to the nations and to make recommendations thereon to the governments."

Nothing much happened. But then in September 1904 the request was taken up by the Interparliamentary Union gathering at St. Louis. The issues of the proposed conference were here thus specified: the subjects postponed by the Hague Conference; the negotiation of arbitration treaties between the nations which shall be represented in the Conference; the establishment of an international congress which shall meet at stated periods to discuss international questions.

It must be said that President Roosevelt showed little reserve and lost even less time to further the cause. On 21 October 1904 Secretary of State John Hay addressed a circular note "to the representatives of the United States accredited to the governments signatory to the acts of the Hague Conference of 1899", in which the plan was defined. The embarrassment felt by some at the calling

together of a peace conference at a time when a great war (the Russo-Japanese War) was in progress, was more apparent than real, it was argued here. Events of that sort should in no way impede efforts to prevent future wars.

In the circular note no categorical programme of subjects was proposed, but it should, in all events, include the issues relegated to a future conference in 1899. Moreover, a procedure was suggested to have States who had been absent from The Hague in 1899 made co-signatories and adhering parties to its acts. The Hague was again suggested as the meeting place, also, as it was stated, in view of the "undying memories which cling around it".

The response to the call was favourable; only Russia had its reservations and in fact made its participation dependent on the cessation of hostilities in the Far East. Thereupon, on 16 December 1904 to be precise, a second circular note was distributed from Washington to its representatives abroad in which the nations were called upon to propose specific subjects other than the general ones outlined so far. For practical reasons it was suggested that, whilst awaiting the formal invitation to the nations from the Dutch Government, the International Bureau, under the control of the Permanent Administrative Council of the Court at The Hague, should work out the agenda.

On 5 September 1905 the Treaty of Portsmouth, New Hampshire, ending the Russo-Japanese war was signed, thanks to the mediation of President

Roosevelt. The following week Russia, through its Washington ambassador, declared itself prepared – not only to attend, but "… to assume the responsibility of summoning a Second Hague Conference". With characteristic chivalry Roosevelt then renounced the honour to the Czar. He made a single reservation, however: he insisted on having all American States invited to the Conference and it being held at a juncture which did not conflict with or compete with the importance of the Third Pan-American Conference that was to be held in Rio de Janeiro in the summer of 1906. Besides, he pointed out, a formula of adherence to the conventions of the First Conference had to be devised on behalf of the Latin American nations, in particular regarding the first, so-called "closed" convention for the peaceful adjustment of differences, which was in fact a kind of contract between parties and therefore of no effect upon non-signatories. These matters were regulated in perfect harmony in April 1906 and on the eve of the Second Conference, on 14 June 1907, the States which had not signed the 1899 Act, without exception signed the protocol of adherence at The Hague.

The Programme

On 12 April 1906 Russia presented an elaborate and apparently definitive programme for the Conference, including the following topics: improvements to the 1899 convention regarding the Court of Arbitration and the international commissions of inquiry; additions to the 1899 convention regarding the laws and customs of war and revision of the 1899 declarations; framing of a convention relative to the laws and customs of maritime warfare; and additions to the 1899 convention for the adaptation to maritime warfare of the principles of the 1864 Geneva Convention.

As in 1899 it was decided that questions not directly bearing on the said issues were unacceptable for debate. This latter restriction, however sound, led to complications when in reply to this programme on 7 June, the American Secretary of State, Elihu Root, proposed two more topics, to wit the limitation of armaments and the restriction of force in the collecting of contract debts. St. Petersburg showed little willingness to consent: the acceptance of the proposal would necessitate a second round of consultations, as most of the nations had already agreed to the former programme. Besides, it was argued, the new topics might be unacceptable to some nations and therefore the proposal for their insertion might endanger the Conference. Root, however, insisted, suggesting in a note dated 26 March 1907 that Russia included in its letter of invitation a statement to the extent that the United States Government reserved to itself the right to bring the two matters mentioned up for discussion. To this the Russian Government agreed.

It was then proved that more powers showed an unwillingness to formally restrict debate on the programme presented by Russia. So much at least

appeared from the formal invitation, which was distributed on 4 April 1907 and which fixed the opening date of the Conference on 15 June, following. In it reference was made to, first, a British claim to raise the question of expenditure on armament; second, American and Spanish claims to raise the questions of limitation of armament; third, an American claim to raise the question of the restriction of force in the collecting of contract debts. Apart from this, however, Bolivian, Danish, Dutch, Greek and Japanese claims had come in to submit to the Conference issues not explicitly mentioned in the formal programme, complemented by Austro-Hungarian, British, German and Japanese claims to abstain from the discussion of any points which they deemed unlikely to produce any useful result.

The Conference, it was decided, was again to be held in The Hague, though not in the *Huis ten Bosch* this time. The tiny palace was not large enough to accommodate so large a gathering and its outlying site was felt to have some disadvantages. Another historic site had been reserved though, the Binnenhof, the former residence of the Counts of Holland and the present seat of the Houses of Parliament in the centre of town. Plenary sessions were to be held in the 13th-century *Ridderzaal* (Knights' Hall), only recently restored to its former glory. Delegates were expected in mid-June.

General Outline of the Conference

What then are the figures and statistics for this Second Peace Conference?

The Conference lasted from 15 June till 18 October, which is to say a full four months and indeed twice the length of the former Conference. The number of delegates, too, was more than doubled to two hundred and fifty-six. Some nations were represented by a single, others by no less than fifteen delegates, but taken together they represented forty-four of the fifty-seven nations which at the time claimed sovereignty. More than its predecessor,

A survey of the expenditure spent on armaments in a single year by the world's prominent nations.

therefore, the present Conference could justly claim the titles bestowed on it both of "Confederacy of the World" and "Parliament of Man", though the gathering could hardly be called a parliament in the strict sense of the word. It could, however, boast the attendance of virtually all the "civilized" States at the time – meaning those accepting and applying the principles of international law. This extension, for that matter, was mainly due to the express desire of the United States Government to have the Latin American nations represented. Of the nineteen States claiming sovereignty in the Western hemisphere seventeen were attending, only Honduras and Costa Rica being absent.

Interestingly enough, Africa was no more represented in 1907 than it had been in 1899. The two governments that claimed sovereignty in 1899 but were then banned by a British veto, had in the meantime been replaced by British rule. Asia was represented by the same four governments that attended in 1899, but there was a nasty problem here in the case of Korea. This empire of some 20 million people had been recognized as a sovereign State by the Western powers as early as 1884. It had indeed been invited to the present Conference in the 1904 circular note. In the meantime, though, it had been virtually absorbed by Japan, and that without anything like a European reaction: its Emperor was held captive and Japan was doing its utmost to have nominated as successor a Prince in whom it saw the appropriate marionette of its politics. Accordingly, Korea had not been sent invitations in 1906. Despite all this, a Korean delegation of three, nominated before the crisis and headed by Prince Yi, proudly arrived at The Hague, creating diplomatic embarrassment all round. It vainly claimed its admittance and actually, on 26 June, raised a fierce protest against their banning for all the world to see. Things grew worse when about mid-July the forty-nine year

The opening session of the Second Hague Conference on 15 June, 1907. The arrival of delegations by cars and carriages.

old delegate Tjoune, a highly respected member of the Korean High Court, died suddenly from the results of an otherwise innocent operation to remove an abcess from his cheek. Like so many of his important compatriots at the time, Tjoune had been seriously weakened by starvation, due to his abstinence from food out of protest against the Japanese aggression. His last words: "Save my country! The Japanese will soon have destroyed my land!", which sealed what was in fact a suicide, rang in the ears of the delegates for days and created embarrassment throughout the Conference.

The Old World itself was represented by the same twenty governments as in 1899, though Norway, having won its independence from Sweden in the meantime, now had a delegation of its own. Montenegro was, as before, represented by Russia, but Bulgaria this time acted independently of its Turkish suzerain.

Seats were again arranged in French alphabetical order. Again some prominent diplomats, military men and scholars attended. Among these Joseph H. Choate of America, Marshal von Bieberstein of Germany, Drago of Argentina, Ruy Barbosa of Brazil, Renault of France, Count Tornielli of Italy, Nelidow of Russia, Hagerup of Norway and several veterans of the First Conference, including Bourgeois and Constant Baron d'Estournelles of France, de Martens of Russia, Asser of Holland and the former Prime Minister Beernaert of Belgium.

The Opening Session

On Saturday 15 June, around 2.30 p.m., the *Ridderzaal* was gradually filled by a gathering as colourful as it was venerable. It was a spacious hall, fairly comfortable and splendidly illuminated by scores of electric lights. Some two hundred and forty

seats had been reserved for the delegates, positioned in neat rows and concentric half circles. Some two hundred invited guests overfilled the galleries, from which they had a perfect view of the proceedings, though were hardly able to hear a word due to the miserable acoustics of the hall. Then in they came, one by one: the massive and very impressive German von Bieberstein, who took the best seat on the first row next to the delicate figure of the very cultured and highly intellectual Professor Asser of the Netherlands. In the moving sea of heads one easily spotted the red fez of Turkham Pacha and the blue silk dress of the Siamese delegate. Ladies peered down to get a glimpse of the very handsome delegate Choate from the United States. Attention was drawn, too, to the very respectable Fry, the octogenarian who headed the British delegation. Only fifty places had been set aside for the international press, of which fifteen were allotted to the Dutch, seven only to the British. Still, reporters of repute were noted: Alexandre Ular for the *Revue de Paris* and the *Wiener Zeitung,* Sidney Lo for the *Standard,* George Saunders for *The Times,* and last but not least, dear William Stead.

At three o'clock sharp the Dutch Minister for Foreign Affairs, van Tets van Goudriaan called the Conference to order. In his address of welcome he reminded the delegates of the results of the 1899 Conference. Severe criticism as to details had "not seriously weakened the favourable opinion which had been formed of the work of this Assembly". The best proof of it was the response to the present appeal and the sharp increase in the number of nations represented, nearly the double of the former Conference. He proposed to despatch a telegram to the Czar and, as his predecessor de Beaufort had done in 1899, suggested that the first Russian delegate, Mr. de Nelidow be elected President of the Conference. De Nelidow in his opening speech gave credit to President Roosevelt for his "generous impulses, always inspired by the most noble sentiments of justice and humanity" to the convocation of the Conference. He reminded the delegates of their twofold task, the peaceful settling of disputes and the mitigation of the burdens of war. It was a fallacy, as was so often heard, that the realization of the second task would only hamper the materializing of the first. History proved that no horror of war had ever stopped man or indeed checked the frequency or duration of conflicts, whereas the amplification of humanitarian measures had in no way contributed toward developing a taste for war. The same held good for arbitration. Since 1899, dozens of arbitration conventions had been concluded among the various nations and four major sources of conflict had been taken before the Court at The Hague.

These words all sounded fair enough – and yet some in the audience felt that there was something absolutely wrong in the President's approach. The American delegate Brown Scott for instance read something condescending and belittling from the words of the President. From his gestures and

The President of the Second Hague Conference, Count de Nelidow of Russia.

outward appearance, he surmised, there showed an apparent lack of sympathy with the project in hand. Far from arousing the enthusiasm which had been awakened by the speech of de Staal eight years before, the address of de Nelidow somewhat clouded the opening days of the Conference. For the German press, however, de Nelidow had gone much too far already: as the *Die Leipziger Neueste Nachrichten* was quick to point out: "God, Who had created the iron, provided that swords be made from it, as much as ploughs". Another daily, the *Börsen Zeitung* claimed that "in this world of ours we have but a single companion, our sword". This tried and trusted friend we should esteem, for it was worth more than twenty alliances.

Both sides may have been somewhat biased, for the American delegation bore yet another grief. Amidst the exchange of congratulatory telegrams with the Czar and the Queen of the Netherlands, not a word of thanks was telegraphed to the one they deemed the real initiator of the Conference, President Roosevelt. The Americans deeply resented this "indifference of the proprieties where imperial and royal personages are not involved". Tardy reparation of this blunder was made four months later, at the close of the Conference!

The Procedure of the Conference

In view of the number of delegates attending, it was felt that a strict code of procedure had to be adopted and an efficient secretariat organized for the guidance of the Conference. In this de Nelidow at the second plenary session proposed to follow the procedure of the First Conference, be this with small adaptations. Thus, secretaries and lesser officials were this time not accredited to the Conference but to their delegations. Traditionally, one would almost

say, the Netherlands Minister for Foreign Affairs and Holland's first delegate were made honorary President and Vice-President of the Conference respectively. Again, French was to be the official language of the Conference, though this time formal protest was raised against this procedure from several sides. Some delegates, Choate among them, persisted in addressing their audience in their native tongues throughout the Conference.

Again, a subdivision into commissions was proposed, four this time, due to the increase of numbers and the more elaborate programme. The total number of meetings of these commissions and *comités d'examen* finally amounted to one hundred and thirteen. From this it appears that, not unlike in 1899, most of the work was done here. Consequently, plenary sessions were restricted to a minimum. Only eleven of these were held in over four months. At the first and second session, on 15 and 19 June respectively, matters of procedure were discussed. The third to tenth sessions, on 20 July, 17 August, 7, 21 and 27 September and 9, 16 and 17 October respectively were devoted to the successive discussion of the reports submitted by the various commissions. The concluding plenary session on 18 October was for the greater part occupied by the farewell speeches.

Public Opinion and Outside Contacts

The two most renowned "peace-crusaders" of the period: Bertha von Suttner in a contemporary cartoon (above) and William Stead at his writing-desk in his Hague office (below).

In one respect at least the organizing committee had learned its lesson from 1899. The apparent lack of interest as regards public opinion, which hampered the contacts with the representatives of the press during the First Conference and indeed accounted for much of the sneering and cynicism on that occasion, was virtually absent this time.

Beernaert of Belgium was but one out of many to remind his colleagues of their responsibility to public opinion, "that redoubtable sovereign": "Public opinion is listening to and watching us; and today there is no assembly which must not sit with windows opened, listening to the voices from outside." Baroness von Suttner commented on it in the following way: "That which impresses me most is their (i.e., the delegates') respectful obedience to the desires of public opinion. If they oppose a reform, it is only because they are persuaded that public opinion is indifferent to it. If public opinion should express itself with appropriate vigor, there is nothing the Conference would not try to do ... Public opinion ... that is the master, and even the god, of the Conference."

As before, sessions of the commissions and subcommissions were secret, that is to say closed, but plenary sessions were open to the public upon presentation of tickets to be distributed by the secretary. Up to two hundred guests crowded the gallery at times. Besides, the general secretary of the Editing Committee kept members well-informed. The minutes (*procès-verbaux*) of the sessions of commissions from the day before were distributed daily among the delegates and these found their way in no time to the "ambassadors of the peoples" as the paparazzi liked to call themselves, despite objections to this procedure put forward by several delegations. These minutes were made up in French under the supervision of a Russian delegate, Prozor. They were prepared with remarkable rapidity and typified by James Brown Scott, the young American expert delegate from Harvard who wrote an authoritative concise history of the two Hague Peace conferences, as marvels of accuracy considering the intricacy of detail.

But one other very accurate source of fairly detailed information was at their service, namely the *Courrier de la Conférence de la Paix*, edited by no less a person than ... William Stead. For once again this Crusader of Peace was first among his equals and indeed a central figure of the Conference. In 1899 he had, as one will remember, the Hague *Dagblad* at his disposal to vent his views. This time the *Foundation for Internationalism* at The Hague had provided him with every facility to edit a true journal to be published under the auspices of the well-known firm of Maas en van Suchtelen. Residing in comfortable quarters at Prinsessegracht 6a, Stead, assisted by Baroness von Suttner among others, wrote his daily editorials which justly claimed independence of view and were distributed free among the delegates. Others interested could buy the paper at 14 cents a copy or subscribe at 75 cents weekly – and many they were. The cloth-bound edition of this *Courrier*, available at Dfl. 25 – from the end of October onwards, constituted a full and indeed most impressive account of the Conference. It contained succinct reports of all plenary sessions and gatherings of the respective committees, biographies, portraits and interviews with prominent delegates. Besides, it gave editorial reviews reflecting on daily events; many, many photographs and some fifty caricatures taken from all European periodicals. It featured a lavish display of plans and schemes, drawings, accounts of social events, "faites diverses", "petites nouvelles" and delicious gossip. It is, in a word, a real *Fundgrube,* reflecting both day to day progress and the overall atmosphere of the Conference. Colleagues of Stead made grateful use of it for their own ends.

Reporters were served, too, incidentally, from other sources. At the Café Hollandais at Groenmarkt 23 they could subscribe to all sorts of facilities, such as type-writers, telegraph and the like. The post offices did a good job, too, this time, notably the one at Scheveningen which was generally praised for its speed and competence. Accordingly, the newspaper reporters, at least of journals represented at The Hague, were generally writing far less cynically than eight years before. Again, though, the ones who pretended to know best, had not bothered to come at all.

Critics and Eulogists

Who did attend, though, and indeed in crowds, were representatives of peace organizations and political movements. Communications were received from the *International Bureau of Peace* in Bern, from peace societies over three continents, and from two noteworthy peace congresses, the one held in April in New York and the other in September in Munich. Within the period of the Conference The Hague saw within its walls the opening of international congresses of zionists and anarchists, all appealing to or strongly denouncing the Peace Conference. In an address attended by Mr. de Martens, among others, the inflammable Zionist leader, Max Nordau, stated that the Conference would be a farce and comedy as long as it neglected the cause of the Jews which had been worded so eloquently by Herzl. Reaction from the Conference was laconic. Delegates by far preferred a comedy to the tragedy that would result from the pretension of solving all the world's problems within a fortnight.

Socialists, too, gathered at Stuttgart, and commented fiercely. One of them, Emile Vandervelde, spoke of The Hague "demonstration of impotence and hypocrisy": the Socialist Movement was "never to show such feeble-mindedness and pusillanimity". His colleague Quelch went so far as to call the delegates thieves and murderers. But then he was banned from Stuttgart afterwards by the local police. Still, the Stuttgart congress "declared war on war" and it was felt at The Hague that an unhoped for failure of the present Conference would only invite socialists to violently overthrow the "commercial rivalry of capitalism", which they held was the cause of all misery.

About mid-July a pamphlet called *Ha Ha Ha,* edited by a the Dutch satiric cartoonist Louis Raemaekers and containing some fourteen caricatures of the Conference alarmed some delegates. In the end though they wisely decided not to react. It

The "Café Hollandais" (or rather "Zélandais") at the Groenmarkt, where journalists and pacifists met during the Conference.

was a forewarning of what awaited them if the Conference should fail to reach adequate results in the eyes of the world.

Positive reactions came in in great numbers, too. The International Council of Women, headed by Lady Aberdeen presented the signatures of some two million women from twenty nations, and this was easily surpassed by the Universal Alliance of Women for Peace by Education, who represented over five million members. Ecclesiastical organizations presented the signatures of dozens of patriarchs, the International Federation of Students gave its comments on the Conference. On 4 July, a petition for arbitration was brought in, bearing over two million signatures from Boston only, and thousands of students cabled their names and addresses to the secretary. Thousands of adhesions came in from individuals and dozens of deputations looked to the Conference for the prompt materializing of their ideals. Just as in 1899 people who felt oppressed implored the help of the delegates in great numbers: petitions and demands came in from Albanians, Armenians, Bosnians and Georgians, Boers, Egyptians and Irishmen.

Honourable mention must be made of the Interparliamentary Union, which again was instrumental in the success of the Conference and actually prepared the plan of obligatory arbitration which was offered to the Conference by the Marquis de Soveral of Portugal and formed the basis of the agreement subsequently adopted. All sorts of suggestions were made. Thus, for 1908, the idea was proposed of a Pilgrimage of Peace through Europe. Likewise, on 20 July, President de Nelidow made reference to a highly interesting plan designed by Professor Nippold of Germany to found an Academy of International Law at The Hague on behalf of future conferences. De Nelidow on this occasion called for more Carnegies to help materialize the idea.

Carnegie himself for that matter attended the Conference for some days. On 29 June he looked in for two or three days on his way back to Skibo Castle from his widely discussed interview with Emperor Wilhelm II at Kiel. Rumour had it that *der Kaiser* and the business tycoon had mainly discussed Bruce of Bannockburn and Robert Burns, and on the most cordial terms. At The Hague Carnegie was welcomed as a second Aladdin, whose cheque book served him as a wonder lamp. Only the other day this "contemporary Count of Montechristo" or "Midas Reborn" had proposed a universal League of Nations, not unlike the spontaneous alliance of the European nations in the case of the China crisis. Unfortunately, Carnegie was unable to stay and attend the stone-

A satirical print from the brochure "Ha Ha Ha" by the cartoonist Louis Raemaekers (1869–1956), caricaturing the banning of the Pope from the Conference by monarchs who asked his blessings before making war with each other.

De Kerk in oorlog en vrede.

ALPHONSUS: Het gaat mij toch aan 't hart hem eenvoudig te negeeren; in tijd van oorlog laten we onze wapenen zegenen en ....

NICOLAAS: In tijd van oorlog werk ik ook vrij aardig met heiligen-beelden, maar bij een vredesconferentie ..... dan blijft de kerk thuis.

laying ceremony on 30 July and personally to accept from the hands of Mrs. Albert of Paris the commemorative medal struck in his honour in France.

Finally, offers of all kinds were made to the Conference. On 9 July Barthold, President of the American section of the Interparliamentary Union, presented the Dutch group with a peace flag which was first hoisted on 30 July. On 10 August, a portrait of Nicholas II by the Hague artist Sophie Hirschmann was accepted by the Conference and hung in the *Ridderzaal* awaiting its final destination in the Peace Palace. According to de Nelidow and de Martens the portrait bore a striking, though somewhat flattering, resemblance; obviously it had been taken from photographs dating from 1899! On 15 October a drawing by Holiday and representing the *Guardian Angels of the Pilgrimage of Peace* and accompanying an *Appeal to the Peoples* was submitted to the delegates for their signature. In the same weeks their financial support was invoked regarding the purchase of a huge bronze monument on a black marble pedestal created by Frederick McMonnies and representing *Pax Victrix,* the goddess of peace arbitrating between duelling warriors.

The Social Entourage

The sheer number of delegates at the Second Conference had some implications in matters of logistics. Strict organization was self-imposed on its officers. Veterans must have missed the cosy atmosphere of the *Huis ten Bosch,* the easy going – and the shared – lunches. In 1907 it proved impossible for all delegates to have lunch together each day within the strict time-schedule, that is without disturbing the sessions. The Government therefore provided simple lunches on a take-away basis. But in other respects the reception was as cordial and generous as it had been eight years before.

On the night of 1 July Queen Wilhelmina received the full Conference at the Royal Palace in The Hague. What she had in mind first was a garden party that afternoon at the *Huis ten Bosch.* Inclement weather conditions though, "to which even she had to resign" (Stead) necessitated a last minute switch, however deplored by the more fashionable ladies like Madame Choate, who had fancied to show off their airy ensembles at last. To be sure, there were some eighty ladies from eleven countries accompanying their husbands or relatives to the Conference: eleven from America, nine from Britain, eight from Russia, six from Brazil.

In the evening dozens of carriages drove up to the beds of roses and geraniums planted in front of the palace. Seldom before had The Hague witnessed such a display of style and pomp. Madame Choate in her "robe jaune aux aigrettes d'autruche noires" and Lady Howard in her "vert pâle robe" looked absolutely ravishing. But likewise did the young Queen: elegant and graceful in her light blue empire robe with a necklace of pearls and a tiara set with diamonds she was a treat to look at. She was flanked

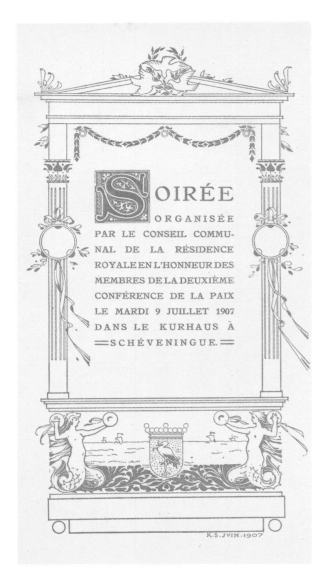

frequented as the sessions themselves. It invited a remark from Drago halfway through the Conference to the extent that "he could digest Obligatory Arbitration and a Permanent Court, but was since long ago fed up with obligatory dinners and permanent salmon". As weeks went by caricaturists tended to depict the delegates as ever stouter: "maigre comme un clou en juin, gros comme un moine à la fin d'Aôut" were the words. The most popular restaurant was in the recently opened Palace Hotel at Scheveningen, harbouring representatives from no less than sixteen nations. The others would lodge in the Kurhaus or Hotel d'Orange nearby in Scheveningen, or in the very respectable hotels in the city centre: the Vieux Doelen and Des Indes.

Up to 1 September some sixty-six dinners from ten up to one hundred places had been celebrated in the Palace Hotel alone. Thirteen of these were given by American delegates, nine by the Germans, eight by the French and Brazilians, one (!) by the Dutch. As already mentioned, the most sumptuous dinners were offered by the Brazilian delegates. Meals would cost some Dfl. 20 per person,

Left: The programme of the "soirée" at the Kurhaus organized by the Hague City Council in honour of the Conference on 9 July, 1907.

Below: Specimens of the delegates' correspondence on notepaper of the fashionable hotels of the time.

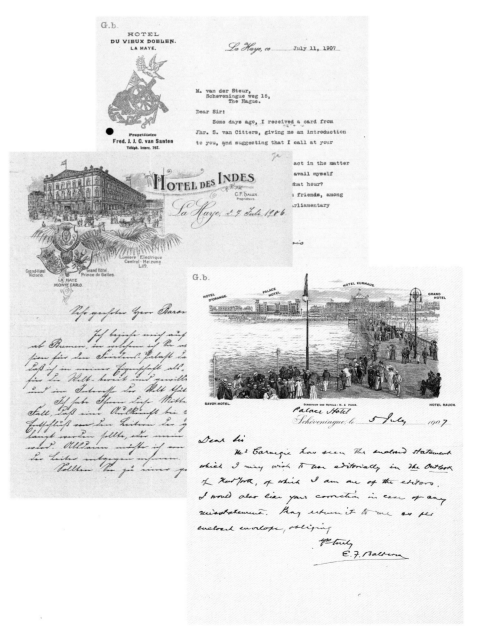

by the Queen Mother Emma and Prince Hendrick, who was afterwards seen in serious debate with Baroness von Suttner. The night was a thrilling one: it could have been taken for a family party. The English and French ambassadors strolled through the salons arms linked, a Russian and Japanese delegate were spotted chatting and as if totally unaware of recent hostilities, all memories of Mukden gone. The pell-mell of colours of all nations were a feast to the eye; that night, for once, they seemed a brotherhood of men.

On 21 July the chief delegates were invited to a State banquet at the Palace in Amsterdam. On Tuesday 27 July, by invitation of the Dutch Government, members went on a tour to the Nieuwe Waterweg, the canal dug from the North Sea entrance at the Hook up to Rotterdam. Fortunately, it was fair weather that day, for otherwise it was an exceptionally cool summer. All along the road the delegates were welcomed by the fluttering flags of all nations, festive speeches from burgomasters, cheering crowds and choirs of children in gorgeous attire with rosy apple cheeks – "like so many flowers of life" as Stead observed.

Apart from all this, delegations vied with each other in proffering hospitality, the Brazilians in particular. The dinners actually were as numerous and as

The former Hotel "Du Vieux Doelen" at the Tournooiveld in the city-center, near the Binnenhof.

wines excluded, but the costs of decorations could amount to some Dfl. 4,000. The average costs of a dinner were some Dfl. 10,000.

The most impressive receptions up till then, with six hundred and five hundred guests respectively, were offered by Bourgeois on the occasion of *Quatorze Juillet* and Buchanan (USA) on 24 August. The *maître d'hotel* of the Palace Hotel was given much credit for dinner, decorations and music alike. As with the excursion to Delft in 1899, on Independence Day, 4 July, the American delegate, Mr. Hill, gave a splendid reception at the Hotel des Indes on the Voorhout.

Then of course there were numerous unofficial contacts: Mrs. Tcharykoff for one, the wife of the Russian Minister, received each Wednesday afternoon at the legation at Lange Voorhout 9. A very

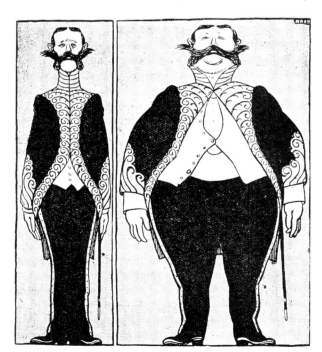

"Maigre comme un clou en Juin, gros comme un moine à la fin d'Août", a satirical comment by Albert Hahn (1877–1918) on the many dinners and receptions during the Conference.

welcome meeting point of another kind for all and sundry was the *Cercle International*. Lectures were given here almost daily by delegates and prominent outsiders. On 29 July it was Baroness Bertha von Suttner who addressed an audience here and afterwards had a congratulatory telegram dispatched to President de Nelidow. It was eight years to the day that the Final Act of the First Hague Conference had been signed.

The most interesting event of all though, attended by all the delegates and many *invités,* and in effect somewhat resembling the laying of the wreath on the grave of Hugo Grotius in Delft in 1899, was the laying of the first stone of the Peace Palace on the afternoon of 30 July. This festive ceremony, which is discussed in detail below in Chapter VIII, inspired the resolution proposed by Baron d'Estournelles towards the end of the Conference: "... that each Government represented at The Hague should contribute to the erection of the Peace Palace by sending, after consultation with the architect, materials of construction and ornamentation, representing the purest example of its national production, so that this Palace, an expression of universal good will and hope, may be built of the very substance of all countries".

The Work within the Commissions

As stated above, the Conference was divided into commissions and sub-commissions:

The *Arbitration Commission* (22 June – 11 October), which held ten reunions and was split into a commission on arbitration plans and warfare, which was attended by one hundred and three members and met forty-seven times, and a second on maritime prizes, constituted by eighty-nine members and meeting six times.

The *Commission of War on Land* (22 June – 9 September), which met six times, and also had two subcommissions: the first discussed laws and customs, was attended by seventy-nine members and met five times, the second covered mainly the rights and duties of neutrals and war declarations, had eighty-two members and met seven times.

The *Commission on War at Sea* (4 June – 4 October), which met eight times and again was split in two, the first subcommission considering bombardments, mines and torpedoes, its four sessions being attended by seventy-three members; the second treating the status of belligerent ships in neutral ports and the application of the Geneva Convention to maritime warfare, its eighty-two members convening five times.

The *Commission on Maritime Law* (24 June – 26 September) was made up by one hundred and fourteen members and met fourteen times, discussing special questions in the field of maritime law.

Chairmen of the commissions were, most of them, "peace veterans": Léon Bourgeois of France presided over the first commission, Beernaert of Belgium the second (with Asser assisting in view of the health condition of Mr. Beernaert), Count Tornielli of Italy the third, de Martens of Russia the fourth. Again, the absence of an American chairman was resented! Reporters were added to each commission to present the overall course of discussions to the full assembly. They included very capable men such as Renault from France.

Two other Commissions were appointed: the *Commission on Petitions* was composed of five members and presented two reports and the *Commission on Editing* was composed of twenty-nine members and presented a single report.

The Arbitration Commission

The justified boast of the First Conference had been the Hague Court and the convention for the peaceful settlement of disputes. From 1899 on, it was argued, a rational solution of conflicts for litigants to resort to lay open. As a matter of fact, in years bygone both Court and Convention had been successfully tested in difficulties susceptible to judicial settlement. As will be remembered, mediation had been applied by President Roosevelt in the Russo-Japanese War, whereas the Court had settled the Dogger Bank incident among others. Something else had occurred though, and a staggering thing it was for critics: within ten years over fifty treaties had been negotiated by which nations pledged themselves to arbitrate their mutual differences. Oddly enough, it had been this convention which, if anything, had been the laughing-stock of critics all over the world. It is perfectly true, admittedly, that the primary aim of the First Conference had been the treaty on compulsory arbitration. This had been effectively grounded by fierce German resistance. The convention finally agreed upon did not really extend the rights to which independent States had been empowered all the time. It was felt to be a needless confirmation of the obvious and was therefore looked upon by many as useless. What it did, however, was to call attention to the idea of arbitration and the fact remains that, maybe due to the moral authority of the Conference only, nations from that moment onwards tended to make use of the provisions arranged. Germany admittedly had only used it once, in the 1904 treaty with Great Britain, but the latter nation had concluded seven treaties of the kind, France eight, Portugal ten and the United States seven. Accordingly, there was solid ground for optimism. At the same time, the commission of 1907 had had ample occasion to amend any inconveniences which a full eight-year practice had revealed. The commission did more, though, and mainly in four ways, concurring with the four issues included in the 1899 convention.

ARBITRATION

If nations proved prepared to conclude compulsory arbitration treaties on concrete subjects with specific nations, it was argued by Bourgeois in his opening address to the Conference, then why not with all nations? And if on so many specific subjects, then why not on all differences which might arise? It will be remembered that in 1899 it was mainly questions concerning "independence, vital interests and national honour" which had posed obstacles and barred a general agreement. A decade afterwards it became evident that the idea of arbitration itself was by now universally approved. Besides, many nations had declared themselves prepared to sign a general treaty – if not on all differences which might arise, then at least on the numerous issues listed in a selection carefully prepared by the secretary on the basis of the proposal of the Parliamentary Union. For some days, therefore, optimism seemed justified, the more so as the German spokesman Marshal von Bieberstein stated that his Government basically favoured the idea of compulsory arbitration, and would examine *sans parti pris* any specified listing of subjects proposed for unrestricted arbitration. In his survey of the Conference, Brown Scott, the American technical delegate recalls this crucial phase of the Conference in gloomy detail.

Only a few days afterwards it appeared that Bismarck's "era of blood and iron" was not yet quite *passé*. Bieberstein himself was of good will, it seems, but the "examination *sans parti pris*" of the proposed list by the stern and austere delegate Kriege had resulted in the rejection of "literally every proposed subject of arbitration, be it large or trivial". On this Drago from Argentina, who was sitting next to Scott, handed the American, a slip of paper, on which was written: "This is the death of arbitration" – and so it was. Many were the delegates who had trouble digesting the German attitude. For weeks the Conference spoke of the *Elephas Germanicus*, the Teutonic Elephant, that most formidable and prudent animal that was never seen crossing a bridge before being fully satisfied with its construction. Though "thirsting for a Permanent Court", it was said with a sneer, and "starving from sheer lack of obligatory arbitration", it could not be induced by heaven or earth to cross the bridge to peace so fitly built for it by the Conference.

CONTRACT DEBTS

Surrounded, if not besieged by traditional enemies Germany did not yet dare to sheathe the sword which had united the nation and defended its independence on so many occasions. Perhaps the French papers calling for *revanche* were too widely read in Prussia. The German delegation did, however, show some willingness to enter into special treaties with carefully selected nations and on certain issues. This became evident in the second project that was brought up for discussion, the proposition for the restriction of force in the collecting of contract debts. Here Germany proved to have prepared a proposition of its own, closely resembling the American suggestion, and which indeed resulted in a very concrete agreement, considered by some as of world-wide significance. Here at least,

Léon Bourgois, the French delegate (1851–1925), banging the big drum.

one heard, was a clear-cut case of obligatory arbitration. In it all nations involved agreed to renounce the use of force in matters of debts, always provided that the debtor nation executed the arbitral award finally reached.

It was this latter restriction which made Mr. Asser, a very critical observer, comment rather cynically upon the value of the treaty. The outcome of the arbitration of any such differences could hardly be questionable, he argued – not even to the debtor-nation itself. Therefore, if the latter persisted in not repaying its debts, which might happen any time, in the end force was to be applied after all …

TOWARDS A PERMANENT COURT OF JUSTICE

The third issue brought up, again under the auspices of the American delegation, was the institution at The Hague of a *Permanent Court of Justice.* A team of expert judges on the administration of law would thus permanently be at the disposal of nations willing to present controversies of any kind. Both Germany and Great Britain favoured the proposal, which was accordingly adopted by the Conference and finally embedded in thirty-five articles. These, however, only proposed the establishing of a court as such; no agreement was reached as regards its composition. It was generally thought that this obstacle would be overrun in due course, to all appearances before the Third Conference would meet …

In the days preceding the final discussions in the second week of September, delegates speculated as to the men likely to be appointed to the court, the Seven Sages as Stead with his rich imagination named them. According to Stead it was not easy to point out a true Solon among the delegates: von Bieberstein was not much of a philosopher, Bour-

geois was more of a strategist, Barbosa was a walking encyclopedia, Choate maybe just a trifle too much of an optimist. Far less difficult would it be to point out seven competent international lawyers – Europeans preferably, that is if the court was indeed meant to reside at The Hague. These would be, in alphabetical order: Asser, Beernaert, Fry, Lammasch, de Martens, Renault and Zorn … but Tornielli, Eyschen and Kapos-Mere would do too. But then, would competence be the only criterion to be applied – or rather be a criterion at all and not rather geographical variety and political influence …

AN INTERNATIONAL PRIZE COURT

The fourth issue tackled by the first commission was the establishment of an International Prize Court. Both Germany and Great Britain had made proposals to this extent, although widely differing and clearly revealing their source. Britain opted for a permanent court composed of judges representing the major merchant marines. Germany sought a court which was only to be constituted upon the outbreak of war and would include among its five members a representative of the belligerent nations and three judges selected from the permanent court. It was the American representative, Choate, who managed to reconcile the parties.

The successful outcome, under the auspices of Germany, Great Britain, France and the United States was a permanent court in which the great maritime powers were to be permanently represented and the minor powers proportionally. However, "the wits had their jest here too", as the keen observer from the State Department, James Brown Scott, did not fail to notice. Whereas the Court of Justice agreed upon lacked its judges so far, the Prize Court was a court without its law. No code of maritime law was supplied which might help judges in solving the problems brought to their attention. The British Government therefore took it upon itself to summon the leading maritime nations to London for a Conference to codify maritime law and custom sometime in 1908.

All in all the resolutions taken by this first commission seemed no meagre results. At the time it was generally felt that with the amendment of the previous 1899 convention on the settlement of disputes, the unanimous recognition of the principle of obligatory arbitration and the foundation of no less than two courts of justice, the first commission had made an essential contribution to the progress of world order.

The Commission of War on Land

Whatever results the 1899 Conference had reached, war was not banished in the least. Indeed, it was as likely to occur in the future as it had in the past. Inevitably therefore in 1907 the attention of the delegates was to be called anew to the problems war involved, its laws and its humanitarian aspects. Both the second and third commissions were fully occupied for weeks discussing these manifold issues. We do not have to cover these endless negotiations in detail, first because they were highly technical and served their goals long ago, second because most of them have already been introduced in Chapter II in our report of the discussions of the first and second commissions of the 1899 Conference. We may therefore limit our account of the proceedings to the main results as worded in resolutions and the kind.

The object of the second commission was to take up the questions pertaining to warfare on land. It aimed, as the programme stated, at (1) improvements in the system of the laws and customs of land warfare; (2) the declarations of 1899 relating thereto; (3) the opening of hostilities; (4) the rights and obligations of neutrals on land.

Two subcommissions were organized, the first to be headed by Beernaert and dealing with the first and second points, the second presided over by Asser and occupying itself with the third and fourth points under consideration.

Not unlike the First Conference, the work within these subcommissions was the domain proper of experts. Progress was made in several fields. The first subcommission revised the 1899 convention. Thus, it also renewed the 1899 declaration on the dropping of projectiles from balloons, the duration of which was continued till the close of the Third Conference.

Likewise, the second subcommission framed a convention on the opening of hostilities, by which the powers bound themselves not to engage in warfare without a formal declaration of intention, and which released neutrals from the observance of their obligations till that moment. Maybe it did not seem too much, but as Brown Scott puts it: "To have corrected, even in a measure, the hardships incident to war; to have eliminated doubt and introduced certainty; to have imposed a restraint upon the rights of the conqueror, and to have protected the vanquished in life and property – are results of which we may well be proud."

Around mid-August the commission was startled by a wild rumour in the Italian press that King Edward VII of Britain, that most practical of men, had initiated a plan for a worldwide truce of non-aggression for the duration of twenty-five years. Since Edward had a political mind which lent itself badly to Quixotic undertakings, Stead in his *Courrier* didn't believe the rumour for a moment: *"non vero ma ben trovato"* was his typical comment. He proved right of course. Still, it is true that the English King did back the idea of a network of mutual pacts and treaties that would ultimately cover the whole world.

A similar idea, incidentally, had been raised by the Brazilian expert Barbosa with respect to the American continent. Five years of abstinence from aggression and observance of the Monroe and Drago doctrines, he observed, would free the Western hemisphere of the threat of all internal and external struggle. Border claims could thus be solved by mutual consent or international arbitration.

The Commission on War at Sea

This commission had to deal with problems of naval warfare. It was headed, very enthusiastically for that matter, by Count Tornielli, the first Italian delegate. On his proposal the commission was divided into two sections. The first sub-commission was presided over by Hagerup of Norway. It discussed the problems of bombardments of ports and cities by naval forces, and the laying of mines. On both points substantial progress was made, though only after embittered debate. Conventions were agreed upon which spoke of the compromising of formerly irreconcilable views: bombardment of undefended cities was forbidden and the use of submarine mines was restricted.

The second subcommission, headed by Tornielli himself, dealt with questions such as the treatment of ships of belligerent nations in neutral ports and the revision of the 1899 Hague Convention in these respects (based as it was on the 1864 Geneva Convention) in view of the renewed 1906 Geneva Convention. The conventions concluded, again, were satisfactory. The rules on the treatment of ships, although being still far from ideal, still meant a step forward, whereas the extension of the 1906 Geneva Convention to maritime warfare was regulated in a really humanitarian set of articles.

Again, the progress made was fought over step by step and covered but a small area of the whole field of warfare. But, as Brown Scott remarked: "We must not reject the minimum solely because it is not the maximum of our desires."

The Commission on Maritime Law

"The fourth commission makes but a sorry comparison with the second and third. Its positive results in conventional form were far from satisfactory, and its failures were even more marked than its partial successes." Thus the severe judgment of this commission by James Brown Scott. In a way Brown Scott was right, though his views were not shared by all, at least not by the president of the commission and the most prominent scholar of the Conference, de Martens. At all events, the outcome, however unsatisfactory to some members, was foreseen by many. The codification of the law on naval warfare which was discussed within this body involved subjects that were highly technical, extremely difficult and virtually without precedent, although one might argue that at the 1856 Paris Conference the codification of maritime warfare had been discussed in passing. Ever since, the issue had invited clashing views of authorities in the field and these in their turn only reflected widely differing State practices.

Several of the questions raised here have perplexed successive generations. However unfortunate and discouraging all of this was, it soon became evident that also within the present quorum of delegates the conflicting views proved beyond all compromise. No acceptable conclusions were reached in matters of contraband and blockade, whereas in matters of capture only an "infinitesimal recognition of a great principle" (Brown Scott) shimmered at the horizon. The convention relating to the status of enemy merchant ships at the outbreak of hostilities "is a distinct retreat by reducing that to a privilege which has hitherto had the sanction of enlightened practice and custom".

Again, as Scott remarks, the failure in the application of land warfare provisions to naval warfare only illustrates "the difficulty of reaching international agreements when material interests of the State intervene". All the same it must have come as a disappointment for Professor de Martens, who in 1899 had been instrumental, along with Beernaert and Bourgeois, in establishing the convention on the laws and customs of land warfare and who by now was one of the undisputed authorities in the field of international law. The commission could only express its hope that a Third Conference would reach more substantial results – not necessarily an idle desire, as Brown Scott claims, "because experience shows that the vœux of one Conference are the conventions of its successor".

Other Issues Raised

These were the results of the work within the bodies of the commissions. One will remember, however, that several States had laid claims to issues which might just be brought up for discussion. One such claim was actually raised by Great Britain on matters of military expenditure. Again no breakthrough was reached here. As stated in the final act, the Conference reaffirmed the resolution adopted in 1899 in these respects.

A last point brought up was the recommendation for a third Peace Conference. A resolution to this purport was proposed by the United States delegation, suggesting as date of meeting the month of June 1914. It was, however, generally considered as an injustice to the Czar of Russia not to leave him the initiative. To this the American delegation somewhat irritably retorted that no wrong was meant, but that, as they saw it, "the welfare of humanity should not be subordinated to diplomatic ceremonialism". The resolution was finally shaped into a *vœu* in the final act, to the extent that a third Peace Conference was to be held "within a period analogous to that which has elapsed since the preceding Conference, at a date to be fixed by common agreement among the powers, and it calls their attention to the necessity of preparing for the work of this third Conference long enough in advance to insure the pursuit of its deliberations with the requisite authority and rapidity."

The Brazilian delegate Ruy Barbosa, or "Mr. Verbosa" as he was called during the Conference. Vice-President and Minister of Finance in 1889. A brilliant internationalist and one of the little-known delegates who positively distinguished themselves during the Conference. He sought for the equality of all States before international law and the compulsory arbitration of conflicts. He was Judge in the Permanent Court of International Justice in 1922–1923.

This text was generally understood to mean that the Conference would take place somewhere in the summer of 1915. At this juncture, Professor Asser took his chance to point out that the one conclusion to be drawn from the two Conferences must certainly be that it was not so much a juridical research which had to precede a Conference like the present one, but rather a political study regarding the issues that could be brought up for discussion with a fair chance of unanimity and success. It was then to be left to the Conference to discuss details. From 1912 onwards commissions were raised in several countries to arrange a proper agenda for 1915. Detailed studies were made of a fairly promising nature. However, the outbreak of *La Grande Guerre* put an end to these lofty ideals.

Some Prominent Men

If you drive a van laden with apples over a bumpy road for some miles, after a while, on stopping, you will find that all the large ones have come to the top, whereas the small ones are down at the bottom. The same tends to happen with delegates at a Conference. At the opening they are all equal, haphazardly thrown together, though some have a reputation to defend, whereas others come in as perfect nonentities. In the course of four months though, all have ample opportunity either to hide or to assert themselves, to keep a low profile or try to catch the eye – but either way round the others cannot help noticing. Thus, it was observed by one delegate that each delegate at the Peace Conference had three faces: his real face, the way he pretended to be, and the way he thought he was seen by others. To the reputation of some of them the prolonged debates on highly controversial and delicate issues proved a true *demasqué*. Like a Spanish delegate remarked: "sous quelques uns de ces beaux chapeaux on ne trouve que de la sciure de bois."

The most negative impression, without the least doubt, was made by Beldiman of Romania. He represented the "perpetual no" and was justly called "le chef des obstructionistes". Though Carlin of Switzerland did his utmost to equal Beldiman, the latter showed more talent; in fact, as Stead observes "he seemed created to this end only".

Two men distinguished themselves most during the sessions, the first during the first months, the latter notably in the later sessions. They were different in all respects, the one a very colossus, the other the most slender of men. As the *Courrier* said: "L'homme le plus colossal et l'homme le plus mince sont les personnalités les plus importants, qui survivront dans la mémoire de leurs collègues."

The first was the German von Bieberstein, the other the Brasilian Barbosa. As weeks passed the first was increasingly handicapped by his fellow delegate Kriege, who represented the strictly Prussian point of view. As the *Courrier* points out: "Son étoile est obscurcie par les nuages de la méfiance et de la stupéfaction, créées par la politique allemande."

Barbosa was totally unknown beforehand. He was not much respected the first weeks either, witness his nick-name, *Mr. Verbosa*. Contrary to the exuberant German, Barbosa was a cool debater: "le coeur si chaud et la main tellement froide" was said of him. Both were very expert in law though, and born fighters, who would not give an inch, no matter how hot or prolonged the debate. Also both were excellent speakers, but in these respects were clearly beaten by two other men of genius, again the embodiment of contrasts. On the one hand the well-known and imposing figure of Joseph Choate, the American first delegate who excelled in long English spoken addresses, on the other the very unknown and slender Perez Triana, the knowledgeable son of a former Colombian President, who distinguished himself by some splendid short speeches in impeccable French. But they stood not alone: Tornielli for instance, the Italian, was a born stylist, Léon Bourgeois was vivid and amusing on whatever topic, whereas de Martens' words always had a ring of sincere emotion. And what to say of the English translations by Baron d'Estournelles!

With Tornielli, the most energetic, and Kriege, the most stern of delegates, we have probably the most influential men of the Conference, just as the American delegate Buchanan made himself known as the manager type, Asser as the wise mediator, and Prozor of Russia, Tsudzuki of Japan and Drago of Argentina as the most charming men of all. These latter were badly needed too, for as Stead observes: "la loi du progrès, c'est la loi du sacrifice."

The Final Act

The Final Act of the Conference, which was signed in the plenary session of October, was substantially longer than the one of 1899. It included thirteen conventions, a signed and an unsigned declaration, a resolution and five *vœux*. The first category, as will be remembered, form contracts proper entered into by the nations involved. The declaration proclaims a principle which may be accepted or not, therefore signed or unsigned, by specific nations. The resolution, less formal again, is

Right: The interior of the Ridderzaal during the 1907 Conference.

Below: The Hague Binnenhof and exterior of the Ridderzaal.

RIDDERZAAL AND BINNENHOF

"This is it", Count Wiliam II of Holland must have exclaimed in 1248, as galloping through the dunes with his retinue on a visiting tour of his lands he came at the crossing of two riverlets and a pleasant lake. And on the spot he built himself a fortress with a majestic Knights' Hall. Hence came 's-Gravenhage, "The Count's Hedge".
This is only one out of many legends to explain the genesis of Holland's administrative centre, the *Binnenhof* or "Inner Court". Actually, the architecture must be slightly younger than 1248, as the findings of archeologists and art historians enable us to see now. Still its age is as impressive as has been its functioning over the centuries. The Knights' Hall was built around 1280 by the architect Gerard van Leyden on behalf of William's son Floris V. It stands out as the largest secular Gothic edifice in the Low Countries, its wide hulk spanned by a splendid vault without any supporting piers. In the Binnenhof area, confined by the *Hofvijver* ("Court's Lake"), Dutch parliamentary history took shape. After the

Counts of Holland had gone, the States General of the Dutch Republic came in and it has remained the seat of the Houses of Parliament ever since. Later centuries tore down old buildings and added new ones of their own. In the middle of the 17th century Jacob van Campen and Pieter Post built the well known *Mauritshuis* (the actual art gallery) and the Houses of Parliament along the Hofvijver. Towards the end of the century Daniel Marot of France redecorated most of the ancient buildings and notably the *Trèveszaal* in an elegant baroque style. In the middle of the 19th century a cast-iron construction was made to replace the original vault of the Ridderzaal. Then, the very decade of the Hague Conferences, between 1896 and 1904, a drastic restauration was put through, restoring the former glory of Hall and Courtyard. But whatever changed with time, the Binnenhof has always remained the administrative centre of Holland and the Netherlands. Here, in September, the Dutch Queen arrives in her lavishly decorated Golden Coach to deliver the "Speech from the Throne" and therewith open the parliamentary session.

the expression of an opinion of the Conference in a concrete question. The "vœux", to conclude, constitute no legal obligations like conventions or signed declarations, nor the acceptance of a principle like the resolution, but the expression of a hope that something may be done on the subject in the future.

The Closing Session

At the closing session of the Conference de Nelidow gave a summary account of the work accomplished and praised the spirit of conciliation and concord which had reigned throughout, in spite of the often diametrically opposed interests of the

great nations. It was the task of conferences such as the present one, he recalled, to bring these conflicting tendencies into accord with the theoretical requirements of absolute law and justice. Hence, ultimately, would grow the moral and material solidarity which was the best shield against warlike enterprises. It was in this respect, probably, that apart from all the conventions agreed upon, the present Conference had made the greatest progress ever of mankind.

He then thanked all the delegates, expressed his gratitude to Queen Wilhelmina and President Roosevelt in telegrams and gave the floor to the Dutch Minister for Foreign Affairs, who, in response to the selecting of The Hague by the delegates as the regular and permanent headquarters of the Peace Conferences, offered the hospitality of The Hague to any subsequent Conference. Another telegram was dispatched to Czar Nicholas, upon which the session was closed.

Conclusions

Not unlike its predecessor, this Second Conference was hailed as a success and condemned as an utter failure. To the laymen and enthusiasts who had failed to learn from the experiment of 1899 it must have seemed disillusionary. As far as the concrete results in figures go, it was a great success. The numbers of nations involved, delegates attending and conventions and the similar concluded, these all were by far surpassing that of the First Conference. Though the effects to be expected from it were about the same. The small margins of progress only confirmed the impression gained from 1899 that no miracles should be expected. Asser, one of the more prominent members of both conferences, was very realistic in these respects. He was highly critical as to its results, yet fully satisfied with the critical urgency of this and subsequent conferences, if only for the furtherance of mutual understanding by personal contacts. In this at least he proved right, as will be seen from the early days of the Court of Justice and the Hague Academy in later years.

Mr. Elihu Root, the American Secretary of State at the time, was not necessarily less realistic, but certainly less critical as he concluded: "The work of the Second Hague Conference, presents the greatest advance ever made at any single time toward the reasonable and peaceful regulation of international conduct, unless it be the advance made at The Hague Conference of 1899 ... The achievements of the Conferences justify the belief that the world has entered upon an orderly process through which, step by step, in successive Conferences, each taking the work of its predecessor as its point of departure, there may be continual progress toward making the practice of civilized nations conform to their peaceful professions ... The question about each international Conference is not merely what it has accomplished, but also what it has begun and what it has moved forward."

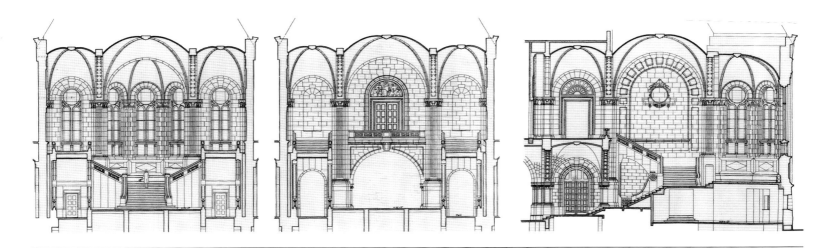

leading colleagues there, who helped him interpret the modifications decided upon by the building committee. As mentioned above, these were numerous and far-reaching; still, most of them were prompted by either stylistic or budgetary reasons. Cordonnier's initial design provided for two separate buildings, court house and library being connected by a covered passage only. In the modified design the two buildings were to be entwined. In the heart of the building a central courtyard would lighten all the corridors. The ground plan became a square now, measuring about seventy-eight metres, its central yard measuring about forty-four metres. The Court of Arbitration now made up the whole of the front, whereas the library constituted the rear of the building. Both were accessible by entrances situated in the centre of the major façades.

If these changes enhanced the balance, others were to detract from it. Thus, the northern belfry and both library turrets had disappeared altogether and been replaced by a turret behind the Great Court Room. The logical consequence of this was that the great and small court rooms were interchanged. Probably the most radical change, however, although hardly noticeable on the surface, was the minimizing of the library and reading room, which formerly had held a central part of their own and now were almost hidden due to the economy measures imposed by Carnegie. This is not to say that efficiency was pushed through relentlessly. Nothing of the sort was to be expected in a "Palace" built in a basically representative style. Still, most of the ornamentation – which Cordonnier otherwise applied throughout his career and with the lavishness worthy of a Carnegie – had been cut down to more earthy proportions. Likewise, his copying in the frontal façade of figures previously used in Dunkirk was struck out by the level-headed van der Steur. Indeed, a new building had come to life!

The Stone-laying Ceremony

Although the Board of the Carnegie Foundation was fully aware it had nothing much to show, it was resolved towards the end of May 1907 to avail itself of the presence of the international Conference

and the willing ears of the world press to draw attention to the newly projected building. Critical comments, both as regards the delay the project had met, and the prize competition and winning design, had urged van Karnebeek and his fellow-members to present the delegates of the Conference with some tangible revenue of their 1899 convention and

The confectioner's, furnisher's and contractor's invoices for the stone-laying ceremony of 30 July, 1907.

Right: The programme for the stone-laying ceremony of 30 July, 1907.

Carnegie's beneficence. To this end a stone-laying ceremony was projected for 30 July, halfway through the Conference's deliberations.

Although not everything went the way the Board had planned, still the ceremony itself was a great success. Van Karnebeek would have given his last dime to have Carnegie attend the ceremony, but the Scotsman decided otherwise. In fact, as mentioned before, he left The Hague for Skibo Castle shortly before the ceremony. Yet another guest of honour declined, namely Queen Wilhelmina. Her Majesty preferred to have the stone-laying act, which the Board had allotted to her, performed by the first representative of the Conference's initiator, Count de Nelidow.

Under and above left: The builder's estimate for the central hall and staircase.

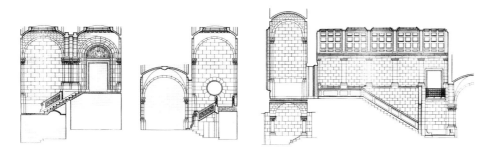

Below: The builder's estimate for the frontispiece.

Even so, the ceremony was a major social event of the season. No costs were spared to impress the audience; according to the accounts in the Foundation's archives, some Dfl. 17,500 were spent on the event. Mr. Viotta, director of the Koninklijk Conservatorium was contracted to conduct the Kurhaus Philharmonic Orchestra and a well-known violin player, Mr. Witek, was invited along with a selection of singers from Hague choirs. Placed in between the speeches by van Karnebeek and Count de Nelidow they performed Händel's "Alleluja", Beethoven's "Benedictus", Mozart's "Hymn" and Wagner's "Wach' auf, es nahet gen den Tag!"

Much work had been done on the tribunes: the speakers' rostrum and the covered-over pavilion – which served the orchestra as a *Coquille St.*

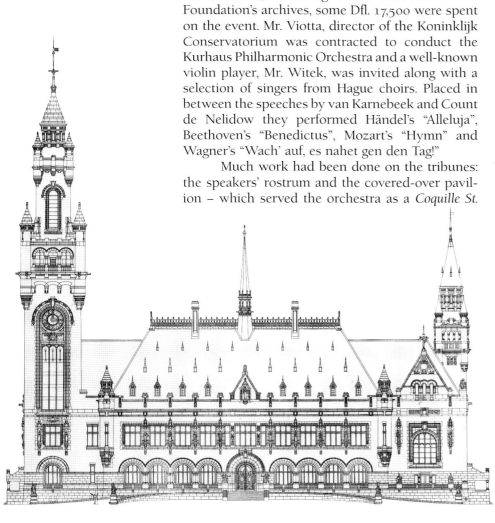

PROGRAMME.

1. „Alleluja". . . . . HÄNDEL.
2. „Benedictus qui venit in nomine Domini." BEETHOVEN.
3. Discours du Président du Comité des Directeurs de la Fondation Carnegie.
4. Pose de la première pierre du Palais de la Paix par son Excellence M. NELIDOW, Ambassadeur de Russie, Président de la Deuxième Conférence de la Paix.
5. „Hymne". . . . . MOZART.
6. „Wach' auf, es nahet gen den Tag!" . . WAGNER.

EXÉCUTANTS.

Direction: M. VIOTTA, Directeur du Conservatoire Royal de Musique.

Quatuor vocal: Mlle VAN LINDEN VAN DEN HEUVELL. Mme VIOTTA-WILSON. M. VAN SCHAIK. M. ZALSMAN.

Violon: M. WITEK.

Choeur: Membres des Sociétés Chorales de la Haye.

Orchestre: l'Orchestre Philharmonique du Kurhaus de Schéveningue.

Jacques as a reporter could not fail to observe – were faced by a wide semicircle of galleries, decorated with garlands and crowded with dignitaries. Along with the delegates, "toute la Haye était là": Royalty, *Corps Diplomatique*, Cabinet Ministers, the Chambers of Parliament and the Municipal Council all attended. Amounting to some eleven hundred in total, they were all neatly seated in compartments of their own. Over their heads, high up in the air and a sport to the wind, all sorts of colourful banners, pennants and standards were floating from sixteen flag-poles. Still, despite all the pomp and glamour, attention was drawn involuntarily to that curious machine in the midst of it all: a huge tripod from which was dangling a heavy, massive stone with the inevitable Latin text engraved on it:

PACI · JUSTITIA · FIRMANDAE · HANC · AEDEM · ANDREAE · CARNEGII · MUNIFICENTIA · DEDICAVIT

At the time, with the first sod not yet cut, the position of the founding stone could only be an estimated one. In fact, in later days, research has speculated heavily on the precise location of the stone that day as compared to its definite position in the outer corner of the great court room. There is no need for us to enter into this debate, as the very act of Count de Nelidow was basically a symbolic one as we shall see. Actually, at the time the only thing to account for any building activities as yet, was the much regretted felling of some majestic oaks and precious beeches on the Buitenrust estate. However, an exhibition arranged in a pavilion on the grounds allowed visitors to gain an impression of the present state of plans and the ultimate effect.

The day was blessed with sunshine throughout, that is, except for the opening minutes of the ceremony. As the orchestra struck up the "Alleluja", a heavy shower poured down, as if consecrating the gathering. In no time hundreds of umbrellas were raised, reminding the reporter of the *Courrier* of the *testudo,* the "tortoise of shields" of the Roman army. However, as van Karnebeek ascended the *rostrum*, the sun was once again peering through. A gifted orator who availed himself of impeccable French, the Board's President outlined the genesis of the idea of arbitration, enlarged on Carnegie's munificence and, repeatedly interrupted by cheers or applause, notably expanded on the moral values implied in the Court of Arbitration: it actually anticipated a world which no longer contented itself with the *jus inter gentes*, but availed itself of this very moral in order to found a true *jurisdictio inter gentes*, the latter to be considered the reflection of the former in the everyday practice of law. Within the walls of this court room all nations, large or small were equal: "Pas d'autre épée ne sera mise dans la balance, que le glaive de la justice." Ironically enough, the one concrete thing that van Karnebeek proudly announced in this context, the intended gift by the Dutch Government of a large allegorical mural panel to be hung in the great court room, for some reason or other never materialized.

The ceremony itself was a succinct one. Count de Nelidow stepped forward and with a silver hammer or hoe tapped the founding stone thrice, in the names of Nicholas, Wilhelmina and the Conference. In the ensuing address, which was as brilliant but no more substantial than was van Karnebeek's speech, he spoke words of thanks to all involved, referred to the Palace as the perfect counterpart of the Temple of Janus in Rome and to its belfry as a pharos guiding the world's nations towards justice. *La Paix par la Justice,* again, was the nucleus of the speaker's message.

Then Mrs. Albert of Paris came up, dressed in the white and blue of the peace movement. On behalf of five million women organized in the ten-year old and very flourishing *Alliance Universelle des Femmes pour la Paix par l'Education* she handed van Karnebeek the commemorative medal that had been struck for the occasion in honour of Carnegie. It featured a female reading the word of Peace from a book to a child on her lap. Choir and orchestra finished it off in style with Wagner's call to the nations. On this same occasion, incidentally, Queen Wilhelmina had conferred upon the Scottish-American benefactor the Grand Cross of the Order of Orange Nassau.

After the ceremony there was champagne for everyone and Krul, the finest confectioners in town, produced *petits fours* to the full. Later that day a "historical pageant of peace" was arranged at the Groenmarkt, it was an exhibition featuring mankind in its development from the cradle of civilization up to modern times, in which, however, critical reporters painfully missed the figure of Carnegie – as for that matter any female figure!

The Invitation to Tender

For five long months after the pavillions of the stone-laying ceremony had been dismantled, the founding stone lay idle in "splendid isolation". So many were the preparatory proceedings which first had to be accomplished before, on 14 December 1907 to be precise, the first tender for the excavation work and enclosure of the site was allotted and entrusted to the contractor J. Knijnenburg of Scheveningen. But once the building activities had started the work was carried out with due swiftness and determination. On 18 April 1908 the construction of the foundation work and basement were allocated to the contractor Nollen & Heymerink of The Hague, some months afterwards the ferro-concrete work for the floors was allotted to the *N.V. Beton-*

On the eve of the ceremony a last minute change in the Latin text on the founding stone was brought about. On the left the original draft by van Karnebeek, on the right the final text.

maatschappij, and in the same period the central-heating works were conferred on Braat in Delft. Mr. Braat accompanied van der Steur and Knuttel on a most satisfying trip to Cologne, Berlin, Copenhagen and Hamburg, where the natural stone and heating installations of major buildings such as the *Dome*, the *Reichstag* building and several town halls were inspected. On their way back they paid a rewarding visit to the Obernkircher quarries. As for the heating, it was notably the large windows, they were given to understand everywhere they went, that posed major problems. Braat, however, felt satisfied that his firm was equal to the job. On 2 January 1911, when the first try-outs of the central-heating system took place, he was proved right.

Inconspicuously, on 1 May a certain J. Scherpenhuyzen entered the service of the Foundation as surveyor and draughtsman. We refer to it because it was this man who, twenty-five years afterwards, would produce an account of the building history of the Palace, from which we draw on here.

On 22 February 1909 the order for the supply of "Obernkirchen" sandstone was given to the *Rotterdamsche Steenhouwerij*. Interestingly enough, the stone was transported by rail straight from the quarry to the site. The building managers had been able to construct a side-track from the steam-tram station down the road, along the Anna Paulownastraat, which rendered excellent services for a couple of years. The 1,900 cubic metres of stone were cut into pieces by a wire-saw on the site and

placed in position by means of a huge crane that had been installed there. These minor data show the resourcefulness applied to the project.

Three months later, on 24 May, the contractors Boersma, of The Hague, were awarded the principal contract concerning the main building. This contract, for which a large number of competitors were on the prowl, gave rise to many conflicts and almost to lawsuits on the part of many dissatisfied contractors. Not bothered in the least about these affairs which the Board had to handle for him, Boersma started energetically building barracks and coffee-stalls for the workmen, carpenters' workshops and scaffolds, and a sixteen-metre platform all around the excavation, on which, afterwards, two electric hoisting cranes were positioned that could work in all directions. Another modern feature installed by this firm during the course of time were two electric elevators in the centre of the frontal and back façade. These hoisted all sorts of building materials up by means of lorries which then could be moved by rail all around the place and on several levels. Furthermore, on top of the elevator shaft at the front, at a height of some twenty metres, a huge water reservoir was placed, which, with the help of an electric pump, drew water from a well beneath to provide the workmen on all floors with water by means of conveniently located taps and tenons.

Projects of this kind tend to run into setbacks one way or another. Something of the sort had already occurred during the first phase, namely in

Summer 1908; the work on the foundation well on the way.

the preparation of the substructure. Experimental borings had revealed a stratum of sand all over the place, which seemed sufficiently firm to carry the building. Just in time and thanks to van der Steur's *Tüchtichkeit* it was noticed that underneath lay a bed of loose sand which would have to be removed first. Consequently, the building was sited three metres below the level originally projected. Then the foundations were laid in some 7,000 cubic metres of "stamping concrete", on top of which came some 2.5 million pieces of stone from the River Waal, covered with 300 cubic metres of "Andvik" granite from Norway – one of the first gifts to be sent. The whole of this substructure, which rose to three metres above the ground, was finished on 1 May 1909.

Another problem arose in the autumn of 1909, in the months when the masonry of the upper structure was carried out. The white stone varieties ("Tercé Normandoux" and "Liais de Larrys") that were to be used in the interior of the corridors and had arrived from Bruges in a kind of prefab finished form, soon appeared not to be frost-proof. Consequently, the work had either to be interrupted for five or six months – or what else? Van der Steur managed to have a shanty built all along the corridors and provided it with stoves to heat all around. More than once resourcefulness of this kind proved essential to the progress of the project, for even without setbacks it was no easy task to keep work on schedule and things in line. For instance, the work on the library part was evidently less compli-

cated than at the front of the building and therefore made better progress. On 20 May 1910, to pick a date, the façade at the back had reached the level of the ceilings and the ferro-concrete floors were about to be poured, whereas in the left and right wings only the first floor had been reached. At the front, understandably, the columns in the great hall were only just being placed in position.

The finishing of the roof took eighteen months. In June 1910 the first iron girders in this modern construction had been hoisted up in position in the library part at the rear, six months later the last one had been riveted in the front façade. Then, between September 1910 and December 1911 the Welsh slate was added. On 8 December the building was waterproof and before the year was over capable plumbers' hands had fastened the gutters and the sun was reflected by scores of elegant red brass ornaments. These, incidentally, also were made part of the ingenious lightning rod system: pinnacles, garret-windows, pirons, ornaments and the similar, all had been linked through the brass outlet pipes to the conduct pipes of galvanized iron which lay three feet deep all around the Palace.

From 1911 onwards, accordingly, it was the furnishing and decoration of the inside that drew the main attention. Brazil, the United States and the Dutch Indies had sent all sorts of precious wood, which was shipped in at Rotterdam and then transported to the saw-mills at Leidschendam, where the tree-trunks were cut into boards. In the rear premises of the Palace, the library part, a joinery workshop was built, where some thirty master carpenters, cabinet-makers and sculptors were kept busy over two years modelling, carving and chiselling the one hundred and seventy cubic metres of teak from the Indies, a similar quantity of cedar, palisander and ebony from Brazil, mahogany from Tahiti and fine timber from San Salvador, all to be applied on ceilings, boarding and panelling. Only the panelling of the two court rooms was, in 1912, given to other firms, among whom were the well-known H. Pander & Sons of The Hague.

Artistry and Craftsmanship

Apart from resourcefulness, other qualities were also needed. The building history, as for that matter the Palace itself, testifies in many ways to the craftsmanship of the workmen. One may speculate on the artistic value of the work done, one may question the style of the building, but one can only admire the care and dedication applied to the work by so many. A first example of this is found in the sculpture by W. Retera of the Amsterdam Academy of Arts. His early works were the models for the marble bases and capitals of the columns in the great hall. For over two years he laboured undauntedly in his workshop at Buitenrust and in close touch with van der Steur. Helped by Eikenhout and his team of twenty-five sculptors he produced marble, sand-

Right: 1910; one of the electric hoisting cranes at work.

Autumn 1911; the last Welsh slates being fixed on the roof. A view from the inner courtyard.

stone and white-stone works, then proceeded with the wood panelling and the furniture. Inspiration and endurance went hand in hand here. The same holds true in a way for the terracotta decorations along the windows of the inner-courtyard that were produced by Brouwers Aardewerkfabriek at Leiderdorp. These, too, required two years of incessant labour, from 1909 to 1911.

Halfway through 1911, inconspicuous and shy, another fine craftsman came in. He was a mere youngster at the time, yet bound to leave a noticeable mark on the building. His name was Herman A. Rosse, an artist's son and a native of The Hague. It was this Rosse, who in the two years to come, and in consultation with van der Steur, made the designs and supervised the execution of nearly all of the elaborate decoration on the ceilings and vaults. To this accomplished artist indeed we owe some of the most elegant and charming features of the building such as, to name one, the fine reliefs in gold leaf along the posts of the Japanese Room. He was indeed a versatile craftsman: from his hands came most of the stained glass windows, murals and painted ceilings and, for that matter, the superb tile-panels along the walls of the corridors in the rear of the premises. In fact, it is on the grounds of his work in the Peace Palace that young Herman Rosse entered upon his most distinguished career. And yet, it is on another event mainly that he himself drew tender memories from the place – for here it was where he met his beloved Sophia ...

Herman Rosse and Sophia Luyt

He was only twenty-five at the time, but a promising apprentice. He had already gained degrees at the Hague Academy of Arts, the Delft Polytechnic, the South Kensington School of Art

A detail from one of the rich ornamental ceilings in the drawing-rooms of the Palace, designed by Herman Rosse.

Opposite left: The huge jasper vase presented by Czar Nicholas and bearing his initials and emblem, the double eagles of the Romanovs. The vase weighs about 3,200 kilograms.

The commemorative medal presented by sir Cuthbert Grandy of Blackpool to all collaborators on the opening of the Palace in August 1913.

vase was to be shipped to The Hague. On its arrival in July the gold-handled jasper vase, with a height of about five metres, proved to weigh 3,200 kilogrammes. Therefore a site had to be chosen and the concrete floor reinforced. The spot selected was the entrance chamber to the small court room, right beneath the belfry and visible from the main entrance hall.

Two months later the Swiss gift arrived, a most impressive clock, both in precision and size, and to be hung in the belfry. The face alone was about eleven feet across (3.75 metres) and the length of its hour hand some seven feet (2.25 metres). It struck twice an hour and ran for eight days at a stretch. In later years its works were replaced by a modern mechanism.

The year 1913 opened with the arrangement of the so-called Ferdinand Bol Room, a representative hall on the second floor named after the artist who had produced the exquisite paintings on biblical themes that were hung in the room. They were on loan from the Dutch Government.

More works of art were put on the ceiling of this room: notably some paintings by another Dutch master, Gérard de Lairesse, which the Carnegie Foundation had purchased, and representing the *Triumph of Peace*, as it was thought at the time. The room was completed with the fixing of the oak panelling, another product of van der Steur's workshop, and of the sculptured leaves in the ceiling, cut in lime-wood that came from linden trees in the grounds which were felled in the building process of the Palace.

Another gift of the Dutch Government was seven stained glass windows which in February 1913 were installed in the apse of the main hall.

For ceremonial reasons the official date of the opening had to be announced well in advance. As is only natural with such large projects, in the final months a large number of minor things had still to be

settled, causing stress, tension and, at times, panic. Having initially been arranged for June and later on postponed until August, already there was a rumour that the opening was again likely to be postponed. This was considered generally most unfortunate, as the summer of 1913 marked the first centenary of Dutch independence. What better occasion possible for having all peace-loving nations summoned to a Hague pilgrimage!

Unperturbed by this or any other rumours van der Steur laboured on – frenetically. *De Porceleyne Fles* of Delft had only just started the most delicate work of placing the precious tile tableaux in the rear corridors and the *grès* panelling near the Russian vase, as engineers from the telephone company rushed in, swarming all over the place and pulling cables. Next day it was the *Panzer Aktiengesellschaft* of Berlin hastily arranging the archives and stacks for the Court and Library. In the midst of all this the national gift of Belgium arrived: wrought-iron, bronze-framed entrance doors along with bronze inner-hall doors. These were positioned in the very weeks the removal contractors brought in the household effects of the Permanent Court of Arbitration from their former lodgings on the Prinsegracht. Minor presents like busts and statues were brought in by the dozen along with the national gift of Argentina, a large statue of Christ copied from the one high up in the Andes mountains. A last minute arrival, too, was the Japanese gift, the superb silk panels especially designed for the room of the *Conseil Administratif* of the Court which was hence called the Japanese Room.

Indeed, van der Steur and his staff had to divide their attention between inside and outside for, to be sure, the gardens, too, needed intense supervision. Loads of plants: bulbs and bushes, annuals and perennials, seedlings and cuttings were brought in pell-mell. In spring 1913 the rose society *Nos Jungunt Rosae* of The Hague had offered 4,500 rose bushes which were subsequently planted in the two rosariums which ran parallel to the "ornamental lake". As for the latter, the base of this pond was made of strengthened concrete and the refreshing and drainage of the water was arranged by leading the Beek in an annular sewer underneath. Gates at both ends of the pond see to the water level and water replenishment. These matters, too, were arranged during the last months.

Finally, around mid-August it became evident that but for the finishing touches, the work of six years had drawn to its close; the Peace Palace could indeed be duly opened within a fortnight. All in all, a total of thirteen million bricks, 1,850 cubic metres Obernkirchen sandstone, 680 cubic metres granite, 1,400 cubic metres limestone, 8,000 cubic metres concrete for foundations, 6,500 square metres slates for roofing and 150,000 kilograms of lead for gutters, roofing and the kind had found their way into the construction. Upon the completion a commemoration medal, a gift of Sir Cuthbert Grandy of Blackpool, was presented to all who had contributed thereto.

1913: The Opening Ceremony

The inauguration of the Peace Palace in August 1913 played a major part in the ceremonies and festivities to commemorate the hundredth anniversary of Dutch independence that summer. On the poster on the opposite page, Dutch prosperity is represented by the horn of plenty and the mercantile fleet in the background. On the poster below attention is drawn to Holland's many connections over land and sea with the world abroad.

The summer months of 1913 were heydays of social life in Holland. The opening of the Peace Palace coincided with the first centenary of Dutch liberation from French rule in Napoleonic times. The year 1813 had marked the retrieval of independence, the return of the House of Orange and the drawing up of the constitution. Accordingly, in August-September 1913, The Hague was literally inundated with ceremonies. Historical pageants crowded the squares, sparkling fire works were let off every night, and people feasted their eyes upon dignitaries in ceremonial dress being driven in coaches and pairs to splendid balls and receptions. The opening of the palace was to take place on 28 August, the new cabinet was to be installed on 29 August, and 31 August was the Queen's birthday – that year being the fifteenth of her reign. Together these events gave rise to perfectly justified exultancy.

The impression of a mondain capital was heightened too by the presence of hundreds of celebrities attending one of the many conferences that were held at The Hague during those very weeks, precisely because of the imminent opening on 28 August. Thus, from 18 to 23 August some 500 pacifists from all over the world, headed by de Louter and Lafontaine, attended the XXe *Congrès Universel de La Paix* held in the Ridderzaal by the Dutch society *Vrede door Recht* and the Roman Catholic peace movement, while on 5 September the Interparliamentary Union planned to convene here for its eighteenth conference.

These conferences, in their turn, had evoked other events. Thus, for one, Dutch suffragettes had arranged exhibits on the status of women through the ages. All in all, it looked very much as if the whole universe of pacifism had gravitated to The Hague – indeed, the atmosphere around the Binnenhof and the Hofvijver was that of a joyful world reunion. The very presence of Bertha von Suttner, Alfred Fried, Bourgeois, Constant d'Estournelles, Renault, and so many veterans of the Second Hague Conference recalled the summer of 1907. This idea was also strengthened by the programme of the current peace congress, which featured high on its agenda the drawing up of issues for the Third Hague Peace Conference. This conference was projected here for somewhere in 1915 ... Little did one know at the time that history was to play tricks on man once more.

But even so, amid all the cheers there was cause for sadness too: if only in the personal sphere. The reunion could not hide the absence of the many combatants for peace that had died in the past years. De Martens, Asser, the other day only (on 29 July to be precise), den Beer Poortugael, that placid military man – and then William Stead, one of the many who (one and a half years ago already, how time did fly!) had expectantly stepped aboard the *Titanic*. "Expectantly" was the word indeed, for had not this medium himself prophesied his drowning?

Yet in the public sphere there was much to deplore as well. Once again the clouds of war had blown over – only for how long this time? In a competent analysis of the past year's events Gobat of Bern had lectured the congress on topical controversies. He expanded on the Turkish situation; the Treaty of London which had finally put an end to the First Balkan War had promptly been trodden on first by Austria, and now again by Italy – ironically enough on the strength of the Austrian precedent. Thus, with Western diplomacy standing aloof, another piece of the world cake had once again been snatched away and the urchins gone unpunished. The present state of the Balkans was explosive if anything, Serbia for good reasons felt betrayed by the allied powers; Libya and Morocco obviously no longer took the rule of their colonial masters for granted; the Finns had much to complain about and Mexico, having enjoyed a quarter-century of peaceful prosperity under Porfirio Diaz, seemed once again set on a succession of revolutions, forty of which had already devastated the country in its single century of independence.

Probably even more alarming though were the severe cracks in the varnish of the European Concert: tension between France and Germany was rapidly building up, the armaments race gained pace anew, and Britain and the United States were on most unfriendly terms over the Panama Canal. It seemed that, after all, the Americans did not back the idea of arbitration as wholeheartedly and unconditionally as they had given the other nations to understand in the past years. Actually, with the Hague Court as a beacon at sea, one wondered indeed at the number of ill-guided helmsmen.

Still, all was not yet lost. The Permanent Court had proved itself in several instances, and the peace plan recently developed by Bryan, the American Secretary of State, to have international commissions of inquiry installed, plus the circumstance that even *der Kaiser* seemed favourably disposed towards the idea, were stimulating facts indeed. Most heartening of all perhaps was that, seemingly unwavering despite all the setbacks, man's innate idealism came up with ever new ideas. Thus it appeared that the idea of the late Professor Asser to launch an Academy of International Law, to which end he had actually voted half of his Nobel Prize fee, was to materialize after all, albeit too late to have the Academy inaugurated on the opening day of the palace, as its initiator's dream had been. The opening of the International Bureau of Statistics in Holland the same year was another promising sign. It was mixed feelings therefore that occupied the minds of the dignitaries at The Hague those weeks.

Still, the presence of so many eminent men and women quite naturally prompted all sorts of joyful events in the days preceding and following the opening ceremony. Actually, the latter event was virtually embedded in commemorations and similar events. Several of these took place on the premises of the palace. Thus, on 21 August, the members of the World Congress for Peace paid a visit to the palace and through their president, de Pinto, presented a bust of Hugo Grotius, sculptured after the Mierevelt portrait. On this occasion La Fontaine made a brilliant speech. Surrounded by his deeply moved audience, he congratulated the Board on the work that had been done and reminded it of the course that lay open to realize its ideas. Boldly, though not quite unjustified, he declared the attendance of this gathering of pacifists as the unofficial inauguration of the palace. The next day they were off to Delft to lay another wreath at Grotius' statue ...

On 27 August, Dutch science paid homage to three men who, by their work for international organization, had made the world their debtor: Fried, Renault and Elihu Root were granted the honorary doctor's degree by Leiden University through Professor van Eysinga. The following day then, finally, the world of politics, learning and pacifism crowded together within the Palace walls.

The Opening Ceremony

Apprehensively peeping through their hotel windows that morning of 28 August, those who had attended the 1907 Conference breathed sighs of relief. They had learned to appreciate the whims of the Dutch climate, but for once nature was willing to favour the opening ceremony: the day appeared to be glorious. Actually, despite evil forecasts of thunder and storm, 28 August turned out to be one of the fairest days of the year. From one o'clock on, a seemingly endless cortege of guests passed the entrance gates and the Hague police officers who kept cheering crowds from overrunning the terraces. The old and the new world met on this sunny day in August as dozens of shining coaches along with puffing automobiles drove up in an endless parade and the Scottish-American benefactor bowed the knee to the Dutch Queen. One man arrived in a most singular way. This was a certain van Steyn who flew in from Paris in his aeroplane, circled over the Palace, landed nearby and attended the meeting.

But no doubt about it: to the Dutch population it was Carnegie who was the key figure that day. He and his wife had lodgings at the American Legation on the Voorhout and their ten minutes' drive to the palace must have been like a Fifth Avenue ticker-tape parade to them. Rarely have foreigners met with such spontaneous applause in Holland – and not one of the dozens of political cartoons and venomous articles that had appeared in the leading European papers those months could detract from that fact. It must have been a comforting experience to the Scotsman, for, to be sure, few international events had evoked so much satire. As pacifists did not get weary from pointing out, with Carnegie's philanthropy it was as with Galileo, or for that matter any man who first introduced anything out of the ordinary, be this an aeroplane or umbrella: they all were likely to be ridiculed by the masses.

Whatever others may have thought of it, there is little doubt that Carnegie himself was sincerely impressed by the thrill of the moment. The entry in his diary that day reads: "Looking back a hundred years, or less perchance, from today, the future historian is to pronounce the opening of a World Court for the Settlement of International Disputes by Arbitration the greatest one step forward ever taken by man, in his long and checkered march upward from barbarism. Nothing he has yet accomplished equals the substitution for war, of judicial decisions founded upon International Law, which is slowly, yet surely, to become the corner stone, so long rejected by the builders, of the grand edifice of Civilization."

The two-minute 70 mm. movie that recorded the opening, shows Carnegie and his wife upon entering the palace: a grey, small figure, but cheerful and resolute, and proudly wearing the decoration of the Grand Cross of Orange-Nassau. Inside, the couple was heartily welcomed by cheers from the four hundred guests, who from half past one had

Queen-Mother Emma (1858–1934) on entering the Palace to attend the opening ceremony. A scene from a contemporary movie.

Just another tribute to the greatest of Dutch international lawyers. On 22 August a bust of Grotius was unveiled in the Palace.

On entering the Palace Carnegie seemed somewhat disconcerted by all the stir and bustle. As the movie camera was pointed out to him a broad smile appeared. Two scenes from the documentary movie of the ceremony.

The ornamental key to the entrance gates of the Palace that was presented by van Karnebeek to the Administrative Board of the Permanent Court of Arbitration.

rapidly filled the Great Court Room, which that day seemed great in name only. It was a splendid sight! The silk, satin and lace, and the ostrich feathers, towering coiffures and jewelry of the ladies *en grande toilette* rivalled the sparkling uniforms of military men and the colourful dress of foreign diplomats. Scholars and politicians, among whom were the members of two cabinets in cheerful conversation, looked definitely sober in their ceremonial dress. The sun beamed through the four stained glass windows, reflecting a myriad of colours on the light oak panelling. Six brass and crystal crowns of light illuminated the polychromic ceilings. Then, at half past two sharp, and announced by the national anthem, in came the royalty.

The ceremony itself was succinct and mainly symbolic. It consisted of van Karnebeek's handing over of the key to the palace gates to the president of the *Conseil Administratif* of the Court, the Dutch Minister for Foreign Affairs van Swinderen. This ceremony was placed in a setting of speeches and musical interlude. The choir, directed by Anton Haverkamp, opened with Palestrina and Valerius; then van Karnebeek rose. In his address, which was as witty and polished as ever, the aged President expanded on the Court of Arbitration, discussed its successes and handicaps, reminded the audience of the call for obligatory measures, an armed coercive force, and permanent and special tribunals. He switched to English in order to address some personal words to Carnegie, which evoked warm applause, paid homage to the architects and proudly listed the many gifts from foreign nations the Foundation had already received. His last words had a ring of prophesy as he said: "This Palace will be a Temple of Peace, in which, even when the waves of war arise on the horizon, better sentiments can find a resort in order to resume their flight after the gale like the doves of Noah's Ark."

Van Swinderen in his response paid compliments to van Karnebeek and likewise had some words for the grey Scot: "By the co-operation of the world powers, your initiative has got the sanction which you deemed necessary ... That is the check, Mr. Carnegie, which I beg you to accept from my hands, that means through my words, from the entire complex of Europe, Asia and America here represented at Her Majesty's Court. It's a draft on the future, but I trust you will consider the drawer good for it." In his autobiography Carnegie would call his "Temple of Peace ... the most holy building in the world ... because it has the holiest end in view. I do not even except St. Peter's, or any building erected to the glory of God, whom, as Luther says, 'we cannot serve or aid; He needs no help from us ...'. The highest worship of God is service to man. At least I feel so with Luther and Franklin."

After the ceremony the Board's secretary, R. J. H. Patijn, led the audience on a guided tour of the premises. Royalty and diplomats in a cavalcade visited the Japanese and Bol rooms, the gardens and rosarium. In the evening, the special guests and the *corps diplomatique* were entertained by the Dutch Government at a gala dinner in the Ridderzaal and were received by the Queen at the Royal Palace.

On the following day Andrew Carnegie came over to the Palace once more to unveil a bust of William Randal Cremer, presented to the Carnegie Board by the International Arbitration League, of which Cremer had been the founding father as far back as 1870. On that occasion Carnegie and Lord Weardale, Chairman of the Interparliamentary Union digressed on the merits of the British pacifist who, in 1888 and along with Frédéric Passy, also had taken the initiative towards the establishment of Weardale's Union. Afterwards a garden party was held in honour of the XVIIIth Interparliamentary Conference. The fair weather allowed the guests, among whom was Mawson in person, to have a closer look at the gardens. These were, of course, still *in statu nascendi*, but the box-wood hedges made the groundplan plain to the eye. With its pond down in the centre and its rosariums near the terrace the garden layout was in the natural English style. If anything, the overall impression was one of quiet stateliness. Whatever the years might add to its splendour, it was thought that the time-honoured oaks and beeches on the slopes in the background made a perfect setting for the Palace.

Still other ceremonies followed in the subsequent days – and not all of these necessarily of an international or even public nature. Thus, on 30 August the population of the Zorgvliet quarter paid tribute to the Board in the person of its grey chairman by the erection of the "van Karnebeek Fountain" along the public road adjoining the palace grounds. During the speeches the fountain, designed by Brouwer and featuring the names of the Board-members, was presented to the Hague municipality. From 4 September onwards the palace was opened to the public upon presentation of a card of admittance. Millions have passed the gates ever since.

The Carnegie Foundation, 1913–1988

The early years of the Peace Palace are full of memorable incidents and interesting anecdotes. As early as 1913, both as regards to staff and court, with respect to garden and library, and even in matters of gifts, all sorts of setbacks and minor quarrels arose. The man who managed to untangle all those problems, be they tiny or formidable, with firm resolution and distinct competence, if perhaps not always without some rigidity, was Jhr. Mr. A. P. C. van Karnebeek, who served the Foundation for a full twenty years as its inspiring president (1904–1923). Without in the least detracting from the merits of his colleagues, van Karnebeek was in all respects the *primus inter pares*.

The Contacts with the Courts

Of all the issues van Karnebeek had to settle in those early years, perhaps the most delicate and by all means the most relevant ones concerned relations with, first, the Permanent Court of Arbitration and, then, the Permanent Court of International Justice. The regulations he pushed through have remained in force to the present day.

The first formal contacts between Court officials and the Carnegie Foundation had been made as early as the summer of 1904. In the notarial act of the Foundation's regulations, dated 4 June of that year, the *Conseil Administratif* of the Court was empowered to nominate one of the five members of the Board of the Foundation. On 20 June following, Mr. W. H. de Beaufort was elected to this post. The Conference veteran and former Foreign Minister of the Netherlands was to serve the Board for fifteen years. Among the first things to be done in view of future close relations was the setting out of the mutual rights and obligations of Court and Foundation. Strictly speaking, that is according to the Skibo Castle Deed, the Foundation's purpose was none other than that of "building, establishing and maintaining in perpetuity at The Hague a Court House and Library (Temple of Peace) for the Permanent Court of Arbitration". However, if only for practical reasons, the Board was disposed to extend its province to such matters as the layout of the grounds, the upkeep of the Court's lodgings and furniture, the regular supplementing of the library, in short all those services which strictly speaking exceeded the Foundation Deed – and which accordingly, could not be borne by the Foundation – but

for the execution of which, the staff of the Court of Arbitration was certainly not equipped. In order to bear the expenses involved with its services, the Board requested an annual grant of Dfl. 49,504 to be shared between the Contracting States according to their quota. A regulation to this end was proposed in June 1912. In December, and only after lengthy negotiations, this financial issue was settled, and not without the Board having pledged to submit its accounts and balance sheets to the Court's Administrative Council for its information.

A second controversy emerged soon after the ceremonial transfer of the keys by van Karnebeek to the Court's Secretary-General Michiels van Verduynen on the occasion of the opening of the Palace on 28 August 1913. In the autumn it appeared that the Council (read: some Contracting Nations, *in casu* England and France) made objections to the Board's policy in matters of administration and in not consulting the Council in advance on such varying matters as the unveiling of a bust of Stead or the appointment of the Director-General of the library. The incident assumed painful proportions and led to sharp memoranda, such as the one by the Board dated 7 May 1914: "… if the Administrative Council might not consider itself any longer bound by the 1912 agreement, the Board would consider itself free, on its part, from the obligations of that agreement; consequently it would confine itself to the obligation of the maintenance of what had been built, the sole thing imposed upon it by the Foundation Deed and the Regulations, and leave all the rest to the care of the Administrative Council; it would be led to withdraw from the Palace with its offices, establish itself elsewhere and only occupy itself with the upkeep of the building … It is beyond doubt that in that case the Administrative Council would have to provide for considerably higher expenditure than the contribution fixed by the 1912 agreement."

Stag versus stag indeed! It was these conflicts, incidentally, which first made van Karnebeek appreciate the risks of having his Foundation financially dependent upon the benevolence of (at the time) forty-two nations. This led him to approach Carnegie, for a second time within a few years, for a supplementary donation. As with his first endeavour, however, the request proved fruitless.

As a matter of fact, this is not to say that misunderstandings and unworthy quarrels ruled the mutual relations over the years – far from it. Harmonious co-operation has marked the relation-

Jhr. A. P. C. van Karnebeek (1836–1925), the first President of the Carnegie Foundation (1903–1923), portrayed in the year of his resignation.

Opposite left: The inner courtyard of the Peace Palace with the fountain that was presented by Denmark in 1922. Also note the red tile wall ornaments by Brouwer and the decorative brass border on top of the front roof.

ship of Board and Courts throughout. Understandably though, a proper *modus vivendi* had to be found at first. Almost predictably therefore, a similar incident occurred in 1921 on the arrival of the Court of Justice of the League of Nations; this Court in a way impaired the privileged position which the Court of Arbitration had enjoyed over the years, something that certainly had not been foreseen in the 1903 Foundation Deed. The arrangements suggested to the newcomer by the Board included the transfer of rooms which, though left unoccupied up to then, had formally been put at the disposal of the Permanent Court. The Administrative Council was disposed to give up these rooms on the assumption that the newcomer would enjoy the Court's hospitality – rather than that of the Foundation. Now the staff of the Court of Justice would hardly have noticed the difference, far less appreciated the controversy, if it were not for the financial dispute which lay at the base of it all. The result of it, agreed upon somewhere in the summer of 1923, was that the Foundation virtually took over full responsibility for the upkeep of the Palace, including all the costs of heating, lighting and maintenance. To this end it also took over the staff-members of the Court involved with these matters. These regulations have remained unaltered to the present day.

The Upkeep of the Gardens

In the early months of 1915 the last bills submitted by Mawson & Son were dealt with by the Board (not without some controversy, incidentally!). Van Karnebeek and his colleagues leaned back at ease. They felt justly satisfied with the result of the layout of the park, which for once had also been favourably reviewed by the many critics who had attended the garden party on 29 August 1913. Though still fervently debating as to whether the overall appearance of the park was more in line with French or English landscape traditions, the critics were in accord that the lawns were a feast to the eye. The wealth of colours in the rosarium twin beds, crowned by the two precious marble vases that called back to memory the proud 17th-century owners of the stately Zorgvliet and Rustenburg

villas, stood out magnificently against the fine red brick of the terraces on which, again, eight elegant vases of fine *grès* caught the eye. Further down, the lake – bordered by romantic, ivied pergolas – its stately calm only rippled by occasional bubbles and splashes of tail-whisking fish. Varieties of flowers, both indigenous and exotic, spread their perfumes all around. Selected shrubbery and bushes covered the decorative slopes. And in the background one saw the massive and imposing outlines of the four hundred and thirty-five time-honoured oaks, beeches and elm trees that had been planted by the first lord of Zorgvliet, the poet Jacob Cats, which had since calmly looked upon three centuries of human turmoil. Those who knew could still discern the two beeches in the western part, near the lake, in which were carved the now partly overgrown signatures and mottoes of the two "Guillaumes", King William I and his son William II, dating back to 1837 and the days of Anna Paulovna. Speaking of hidden treasures: only a few people knew the secret of the tiny *hedera* that bravely clung to the terrace wall of the rosarium, a cutting from the ivy that was planted by George Washington on Mount Vernon, and had been given in 1914 by "The Daughters of the American Revolution" and been planted with infinite care by Mawson's assistant, the young landscape designer Sophia Luyt, now Rosse. The restful atmosphere of the park seemed an abode of eternal peace. It was not to be, though: soon the Board's dream would turn into a veritable nightmare.

The Calvary started in the spring of 1915, when the Board was confronted with an official protest by the Chilean Minister over the position, back in the central axis of the rear garden, of his

Left: The rose gardens in the early years.

Part of the commemoration of the 75th birthday of the Palace is the introduction of a rose named after Andrew Carnegie which was sponsored by the Carnegie Foundation.

A view of the ornamental lake through a vine-clad pergola.

Palace and gardens on a fair summer day.

nation's contribution. This impressive bronze monument, created by the sculptress Rebecca Matte de Iniguez, echoed in extremely vivid and realistic tones the horrors of war as experienced by the mothers and wives of butchered soldiers. Soon afterwards, in the summer of 1915, new setbacks presented themselves, as it proved that the rosarium had suffered dramatically from the poor soil and the sterile dune water with which it had been watered, and had for the greater part to be replaced. The same held good for other plants. The estimated costs of restoration amounted to some Dfl. 10,000. (The instant remedy, incidentally, proved to be to water the gardens from the lake).

On top of this, trouble arose with the head gardener when the supplier of free begonias stopped furnishing the tubers when he noticed that they were consistently put in the wrong spots. As it turned out, the head gardener was a notorious drunk who had borrowed money from suppliers, fiddled with the cash-book and regularly sold plants for his own profit. As a means of revenge, in the days before his dismissal, the man managed to order enormous

quantities of plants costing some Dfl. 6,000, for which the Board was compelled to pay. This having been taken care of, the next year tens of oaks and majestic beeches in the park proved to be sick and had to be felled.

At this point, the Board was wise enough to call in the help of the municipal parks superintendent, the well-known Westbroek. He, and later his successor, Doorenbos, would serve the Foundation with their invaluable advice for many years to come. Accordingly, setting apart the cumulation of disasters in the first decade, the pleasure and splendour of the gardens have always by far outweighed its financial burden. The rosarium was to be replaced several times, most recently in 1987, as the soil proved once more infected throughout with the ill-reputed little eels. All other setbacks, however, were minor incidents and no one's fault. In 1968, unfortunately, again two score of old trees had to be felled, which left the number of 17th-century giants at three hundred and seventy-five. Another dozen succumbed to the fierce storm of 2 April 1973, breaking down walls and demolishing buildings. Again, five

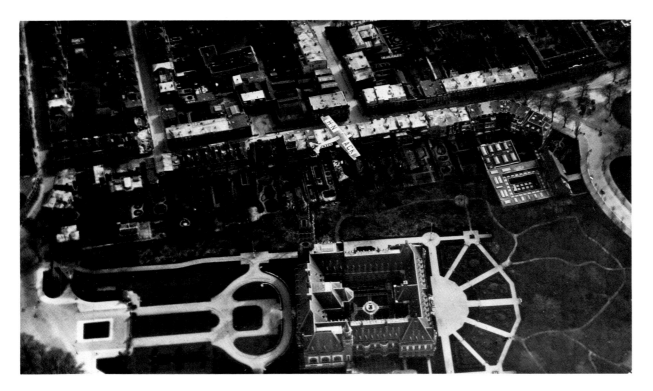

Air photograph from the days before the construction of the new bookstores and Academy building in the late twenties, showing the original groundplan of the rear gardens. The photo was taken from a Zeppelin in 1927.

Below: P. W. A. Cort van der Linden (1846–1935). He was Minister of Justice, 1897–1901 and Prime Minister, 1913–1918. In his later years van der Linden was Minister of State. He was President of the Carnegie Foundation from 1923 to 1935.

years later, another score came down with loud moans, by man's hands this time, on the erection of the Court's new premises.

All in all, though, these setbacks did little to distract from the charms of the Palace gardens. For seventy-five years now, tens of thousands of visitors have stood staring at its summer splendours. Generations of students of the Hague Academy have strolled along its lawns between their sessions – and many are the judges and scholars who have learned to appreciate its many hidden corners and shady seats, indeed the perfect scenery to weigh nature's endless wonders against man's eternal folly.

Today, blessed with an energetic team of young gardeners and with a novelty in their midst, being the brand new Carnegie rose in the rose-beds the park holds the promise of many more seasons of comfort and splendour.

The Twenties and Thirties

The regulations drawn up for the Courts were the last major feat of President van Karnebeek. Sadly enough, his physical condition no longer allowed him to attend the ceremonial opening session of the Permanent Court of International Justice. In twenty years he had presided over one hundred and twenty-five meetings of the Board. At the first Board meeting after his departure, on 31 May 1923, it was decided to have his portrait hung in the Board's room. The proposal, incidentally, was submitted by the young Mr. J. P. A. François who had only recently succeeded Mr. J. A. N. Patijn as Secretary-Treasurer to the Board. François was bound for a most impressive record: he would serve the Board in that capacity for forty-two years. Meanwhile, van Karnebeek was succeeded by the former Prime Minister Mr. P. W. A. Cort van der Linden (1923–1935).

One major event relating to the new president's term concerned the reconstruction of the Palace in the late twenties and early thirties in order to give more room to the ever-expanding Court of Justice – no minor feat in those years of world crisis. Circumstances also prompted the addition of book-storage areas and the creation of new headquarters for the Academy – these events will be told more suitably in the surveys of these institutions. It was under the presidency of Cort van der Linden too, that, in 1934, the first official history of the Peace Palace, edited by Dr. Lysen, was published. Cort van der Linden's term of office is further noteworthy for the addition of a post office and telephone exchange in the building and the launching of the Wateler Peace Fund.

The Wateler Peace Fund

Though by far the most generous private patron of the Peace Palace, Andrew Carnegie is by no means the only testator to the furtherance of peace

One of the many demonstrations held at the entrance gates over the years. In this case the Women's Society for Peace and Liberty makes an anti-war appeal to the world's governments supported by one hundred thousand signatures.

Among the numerous official guests and VIP's who have visited the Palace over the years, the visit paid in 1930 by the Indian Big Chief White Horse Eagle and his squaw was certainly a colourful one.

at The Hague. Among major and minor legators at home and abroad, there also features a Dutch banker, Mr. J. G. D. Wateler (†1927). In the midst of war, in 1916, this manager of the Oranje-Nassau Hypotheekbank, a mortgage bank at The Hague, made testamentary disposals to have his considerable capital – upon his death – placed at the service of peace. What these disposals were became evident on 22 July 1927, as the Dutch State found itself bequeathed with a substantial sum under the proviso that the annual revenue accruing therefrom would be expended upon the awarding of a yearly prize to private persons or institutions, alternately Dutch and foreign, who had notably furthered the cause of peace by word or deed, in their writings or works of art. Upon acceptance by the State, the selection of prize-winners was to be carried out by the Second Chamber, and in case of non-acceptance, the legacy was to fall to the Carnegie Foundation,

which then would award the prizes, be this with or without previous consultation with the Second Chamber. On non-acceptance by the Carnegie Foundation, the Hague Municipality would become the beneficiary.

On 20 March 1928 the Dutch Government proposed the rejection of the legacy, considering that the awards had not to be imbued with political influence. Of the three nominees mentioned in Mr. Wateler's will, it deemed the Carnegie Foundation the most suitable beneficiary. In August the two Chambers of the States General proved to be in accord in these respects.

Though fully appreciating that the acceptance of the legacy did not strictly conform to the regulations of the Foundation, the trustees thought it certainly in accordance with Carnegie's intentions "to promote anything that must ultimately banish war". Accordingly, in May 1929, authorized by the Supervisory Council, the Board accepted the legacy, and the Foundation took possession on 30 September 1930. In 1931 the prize, amounting to Dfl. 25,000 was awarded to Sir Eric Drummond, Secretary-General of the League of Nations "for his valuable services in the cause of the organization of the community of nations". Sir Eric accepted, but stipulated that the Board would use the money to further the League ideal – international co-operation.

From 1931 until the present day the prize has been awarded yearly, with the exception of the years 1940–1946. The amount has been gradually increased to Dfl. 40,000. In later years, and as a rule, prizes are awarded in the autumn, and handed over in the large court room of the Peace Palace. Since 1981 a Charter has been added to the prize.

H.R.H. Prince Bernhard of the Netherlands handing the Charter of the Wateler Peace Prize to the former Foreign Minister Dr. J. H. van Royen. Attending are Mrs. van Royen, Baron van Lynden (the laureate's successor as president of the Carnegie Foundation), and Mrs. van Lynden.

*Four busts of peacemakers
and internationalists
presented in the course of past
decades. Above right the bust
of Mahatma Gandhi, unveiled
in 1951 with Prime Minister
W. Drees (1886–1988) at-
tending; in the middle the bust
of Albert Schweitzer, unveiled
in 1958, with the aged van
Eysinga attending. Below left,
the bust of Andres Bello,
presented in 1978 by the
Venezuelan Government.
Below right, the bust of Carlos
Calvo, a gift from the Argentinian Government (1987).
Above left: One of the vases
presented to the Board by the
City of Amsterdam.*

GIFTS AND GUESTS

*Three more gifts. Above:
the bust of Henry Dunant,
presented by the Red Cross in
1967. Below left: a detail of
the Danish fountain in the
inner courtyard of the palace.
Below right: the bust of
Edward VII (1841–1910), the
English King (1901–1910)
and peacemaker, positioned in
the vestibule near the Russian
vase. Edward was a natural
diplomat, who travelled
extensively through Europe in
order to promote peace efforts.*

Many are the gifts that have come in over the years. They were literally shipped from all over the world: a desk and gilded ink pot from Australia, elephant tusks from Siam, a duplicate of the Knossos throne from Greece, fine woods from Haiti, vases from Hungary, a marble statue of Justice by Bartlett from the United States, antique Bohemian lamps from Czechoslovakia, silver ink pots from Portugal, a tiny book chest with rare editions of Grotius' works from Nijhoff, the publishers, a charter from the Women's League for Peace.
Not all the gifts arrived in time for the opening and not all of them found their "natural" place in the Palace. The Danish fountain for instance, which was meant for the inner court, arrived too late and could only be installed after all sorts of technical problems. Once it was functioning, the Danish Minister objected to its position. The same happened with the Chilean contribution, as was mentioned before, and the Argentinian gift. The latter incident is noteworthy for reason of the protest being raised by the Dutch Queen Wilhelmina, and that on the very day of the opening. Argentina's gift was a two-metre copy of the eight-metre statue of Christ on top of the Andes. The Board had decided to put the statue at the top of the marble staircase, itself a gift from the Hague municipality, opposite the Japanese Room. Queen Wilhelmina argued that the Christ must be given the place of honour in the entrance hall, to which van Karnebeek riposted that the statue did not represent the Christ as Redemptor but as Pacificator. But Wilhelmina was not the woman to take no for an answer. As late as 1958, in the volume of memoirs *Eenzaam maar niet alleen*, the aged Queen found occasion to repeat her objections which then invited some critical reviews in the papers.
A similar incident was to occur in later years (1938) with the Erasmus statue by Hildo Krop, which was offered by the Dutch Government, and on arrival proved much less impressive in height than was anticipated. Its original place, in the rosarium, invited so many protests that finally the statue was put on a plinth.

Numerous, too, were the busts of internationalists that were offered. The London Peace Society donated a bust of King Edward VII as Peacemaker, Dutch friends of Carnegie presented the Board with a bust of the benefactor, the Interparliamentarian Union offered a bust of its founder, Sir Randal Cremer, and in 1914 a peace committee unveiled the bust of William Stead, two years to the day after the *Titanic* disaster where Stead lost his life. A bust of William Penn was promised from America, Hugo Grotius was honoured, and at the same time the sculptor Odé was working on a statue of Tobias Asser which, some years later, and on the initiative of Mr. Politis, was placed side by side with the statue of Renault. The statues now feature on either side of the double doors of the Japanese Room.
In later years many busts were to follow: Lyon-Caen (1936, another initiative of Politis), Mahatma Gandhi (1951, courtesy of the Indian Government), Albert Schweitzer (1958) and Henry Dunant (1967, courtesy of the Red Cross). In recent years a trio of Latin American internationalists were added to this hall of fame: Ruy Barbosa (1978, courtesy of the Brazilian Government), Andres Bello (1978, courtesy of the Venezuelian Government) and, in the last weeks of 1987, Carlo Calvo (courtesy of the Argentinian Government).
In fact, the offers of gifts have been so numerous over the years that at a fairly early stage it was decided, if only to adopt a criterium, not to accept presents made by individuals. This policy, which otherwise is sound, once

led to the anomaly where three Rozenburg vases which were made on the occasion of the 1899 Peace Conference and were offered by a private person in 1953 were refused, only to be accepted years later when they were again offered, this time by the Amsterdam municipality. The same policy is maintained with respect to conferences. From 1913 onwards innumerable requests have come in for conferences and meetings to be held on the premises. Here again the Board had to adopt a conservative line, restricting admission to organizations operating in the fields of international law and diplomacy. Even so, the number of yearly meetings has been most impresssive. Regular meetings over the years have been the Hague Conference on Private International Law, conferences of the International Academy of Comparative Law and the International Law Association, the Interparliamentary Union, the Red Cross, meetings of committees of the League of Nations and, later, the United Nations, and the Telders and Jessup students' moot courts. The Telders International Moot Court Competition, named after the Leiden Professor B. J. M. Telders (1903–1945) was first organized in the Peace Palace in 1977. In the past years participation has expanded to thirteen teams from universities throughout Europe. Members of the International Court of Justice, of the Board of the Carnegie Foundation and university Professors sit as judges in this Moot Court, which rapidly grows into the Dutch equivalent of the famous Jessup Moot Court in the United States.

WATELER PEACE PRIZE – 16 APRIL 1981

All fervent wishes for happiness + Peace

Danny Kaye

Over the years there has been lively debate among the Board members as to whether institutions or private persons should be chosen as nominees, and among the latter rather people of well-known repute such as politicians, or preferably distinguished scholars and field workers. Looking back, the majority of prizes has been presented to private persons, though they were often nominated in their capacity as representatives of institutions. All in all, their names make interesting reading. Among the foreign private prize winners are: Arthur Henderson, President of the Geneva Disarmament Conference (1933), Lord Baden-Powell, on the occasion of the World Jamboree at Vogelenzang (1937), Monnet, the architect of the European Community (1952), Sir Anthony Eden (1954), the Dag Hammarskjøld Minnefonds (1962), the Communauté de Taizé (1966), the widow of Martin Luther King for her work on behalf of the Southern Christian Leadership Conference (1968), Henry Kissinger (1974), Judge Lachs, President of the International Court of Justice (1976) and Danny Kaye for his work on behalf of Unicef (1978). Dutch prize-winners have been: the Hague Academy (twice, in 1936 and 1949), Mr. Udo Stikker, the Foreign Minister who was instrumental in settling the conflict with Indonesia (1951), W. A. Visser 't Hooft, President of the World Council of Churches (1961), Professor Röling, the polemologist (1971) and Dr. J. H. van Royen, who arranged first the agreement on Indonesian Independence, later the transfer of sovereignty over New Guinea (1981).

The War Years: 1940–1945

On 20 December 1935, after forty meetings to be precise, Cort van der Linden, who was almost a nonagenarian at the time, handed the chairman's gavel to another man of undisputed credentials, Jhr. Mr. Dr. H. A. van Karnebeek, the son of the Foundation's first president. During his brief presidency (he died in the early months of 1942), another Board member was appointed and would earn prestige on the premises in years to come, Mr. S. J. R. de Monchy, the Hague Mayor and future president of the Foundation, who was installed in 1939.

In 1938 the shortage of funds precluded the celebration of the silver jubilee of the Palace. Contacts were made with the Rockefeller Foundation during these years to obtain funds on behalf of the library. Before these came to anything, quite other priorities were to prevail, as on 10 May 1940 the Germans invaded the Netherlands.

Probably the first indication of the Board's awareness of a storm brewing is found in the records of 1938, as van der Steur was ordered to ensure that the new bookstorage areas he was designing would be bombproof and serve as an adequate shelter for man and valuable objects of art in case of air-raids. Again, in the opening weeks of 1939, an urgent call was made by the Board for fire-extinguishers, or the digging of a well, or the laying of conduit pipes to the lake as in wartime the fire brigade was not to be depended upon. Treasures were meanwhile carried into the vast basements, the Grotius collection was microcopied and a first aid team formed. During the summer courses at the Academy, in July and August, a certain uneasiness prevailed among the students of the Academy and most American students hastened their departure. In subsequent months, tension rapidly built up and from the moment the German armies invaded Poland an atmosphere of gloom and loneliness surrounded the place. The judges and Registry were frantically packing their bags whereas the Dutch staff of the Foundation was virtually decimated as more clerks, gardeners and stokers enlisted. In May 1940, a delightful sunny month with parks and lanes in spring foliage, the grim truth finally dawned upon Holland. Within twenty-four hours of the capitulation by General Winkelman on 15 May, a German motor convoy drove up the entrance path brazenly and with the clear intention of occupying the place.

Oddly enough, at this juncture the exact legal standing of the grounds and personnel were not perfectly clear, neither to the aggressor nor to the Board itself. The premises of course were Dutch property, the Courts, however, were international organizations. Now, the staff of the Court of Justice had left the place to some officials headed by the Dutch Judge van Eysinga in his capacity as Vice-President of the Court, but the staff of the Court of Arbitration was for the greater part functioning normally as were for that matter the library officials. At length, being the outcome of informal dealings in which the Board maintained that the international standing of the Courts had never been questioned by the German Government, the occupier preferred to respect the status of the Palace if only for its symbolic stature, and they maintained this pledge throughout the occupation.

Meanwhile, library proceedings continued normally and the German military staff were among the most frequent borrowers. Naturally, all sorts of restrictions were ordered soon enough: thus, "Deutsch-feindliche" books were to be listed and locked away and, predictably, Jewish scholars were to be struck from the users' files. Again, on 2 December 1940, the Carnegie Foundation, being a

Jhr. H. A. van Karnebeek (1874–1942), a statesman as his father was. He was adjunct-delegate to the 1907 Peace Conference, Burgomaster of The Hague since 1911 and Minister for Foreign Affairs in four successive cabinets from 1918 onwards. He became a Minister of State in 1929 and was President of the Carnegie Foundation in the years 1935–1942.

Jhr. A. M. Snouck Hurgronje (1882–1951), Secretary-General at the Dutch Foreign Office (1921–1947) and President of the Carnegie Foundation.

subsidized organization, was ordered to hand in a list of Jewish staff members. To this, the Board objected on formal grounds, arguing that the municipal grants (Dfl. 20,000 yearly at the time) were not essential to the Foundation's functioning. In the end, it never submitted the names of the two staff members under consideration.

Meanwhile, all the time, German officials showed a keen interest in the place, be this only from a suspicion of irregularities. Similarly, German authorities paid regular visits to the Palace. Thus, on 17 November 1941, *Reichskommissar* Seyss-Inquart inspected the grounds along with *General-Kommissar* Wimmer and Dr. Plutzar. On 25 June 1942 *Oberst Freiherr* Rüdt von Collenberg, head of the *Heeresbüchereien,* visited the Library along with his deputy von Rundstedt, while on 17 October of that year the wife of *Reichskommissar* Seyss-Inquart made a tour, followed by some fifty admirals and naval officers ten days afterwards. The last visit by a prominent Nazi was made on 24 May 1944, as Minister Alfred Rosenberg drove up the entrance driveway to have cinecameras record this "historic" moment; actually he never entered the Palace.

Generally speaking though, the Germans never interfered with the daily proceedings at the Palace. As a matter of fact, to the library officials, the

Formal declaration prohibiting the military forces of war-waging powers from entering the grounds of the Peace Palace. Signed by van Eysinga, the Vice-President of the Permanent Court of International Justice in the war years.

Friedenspalast.

Ständiger Internationaler Gerichtshof.

(Deutsches Reichsgesetzblatt, 1927, II, S. 227).

Das Betreten des Friedenspalastes, seiner Nebengebäude und des Gartens, Sitz des Ständigen Internationalen Gerichtshofes, ist, auf Grund der diesem Sitz zustehenden Unverletzlichkeit, jedem Truppenteil der Kriegführenden untersagt.

Der stellvertretende Vorsitzende des Ständigen Internationalen Gerichtshofes:

Vredespaleis.

Permanent Hof van Internationale Justitie.

(Staatsblad van het Koninkrijk der Nederlanden, 1921, No. 1049).

Het betreden van het Vredespaleis, van zijne bijgebouwen en van den tuin, Zetel van het Permanente Hof van Internationale Justitie, is, op grond van de onschendbaarheid van dien Zetel, aan alle troependeelen der oorlogvoerenden verboden.

De waarnemend President van het Permanente Hof van Internationale Justitie:

V. Eysinga

early war years in a way must have had a distinct charm of their own. As the "Nationale Bibliotheek" (as the Royal Library was renamed) and the *Rijksarchief* were closed down with increasing frequency, prominent scholars from far and near, among them the *Rijksarchivaris* himself, frequented the cosy and centrally-heated reading room at the Peace Palace. From 1944 onwards, and notably during the "hongerwinter", there were many who found refuge in the warmth of the Palace, also for less honourable reasons, as Board member de Monchy was to find out when once on leaving the library he found his galoshes gone.

Communications with publishers abroad were for the greater part disconnected and library officials spent much of their spare time in rearranging the collection. It was in these years also that ter Meulen and Diermanse launched their extensive Grotian studies. The Palace's cellars, for safety reasons, welcomed extensive collections from the Ministries of Foreign Affairs, Colonies, Justice, and Education, as well as private collections from refugees. Meanwhile, ter Meulen, resourceful as ever, made arrangements for collecting duplicates of rare books, which he thought would serve usefully in the years after the war. By a twist of fortune, in 1951 these books were gratefully accepted by the German librarians whose collections had been destroyed by bombing.

In 1944 things changed for the worse. In fact, the last year of the war was absolute hell to all concerned. The launching-pads of the experimental V-weapons nearby in the dunes represented a dangerous risk indeed. The frequent failures in launching operations held the population in constant fear as every now and then projectiles flew over with high-pitched, whistling screams. Twice, in the dead of night of 2 November 1944 and 5 January 1945, the Foundation officials on nightwatch panicked as hundreds of windows were shattered and, all over the place, wooden panels came tumbling down with the shock of untimely exploding projectiles. Hastily, all valuable objects were assembled in the sousterrains and the gaping windows were boarded. On 25 January 1945, another V-weapon exploded and hit the house of librarian ter Meulen in the nearby Archipelbuurt.

However, ironically, in the end more damage was done by the Allied Forces who constantly bombed the close surrounding areas of the Palace in order to eliminate the German launching installations. As is well known, these desperate attempts to save Britain from the devilish products of the *totaler Krieg* were not always successful and often lacked precision. On 3 March 1945 the Bezuidenhout area was bombed with enormous casualties without damaging the launching installations in the least. The Palace was spared such a fate. All in all, the V-weapons and allied raids from 2 November 1944 to 30 April 1945 destroyed some 210 square metres of windows, breaking 320 stained glass pieces. Fortunately, these could all be replaced and no serious damage was done to the building, not even by a most welcome raid on 11 April 1944, which was indeed planned and executed with the utmost precision and diligence. On that day the Gebouw Kleykamp opposite the Palace, being the headquarters of the hated registers office which endangered the lives of so many patriots, was effectively bombed. For months this raid had been minutely prepared by the RAF which, in a field near London, had carefully simulated the geographical position – with excellent results.

Like the whole of the Hague population, in the last year of the war, the Palace officials suffered much from the shortage of food and fuel, and the Board did its utmost to help its staff. In the grounds some 2,000 kilogrammes of timber were felled and distributed, along with potatoes, beets, onions and wheat. The administrator Intres, who had already served the Foundation for forty years, proved worth his weight in gold when shopping on the black market. Among the staff many showed distinct bravery in those years. Several of them, such as Schippers and Westgeest, were deported to Germany, but were lucky enough to return in the summer of 1945. Conservator Chotzen, however, who had distinguished himself at the Grebbeberg, the Dutch line of defence in May 1940, was arrested in January 1945 and never came back. Only years later was it established that he had perished in the "Oranje-Hotel", as the Scheveningen convict prison was ironically called in those days. Van der Steur, the Palace's architect, was killed during skirmishes in Steenwijk in February 1945. Again, Mazel, the initiator of the Hague Academy, came to a tragic end under similar circumstances. Inevitably, the staff also had its collaborator. The man slipped out on 5 September 1944, "Dolle Dinsdag" ("Mad Tuesday"), as the withdrawal of the Germans appeared imminent, to brazenfacedly reapply for his previous position in 1948 …

Puzzling to many had been the fate of Miss Ada Belinfante, who had disappeared in the May days of 1940 only to re-emerge in the summer of 1945. As is told elsewhere in greater detail, she had been based in London, collecting vast piles of books on the Library's behalf for after the war purposes.

The Second Phase: 1946–1988

At the 182nd meeting of the Board, on 27 April 1942, Jhr. Mr. A. M. Snouck Hurgronje, Secretary-General at the Foreign Office, was elected President, initally *ad interim* (1942–1951). During the war years no memorable activities were undertaken other than to preserve the building and its treasures. When, on 28 November 1945, the first meeting after the German withdrawal took place, the balance was established and the losses in personnel and finance proved by far to outweigh the material damage. New Board members had to be elected (van Wyckerheld Bisdom, van Hardenbroek, both 1946), a new architect had to be appointed (Luthman, 1946), a new library staff recruited, and both Courts were urgently requested to meet the outstanding debts. Altogether these debts amounted to more than Dfl.

The bombardement of the Kleykamp, the despited German registers office opposite the Palace, by the RAF on 11 April 1944.

500,000. Since the United Nations had declared themselves unwilling to take over any debts of the League of Nations, there was ample room for pessimism as to the Foundation's future. In the end, though, nearly all the arrears were paid. Only China, Japan and Germany refused to fulfil their debts to the Court of Arbitration. In 1949, after major restoration and renovation, some Dfl. 250,000 were left for investment. But then a sharp inflation set in and prices and salaries went up tremendously, which again made economies imperative. At this juncture ter Meulen requested the expansion of the library in the scholarly sphere. This invited the evaluation of his institution by a committee that ironically pleaded for modernization and the prevalence of administrative aspects over academic ones. So much for Diermanse and his Grotian studies! Within a year ter Meulen resigned.

In the same year, 1951, Snouck Hurgronje died and was succeeded by de Monchy (1952–1958). His term of office is memorable mainly for the attempt to get the Schuman Court of the European Community of Coal and Steel installed on the grounds, and for a large scale restoration of the Peace Palace.

The first discussion of the Schuman Court is recorded in a special meeting of the Board in July 1951, pursuant to a request from the Foreign Office as to the Board's willingness to harbour the new Court. The Board was given to understand that the Government would look favourably upon the financial aspects. Architect Luthman was then ordered to make some designs for a new building in the grounds. Luthman's model consisted of a modern building in the back garden with a front-entrance in the Carnegielaan. However, the Board always retained its reserves as to the idea, which it argued would impair the Foundation's primary objectives and therefore demand the structural reorganization of its finances. At length it became manifest that any decision as to the Court's settlement would be a provisional one only, upon which any initial warmth the Board may have had, abated altogether. Being in great strain as to how to balance the budget of the old

S. J. R. de Monchy (1880–1961), President of the Carnegie Foundation (1952–1958).

Jhr. A. W. L. Tjarda van Starkenborgh Stachouwer (1888–1978), former Governor-General of the Dutch East Indies (1936–1945) and President of the Carnegie Foundation (1958–1963).

building, it did not in the least intend to erect another building, the exploitation of which, it anticipated, might well pose problems of its own and would in all events endanger the Foundation's independence.

At the same time, in 1954–1955, the ageing building, forty years after its construction, badly needed major repairs, owing to wear and tear, leakage and the sinking of floors. Rust-eaten gates and conduit-pipes, outdated technical installations and lifts, insufficient heating, and lack of book storage space did not make it the proper entourage to house the International Court, as its Registrar politely emphasized. The estimated costs of renovation amounted to some Dfl. 300,000. In a major effort which lasted over four years and was a financial *tour de force,* the Board managed to appease the Court's complaints and, at least for the time being, put a halt to the rumours as to the Court's imminent migration to Geneva ...

At the 221st meeting of the Board, on 14 February 1958, the diplomat Jhr. Mr. Dr. A. W. L. Tjarda van Starkenborgh Stachouwer, former Governor-General of the Dutch East Indies, succeeded the aged de Monchy. During his term (1958–1963) again new ways were sought to somewhat relieve the financial burdens of the Foundation. In view of its substantial interests in the Middle East,

Shell was willing to offer the library Dfl. 300,000 over a five-year period to improve its collection and research in that specific area. The Board did not fall in with the idea which would again have impaired the Foundation's independence. It did, however, back the subsequent suggestion to create a foundation in support of a documentary centre on foreign law in the Peace Palace Library. The Supervisory Council of the Carnegie Foundation also showed its sympathy with the idea when discussing the proposal in a session presided over by the Dutch Foreign Minister, Mr. J. Luns, on 17 November 1959. It made the suggestion to interest international companies and university centres at home and abroad. At length it proved impossible to raise the necessary funds. However, in these same years the *Centre d'Etudes* of the Hague Academy was launched.

Another major issue during these years was the ever greater need for space for the Court of Justice. Having dismissed Luthman's previous ideas of creating additional rooms in the attics of the Palace and, later on, build a new wing adjoining the old premises, the Board in 1961 instructed the architect to estimate the costs of (*a*) transplanting the library to the Academy building, (*b*) having new headquarters designed for the Academy itself, and (*c*) arranging new rooms in the former library on behalf of the judges. Nothing came of it, initially. At that moment, matters of finance represented insurmountable problems. From then on, however, the idea of creating additional rooms was never lost.

The succession of President Stachouwer by the former Prime Minister Professor Dr. J. E. de Quay, in May 1963, coincided with the commemoration of the golden jubilee of the Palace, that summer. For once a true exhibition was arranged in the Academy building, which attracted thousands of people. The festivities, though well-deserved, were succinct: soon afterwards the Board was once more struggling with the endless dilemma of finance and space. In the winter of 1964–1965 Sir Percy Spender, then President of the International Court of Justice, approached Secretary-General U Thant at the United Nations Headquarters in New York with a list of complaints regarding the provision of accommodation for the Court and made an urgent appeal for additional subsidies. It was here, too, that for the first time, the idea of a new wing was launched. Sir Percy even made the suggestion to use Luthman's old plans for the Schuman Court.

On 11 February 1965 the Foundation's Supervisory Council drew the following provisional conclusions: a new building had to be provided for the International Court of Justice, at the earliest convenience, if only to prevent the one prominent international body in the Netherlands from accepting lucrative offers from abroad. Pursuant to the 1903 Deed and in view of the current financial crisis in the United Nations, the costs evidently had to be borne by the Dutch Government, not unlike when the Swiss Government had taken responsibility for the renovation and extension of the old *Palais des Nations* in Geneva. Thereupon, a committee was

"The Christ of the Andes," J. Lagae (Brussels 1913), presented by the Argentinian Government.
A replica of the much larger statue on top of the Andes Mountains on the border with Chile. The original commemorates the peace between the two nations and was made in 1905 from the melted bronze of the canons used in their previous war.

established but, curiously enough, nothing was heard of the project for three whole years. The conclusions drawn by the committee as to the desirability of new headquarters were apparently set aside. In November 1968 the Court in its turn applied to the Board with a request to have at least the most urgent repairs carried out. On 9 December following, the Supervisory Council was in agreement with a major project of renovation, which was indeed executed in the subsequent years: walls were aligned and readjusted, new bookstorage areas dug out in the cellars at the front side, and electrical equipment modernized.

Meanwhile, in the autumn of 1971, yet another committee to investigate the feasibility of additional buildings was put into motion. In October 1972 the International Court of Justice, for its part, submitted specifications as to numbers of staff and rooms required. Again a year later, on 30 October 1973, during a meeting in which, significantly, the Board felt compelled to sell some "securities" in order to balance the budget, the final decision was taken to have a new building erected in the grounds of the Palace. In the spring of 1974 three models were submitted by competing firms. At length, on 30 October 1975, the entry "Hortus Nato" of the Arnhem Architects Bureau Brouwer & Deurvorst was selected: in their explanatory note the architects maintained that the new wing should in no way surpass the principal building in height and should respect the lay-out of the garden. Construction activities started the following week under the supervision of the architects Ir. T. T. Deurvorst and Ir. J. Schrieke with the assistance, on behalf of the Carnegie Foundation, of S. A. W. Mies. And under a lucky star it was! In December 1976, on reaching the top of the building, the "pannebier" was poured and in the summer of 1977 the decoration of the interior was begun. All bills were honoured by the State of the Netherlands, and on completion, the building was presented to the Carnegie Foundation as the proper administrative institution.

On 4 April 1978, a chilly morning – with the Secretary-General of the United Nations, Dr. Waldheim, the Secretary-General of Nato, Mr. Luns, the Dutch Prime Minister Mr. van Agt and a bevy of diplomats and dignitaries attending – the new wing, harbouring conference and study rooms for the judges, was effectively inaugurated by Her Majesty Queen Juliana, sixty-five years after her mother, Wilhelmina, had performed the same with the main building. On this occasion Dr. van Royen, President of the Board of the Carnegie Foundation, transferred the building to Secretary-General Dr. Waldheim for the exclusive use of the Court. A plaquette was unveiled by the Court's President, H. E. Jiménez de Aréchaga from Uruguay, bearing a quotation from Cicero: "Fundamentum est justitiae fides, id est dictorum conventorumque constantia et veritas" ("The basis of Justice is credibility, that is to say, the immutable validity of agreements and conventions"). To conclude, luncheon was offered in the Palace by the President of the Court.

The interior of the new wing that was built in 1976–1978 on behalf of the International Court of Justice.

Professor J. P. A. François (1889–1978) who served the Foundation as its Secretary from 1922 to 1968.

Given the circumstances, the design, situating the new building on the crossroads of ornate rose-beds and rhododendron alleys, is a happy one indeed. The architects have managed to spare the precious greenery and preserved the visual relation between terrace garden and Palace. With its noble outlines of Brazilian marble and glass, the 3,760 square metre structure links, in fact, elegance to the utilitarian element. From the delicately decorated interior it offers splendid views on gardens, lake and Palace. It has an underground parking area and a functional connection with the main building and the Court Room by means of a covered corridor, leading to the library quarters.

In hurrying to bring this good news, we have somewhat anticipated other events: on the installation of a Library Council, for instance, which was launched in 1965, pursuant to complaints about the internal organization of the institution; on the retirement, furthermore, of Luthman, the Palace architect, none of whose many designs were ever executed; again, on the retirement, in November 1968, of that officer of long standing, the Board's Secretary, Mr.

United Nations' Secretary-General U Thant (1909–1974) visiting the Court in the sixties.

François, who was succeeded in this capacity by Drs. J. G. Bruggeman, and on the retirement of President de Quay in 1972. Finally, we have anticipated the creation of a new position, to wit the Directorship of the Peace Palace. From spring 1974 onwards it was this new functionary, Mr. H. C. Vaandrager, who controlled the daily affairs of the increasingly complex administration. It was under the presidency of Dr. J. H. van Royen (1972–1981), therefore, and with the effective help of a new director, Mr. W. A. J. Wevers (who succeeded Mr. Vaandrager in 1976), that most of the aforesaid building activities proceeded. The years under consideration saw also the rapid succession of Board members, some of whom had become figures of long standing. In 1978 Mr.

C. R. C. Wyckerheld Bisdom, a Board member since 1946, was succeeded by Mr. M. van der Stoel, again a former Foreign Minister (1973–1977). In October 1980 S. J. Baron van Tuyll van Serooskerken, Board member since 1952, was succeeded by Dr. G. A. Wagner. In the following year President van Royen was succeeded, first, in May, by Mr. van der Stoel, soon afterwards, upon the latter's renewed appointment as Foreign Minister in September, by D. W. Baron van Lynden, Her Majesty's former Ambassador to Bonn. In 1981, also, Professor Mr. P. H. Kooijmans of Leiden University and former Secretary of State was made a member of the Board. Since 1976, the representative of the Permanent Court of Arbitration has been Professor Dr. E. H. van der Beugel.

The new team, during the past years, has achieved some memorable feats. Essential to the future functioning of the Palace has been the updating of the maintenance of the building, including the installation of a new restaurant and the renovation of washrooms, etc. In 1983 a Grotius commemoration was held featuring a conference and exhibition. In May 1984 an "open house" was organized which attracted some 25,000 people. In the following year the urgent needs of the Hague Academy were eased by the increase of the subsidies from the Dutch Government and the United

Nations. Between 1983 and 1986, with the generous help of the Japanese Government, the tapestries in the Japanese room were restored to their former splendour. In 1987 a revision of the statutes of the Foundation was projected to bring these in line with modern day insights of effective administration. On 1 December 1987 Baron van Lynden was succeeded by a former colleague Board member, Mr. van der Stoel, who had been the Dutch Ambassador at the United Nations from 1983 to 1987 and is at present a Councillor of State. It is therefore under his aegis that the Board now sets out to steer the Hague international institutions into a new age of international law.

Finance

"... for the finances form, and have always formed, the vulnerable spot in the organization of the Carnegie Foundation". Thus ends the chapter which Dr. A. Lysen in his 1934 survey devotes to the Foundation's finances. A chapter which opens with the *captatio benevolentiae* stating that the author is now to deal with "a less attractive subject ... which, moreover, cannot be in a lively tone" ... "the Board having at almost all stages been hampered in the execution of its task by the scarcity of its funds".

Undoubtedly, the words have a ring of truth. Indeed, in a sense, they hold good to the present day; with regard to finance, the Board's records make for the perfect jeremiad. Matters of finance lay at the basis of nearly all the problems the Foundation has suffered from in the past decades. Perhaps this is not surprising, really, and somewhat innate to organizations of the kind. The Carnegie Foundation was launched in the time of the great entrepreneurs, the American business tycoons who constituted just another example of the Maecenas of all times. Keen as always, Carnegie, in donating his astounding one-and-a-half-million dollar gift, simply intended to start a project and give it its initial impetus, but not to finance it for years to come. Once off the ground, he reckoned it would obtain the backing of governments, and if not, enforce their contribution with the help of public opinion. The more so as the very idea of an International Court was a governmental matter rather than in the line of private enterprise, as he was himself told time and again at the conference table.

The last appreciation was right of course, but even so the construction is a hybrid one and the Palace has been called the child of a misalliance. The Palace was built from private funds, on land offered by the Dutch Government, in order to harbour international organizations mainly. It was to be administered by a supposedly independent Board that was to be Dutch and supervised by a Council in which the Dutch Minister for Foreign Affairs presided over colleague Ministers and representatives of both Chambers and the Judiciary. This peculiar construction is reflected in matters of finance. The Foundation's revenue is made up from four sources: the accrual of interest on its basic capital, contributions from the Court of Arbitration and the United

Nations, subsidies from the Dutch State and the Hague Municipality, and the proceeds from admission ticket. Its balance sheets again feature four items: the maintenance of the Palace, the upkeep of the grounds, the support of the library, and salaries. Originally, the State subsidies were intended solely for the support of the library and its staff.

The "four-in-hand" has not always been easy to rein in. Thus, in periods of crisis such as the world wars, the contributions of the Courts have proven as risky a base as the entrance tickets. Some nations have been far from punctual in their support of the Court of Arbitration, whereas others in the course of time underwent drastic changes in their political status. Thus, in 1940, the Secretary-General had the choice either to pay the Court's debts to the Foundation or salaries to his staff. Besides, the increase in the Courts' contributions never kept pace with the costs of maintenance for the ageing building, which literally exploded after 1945. Again, the United Nations never showed much sympathy with the hordes of tourists that crowded the grounds to disturb the cerebral atmosphere. Finally, the formal links with Courts and governments at times precluded the acceptance of funds offered by private organizations thanks to the initiatives of Board members and librarians. Given these basic conditions, the formal independence of the Board has often been curtailed.

How, then, came the constituent parts of the Foundation's revenue into being? Towards the end of 1910 the accrual of interest on the basic capital of Dfl. 3,712,008 deposited in 1903, amounted to some Dfl. 1,500,000. The Board determined to invest this sum in securities. From 1 September 1913, with the Palace opened and the keys duly delivered to the Court of Arbitration, pursuant to an agreement with its administrative council, the Court pledged to pay a yearly contribution of Dfl. 49,504 to cover the expenditure borne by the Foundation. This put the total revenue of the Board during 1913, consisting of interest on the basic capital (Dfl. 55,640.46) and contributions at about Dfl. 105,000. Soon enough, that is directly after the First World War, this amount proved insufficient to pay proper salaries to the staff and only by not replacing Albéric Baron Rolin, the general director of the Library, upon his leaving in 1920, did the Board manage to survive.

A momentous event in 1985 was the visit of H.H. John Paul II. On the steps of the Palace His Holiness was welcomed by Mr. W. A. J. Wevers, director of the Carnegie Foundation.

A gilt, silver and enamel inkstand presented by the Australian Government.

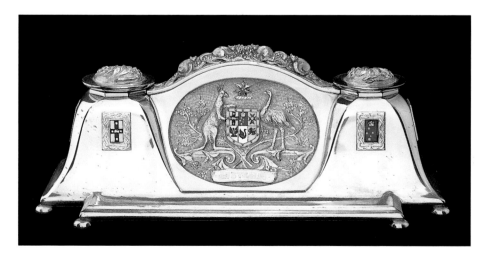

Desiderius Erasmus of Rotterdam, the great humanist scholar (1469–1536). The statue was made by Hildo Krop (1884–1970) and unveiled in 1938. It stands in the gardens in between the rose-beds.

With the arrival of the Permanent Court of International Justice in 1922, the Carnegie Foundation secured a second annual contribution which, after initial provisions for Dfl. 50,000, was soon settled at Dfl. 40,000. This amount was meant to cover the defraying of the higher expenses the Foundation was bound to incur. However, despite the decline in prices, the costs of heating, light and cleaning, which in 1921 had amounted to only some Dfl. 4,000, in 1933 amounted to Dfl. 21,895.29. Similarly, telephone costs over the same period had risen from a meagre Dfl. 770 to Dfl. 5,500.

Apart from this, the staff of the Foundation, too, had increased considerably, if only to properly serve the new Court. Again, pursuant to the new arrangements concluded in 1922, the Foundation, which then virtually took upon itself the overall administration of all Palace proceedings, had also taken over the greater part of the staff of the Court of Arbitration. The shortage of funds therefore soon became alarming. Van Karnebeek was a resourceful man, though. Since the admission ticket funds, which up to then were retained by the Court of Arbitration, and were applied to a relief fund on behalf of its staff, van Karnebeek argued that it was only reasonable for the Foundation to take over also the revenue from these entrance tickets which only in 1914 amounted to some Dfl. 22,000. This is how, after lengthy negotiations, the admission ticket fund was obtained which, ever since, has served as a "relief instrument", though the increase of prices at the gate has been moderate: tickets were sold at 50 cents in 1950, 60 in 1956, 75 in 1960, 100 in 1965, 125 in 1972, 175 in 1983 with all kinds of reductions for groups, children and invalids. Over the years, the investments have been a matter of serious concern as well. From 1904 on, investments were made in funds at home and abroad.

The fourth constituent part of the Foundation's basic revenue is the governmental and municipal subsidies which came into being on 1 January 1931 and amounted to Dfl. 5,000 and Dfl. 2,500 respectively. Both were made on behalf of a revision of salaries of the library staff and both were, within two years, curtailed due to the worldwide crisis. From then on, however, the library staff, at least in theory, enjoyed the same remuneration as the staff of university libraries. Unfortunately, the Foundation was not always in the position to keep the salaries and pension funds in pace. Thus, salaries had to be readjusted in 1946, in which year also the pensions were increased to something over 50 per cent, although remaining well below the national level up to 1953. This situation lasted till 1971 before the State of the Netherlands took over the staff salaries.

Over the years, and notably after the Second World War, the Dutch Government took over an increasing percentage of the Foundation's expenditure. The sharp increase in prices outran by far the fixed revenue of the Board's own means and for instance increased expenditure from Dfl. 183,000 in 1946 to Dfl. 338,000 in 1955. In 1965 the subsidy amounted to about half of the expenditure, again a decade later the Government took care of the inevitable construction of a new wing in the rear garden on behalf of the International Court, which cost about Dfl. 16 million.

This is far from saying that the Court itself, that is the United Nations, did not live up to its own responsibilities. Most renovations, such as the installation of cabins for simultaneous interpretation or the replacement of outdated microphones were executed on a fifty-fifty basis. Again, the annual contribution of the Court was gradually raised from the initial Dfl. 40,000 in 1922 to Dfl. 896,900 in 1988. To compare with this, the current yearly contribution of the Permanent Court of Arbitration is Dfl. 112,000, the subsidies of the Hague Municipality amount to some Dfl. 20,000, whereas the State of the Netherlands contributes Dfl. 2 million.

The perennial shortage of funds is manifest throughout in the Board's records and becomes apparent in various sad and funny ways. Out of the many occasions to commemorate historic events relating to the building virtually none ever prompted large scale festivities and only one or two invited proper ceremonies: in 1928, the international crisis stopped the Foundation from commemorating the twenty-fifth anniversary of Carnegie's gift. The same happened with the hundredth anniversary of the birth of the Scot in 1935, the tercentenary of Hugo Grotius' death in 1945, as for that matter the fiftieth anniversary of the 1899 Conference in 1949, of the Foundation in 1953 or of the 1907 Conference in 1957. The twenty-fifth anniversary of the Palace in 1938 was restricted to some references in local papers. Only twenty-five years afterwards, in 1963, a comprehensive and well-arranged exhibition was held in the Academy building, whereas in 1983 Grotius' four hundredth anniversary was commemorated with a conference and a display of books.

From 1914 onwards complaints are heard about the wearing away of floors and carpets due to the hordes of tourists. The fine rug in the Japanese Room was then protected with a carpet, but throughout the twenties no means were found to bear the cost of covering the Italian marble with rubber mats. In 1962 the first call is heard in the records for asphalting the entrance driveway. Though repeated several times, notably in 1983, it is only in the present commemorative year that the necessary funds were found.

To conclude, in recent years the financial standing of the Carnegie Foundation has improved considerably. At least it has a relatively sound basis now, and if certainly restricted in their expenditure, the Board and its director are now in a position to meet the first needs of the resident institutions. In the past decade many investments were made to this end. The new wing built on behalf of the International Court was opened, which put an end to decades of justified lamenting; most of the staff rooms were redecorated and cloak rooms renewed, and the old refectorium was renovated and is now well equipped to serve the staff and the hundreds of Academy students in summer time.

The Permanent Court of Arbitration

At the first Hague Conference of 1899 the inclusion of the issue of arbitration as an additional point on the programme had been a last minute change only. If anything the idea was suggested to counterbalance by a feasible success in this area the forestalled failure of the disarmament talks. As it turned out, the idea proved providential and the Permanent Court has justly been claimed the triumph of the Conference. Still, the idea was not altogether incidental. Actually, the very term arbitration should be deemed one of the key-words of the era and the treaty concluded at The Hague in 1899 was indeed the crowning of a long process, which had unmistakably gained momentum in the preceding decades.

The idea of arbitration itself, to be sure, was nothing new and even the Court proposal was anything but innovative. Herodotus tells of King Darius presiding as arbitrator; Solon and Themistocles acted similarly in cases of dispute among the Athenians, and the thirty-year armistice of 445 BC between Athens and Sparta featured a true "compromissory clausule", subjecting any future quarrel to arbitration. The intermediary role of popes in medieval times is well known, though it is often hard to establish formally whether their verdicts had the binding force of an arbitral award or merely the facultative, advisory function of the mediator. In practice, however, the temporal authority of the popes warranted the enforcement of their wishes to the letter! Similarly, the Swiss cantons kept an arbitration board all along and so did the German Hanse.

Of the numerous peace designs referred to in the introductory chapter, there are few that have no inkling of, and many that contain outspoken projects of, international courts of arbitration or justice proper. Erasmus, to name one, advocated the idea and though Grotius did not, his colleague Pufendorff in his *Jus Naturae et Gentium* of 1671 outlined a detailed sketch of an international court. In those same days, Landgrave Ernest of Hesse championed a permanent court at Lucerne. Most of these plans, however, had a strong political bias. Interestingly enough, it was the very prince of pacifism, the Abbé de St. Pierre, who, at the beginning of the 18th century, with admirable foresight ventured that it would probably take the world two more centuries to accept the notion of an international court. Leibniz, having experienced the political failure of the project outlined in his *De Jure Suprematus,* had to agree with him – and so did Rousseau, reluctantly.

Voltaire, in his turn, was positively deterred from launching any plan of the sort, as he said, by the prevailing egotism of rulers in his day. Time and again the idol of national sovereignty proved an unsurmountable barrier to any international undertaking. It was only with the changing of international life and the increase of global contacts through trade and traffic in the 19th century that new ideas came to the fore. Economic pressure then came to overturn all previous political insights, as for that matter Jeremy Bentham had correctly predicted. It was at this juncture, too, that the very notion of arbitration underwent a radical change.

The Nineteenth-Century Appraisal of Arbitration

Up to the 19th century arbitration had been generally deemed a suitable instrument to *end* a dispute. In other words, it was never properly considered *before* the outbreak of hostilities. It was only around 1800 that the urge for a more durable peaceful coexistence of man and the firmer foundation of society gave rise to the idea of applying arbitration to the *prevention* of disputes. The best way to do so was by concluding treaties which made provision for arbitration in case of a dispute over certain stipulated issues. Interestingly enough, this notion was not born in Europe, but among politicians in the young South American republics that had only recently liberated themselves from the Spanish yoke. Simon Bolivar was the central figure at the 1826 Conference in Panama which concluded (but never ratified) treaties between Bolivia, Colombia, Chile, Mexico and the United States that even included the compromissory clause. It was this Conference which initiated, first, two decades of South American treaty-making covering virtually the whole of the Western hemisphere and, second, in the latter part of the century, similar arbitration dealing with European powers. Arbitration was even inserted as a premiss to warfare in the constitutions of many of these young republics. In September 1880 Colombia and Chile concluded a "general, permanent and absolute arbitration treaty" which outdated by far any undertaking of the sort in the Western World.

Another step forward was the outcome of the First Pan-American Conference at Washington in 1889, which concluded a similar overall treaty for the Continent – that is to say, on certain conditions. For here we meet the restriction which would play such a prominent role at the Hague Conferences as to virtually wreck all constructive debate. The treaty so concluded excluded from arbitration any issues which involved the "national honour and vital interests" of a State. And this, whereas throughout the era it was argued time and again by the most prominent international lawyers all over the world that if anything it was precisely the submitting of these issues to international judgment which involved the very existence of a nation, that would properly manifest the nation's belief in legal order and justice. These claims were all in vain: understandably perhaps, no nation was found willing to concede an inch on its sovereign rights.

Oddly enough, for the time being no help was to be expected from Europe either. Although here, too, the increase in the application of arbitration to disputes was considerable over the period (running from a meagre twelve instances over the first two decades of the century to an impressive one hundred and eleven over the twenty concluding years), all of them involved the settlement of existing dispute, not its systematic prevention. This is not to say that no substantial progress was made here. Fresh ground had been broken as early as November 1794 with the so-called "Jay Treaty" between the United States and England which first regulated through arbitration quite a range of hot issues.

By far the most interesting treaty of the following century was again concluded by these two nations in the so-called "Alabama Treaty" negotiated in Geneva in 1873 which defined the rights and obligations of neutrals in the wake of incidents which had occurred during the American Civil War. Thus, little by little, the belief in arbitration gained impetus. The success of the compromissory clause, which in the last quarter of the century became virtually inherent to any treaty concluded and which bound nations in advance to subject any differences of opinion resulting from that treaty to an arbitration committee, quite naturally led to the call for similar regulations of a more general import. Thus, treaties of friendship were corroborated by the inclusion of a clause extending to virtually all mutual relations. the United States for instance in the nineties energetically devoted itself to the conclusion of this kind of treaties with all major European powers. Hence it was a minor step to the so-called "permanent arbitration treaty", which not only specified the conditions and area of the arbitration agreed upon, but also matters of procedure. This, too, was a major improvement on the nervous and suspicious atmosphere which, up to then, used to surround similar proceedings on the eve of imminent combat. And, of paramount interest indeed, it was the unmistakable sign that the day of general *obligatory* arbitration was soon to dawn.

It was at the 1899 Hague Conference that the first attempt was made to effectively materialize such an "obligatory" convention on a global scale. We have also seen the reasons for its failure (German opposition) and similar wrecking of the idea in 1907. However, in its Convention of 29 July, signed by twenty-six States, the First Hague Conference firmly established the idea of the *permanent treaty,* as much as the Second Conference at least warranted the universal acceptance of the *idea* of obligatory arbitration. Thus, step by step, order was wrenched from chaos and emotion, leading inevitably to war, replaced by logic which would finally result in law. Admittedly, the road to peace started from minor, even insignificant issues … but so did most wars!

Legal Internationalism

We now see how the notion of arbitration and the Permanent Court did not arrive out of the blue, but emerged quite naturally from the thought of the day. Indeed, the idea was in the air, as may be gathered from a glimpse at the peace movement of the time: it was the area of the "legal internationalists". Through meetings, public lectures and a variety of magazines, pamphlets and journals, these (mostly middle class) activists from government, business and the professional world alike sought to popularize the idea of an international organization, propagating a systematic alternative to war through a series of legal regulations. As they saw it, the socially useless and, besides, extravagant investments on armaments could, with the passage of time, be replaced by a code of international law and the eternal human dream of peace thus achieved in a "slow, evolutionary, legal and practical manner" – indeed, in much the same way as law had substituted feudal violence at the dawn of modern times. They were seers, yet the best of them were practical thinkers, too, realizing they had to steer their course through many obstacles.

Though firmly believing in the progressive enlightenment of public opinion, they were sensitive to the fact that their ideas of a universal political brotherhood would easily be taken for the simpleminded ravings of utopians. At the same time they were keenly aware of the strong reserves felt in circles of chauvinistic officials with regard to any supra-national bodies, which only reminded these passionate nationalists too painfully of the chimera of Habsburgian and Napoleonic imperialism. In propagating arbitration the internationalists therefore stressed its voluntary aspect, being careful to present the issue as a strictly non-political *modus operandi*. Similarly, in drawing up a universal code of law, they wisely held back from referring to the establishment of a political body such as a global government.

Still, it was to arbitration they clung: it was the central issue on the agenda of the Brussels, Paris and Frankfurt Peace Congresses of 1848–1850, and the same held good for the meetings of the Interparliamentary Union which from 1889 onwards were held yearly and were concurrent with the Peace Congresses. It has even been argued that it was precisely the narrow focussing on arbitration as a short-term

William Randal Cremer (1828–1908), Secretary of the International Arbitration League (1870) and co-founder, with Frédéric Passy, of the Interparliamentary Union (1888). Cremer was a major figure in 19th-century pacifism. Nobel Prize laureate in 1903, he was knighted in 1907. The bronze bust by Paul R. Montford in the Palace corridor was unveiled by Andrew Carnegie on 29 August 1913.

ratified. Accordingly, it is safe to say that the peace movement has been very much instrumental both in the shaping of the idea of arbitration and the study of the implications of the Permanent Court. Actually, the scheme subjected to the *Comité d'Examen* of the Third Commission at the First Hague Conference was outlined along the lines of the Union's proposal and of Descamps' famous *Mémoire* – and small wonder it is, as its members Beernaert, Rahusen and Descamps himself as delegates helped to draw up the Convention.

Indeed, in the years under consideration the pressure on politicians grew rapidly to the point of saturation. Admirably enough, pacifists all over the world were supported by eminent scholars like Bluntschli, Lorimer and Fiore, who each designed models for a permanent international magistracy, as often as not divided into civil and criminal courts. In this they – oddly enough and contrary to most proposals from previous centuries – anticipated a Court of Justice which was not embedded in any international organization. Though strictly theoretical most of them, these plans had distinct merits. It is only to be regretted that in their zeal the authors were invariably outdone by the apparently infinite number of dilettant publicists who incessantly showered dozens of brochures on the heads of politicians, featuring the most bizarre and quixotic projects and thus literally obscuring more serious proposals.

All in all, these were the premises which the 1899 Hague debate in its opening sessions found concocted into Russian, British and American schemes for a Court and also some urgent proposals for obligatory arbitration on the base of a so-called permanent treaty. As we have seen, the outcome of this debate in the otherwise highly competent *Comité d'Examen* under the stimulating guidance of the French tactical genius Léon Bourgeois was satisfactory in the first and disillusive in the second respect. We may now concentrate on the more successful one, the institution of the Permanent Court of Arbitration.

means of stopping warfare which made pacifism at the time lose sight of its ultimate goal, the improvement of the international order. Be this as it may, in London in 1890 the arbitration clause was agreed upon as a *sine qua non* of any treaty and in Bern in 1892, during the very meeting that saw the founding of the International Peace Bureau and the Interparliamentary Bureau, President Schenk felt sure that a general treaty to prepare a Permanent Court would not be long in coming. In between, Hodgson Ladd in America and Richard Cobden and Henry Richard in England, to mention only some of these "apostles of peace", paved the way for the idea. Suggestive of the universality of the notion, incidentally, is the work of Morelli and Mancini in Italy or Passy, Noyet and Victor Hugo in France.

Hopeful signs in governmental spheres were welcomed too. As early as 1887 the United States Government initiated the proposal to discuss with the European powers the launching of an "International Court", and in June 1893 even Gladstone himself, much impressed by a petition from another prominent pacifist, Randal Cremer of London, which was backed by 2 million signatures, admitted the feasibility of such a Court in the near future – which statement at the time was strongly ridiculed in the *Reichstag*. In 1894 Lord Weardale reported on a similar plan which had been raised in the Interparliamentary Union by Edouard Descamps of Louvain. This plan was effectively outlined during the Union's 1895 meeting at Brussels and warmly championed at the 1896 Budapest meeting by Randal Cremer, who insisted on approaching governments directly. In 1897, again at Brussels, the Belgian minister Beernaert pressed anew the idea on his audience.

The absolute heyday in respect of these efforts was the signing on 10 November 1896 of the far-reaching Anglo-American arbitration treaty, which excluded only vital interests. But it was never

The 1899 Convention

In the 1899 "Hague Convention for the Pacific Settlement of International Disputes", which amounts to sixty-one articles, the Permanent Court is treated under the second and third parts of the fourth title, more specifically in Articles 20 to 29. (In the revised but as far as contents go basically unaltered numbering of 1907 these are Articles 41-50). After a preliminary statement of intention (Article 20) and some matters of competence (Article 21), attention is drawn to the judiciary aspects of the Court (Article 23) which we shall enlarge upon in some detail below. Articles 22 and 28 discuss the secretarial and administrative bodies of the Court, the International Bureau and the Administrative Council. As the seat of the Court (Article 25) The Hague was chosen, it being also the seat of the Inter-

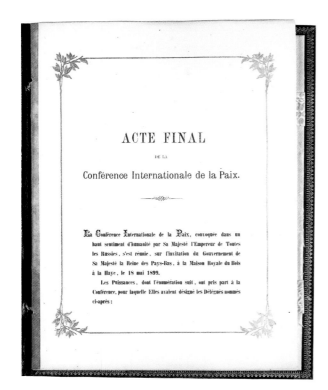

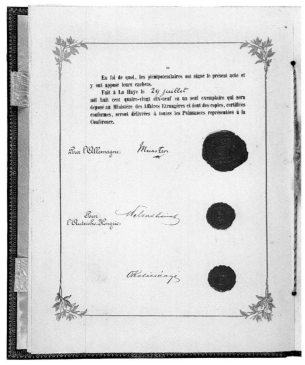

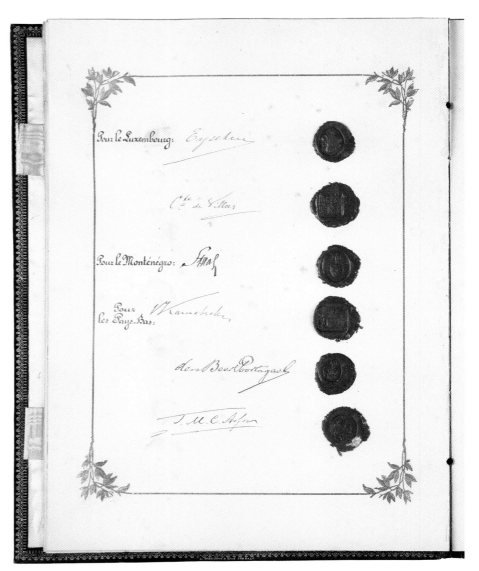

national Bureau. Its court rooms, incidentally, were opened not only to law courts of the Permanent Court but indeed to any court or arbitrator that wished so. Actually, the first case that came up concerned the Behring Street incident in which the Dutch Professor Asser was appointed as the sole arbitrator by the parties.

Article 27 contained what had undoubtedly been the most controversial issue during the deliberations of the *Comité d'Examen*. As stated elsewhere, it was raised and ingeniously defended by Léon Bourgeois and Baron d'Estournelles and was meant to authorize the Secretary-General to draw the attention of the conflicting parties to the Court as a peacemaking institution. In its final phrasing the

Article "reminded the contracting parties of their duty to draw the attention of parties to the Court". In 1907 the Article (48 in the new numbering) was extended, empowering one of two conflicting parties to direct a note to the Bureau stating its willingness to submit the issue to the Court; this note then is forwarded by the Court's Secretary-General to the other party.

The concluding Article 29 concerns the costs. The contributions of the specific nations were regulated on the lines of the International Postal Union, which actually served many international organizations. Pursuant to this schedule States are divided into eleven categories, paying one-half to fifty units, the total representing the number by which the yearly expenses have to be divided.

Some Remarks on the Hague Convention

What to think of the institution herewith created and the regulations agreed upon? As is well known, the most striking aspect in the constitution of the Court is the intrinsic anomaly between its name and its actual functioning. If a proper "court" at all, it is certainly not a "permanent" institution one

The Final Act of the First Hague Peace Conference, signed on 29 July 1899. The pages feature the signatures of Count Münster, de Staal, van Karnebeek and Asser among others.

deals with here. Nothing like a standing court was constituted. The organization created can indeed best be described by the term "permanent arbitration service". At best it is a list of legal authorities. This "List of Members" is compiled by the Bureau according to the selection made by the Contracting Powers, each of whom is invited to submit at the most the names of four persons of known competency. In each case an arbitral tribunal is constituted from this list.

Again, the idea of the Court itself having sprung from widely differing views at the conference table, the procedure agreed upon, even if rather complicated, was very deliberate. In cases of conflict the differing nations are each to appoint two arbitrators from the list. These four arbitrators then proceed to appoint, if needs be with the help of one or two other nations, eventually by the drawing of lots among several candidates, a fifth, their head arbitrator. The parties then formally inform the Bureau of their intention to apply to the Court and submit the names of the arbitrators. The Court then convenes at a date agreed upon by the parties.

From this outline it is seen that, in many respects, the role of the Court is a passive one; the sovereignty of the conflicting parties is respected in every way. Any "permanency" of the Court is found in the list of names – of arbitrators who actually never meet in plenary session. The choice, again, was a deliberate one – and a compromise in itself. Actually, at the conference table the choice of the British scheme was made for the very reason of its conciliatory qualities in front of pluriform, if not hostile views. First of all it was taken on practical grounds, or rather the institution of a court proper was objected to from many sides for practical reasons: among others, it made little sense to have the world's top international lawyers picked from all over the globe for six years at a stretch, only to settle a case once in a while.

Another point was, no doubt, that the body had to be invested with legal authority, but least of all with plenary powers, far less political influence.

Indeed, the utmost care was taken not to deter parties by infringing their autonomy. The very idea of arbitration was adhered to in the first place – and preferred to jurisdiction proper – due to the almost panicky fear of nationalistic governments to surrender their sovereignty. Eight years later, in 1907, Choate's proposal to form a fixed Court, thus better to establish international jurisprudence, was wrecked for those very reasons.

Interestingly enough, the psychological advantage of this specific form of arbitration over the standing court – and for that matter the Court of Justice – an advantage which made itself clearly felt over the years, is the right of nations to appoint arbitrators of their own. Fortunately, this procedure has never translated itself into political pressure, so far. In practice, only once or twice have arbitrators appointed by litigants dissented from majority verdicts. To be sure, any political notion, like, for that matter, personal bias, would be fatal, as was generally felt. The Court is meant to represent the conscience of the civilized world, to further the cause of justice and by its verdicts to create a code of international behaviour. These lofty notions require prudence, as was well understood from the very beginning. These goals also suggest caution on the part of its designers and flexibility on the part of the institution. With the founding of the Court the instrument, the mechanism, the tools were all furnished to create a new international order – and they were found solid. It was left to the initiative of the nations to prove its worth by their craftsmanship.

Reception of the Idea

How did the nations perform? It is of interest to note that in the eyes of the world at large and of their spokesmen, the news media, the genesis and first years of the Court met with the same initial scepticism that was faced by the Conference that created the Court. It was a mixture of feelings really, prompted by overstrung expectations on the one hand and total disbelief on the other, and often misguided by sheer ignorance as well as lack of insight or deeper interest. Be this as it may, numerous were the newspapers predicting that the silver inkstands would never see proper use, that any money spent on the project was wasted and, after the first cases had been successfully concluded, that submitting a conflict to the Court was much too expensive. As to the latter point, nothing was easier than to verify these rumours and disavow them from the figures published in the yearly reports. Pursuant to regulations litigating parties faced the costs of their own defence and shared the costs of the Court proceedings, which seemed only fair. And as far as contributions went, in 1920 the maximum quota to be borne by the five major powers – Germany, the United States, Russia, France and Britain – only amounted to a meagre Dfl. 5,151.50. At present, major powers pay fifty out of the seven hundred and sixty-one units, which on a balance-sheet of about

A postcard featuring Paul Kruger carrying the martyr's cross and a prayer to Czar Nicholas begging the Imperial Promotor of Peace to put a halt to the British onslaught in the Boer Republics. Petitions of the kind were an instrument typical of the peace movement at the time.

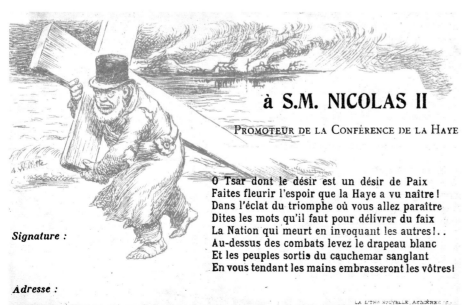

à S.M. NICOLAS II

PROMOTEUR DE LA CONFÉRENCE DE LA HAYE

O Tsar dont le désir est un désir de Paix
Faites fleurir l'espoir que la Haye a vu naître !
Dans l'éclat du triomphe où vous allez paraître
Dites les mots qu'il faut pour délivrer du faix
La Nation qui meurt en invoquant les autres !..
Au-dessus des combats levez le drapeau blanc
Et les peuples sortis du cauchemar sanglant
En vous tendant les mains embrasseront les vôtres!

Signature :

Adresse :

Dfl. 320,000 amounts to some Dfl. 21,000 on a yearly basis. As for the ultimate sceptics: no, the Court certainly did not put a halt to all warfare, nor did it on its own settle each and all major differences henceforward. Those, for instance, who expected – if not demanded – the Court to make short shrift of the Boer War, and numerous they were, had missed the point completely. Vested with the powers agreed upon by the Signatory States, which was facultative arbitration only, the Court was merely a first step towards a truly international judicial body. If anything, it was a symbol to the world that a new era of jurisdiction had finally dawned upon mankind. It was not by far that World Court itself, long-awaited by many, that was authorized, prepared and able to interfere of its own accord into conflicts on behalf of Law and Righteousness. Indeed, no intimate of international jurisdiction ever seriously considered such a body for a long time – in 1907 Beernaert at least called it a "redoutable utopie".

Of a quite different nature and indeed much more alarming than the gossip of sensation-seeking newspapers these first years was the repeated disavowal of the Court's very existence by conflicting nations signatory to the Convention. Thus France, running into conflict with Britain over some minor African matters, chose to have the issue settled through the mediation of a single arbitrator. Interestingly enough it was an eminent Austrian diplomat who at this juncture opened a campaign in the authoritative Paris *Temps* against this procedure … to be promptly backed by – who else than – the Baron d'Estournelles. Indeed, if anyone is to be acclaimed for supporting and propagating the cause of the Court during those early years, it is this

prominent and militant French senator. Even more embarrassing, notably to the British partisans of arbitration who had been so instrumental in drawing up the 1899 Convention, was England's flat refusal to have the issue of the Boer War submitted to the Court. It goes without saying that many critics of the idea eagerly jumped on this setback.

Instances like the ones cited here though were few and became scarcer with the years. Besides, they were by far outweighed by signal successes and, if anything, a growing overall tendency to stipulate

The first housing of the Court (1901–1913) at the Prinsegracht 71, in the centre of The Hague.

The richly furnished drawing rooms at the Prinsegracht. On the walls the portraits of pacifists and delegates to the 1899 Conference.

specific reference to the Hague Court in the compromissory clauses and permanent arbitration treaties that were agreed upon in ever greater numbers by ever more nations. Thus, pursuant to the 1901 Pan-American Conference in Mexico, all South American nations that had been "banned" from the 1899 Conference became *en bloc* signatories to the Hague Convention.

The Installation and Early Housing of the Court

In the Hague Convention of 29 July 1899 the initiative for the constitution of the Court was left to the president of the Administrative Council, the Netherlands Minister for Foreign Affairs *qualitate qua*. This initiative, however, was subjected to the formal ratification of the treaty and the actual entry of nations. As early as September 1900 Minister de Beaufort deemed the number of nations that had joined the Treaty as satisfactory and on the 19th of that month the Administrative Council was

Professor Asser of the Netherlands was tho sole arbitrator in the dispute between Russia and the United States over whaling ships that came before the Court in 1900–1902. In the photograph he is surrounded by staff members of the Bureau.

L. P. M. H. Baron Michiels van Verduynen (1885–1952). He was Secretary-General of the Bureau from 1905 to 1929.

installed. Contracting Powers were duly notified and on 9 April 1901 a first meeting was summoned to appoint functionaries.

To the post of Secretary-General of the Bureau was called R. Melvil Baron van Lynden, who soon had to be replaced due to his installation as Minister for Foreign Affairs, to be succeeded by L. H. Ruyssenaers, Secretary-General of the same department. Ruyssenaers in his turn was soon succeeded by L. P. H. M. Baron Michiels van Verduynen. Along with his tried and trusted first secretary Jhr. Mr. Dr. W. Röell, Michiels van Verduynen would serve the Council for many years to come.

Once the Council had been installed, one of the first steps to be made was the finding of proper accommodation for Court and Bureau. Accommodation was found in one of the typical Hague manorhouses on the Prinsegracht, former habitat of the aristocracy. The busy and indeed rather vulgar traf-

fic artery of modern times is but a poor reflection of what for ages – and up to the first decades of this century – had been one of the smartest thoroughfares in town. The Court kept its headquarters here for more than ten years, from 1901 to August 1913, when it moved into the Peace Palace.

The rooms and salons at the Prinsegracht were stylish and fashionable and breathed a quiet dignity. They were in fact well suited to harbour the decorous diplomats and eminent scholars who were meant to frequent them. Besides, they were well furnished with all sorts of melancholy souvenirs of conferences and symbols of peace and international law. A photograph of the day shows the elegant Professor Asser seated here among staff members. The offices and court-rooms were not too spacious though, and simply lacked the capacity for the public that came to attend Court. It soon became clear that with the presumed growth of the institution and the ensuing increase of cases logistical problems would come to the fore or, as William Stead put it in his typical uncompromising way: "The Bureau as an office is commodious, supposing that arbitrations are occasional ... the prudent Dutch Government and the somewhat sceptical members of the Council decided to proceed tentatively, and so they have provided for the headquarters of the tribunal modest premises which can be procured at a minimum cost, but are in singular contrast to the hopes entertained by those who founded the Hague Tribunal."

However, Carnegie's monumental donation on White's suggestion anticipated any crisis and fully satisfied Stead's express wishes. Though it would take a decade before the temple was to be effectively inaugurated, the very prospect kept the members of the Bureau satisfied with their all too modest housing.

The first formal contacts between Court officials and the Carnegie Foundation were made in the summer of 1904. In the notarial deed of the Foundation's regulations, dated 4 June of that year, the Administrative Council of the Court was empowered to appoint one of the five directors to the board of the Foundation. On 20 June following W. H. de Beaufort, the Conference veteran and former Foreign Minister of the Netherlands was elected; he was to serve on the board for fifteen years.

History of the Court

The history of the Permanent Court of Arbitration up to the present day can be divided mainly into four periods. The first covers the years from 1901, the installation of the Court, till the amendment of the Statute in 1907 (four cases); the second spans the years up to the outbreak of the First World War (eleven cases); the third constitutes the *interbellum* period of the League of Nations (1919–1939; eight cases); the fourth is running and spreads over the years from the foundation of the United Nations (1946–; three cases). The Permanent Court of Arbitration now has a tradition of well over eighty-five years. Of these the years between 1907 and 1914, constituting the Court's second phase, have unmistakably been the heydays of the institution. Rather surprisingly, one should add, for – as we have seen – the Second Hague Conference left a bitter tang with the public at large, precisely because of its failure to resolve the obligatory element.

Still it was these years preceding the opening of the Palace which showed a distinct increase in the number of cases brought up, presumably testifying to the fact that most governments at the time were indeed fully satisfied with the machinery as it was: facultative, but morally authoritative. Together with the ever-rising number of arbitration pacts between powers these developments warranted the supposition that arbitration had become firmly rooted among politicians. Sadly enough, this development was soon to be stopped by the bankruptcy of the political system itself with the outbreak of war. It is only feasible that the deception of "the Great War" left its traces on the credibility of the Court too. At least no cases were brought up between 1914 and 1919, inspiring cartoons featuring the Hague Palace "for sale or to let". As, finally, new optimism peeped through, sound reason invited the construction of a more reliable and far-reaching system, resulting among others in the foundation of the very League of Nations which up to then had seemed chimerical to all and sundry. But the massacre on the Somme had swept away all reserves in the field of diplomacy as well and made obsolete any trust in facultative treaty making. Hence, a true international network was to link the globe and one of its main tentacles soon spread to The Hague: the Permanent Court of International Justice.

Ever since, international lawyers have advocated either the abolition of the Arbitration Court or its retreat to (or extension to cover) other fields, such as strictly financial or commercial issues or conflicts between nations and enterprises in the field of private international law. In practice, however, the Court has been well proven to be viable alongside the International Court of Justice. Nevertheless, the Court went through a gloomy period of more than fifteen years (1938–1954) during which not a single appeal was made to the Court, and since then a single case per decade has been its somewhat meagre score. But to a certain degree the same holds true for the International Court of Justice as well. Even after many decades of experience with the Courts, States are still reluctant to submit cases which may even slightly affect their vital interests in an unfavourable way. On the whole, the role of the Arbitration Court alongside the successive Courts of Justice has proven consistently valid – if only thanks to formal and procedural differences. Major differences are that, just as the International Court of Justice has competence in one aspect of jurisdiction which the Permanent Court has not, namely its power to give advisory opinions (Article 96 of the United Nations Charter), likewise the former lacks the competence of the Permanent Court to settle

PROCEDURE OF ARBITRATION

In the Articles 30-57 of the Hague Convention of 1899 the rules of arbitration procedure are outlined. For the greater part these were taken from current treaties, but they were scrutinized thoroughly, amended and adjusted – in short adapted to the specific needs of the Court. They were amended in 1907, the creation of a summary procedure for simple cases being the most conspicuous change. They came in handy again in 1920 to serve the Permanent Court of International Justice.

The first act of parties, actually preceding the lawsuit, is the submission of the so-called "compromis", stating the issue and the competence of the arbitrator(s). Setting aside all formalities, the incidental and the varying element, the lawsuit itself falls into two parts basically: written pleadings and oral discussions. During the first phase the agents and barristers of parties submit and exchange all relevant documents corroborating their case. In the second phase these are verbally explained and commented upon by the arbitrators. The Court then retires to deliberate and conclude the case by a simple majority of votes. The verdict in the writ, possibly including the dissenting views of a minority of arbitrators, is then undersigned by president and secretary (previous to 1907 by all arbitrators) and read at a public session to which the agents and lawyers of the parties are summoned. The award is binding on the parties and no appeal is allowed. However, a minor restriction for revision is made in case fresh evidence of a decisive nature has come up in between the debate and the award. Naturally, any decision as to its relevance and the subsequent admission of the request is up to the Court, while the compromis fixes the period within which the demand for revision must be made. It is this Article 55, incidentally, which led to heated argument within the body of the Third Commission in 1899.

THE ADMINISTRATIVE COUNCIL

In a way the council is the chief executive body of the institution. It has mainly an administrative function in controlling the International Bureau, salaries and budgetary matters, and the editing of a yearly report on the activities to the Contracting Powers. The Council is composed of the diplomatic representatives accredited to The Hague of the nations which have adhered to the Hague Conventions of 1899 and 1907, seventy-six at present. The Council is presided over by the Foreign Minister of the Netherlands, the depository State of the Hague Conventions. Since 1907 nine members attending form a quorum. It is this body which nominates the Secretary-General, being the chief executive, as head of the International Bureau and Registrar to the Court. His term is five years, which can be renewed.

The Contracting Powers together also create the Court proper. To this end each power is entitled to select a maximum of four arbitrators. Their names are put on the list, which is drawn up by the Bureau, for a period of six years, after which their term can be renewed. It is from this list that the arbitrators for any specific case in question are chosen. On 1 January 1988 the number of arbitrators on the list was two hundred and forty-four. On the founding of the Permanent Court of International Justice, it was provided in the Statute of the League of Nations that candidate-judges for this Court were likewise to be elected from the list submitted by the "national groups" (the maximum four arbitrators selected by each Contracting Power) in the Permanent Court of Arbitration. And the same holds good for its successor, the International Court of Justice, whose members are likewise chosen by the General Assembly and the Security Council from a list submitted by the national groups in the Permanent Court of Arbitration. The members of the Court can also propose candidates for the Nobel Peace Prize.

disputes between States and private organizations: here both parties need to be States. In practice, however, there have been several other considerations which led parties to prefer submitting their case to the Permanent Court.

Among the Permanent Court's attractions to litigants, a major pull – as said above – has always been the allowance to have arbitrators of one's own choice nominated on the Court. The advantage is mainly psychological, to be sure. As both parties designate arbitrators, none of them enjoys full confidence on either side, whereas within the International Court of Justice parties may also have a arbitrator of their nationality sitting during the full course of their case. There is one point here though: the Permanent Court permits a regional choice of arbitrators, which may appeal to parties and increase confidence in arbitrators in cases of peculiarly regional import. What may strengthen the parties' confidence too is the smaller compass which may just seem preferable over a bench of fifteen representing judicial systems from all over the world.

The office of the Secretary-General of the Court. The mantelpiece, the writing desk and some of the furniture date from the Prinsegracht. On the wall a photograph of the Arbitration Commission of the 1899 Conference. Below: a detail from the ornamental grille in front of the fireplace.

THE INTERNATIONAL BUREAU

Perhaps a few words should be added here as to the character of the Bureau, as its tasks differ considerably from those of seemingly similar international bureaus in those days which were to be found in Bern, Paris and Brussels – such as for instance the bureau of the Postal Union. The Hague Bureau, for one, does not of its own accord oversee the fulfilment of the Treaty; in fact it has no advisory function whatever in these respects. Neither does it compile statistics or edit periodicals. It is not, to put it shortly, the quintessence of the "Work of The Hague", but strictly subordinate to it.

In practice however it proved most essential and the very premise to the functioning of both Court and Council – and small wonder this is. Constituting the only really permanent part of the institution, it was soon due to become pivotal to everything.

According to its regulation, drawn up on 8 December 1900, the Bureau's chief functionary is the Secretary-General. His responsibilities are mainly the correspondence and the yearly budget and in this he is assisted by a First Secretary and three other functionaries. In fact, he is both Chef de Bureau and Registrar to the Court.

This double function is reflected in the Bureau's activities, the functioning of which is also basically twofold. First, of course, it is secretarial, looking after the routine matters of daily affairs, handling inquiries and communications. This aspect also covers the preservation of the Court's archives, being the universal storehouse of arbitral projects. Time and again this has proved of extreme value both to scholarly research and (more particularly) to arbitrators settling subsequent disputes. It was this

consideration which, even during the Conference, led to the suggestion by the American diplomat Frederic W. Holls to have the documents in the archives published or at least opened to public study and requiring the Bureau to furnish any one paying the cost of transcription and certification, with duly authenticated copies of any papers filed in the record office. It was generally felt, however, that subsequent publication or, for that matter, any publicity would precisely deter nations from submitting cases to the Court because of diplomatic or political considerations. It was therefore resolved that official communications and sentences only would be brought into the open.

Noteworthy in this context is that parties are under an obligation to submit copies of any laws proceeding from the Court's sentences or of measures subsequently taken to the International Bureau. This lends the Bureau a check mechanism of its own as regards the observance of verdicts by parties.

Pursuant to an arrangement concluded between the Permanent Court of Arbitration and the International Centre for Settlement of Investment Disputes (ICSID) the International Bureau from time to time undertakes the organization of hearing sessions of this institution. The same applies to hearing sessions under the auspices of the Arbitration Court of the International Chamber of Commerce and other arbitral tribunals.

When the Court is in session the Bureau becomes a registry, taking care, through its Secretary-General, of the exchange of documents between parties and agents (such as memoirs, conclusions, claims and counter-memoirs), its functionaries attending sessions,

assisting judges, drawing up interlocutory judgments and performing intermediary tasks between the Court and the respective parties. From this it is clear that any political involvement of the Bureau and more particularly of its Secretary-General is odious. This does not necessarily mean that the staff of the Bureau had no say in the proceedings of the Court. By the use of tact the competent diplomat found many ways lay open to further the cause of his institution!

Apart from his activities as Head of the International Bureau the Secretary-General has certain special competences. These derive mostly from the standard rules for commercial arbitration set up by the United Nations Commission on International Trade Law (UNCITRAL). These rules stipulate that, if one party fails to appoint an arbitrator or if the arbitrators appointed by the parties cannot reach agreement on the choice of the third arbitrator, the failing arbitrator shall be appointed by a so-called appointing authority. If the parties have not agreed beforehand on the choice of this authority, he shall be designated by the Secretary-General of the Permanent Court of Arbitration. In international private contracts the "UNCITRAL Rules" are often made applicable for the solution of a dispute by arbitration and the Secretary-General is frequently called upon to designate an appointing authority.

It also frequently occurs that in private contracts or in international agreements between States or between a State and an international organization the Secretary-General is mentioned as the authority who can be requested to appoint an arbitrator directly if a party fails to do so or if the party-appointed arbitrators fail to agree on the choice of the third arbitrator.

THE JAPANESE ROOM

On speaking of the accommodation of the Permanent Court, attention must be drawn to the major salons put at its disposal by the Foundation. The first is situated on the first floor, in the central front next to the stylish offices of the staff of the Bureau. This so-called Japanese Room is justly considered by many the most decorous and elegant chamber of the Palace.

The Japanese Room owes its name to the national gift presented to the Foundation by the Japanese Imperial Government and to be found there. The precious gift consists of a series of indeed superb silk-tapestries, named *Hundred flowers and hundred birds in late spring and early summer* and designed in the tradition of the *Tsuzure-Nishiki* style by Jimbei Kawashima II. The work represents a fine specimen of the Japanese tradition, linking artisticity with craftsmanship. Indeed, the *Tsuzure* style is considered by intimates "the art of arts", the most refined, the most complex and therefore the most laborious technique by far of silk fabrics, physically exerting to the naturally delicate, dexterous and agile fingers of Oriental artisans. Contrary to popular belief though, the technique is not really innate in Japanese art, but

was imported from the West around the 12th century and inspired by the French *gobelins*. The art was recreated in the 1840s by Kawashima I, a court artist who travelled extensively through France.

It was his son who, in the summer of 1909, was commissioned by his Government with this crowning endeavour of his life. As rumour has it, he designed the composition overnight, jumped in a rickshaw to commission his friend Hobun Kikuchi the great flower and bird painter, and began constructing a special workshop. Here a team of 48,600 dedicated men and women in total worked in shifts for more than five years, spending much energy over the four large and two somewhat smaller panels, measuring 4.50 × 4.80 m. and 4.50 × 2.70 m. respectively. Only halfway they were laconically implored by Mr. van Karnebeek to produce another set of three minor panels to suit the opposite wall. Apart from the strict time-schedule, it must have required much brain-racking from Jimbei and Hobun to produce a satisfactory result from the artist's point of view for the unlikely measurements that where ordered: 0.83 × 3.26 m. and 0.83 × 7.66 m. They managed wonder-

fully though, applying only the best of products: brilliant alizaline tinctures of rich coloration to dye the precious Gôshû silk, and gold threads in dozens of shades. The scenes of the six major panels represent a landscape of an exceptional vivacity and naturalness: among a lustre of Oriental trees, beds of flowers and plants in the full bloom of late spring (blossoming cherries, azaleas and magnolias in between oak and Japanese cedars), a myriad of birds are chirping and twittering: pigeons and pheasants in many varieties, swallows and peacocks proudly spreading their gorgeous feathers. The work is probably the most noteworthy among the treasures to be found in the Palace. It is only regrettable that Kawashima himself died before seeing the tapestry completed.

A part from the Japanese tapestry, gifts from two other nations decorate the room: four cloisonné vases of gold-plated copper from China and a set of elephant's tusks on a pedestal presented by Siam. Finally, the room is remarkable for its rosewood panels (a gift of Brazil) featuring intricate intarsia with golden geometrical patterns, and its delicately painted ceilings, another design by Herman Rosse.

German Consul awaiting further diplomatic steps. The Court saw no grounds, however, to deliver the deserters to the Germans, as they had pleaded. Both the verdict and the tact applied to it were admired even among German scholars: no winners, no losers.

Another important case in these respects was the North Atlantic Coast Fisheries case between the United States and Britain, case No. 7, submitted in January 1909 and decided in September 1910, whether Britain was allowed to unilaterally impose "reasonable regulations" upon a "liberty to take fish", which had been granted forever to the United States inhabitants by a Convention of 1818 between the two countries.

Apart from settling such thorny political issues as the aforegoing, the Court also dealt with intricate juridical problems, as was the case with the Orinoco, Savarkar and Isle of Palmas incidents. In the Orinoco case a first attempt was made to have a verdict revised. The question concerned a claim by the American Orinoco steamship line against Venezuela, which had been discussed by a mixed commission in 1903 and finally been settled by a Dutch supreme arbitrator in 1904. It was brought up for revision by the United States on the grounds of formal and factual errors in the previous verdict and incompetence of that court. This verdict given in 1910 which accepted the claim gave rise to heated debate among international lawyers.

No less controversial was the outcome of the Savarkar case which arose that same year between France and Britain. An Indian, Savarkar, was on board the British steamer *Morea* awaiting trial in Britain on a murder charge. The French Government was informed of this. During the steamer's stay at Marseilles Savarkar managed to escape, but was taken by the police and duly – or was he? – delivered to the British. On second thoughts the French Government thought he wasn't and asked London for his return. The Court's tribunal argued that the French were basically right: the surrender at Marseilles had been irregular. On the other hand there was no rule in positive law that could enforce the British to deliver their prisoner under the circumstances. Van Hamel, for one, thought otherwise: at Marseilles a positive law had been damaged, he argued, and the *restitutio in integrum* should be enforced. There were many who shared this view. A very similar incident occurred in 1945 between Switzerland and Austria over a spy.

The Isle of Palmas case (1928) was of special interest for jurisprudence in matters of territorial sovereignty. The litigants were the United States and the Netherlands, the issue a small island in the Philippine area and Mr. Max Huber of Switzerland the sole arbitrator in the case. The island had been conceded to the United States by Spain at the Treaty of Paris in 1898, but oddly enough proved effectively to be in Dutch possession. When the Americans arrived some years later to claim their rights, these were contested by the Dutch who claimed effective rule over the island for well over two centuries. Huber concentrated mainly on two matters: the

rules of sovereignty and procedural questions. Effective sovereignty, he argued, was nothing theoretical and, though subject of course to circumstance, had to be manifest from the durable exercise of political powers. This is to say that any alleged Dutch negligence in not notifying the Americans of their possession at their earliest convenience in 1898 could not be held against them, always provided they were indeed in possession of the island.

Against this the Americans held that the Spanish had discovered and first explored the island. This, however, was not deemed identical to "sovereignty", not even by lawyers at the time of the discovery, without the effective taking possession of the territory. Another American claim for sovereignty, the island's adjacency to the Philippine mainland which was in their possession, also proved invalid, by the simple fact that territory implied *terra firma* only, not widely surrounding waters. Besides, Dutch claims proved to stem from a treaty with the native inhabitants dating back to 1677 – which treaty had never been seriously contested by the Spanish. Huber therefore awarded the island to the Dutch.

The judgment in 1970 was followed by a new decade of lethargy and enforced inertia. Then, in 1981, the International Bureau became involved in – and very much occupied with – the Iran-United States Claims Tribunal.

In January of that year the serious problems which had arisen between Iran and the United States as a result of the occupation of the United States Embassy in Tehran in 1979, were finally solved by an agreement reached through the intermediary of the Algerian Government. This agreement contained two declarations. Pursuant to the second declaration an international arbitral tribunal was established to settle the claims of United States nationals against the Government of Iran and vice versa. This tribunal would consist of nine arbitrators, three appointed by each of the two parties and the remaining three to be chosen by the six party-appointed arbitrators. This selection took place in the Peace Palace in May 1981 under the auspices of the Permanent Court of Arbitration. The meeting could be considered a historical event as it was the first time since the beginning of the dispute that representatives of the two countries faced each other at a conference table. The president elected was Mr. Gunnar Lagergren of Sweden, a judge in the European Court of Human Rights at Strasbourg and a member of the Permanent Court of Arbitration.

The regulations of the Tribunal are based on the UNCITRAL Arbitration Rules as adapted in order to meet the Tribunal's specific needs. The claims are dealt with either by the full bench of nine or by one of three chambers consisting of three arbitrators. At the request of the Governments of Iran and the United States the offices and the staff of the International Bureau were placed at the disposal of the Tribunal. The inaugural session took place in the Court Room of the Permanent Court on 1 July 1981 and subsequently all meetings and sessions of the Tribunal were held in the Peace Palace during the following

Max Huber (1874–1960), portrayed by Jan Toorop (1858–1928) in 1927. Huber attended the Second Hague Peace Conference, was Judge and President of the Permanent Court of International Justice (1921–1930), where he left a deep impression on his colleagues, and was member of the Permanent Court of Arbitration from 1923 to 1940. He successfully arbitrated the "Isle of Palmas" case as single arbitrator.

A meeting of the Iran-USA Claims Tribunal in the Small Court Room of the Palace in 1987.

nine months. The Court Room was transformed into a registry, where nearly 4,000 claims were received. During this period the International Bureau took care of the correspondence of the Tribunal, of its archives, accounting, recruitment of interpreters and other personnel, contacts with the press, protocol matters, personal services for the members of the Tribunal, etc. Gradually the Tribunal recruited so much staff of its own that it could no longer be accommodated in the Peace Palace. In March 1982 it moved to its own building, elsewhere in The Hague, but the organization of the International Bureau remains at its disposal. Several times each year hearing sessions of the Tribunal are held in the Court Room of the Permanent Court when so many people attend the hearings that the rooms in the Tribunal's building are too small.

Perspective

Though in a succinct way, we have discussed herewith at least some of the cases that have occupied the Court in the past eighty-five years. Though, admittedly, not all of them are that spectacular, several of the above-mentioned have become classics in the field and have entered the realm of positive law. The verdicts given have found their way into the textbooks, from Verdross and Guggenheim to Nussbaum and have earned respect in practice as well. Never yet has any verdict of the Court been ignored or disavowed by any party. Thus, slowly but steadily, the world is learning "the alphabet of righteousness and peace". There can be little doubt therefore as to the Court's historical role.

Quite another thing is whether the Court has to claim any future role. Formally, its organization is sound. With Nigeria adhering to the Convention since December 1986, the present number of signatory States has risen to a comfortable seventy-six. Still, it goes without saying that the Court's functioning is somewhat obscured by that of the International Court of Justice and the European Courts in

Strasbourg and Luxembourg. Besides, a distinct tendency has been noticeable in past decades to politicize disputes: to this, incidentally, testify the most recent cases before both Hague Courts. On the whole, settlement through judicial or arbitral means, if attempted at all, is preferably sought within political frameworks such as the United Nations or the European Communities, which are often thought to serve better the States' interests.

Another handicap to the proper functioning of the Court may just be that, contrary to the Latin American States, most African and Asian countries look upon it – and rightly so in the historical perspective – mainly as a Western and basically European institution. Few of them are members and they were parties to only two or three cases. If wishing to submit cases for arbitration they would probably prefer the regional systems offered by the Arab League or the Organization for African Unity. These facilities, however, are not frequently applied to either.

Unfortunately, after the Second World War the initial enthusiasm of the Latin American countries has abated as well. Regional arbitration systems have been attempted in this area, notably through the Bogotá Pact of 1948, and these have resulted finally in the facilities offered by the Organization of American States.

Naturally, efforts have been made to ameliorate the situation. Rules of adherence have been simplified and the submittal of an adherence act facilitated. Pursuant to a meeting on 2 December 1959, United Nations members which acknowledge their wish to ratify, are *ipso facto* considered party to the Convention.

In February 1962, the Court's Bureau presented a new set of rules, based on general stipulations derived from practice and elaborated to have the Court play a more active role in the settlement of disputes. From then on, private persons or companies were allowed to submit disputes with Signatory States for arbitration or conciliation.

To conclude, it may be safely said that the Court itself has taken better care in adjusting itself to time and circumstance than have the nations in using the mechanism furnished. It is true that other institutions have partially taken over the original function of the Permanent Court. It may be true as well that the belief in the instrument of arbitration has decreased in past decades. But this is certainly not to say that the need for such a body is beyond us. One might seriously ask oneself whether any institution of the sort was even given a fair chance in practice. Working within a field of its own and confronted by an international society which is growing ever more complex and in which even essentially legal conflicts tend to become increasingly subject to national political prestige, the Permanent Court of Arbitration seems invariably well-equipped to meet the call for an independent arbitrator. After eighty-five years the question is still not so much as to whether it is the perfect instrument as rather whether we can reasonably do without it.

The International Court of Justice

Today, there can be little doubt as to the image of the Peace Palace, if not The Hague itself, in the world at large. In modern times the functioning of the Palace and, to a degree, the town's renown abroad are virtually identified with the proceedings of the institution that has come to be known as the "World Court". Though perhaps somewhat lacking in nuance, as often with the people's belief the general impression is fully justified. The prevalence of the International Court of Justice over the other international bodies residing in the grounds is obvious and plain to all. So much so, indeed, that few people nowadays realize that the coming of the Court to The Hague in the early twenties was due to the reputation the town had made for itself in the field of international law before that time: through Professor Asser's conferences on private international law in 1893–1894, through Czar Nicholas' innovating idea of the Hague Peace Conferences, through the lustre of Carnegie's "Temple", opened in 1913, and not in the least through the rising influence of the Permanent Court of Arbitration, installed in 1900 as the lasting result of the 1899 Conference and the motive for the building of the Palace in the first place. It has been the merit, maybe slightly disregarded in modern literature, of the Hague Conferences to have created and in a way conditioned the network of international relations and personal contacts that a decade later brought into being the League of Nations and, subsequently, the Court of Justice and the Hague Academy.

Once in operation, in 1922, it did not take the Court of Justice long to gain its prominent position in the Palace. In fact, it was obvious from the beginning that the forum about to be created here was a marked step forward in man's quest for an international order. However this was not the main concern of the Netherlands Foreign Minister H. A. van Karnebeek when, on 15 November 1921, he was first confronted with a letter from Sir Eric Drummond, the League's inspiring first Secretary-General, suggestive of establishing the seat of the Court at The Hague. However flattering, tempting and gratifying the proposal was, van Karnebeek instantly and fully appreciated the total upheaval that would ensue of all that had been achieved by his father, arranged and negotiated in the Palace in the past decade. In previous chapters we have described what the outcome was to be: it resulted in the "banishing" of the Hague Academy, that other recent creation, and of large parts of the Carnegie Library to a new wing. It led to

the withdrawal of the Court of Arbitration into the upper front façade of the Palace. It brought on financial complications and personal frictions – but even so it certainly proved worth the trouble. Already in 1934, the first historiographer of the Peace Palace summarized his survey of the establishment of the Court in the Palace with the memorable words: "It has produced delicate problems, heavy financial burdens and risks, it has made serious demands on organization and staff, driven older institutes into a more modest section of the original Palace buildings, or even away from it, into a supplementary building ... But all of this is the result of a gratifying course of development, and also evidence that the Peace Palace is the beating heart of a vital and growing organism, a living centre of international law."

Meanwhile, the reader will have observed that in these introductory lines we speak of the "Court of Justice" indiscriminately. Naturally, in this survey we must make proper distinction between the Permanent Court of International Justice of the interbellum period, and its post-war successor the International Court of Justice. As regards details of internal organization the Courts cannot fail to differ in many ways, and the same holds good for their relations with their originating institutions, the League of Nations and the United Nations respectively. However, in their proper functioning, they are very much alike. More than this, they operate formally on the basis of the same Statute. For these and other practical reasons we feel justified in maintaining a historical approach throughout this chapter. First, therefore, we shall discuss the external history of the successive Courts in a chronological survey, then deepen the insight by outlining their basic principles and functioning.

The Permanent Court of International Justice (1922–1946)

GENESIS OF THE COURT

In previous chapters we have recorded man's ideas regarding international leagues and courts over the centuries. For, to be sure, the idea of a court as projected here was anything but new in itself. Still, in retrospect, the roots of the Court of Justice that opened in 1922 lay with the Hague Peace Conferences. It was here at least that the first concrete steps were taken towards its launching: tentatively at first during the first Peace Conference in the Hague Woods, more precisely and circumscriptively in 1907. Thus, the United States Secretary of State, Elihu Root, had formulated some ideas as to a "permanent court of arbitral justice" in his instructions to the American delegation to the Conference – and soon he proved not alone in his endeavours. In the opening weeks of the Conference a joint proposal was submitted by the United States, Britain and Germany and during the sessions the idea was pleaded eloquently by the Belgian delegate Descamps. In an address occasioned by the laying of the foundation stone of the Peace Palace, on 30 July 1907, the President of the Carnegie Foundation, A. P. C. van Karnebeek, in fact voiced everyone's ideal when exclaiming: "This will be the Palace of International Justice!" Optimism prevailed in those days and alongside the Convention on an International Prize Court, the Recommendation of a Judicial Arbitration Court was in fact one of the most tangible results of the Conference. Both reflected the need, which was generally felt among attenders, of permanent judicial bodies with salaried judges put at the disposal of States to solve disputes and by doing so in due course create a code of international law.

However, for a decade it seemed that, as so often before, the many sceptics would prove right again and that practical objections and matters of procedure would stand in the way of the immediate materialization. In all events, nothing much came of the Courts, initially: the Convention remained unratified and the Recommendation never developed into anything more than that. The idea had stuck though, as witness also the experiment of the Central American Court of Justice which opened in 1908. In retrospect one may safely say that the idea has never been quite out of sight since. Thus, it was envisaged to feature as a major issue on the agenda of the Third Hague Conference. This conference was projected for 1915, but had to be cancelled due to the outbreak of war. Ironically though, it was the very horrors of this war that finally cleared the way, in a perfectly astonishing manner, for the creation of what had only the other day seemed a phantasm of idealists, the true international system of a League of Nations. It was within this organization, predictably, that the idea of the Court of Justice was to crop up again, in the famous Article 14 of the Covenant: "The Council shall formulate and submit to the Members of the League for adoption plans for the establishment of a Permanent Court of International Justice. The Court shall be competent to hear and determine any dispute of an international character which the parties thereto submit to it. The Court may also give an advisory opinion upon any dispute or question referred to it by the Council or by the Assembly."

The paragraph is fundamental to the better understanding of the Court's proceedings, for here, in a nutshell, we have the essentials of the Court's functioning over the years and up to the present day, its judicial duties to States and its advisory functions to international organizations.

In February 1920 the League's Council proceeded to appoint a Committee of ten prominent jurists to produce a "draft scheme". Among these were the Spaniard Altamira, the Belgian Baron Descamps, the Norwegian Hagerup, the Dutchman Loder, the Englishman Lord Phillimore and the American Elihu Root. Worked out at The Hague, in the Peace Palace, in June and July, the draft was submitted to, and with slight modifications adopted, by the League's Council during its meetings at San Sebastian and Brussels in August and September 1920. On 13 December the text was unanimously approved by the Assembly and recorded in a Protocol on 16 December; it thus obtained the status of an international convention, the coming into force of

Above: The "Committee of Ten" assembled in the Japanese Room. In June-July 1920, at the Peace Palace, this committee worked out a first draft scheme for the Permanent Court of International Justice.

Below: The first official sitting of the Court, in the Bol Room of the Peace Palace, on 15 February 1922.

which was subject to the ratification of the Protocol by the necessary majority of nations. This was obtained by September 1921, after which the Assembly duly proceeded to the election of judges. The Court first assembled in a preliminary session on 30 January 1922 and on 15 February 1922 met for its first official sitting, presided over by the Dutch jurist Loder.

With the constituting of this Court, it was generally felt, a new heyday in man's efforts to settle disputes in a non-violent way was attained. Among the several methods applied over the centuries and discussed in our opening chapters: negotiation, enquiry, mediation, arbitration and judicial settlement, the latter was universally acclaimed to be the most impartial, sophisticated and strict method. And here it was: a Court more representative of the world's varying legal systems than any previous one had been; a permanent body at that, and assisted by a permanent registry which warranted the development of a constant practice in its public proceedings; a body besides, that in principle was open to all States. And, best of all, that had managed to settle nicely the thorny problem as regards the election of impartial judges, which had been the major bone of contention fifteen years before at the Second Peace Conference in The Hague. The choice of judges was attributed to the Council and the Assembly of the League of Nations alike, in simultaneous and independent ballot. For, to be sure, the new Court was to be closely associated with the League – though not as an integrated part of its system. It was to operate in a purely advisory function for this organization, its independence duly warranted. Best proof of this: the Court's Statute was not to be part of the League's Covenant.

The Statute of 1922 proved a workable scheme indeed. Only once was it amended, that is to say by another Committee of a dozen experts and in

pursuance of a resolution of the League's Assembly in December 1928. The report of this Committee (featuring the American Elihu Root, the Frenchman Fromageot, the Englishman Sir Cecil Hurst, the Greek Politis, the Dutchman van Eysinga and the Japanese Ito) was submitted to a Conference of States, then approved by the Assembly and finally embodied in a Protocol dated 14 September 1929; this came into force in February 1936. Side by side with a body of "Rules of the Court", a growing set of resolutions of the Council and Assembly, and a variety of international agreements, this Statute has remained the main instrument to the Court's operating in the broadest sense. From the beginning there was dissonance. At the time the Statute was ratified by forty-eight States, but the United States was not among these. Though it duly signed the Protocol, the required two-thirds majority in the Senate was never obtained.

THE COURT'S PROVINCE: A SURVEY OF CASES

During the years of its active existence, that is from 1922 to 1940, the Permanent Court rendered thirty-two judgments in contentious cases among States, delivered twenty-seven advisory opinions to the League and made one hundred and thirty-seven orders. Twelve cases were discontinued as applicants withdrew their claims before a judgment was rendered. Several hundred treaties, conventions and declarations conferred jurisdiction upon it over specified classes of disputes. In other words, as far as statistics go, the Court functioned in a practical and effective manner and easily demonstrated its value to the international community. It helped to resolve some serious international disputes, and in doing so clarified some previously unclear areas of international law. Along the line, it developed a true judicial technique and steadily drew up a sophisticated internal procedure.

The first time in history of an inter-state dispute being submitted to an international court of justice and therefore a historic moment occurred in 1923 in the matter of the *S.S. Wimbledon*. On 21 March 1921 the British vessel of that name, carrying munitions on behalf of a French company, was refused access to the Kiel Canal by the German authorities, who, to uphold their conduct, referred to the German Neutrality Regulations. However, free access to the vessels of all nations at peace with Germany was stipulated in the Treaty of Versailles (Article 380) and at length the German authorities were ordered to pay indemnities.

In the course of two decades, the disputes that were submitted to the Court concerned such varied questions as Brazilian and Serbian loans issued in France (both 1929), Palestine Concessions (Greece v. Great Britain, 1924, 1925, 1927), frontier disputes (Czechoslovakia v. Poland, 1923; Albania v. Yugoslavia, 1924; Turkey v. Iraq, 1925), lighthouses awarded to France on the Greek coasts in the wake of the Balkan Wars (Greece v. France, 1934 and 1937;

Left: The Dutchman B. C. J. Loder (1849–1935), Judge (1922–1930) and first President (1922–1925) of the Court. Loder presided over both the deliberations on the Court's Statute and the advisory committee that prepared the draft scheme in 1920–1921. He was a member of the Permanent Court of Arbitration and a specialist in the Law of the Sea.

Above right: Henri-Auguste Fromageot of France (1864–1949), Judge on the Permanent Court throughout its existence (1922–1945). He also handled three important cases heard before the Permanent Court of Arbitration (Venezuela case, 1903, Japanese leases, 1905 and the Dogger Bank incident, 1905).

Below right: Jhr. W. J. M. van Eysingsa (1978–1961), member of the Permanent Court of Arbitration from 1926 onwards and member of the Court from 1931 to 1946. He was a prolific author and outstanding scholar. He represented the Netherlands in many international conferences and was on the board of numerous commissions of the League of Nations.

this case was submitted to both Courts of Justice and Arbitration, and finally settled in 1956!), and claims on Eastern Greenland (Norway v. Denmark, 1933 twice). Frequently, matters of interest to the International Labour Organisation were discussed, such as the conditions of agricultural labourers or methods of production, the appointment of delegates to conferences (all in 1922), the personal work of the employer (1926), or the convention of 1919 concerning night work for women (1932). International rivers caused trouble too! In 1927 the jurisdiction of the European Commission of the Danube, established in 1856 to ensure the navigability of the Lower Danube, was vainly contested by the Romanian Government. In 1932 a very similar dispute arose over the territorial jurisdiction of the International Commission of the River Oder that had been initiated at Versailles. Another incident occurred some years later between Belgium and the Netherlands over the River Meuse.

Many disputes resulted indirectly from the First World War and the Peace Treaties of Neuilly, Versailles and Trianon. This held good for the controversies between Greece and Bulgaria concerning the interests of the latter's nationals, regulated at Neuilly, which cropped up several times in 1924, 1930 and 1932, or the conflicts between France and Switzerland over the Free Zones of Upper Savoy (1929). By far the most debated issues, however, concerned Polish questions, more particularly its relations with Germany and Lithuania, the treatment of German minorities (settlers, interests, schools, taxes) and the position of the Free City of Danzig (Gdansk). Between 1923 and 1935 these issues cropped up 17 times!

As can be seen from this survey, the twenties and early thirties were busy years for the Court. The later thirties, however, saw a period of clearly diminished activity, if not crisis, till with the outbreak of war in September 1939 the inevitable end came. There were good reasons for this crisis and they were both internal and external. A first unsettling factor in the Court's history was the virtual absence of the United States. This was the more deplorable as through the influential Elihu Root this nation had substantially contributed to the drafting of the Statute in 1921. Although represented on the Board with successive competent judges such as Bassett Moore, Hughes, Kellogg and Hudson (the latter, incidentally, being one of the best historiographers of the Court), the American Senate on several occasions, and finally in 1935, withheld its consent from the Statute, even in its redrafted version. As a consequence, the United States never took a real

Three out of the four American Judges on the pre-war Court. From left to right: John Bassett Moore (1860–1947), who was Judge from 1921 to 1928 and member of the Permanent Court of Arbitration during 1912–1938. Frank B. Kellogg (1856–1937), Nobel Prize laureate in 1929 thanks to his well-known "Pact" and Judge during 1930–1935. Manley O. Hudson (1886–1960), Judge from 1935 to 1939 and author of handbooks on the Court. The fourth American Judge was Charles Evans Hughes (1862–1948), who served the Court from 1928 to 1930 and the Court of Arbitration from 1926 to 1930.

PROCEDURE OF CASES

It is generally felt that in matters of procedure the Court has maintained a happy combination of simplicity and informalism in laying down the rules and a high degree of flexibility in their application. In view of the many legal traditions represented in the Court, the Statute provides for the combining of the two major types of procedure in civil and common law traditions, therefore dividing proceedings into a written and oral stage.

Basically, cases come before the full Court, in which nine judges form a quorum. However, the Statute also provides for Chambers, one for Summary Procedure, comprising five judges and constituted annually, and Special Chambers, comprising at least three judges and originally meant to solve labour issues and questions of communications arising from the Versailles Treaty. Until recently, the Chamber for Summary Procedure was the only one to have been constituted. In recent years, however, and with the changing of the Rules on the Chambers, special chambers have been formed in four cases: in 1982, in the Gulf of Maine dispute between Canada and the United States, in 1985 in the Frontier Dispute between Burkina Faso and Mali, in 1987 in the case concerning Elettronica Sicula between the United States and Italy and in the frontier dispute between El Salvador and Honduras.

States have no permanent representatives accredited to the Court. Usually they communicate with the Registry through their Ministers for Foreign Affairs or their Ambassadors in The Hague. Where they are parties to a case they are represented by an agent, normally the Ambassador or a legal adviser to the Ministry. This agent takes care of all formal acts and as a rule opens the argument at the oral proceedings. States may also appoint deputy-agents and, of course, counsel and advocates – either or not of their own nationality. States nowadays tend to decrease the number of counsel if only to reduce the costs and the Court's new Rules of 1978 are helpful in that respect. The procedure opens with a submission of written pleadings by the parties.

Normally they consist of a Memorial by the applicant to which the opposite party replies with a Counter-Memorial. These are often followed by a second round, featuring a Reply responded to by a Rejoinder. Once this written stage is completed, new documents to the case can be submitted only in exceptional circumstances.

After an average interval of three months the case is ready for hearing. Unless decided otherwise these oral proceedings are public and usually take two to three weeks. They are held in the Great Hall of Justice and are an impressive sight, featuring the bench of judges in their black gowns and white jabots, faced by the agents and counsel in their national legal robes.

Proceedings consist of speeches by counsel, hearings of witnesses and experts, and final questions by judges. The Court then withdraws to consider in private and draw up the judgment. The course of events outlined here can be interrupted in several ways though. First by Preliminary Objections: on being informed by the Registry of the applicant's case, the respondent may raise objections, challenging the Court's competence. This may start a legal tilt by counsel and a trial within the trial. Since 1946 eighteen instances of the kind have occurred and about two-thirds of these protests have been upheld by the Court. Second by Non-Appearance: this may occur at every stage of the proceedings. It occurred recently in the United States Diplomatic and Consular Staff in Tehran case. Third by Interim Measures of Protection: if the applicant State considers its disputed rights in immediate danger, it may make a request for speedy interim measures to restrain the respondent from acts that may jeopardize the Court's decision during the process. This option has been increasingly used by parties in recent years. Fourth by Joinder of Proceedings: by initiative of the Court two proceedings on the same arguments may be joined if only to spare time and costs. Fifth by Intervention: third parties may find their interests involved in a case to which they are not a party. They may then request permission to intervene.

There are two other ways in which a case can be concluded prematurely and these are, first, a settlement between parties, which incidentally did not happen after 1946, and second, the discontinuance of a case if both parties agree to withdraw. This in fact happened several times. The usual way to end a case, however, is the proper judgment of the Court at the end of its deliberations. These latter consist of, first, the study of the arguments and a brief exchange of preliminary views, whereupon each judge prepares a written note. These notes then invite a first round of deliberations and an exchange of views, resulting in the constituting of a Drafting Committee of three. This committee prepares a preliminary draft judgment, which is circulated, resulting in an amended version which is again amply discussed and finally adopted. Decisions are taken by absolute majority with the President having a casting vote. The results of the votes are recorded in the minutes.

Unlike in arbitral procedures, the judgment itself is read in open Court and given maximum publicity. At the very moment of delivery of the judgment by the President, agents of the parties are handed a sealed copy of the text; a third copy is kept in the archives of the Registry. After the session, journalists present are handed a press release summarizing the judgment. The full text is published as soon as possible, both in French and English. It also includes dissenting or separate opinions of judges.

According to civil law practice the text comprises an introduction featuring factual data, then the grounds for the Court's decision with arguments set forth in detail, and finally an operative paragraph formulating the decision properly speaking. In all cases the judgment is binding, final and without appeal. Revision can be applied for in view of the recent discovery of relevant facts hitherto unknown to the Court and to the parties. Appeals have to be made within ten years from the date of the Judgment and within six months from the discovery of the unknown facts.

part in any litigation. A second aspect was the increasing international unrest and dissatisfaction resulting from the financial crisis in the early thirties. The ensuing nationalism and radicalism which came to the fore in Italy and Japan and which in Germany swept the Weimar Republic, soon held the authority of the weakened League of Nations in absolute scorn.

In the final appreciation of most commentators though, it is the Court's own attitude in the second decade of its existence that undermined its authority and made it liable to severe criticism. The nadir of the Court was undoubtedly reached in 1931 when it was lured into rendering an advisory opinion on the openly political issue of the Customs

Union between Germany and Austria. It was this case which seriously undermined the belief in the effectiveness or even appropriateness of judicial means for the settlement of disputes other than of a purely legal nature. The Court never really overcame the blow and certainly never regained its former credit and authority. And in subsequent years the number of cases slackened alarmingly. Despite all the precautions taken, politization, clearly, had brought the Court down. The last public sitting was held on 4 December 1939. Since then, no business was dealt with and no new judges were elected. In 1940, as the Germans overran the Netherlands, the Court was moved to Geneva, leaving behind its Vice-President van Eysinga and a few Dutch Registry officials. Such then was the end of that "Great Bulwark of Peace", which after a fair start never really fulfilled its high promises. In its downfall it excited as little public agitation or distress as its all too technical proceedings had ever evoked popular support. It was a new Court, with new promises and under the auspices of a new political organization, that would return in 1946.

THE TRANSFER OF JURISDICTION

Already in 1942, London and Washington exchanged ideas as to the continuance or re-establishment of an international court after the war. These meetings resulted, early in 1943, in the raising of an informal inter-allied committee of experts which was to discuss the matter. Headed by Sir William Malkin, jurists from eleven countries met no less than nineteen times that year and on 10 Febru-

ary 1944 delivered a full report recommending the basing of the new court on the Statute of the dormant Permanent Court, suggesting that the advisory jurisdiction should be kept but the compulsory be abolished, and explicitly excepting political matters from its competence. The committee's suggestions were taken over a year later by a broader committee. This committee resulted from the meeting of the allied powers at Dumbarton Oaks near Washington, from 21 August until 7 October 1944. Here definite proposals for the establishment of a general international organization, including a court of justice, had been worked out.

The new committee of jurists met in Washington in April 1945 under the chairmanship of the American Hackworth and represented no less than forty-four States. It drew up a draft Statute to be submitted to the San Francisco Conference which in April-June 1945 was to define the United Nations

Detail from the panel "Aeneas receiving through Venus his new armour from Vulcan's smithy" (Virg. Aen. VIII 370–385).

Detail from the "Offering of Presents at the Building of Solomon's Temple" (I Kings 9:11,14 and 10:25) by Ferdinand Bol (1618–1682).

altogether by 1670. Typically enough, he ended his days in luxury twelve years later.

With Bol, lucrative portraits and groupings of dignitaries alternate with trendy, huge historical pieces on biblical and mythological themes in a classicist mood with increasingly baroque overtones. To be sure, this is not to belittle the obvious quality of anything he set himself to do. The four examples found in the Peace Palace by courtesy of the *Rijksdienst Verspreide Kunstvoorwerpen* (National Loan Collection) and part of the collection of the *Rijksmuseum* are in all respects representative of the artist's style. Three of them are found in the Bol Room, the fourth in the Board's Administration Room downstairs. The first panel (407 × 493 cm.) represents the finding of Moses, based on *Exodus* 2:5-7. The rather striking overall impression of the piece is that of a sensual pastorale. Actually, the piece is a "profanation" of the theme and comes within the classical tradition of the goddess Diana and her nymphs taking a bath.

The second panel (407 × 415 cm.) offers similar problems. It has been known as *Joseph's Cup Discovered in Benjamin's Cornbag*, based on *Genesis* 44:12. However, the panel offers a striking resemblance to another piece by Bol, now in the *Rijksmuseum*, which was produced in 1669 on behalf of the eldermen of the Zuiderkerk in Amsterdam and bears the title *The Offering of Presents at the Building of Solomon's Temple* (based on *I Kings* 9:11,14 and 10:25). The piece is noteworthy for its robust "Jordaenesque" style.

The third panel (407 × 415 cm.) has long been known as *Achilles receiving his new Suit of Arms in Vulcan's Smithy* (based on *Iliad* XVIII 368–616). However, the setting with Amor, Venus' steady companion, leads Blankert (who in 1976 devoted a thesis to Bol's works on which we draw here) into presuming that the infinitely more popular scene in Virgil's *Aeneid* is meant here (*Aen.* VIII 370–385), where Venus collects the armour on behalf of Aeneas. Blankert renamed the panel *Aeneas receiving through Venus his new armour from Vulcan's Smithy*. The setting, incidentally, strikingly resembles a work by Luca Giordano in London.

The fourth panel (407 × 275 cm.) is found in the Board's Administration room. It was long thought to represent *King Amasia and the Man of God*, based on *II Chronicles* 25:7. Again, Blankert, mainly on the strength of a preparatory drawing in the *Rijksprentenkabinet*, renamed the picture *The Prince of the Lord's Army visiting Joshua at Jericho*, (based on *Joshua* 5:13).

As regards the dating of the pieces nothing much can be ascertained: the second was presumably produced somewhere around 1669, the third around 1660. All four of them are by all means from Bol's later years.

THE FERDINAND BOL ROOM

"The finding of Moses", based on Exodus 2:5-7.

A special section should be devoted to the meeting rooms of the Court in the Palace. We have already mentioned that on entering, in 1922, the Permanent Court of International Justice took possession of several rooms which had hitherto belonged to other institutions. Among these was a salon with a 17th-century Dutch style interior, situated on the first floor of the left side-façade and a worthy counterpart to the Japanese Room that was situated around the corner and reserved for the Court of Arbitration. The salon under consideration here is called the Ferdinand Bol Room, after the artist who painted the three masterpieces that cover the walls. It was used for deliberations by the Permanent Court of International Justice. In recent days this function has been taken over by the modern facilities offered in the new wing that was built on behalf of the Court in 1978. The name of Ferdinand Bol has a ring which is mainly due to his affinity with Rembrandt. Bol is generally considered the master's best pupil. Indeed, through the ages the works of the two have frequently been interchanged which has sometimes resulted in painful démasqués. It is only due to the advanced techniques of modern research that art historians can step by step proceed in disentangling the two. And yet, there is little quarrel at least about one thing, as to which was the greater talent, the master's or the pupil's. As much as Rembrandt soon

outreached his own master Pieter Lastman, no less Bol remained forever Rembrandt's pupil.

Bol was born in Dordecht in 1616, a barber's son. At twenty he moved to Rembrandt's bustling studio in Amsterdam to become "a man of his own" about 1640. However, the problem with Bol is precisely that he never really became a master of his own. In his younger years, understandably, he is virtually overwhelmed by the genius of Rembrandt. But later on the Flemish painters, Rubens, van Dyck, Jordaens, take Rembrandt's place with him, and he then proceeds to copy their styles with the same virtuosity and gentle ease that is typical of his style throughout. If anything, it was the artist's soul and obsession that Bol was missing, and perhaps originality – rather than talent or genius anyway. His heydays are the fifties and sixties when he is literally overloaded with commissions and showered with compliments by the Amsterdam regent class. Mantelpieces of his are proudly shown in townhalls all over Holland. Meanwhile, his personal life was less fortunate. Having married a regent's daughter in 1653 but having lost her and three out of four children by 1660, he remarried in 1669, upon which the ample wealth of his new wife enabled him to retire. None too early, one is tempted to say, as the last years up to then had shown little but endless repetition. Never resourceful at his best, his vein had run dry

Charter. Based on the 1936 Statute of the Permanent Court, the draft was examined at San Francisco by fifty States, who gladly fell in with the proposals and Statute, meanwhile definitely voting in favour of dissolving the Permanent Court and creating a new Court. For this they had several sound reasons: first and ideologically, the Permanent Court represented an older social order and an organization (the League of Nations) which was now on the point of dissolution. Worst of all, however, it reflected the no-longer acceptable political and legal dominance of the Old World. Second, and more practical, the present meeting of States did not overlap the member States of the League. Third, the new court was to become a proper organ of the new organization, the United Nations, on the same footing as the General Assembly, the Security Council and the kind. Consequently, all member States of the United Nations were *ipso facto* to become parties to the new Court's Statute.

Accordingly, the judges of the Permanent Court of International Justice met for the last time in October 1945, when they entrusted their jurisdiction, along with their archives, to the new Court, and then – on 31 January 1946 – resigned. On 5 February following the new judges were elected in the First Session of the United Nations General Assembly. Hereupon the Permanent Court was formally dissolved and on 18 April the new International Court of Justice held its inaugural public sitting, electing as its president the last president of the former Court, Judge Guerrero, and appointing in the Registry many of the former officials. A new Court had been established.

The International Court of Justice (1946–)

SOME GENERAL REMARKS

The formal continuance of the succeeding Courts cannot better be demonstrated than by the fact that the revised Statute of 1936 fifty years afterwards still rules the Court's functioning. In 1946, without amendments, its seventy articles were annexed to the one hundred and eleven articles of the United Nations Charter. They were not incorporated, mainly for practical reasons: the present option facilitates the access of non-members of the United Nations to the Court. This Statute still holds unchallenged. There has been no demand for amendment so far.

What has been changed twice, though, in the course of the past forty years are the Rules of Court. These Rules amplify the provisions of the Statute, without of course extending the powers of the Court or stipulating provisions that are repugnant to the Statute. The amendments to the Rules, which were adopted in 1972 and 1978, were mainly inspired by the quickening pace of international life and aimed at increasing the flexibility of proceedings by simplifying and accelerating procedures and reducing the costs for parties.

The Court had good reasons for this. For all the smoothness of the transfer of 1946, the States initially showed considerable hesitance in applying to the Hague Court. As early as 1947 the General Assembly of the United Nations felt the need to devote a resolution on the matter. The same happened fifteen years later when, after flourishing in the fifties, the Court was again confronted with an apparent reluctance of States to submit cases. From an average of two or three cases yearly in the fifties, the Court's activities had almost fallen flat in the early sixties. The Registry received but a single case between July 1962 and August 1971.

Following a summons to the nations by the Secretary-General, then Burma's U Thant, in 1970, the General Assembly saw fit to examine the Court's role, analyse the obstacles to its satisfactory functioning and look for yet unexplored possibilities. The ensuing resolution of November 1974 effectively led to a renewed increase in cases, which ran from one to three per year during 1972 to 1985 with a marked increase in the eighties. In recent years, the average has been four indeed. All in all, in the forty-two years of the Court's existence, which incidentally equals the term of its predecessor, seventy-five cases were filed in the Court, sixteen

October 1945: The last session of the Permanent Court before its resignation on 31 January 1946. The session is presided over by Judge Guerrero.

Left: The Court's President Guerrero at his desk. In the background Blommers' portrait of Carnegie (see also page 36).

Right: The programme of the inaugural public sitting.

of which were discontinued or removed from the list. The Court delivered fifty judgments, twenty advisory opinions and two hundred and forty-seven orders. At present the Court has four cases in consideration.

CASES AND PERSPECTIVE

Above: The inauguration of the International Court of Justice on 18 April 1946. H.R.H. Princess Juliana and Prince Bernhard of the Netherlands listen to the speech of Mr. Paul-Henri Spaak (1899–1972), then President of the General Assembly of the UN.

Below: The first session of the International Court of Justice.

Over the years, and with the development of international law, the province of the Court has widened and deepened. Today there is no judicial organ to be found in the world equal to the Hague Court in its capacity for dealing with the legal problems of the international community as a whole. Certainly, the Court has its limitations, indeed they are many and of great consequence. Thus, the Court's competence does not reach private persons and it can only assist international organizations through an advisory role.

INTERNATIONAL COURT OF JUSTICE

AGENDA

of the public inaugural sitting to be held at the Peace Palace, The Hague, on April 18th, 1946, M. Guerrero, President of the Court, presiding.

1. Opening of the sitting; address of welcome by the President to Her Royal Highness the Princess of the Netherlands and His Royal Highness the Prince of the Netherlands.
2. Reading by the Registrar of Article 20 of the Statute of the Court concerning the solemn declaration to be made by members of the Court.
3. The making of the solemn declaration by each member of the Court.
4. Speech by H. E. M. Spaak, President of the General Assembly of the United Nations.
5. Speech by H. E. M. Kerno, Under-Secretary-General of the United Nations, representing the Security Council, the Economic and Social Council, and the Secretary-General of the United Nations.
6. Speech by H. E. Dr. van Roijen Minister for Foreign Affairs of the Netherlands.
7. Speech by M. de Monchy, Burgomaster of The Hague.
8. Speech by the President of the Court.
9. Closure of the sitting.

At the conclusion of the sitting, tea will be served in the Hall of the Palace.

What the Court is, essentially, is an organ of law, more precisely of international law. It dispenses justice, and this within well-defined limits. In doing so it takes into consideration current international conventions in as far as recognized by parties, makes research into past and present international custom as evidence of a general and durable practice accepted as law, and bases its decisions on the general principles of law as recognized by civilized nations. As further subsidiary instruments, it scrutinizes previous judicial decisions and the teachings and publications of experts. In principle, and if requested so by parties, a decision in the light of the justice and pure merits of a case can be envisaged – in a decision *ex aequo et bono* as it is called.

Over the years, through practice, the Court has covered a wide range of issues and examined virtually all legal systems. Presumably, there are not too many mantraps and pitfalls it has not focussed on some time or other. This is not to say that the Court is working "for art's sake only". It is not an academic institution. Certainly, in investigating international law, it has developed international law. In achieving this, the Court's publications have been extremely valuable, too. Its Judgments and Advisory Opinions have been published since 1922 in parallel series, supplemented by several others, containing documents and speeches, Rules of the Court and collections of treaties that govern its jurisdiction, Annual Reports and Annual Lists of Publications, and a General Index on cases.

The Court's goals in the long run, however, are set higher and are in fact very practical, namely, by affirming the role of law in society, and helping maintain a durable peace and friendly relations

among States. It is here indeed that the Court's primary aims are situated, in that it indicates the legally most feasible solution to existing or future disputes of a given character. In this way, its case-law has often proved pivotal to legislators and codifiers.

We cannot attempt a full listing of cases here. Let us start by saying that among the cases are a number of signal successes. In the Anglo-Iranian Oil Co. case of 1951 the Court competently dealt with a dispute which bore the seeds of an international crisis in it, not unlike the U.S. v. Iran case on the hostages in 1979–1981. In matters of the Law of the Sea the Court has been able to support the successive United Nations Conferences and the International Law Commission. It has defined basic criteria governing the delimitation of territorial waters, affirmed the concept of the "economic zone" as part of international law and applied new principles with regards to the continental shelf issue. The Corfu

Channel, Anglo-Norwegian Fisheries, North Sea Continental Shelf and Fisheries Jurisdiction (Cod War) cases were each of them a major help in these respects. Likewise, the Court has discussed worldwide problems of environmental law and even considered the constituting of a separate chamber on these issues. The previous president, Mr. Nagendra Singh, highlighted this field during the 40th anniversary celebrations of the Court.

In the economic field also, as in matters of foreign investment, the Court contributed to the state of the law by indicating the deficiencies of the applicable law and suggesting remedies. The scope of judgments further involved such different issues as State responsibility (the internationally wrongful act and its consequences), the law of international organizations (Reparations case), matters of asylum, the right of passage and aspects of nationality. The Court has shown considerable flexibility and keen

The "Maiden of Amsterdam" holding the hat of liberty and waiting to be crowned by "putti" with the "corona navalis", illustrating her mercantile power, hence also the escorting Mercury. Detail from the ceiling triptych by Gérard de Lairesse (1672).

GÉRARD DE LAIRESSE'S CEILING TRIPTYCH

Apart from Bol's masterpiece the Ferdinand Bol Room contains another set of paintings which are considered among the best in its genre. These concern a triptych on the ceiling by Gérard de Lairesse. The strange thing about these paintings is that they were bought in 1903 by the Carnegie Foundation (at Dfl. 8,300) on the strength of an interpretation which afterwards proved wrong. The paintings certainly do not represent an allegory on the "Triumph of Peace" or the "Munster Peace Treaty" as was thought. However the purchase did save the works from demolition. They came from a patrician's home in Amsterdam (Herengracht 446) and were auctioned at Frederik Muller's. Gérard de Lairesse (1640–1711) was a native of Liège in Belgium. At twenty-five, an amorous incident forced him to take refuge in the Netherlands, where he soon gravitated to Amsterdam, the flamboyant centre of the arts, then in the heyday of its mercantile and cultural expansion. From 1665 onwards, from his modest lodgings at the Nieuwmarkt, Lairesse had a perfect view of the frenetic building activities all along the ever-widening girdle of canals and the Dam where de Keyser's Town Hall, known today as the Royal Palace and crowning effort of the period, was soon to be finished. Major patrician houses like the "Trippenhuis" (present seat of the Royal Netherlands Academy) arose around the corner. Lairesse soon gained local fame as a painter and engraver and in his turn was enchanted by the charms of the artistic and literary circles. In his work he drew from van Scorel, Goltzius and Romein de Hooghe. Both in matters of subject and style, his canvasses were steeped in the French classicism that rapidly became en vogue in the Amsterdam intellectual circles of the time. Nicolas Poussin and Raphael

were his favourites. Like so many of his contemporaries, he was not particularly charmed by the more natural style of Rembrandt – or for that matter Bol. With the years Lairesse grew on particularly friendly terms with men like Andries Pels and Lodewijk Meyer, major characters in *Nil volentibus arduum*, the Amsterdam chamber of rhetoric and initiators of the *Dietsche Academie*, the first Amsterdam playhouse. Hence came his literary interests, which served him well from 1689 onwards as, a tragic incident, blindness struck him within a year. From then on he earned a living by lecturing on the theory and practice of painting and wrote two monographs *The Art of Drawing* (1701) and *The Great Book of Painting* (1707). It is from these works that we learn more about his techniques in creating the triptych now on the ceiling in the Peace Palace. The work was produced in 1672 on a commission by Andries de Graeff, a former Amsterdam burgomaster, to decorate his newly built house on the Herengracht. Only recently decorators had begun replacing the traditional wooden cassettes in the ceilings (formed by the crossings of beams and rafters) that were usually painted with birds, fruit or flowers, by vaulted arches or flat timber panels which invited larger scenes. Thus, both in the Dam Town Hall and the Trippenhuis allegorical paintings had been installed celebrating the noble feats of their inhabitants among scores of hovering *putti* and alluring naiads. More than this, Lairesse soon perceived, that the modern technical facilities offered new artistic challenges, inviting panoramic vistas on heavens which could be linked quite naturally with images on the adjoining mural paintings. With the commission by de Graeff came his first opportunity to eat the pudding.

Lairesse's work of 1672 is not exactly typical of his later style. It is admittedly an early work, featuring the warm colours which are rare in later works of his hand, as can be seen from later ceiling paintings formerly of the Leper House, now in the *Rijksmuseum*. The present work is, however, outstanding mainly for two reasons. First, it is made on canvas, not wood, which was a novelty at the time. Second, it illustrates the artist's mastery over the perspective – or rather the illusion of perspective, and in this it became a model for many artists to follow. As Lairesse taught, the painting of ceilings required special techniques and many dodges like shortening lines or fading colours to obtain the "natural" effect. In his monographs cited above he pleads the scientific approach that comes with learning and experiment. He expounds on the mathematical perspective founded in France by Bosses, but which had been neglected in Holland up to his day, and tells of his applying mirrors and all sorts of strange instruments to master the art. Incidentally he points out numerous mistakes in the works of predecessors like Correggio and Vouet. Now as to the interpretation of the triptych. In the middle panel (measuring 4.40 × 2.27 m.) a maiden sits on a throne high on the clouds, holding the hat of freedom and flanked by Mercury. She represents Amsterdam's mercantile liberty and is about to be crowned with *putti* with the *corona navalis*. At her feet a roaring lion with flaming sword and heavy shield, on which feature the town's emblem of the three St. Andrew crosses, stands ready to defend the lady's honour atop rocks which feature date and signature. On the left panel (4.40 × 1.90 m.) Concordia tramples down the enchained Mars, whereas on the right panel (4.40 × 1.78 m.), of which incidentally a study in red crayon is kept at the Louvre, the helmeted Minerva is seen vanquishing the three Harpies: Violence, Envy and Fraud. The river gods of Y and Amstel, imperative to Amsterdam's prosperity, feature in the left and right bottom corners. Now, oddly enough, in the Peace Palace the two smaller paintings are interchanged: the river gods flank the Amsterdam lion back to back. This is obviously due to the misinterpretation of the triptych, which in itself is a puzzle as in terms of 17th-century iconology there can be little doubt as to the panel's meaning. Concord, Freedom and Security here are the counterparts of the virtues found in the Amsterdam coat of arms: Valour, Determination and Charity. In later days Glauber copied the ceilings in engravings.
To conclude this Dutch 17th-century style room we find above the door openings, carved in light oak panels again produced by Herman Rosse, the busts of Hugo Grotius and Cornelis van Bynckershoek, the two renowned Dutch international lawyers of the 17th and 18th centuries.

Hugo Grotius (1583–1645) carved by local craftsmen in timber from the grounds. The legend reads: "Melior post aspera fata resurgo" ("Adversity strengthens me").

historical insight in interpreting the law of treaties, thus paving the way for the Vienna Convention of 1969 in this area. Finally, it valliantly faced the juridical technicalities involved with virtually virgin fields such as outer space law and the impact of nuclear power.

Not unlike its predecessor, the International Court of Justice has lived through moments of crisis as well. Indeed, it would be wrong to suggest that today the Court is functioning to the full satisfaction of its critics, internal or external. Obviously, there is still much to be desired in the field of international law and over the years this situation has quite naturally also invited suggestions as to adjusting or extending the Court's competence. What have been the major obstacles to the Court's optimal functioning in past decades?

From the beginning, in 1946, despite all good intentions, major setbacks asserted themselves in the political sphere. The Cold War, which dominated activities within the United Nations in the fifties to the point of frustrating its initial impetus, inevitably had its repercussions on the Court. Some of the Court's advisory opinions on human rights in Eastern Europe in 1949–1950 clearly reflected this atmosphere. Another handicap to the proper functioning of both the United Nations and the Court was the non-representation of the superpower China, in the United Nations until 1971, in the Court until 1985. These, admittedly, were basically external factors. But on top of this came the politicization of the United Nations itself in the sixties, the effects of which did not miss the Court either.

In these respects, reviewing the cases the Court has dealt with, there is one field which the commentator has to single out here, if only for the psychological impact it had, and this concerns the issues of decolonization. No area in recent years better serves to illustrate the need on the part of the Court of a keen eye for the evolution of law as a reflection of social changes. We refer to the four advisory opinions (1950, 1955, 1956, 1971) and two judgments (1962, 1966), the Court rendered on matters of South West Africa and Namibia.

To many commentators, the date of 18 July 1966 will remain memorable as the black day in the Court's post-war history. That day, with the slightest

of majorities, the Court delivered what has been called its "most political and least worthy" judgment, in dismissing a challenge made by Ethiopia and Liberia to South Africa's racial policies and its violation of its mandatory obligations in South West Africa. The uproar this incident caused reminds one of the Customs Union case before the Permanent Court in 1931. The judgment occasioned debate regarding the future role of the Court and led to numerous suggestions for enhancing its effectiveness. At the time it also resulted in the African States' insistence on the reconstruction of the Court's composition and, to all likeliness, in the dramatic, if temporary, decrease of cases submitted to the Court in subsequent years.

Fortunately, the storm died down some years later when, in 1970–1971, in the case of Namibia, the Court availed itself of the opportunity to "rehabilitate" itself and stress its views with regard to the primordial role of the principle of self-determination and of man's fundamental rights regardless of race, colour, descent or ethnic origin. In doing so the Court has stressed its readiness to recognize the evolving nature of law. Likewise, on other occasions, the Court did not fail to point out the States' obligations *erga omnes,* that is the international community as a whole.

Thus, the Court was able to restore its former authority and regain the confidence of the Third World. As a matter of fact, the actual increase of cases in recent years has been also due to the application to the Court by these groups of nations. The election of the present Registrar in 1987 therefore in a way reflects a current tendency.

Meanwhile, the sharp reactions to the Court's "failures", if justly coined so, in the sixties, also bear evidence to the primary role generally, if not preferably, attributed to the institution as "the world's ultimate conscience". If anything, it is in the moral area that, alongside the strictly legal field, the World's Supreme Judicial College is expected to make its authority felt throughout. In rendering judgment and advice, and by its pivotal function in weighing claims for legal change against those for the enforcement of established rights, the Court has the privilege of exerting distinct influence on the progressive development of law.

In October 1983 Burkina Faso (then Upper Volta) and Mali applied to a chamber of the Court in order to have their frontier dispute settled. In January 1986, following grave incidents, interim measures were indicated. The judgement was given on 22 December 1986.

Left: His Excellency Judge José Maria Ruda (born 1924), member of the International Court of Justice since 1973 and President since 1988.

Over the years, discontent with the standing of international law has led commentators to examine the Court's effectiveness. There have been critics who thought that the Court was lacking an adequate theory of change in customary international law. Against this it may be argued that guidance from governments has often been meagre. Any court needs cases to prove its worth, and it is precisely the reluctance of States to submit basic issues to it, if only from fear of losing their autonomy, which in the end must injure the Court's authority.

Again, it has been heard that the genesis of the European and Inter-American Courts of Human Rights or the International Tribunal for Law of the Sea has impaired the Court's authority. The one area, however, is not within the International Court's competence proper, and the other field is growing more technical each day. In both fields, therefore, the new courts are very welcome additions.

Finally, in their quest for a better-organized society, commentators have pondered over the possible expansion of the Court's province by broadening its competence and opening it up to new classes of litigants: to international organizations for contentious cases, to municipal courts for preliminary decisions and to litigants for the review of international law questions decided by municipal courts. Numerous objections can be raised against each of these proposals, though they would indeed mean a sharp increase of cases and thus further international law. Whatever may come of this, within the

Advisory Opinion of the Court dated 27 May 1987 in the "Application for Review of Judgement No. 333 of the United Nations Administrative Tribunal".

boundaries set, today, applying to the International Court of Justice undoubtedly offers the most satisfactory way to obtain a reasonable and depoliticized judgment in matters of international law.

Constitution of the Court: Organization, Jurisdiction and Procedures

COMPOSITION OF THE COURT

In its full flowering, that is since the coming into force of the Revised Statute in 1936, the Court consists basically of fifteen judges; initially there had been eleven only. Occasional suggestions to increase the number have failed so far. The judges are nominated, interestingly enough, on the recommendation of national groups – actually in much the same way as in the Permanent Court of Arbitration. These groups consult their Supreme Courts, Law Academies and the kind. They then come up with four candidates, two of them at the most of their own nationality. Once the lists of candidates have been submitted to the United Nations, the election takes place, simultaneously, but separately, in the General Assembly and the Security Council. Elections are held every third year in the annual autumn session of the General Assembly. New judges enter upon their term on 6 February of the following year. Judges are elected for a term of nine years and are re-eligible.

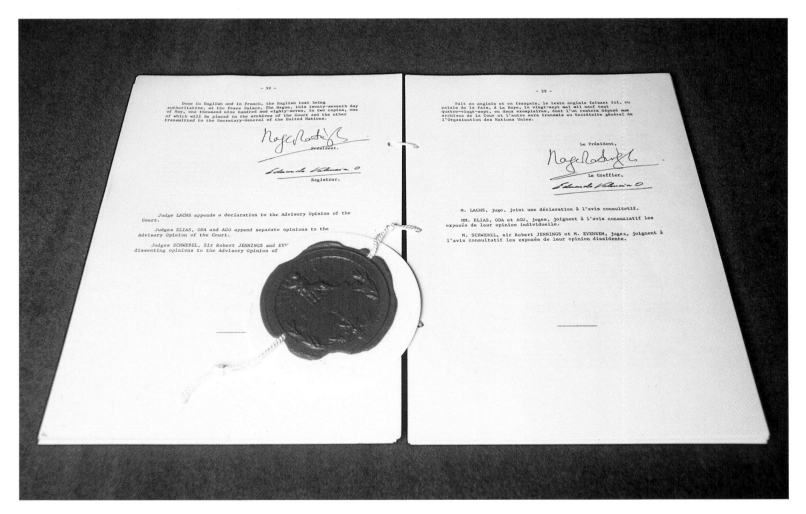

THE GREAT HALL

Above: "La Paix par la Justice" by P. Albert Besnard (1849–1934), one of the gifts of France.

Opposite left: "Peace Achieved". The fourth panel of the stained glass windows by Douglas Strachan offered by the United Kingdom in 1913. The legend reads: "Redeunt Saturnia Regna" ("The Realm of Saturn [= Golden Age] returns", taken from Virgil's Eclogues.

The Great Hall of the Hague Court is an impressive room, if only for its dimensions. It is decorated with exquisite oak panelling, colourful rugs and sparkling chandeliers of Bohemian crystal. Its walls are embellished by lofty latin maxims and notably by a French gift, the painting by Albert Besnard representing *Peace through Justice* and featuring the goddess separating belligerents beneath a scene in which philosophers are disputing. By far the most striking element of the Hall though is the four stained windows by Douglas Strachan, presented by the United Kingdom. The central theme of these highly elaborated and allegorical windows is the Evolution of the Peace Ideal, and this theme is developed throughout in its four phases (from left to right): the Primitive Age, the Age of Conquest, the Present Age and the Achievement of Peace. In the successive windows one discerns the gradual development of human intelligence and civilization based on the firm belief of a World Force greater than man: from self-preservation, through fallacies of military power and industrial suprema- cy, man is led into an age that sees war as a monstrous folly. Keeping in step with this, even the colouring of the windows is allegorical: white is adopted as a background – if only for the lighting of the Court – and seen as symbolic of peace. Likewise the colour schemes of the windows express the mood of the period concerned. The windows each consist of four main panels and separate upper parts.

The first panel of the Primitive Age represents Mother Earth at the First Dawn with the Hunter in the fore- ground. The second panel contains the Keeper of Sheep, who first abstained from killing. Hunter and Shepherd are prototypes of Warrior and Pacifist. The third panel represents the Tiller of the Ground and the Harvesters of the Fruits of the Earth. The mid-distance of the second and third panels are linked and compare the cave-dwelling and early cultivation on the left to the discovery of fire on the right, not unlike the bases where the ship of the adventurous wanderer is put next to the nesting bird typifying the home-loving man. The fourth panel introduces metal working and the strife and slaughter caused by migratory movements. The Signs of the Zodiac at the top parallel man's progress on earth to the larger progression through space. The upper lights represent the mental outlook of the Age, here typified successively in Terror and Worship of natural phenomena, the four elements, the four seasons and the four phases of man.

The first panel of the Age of Conquest contains the energetic Conqueror with Bloodthirst and Greed in the lower sections. The second and third panels are linked again: huge walls protect the Conqueror against invaders. On the barren fields all Industry has vanished and Peace and Love are held in bonds. On the fourth panel, amid ruins of architecture and utter desolation, up comes the Constructive Spirit visionary of Justice and Peace. In the upper lights Bellona, the war goddess, and her hordes preceded by Hunger and Death redden the heavens.

In the first panel of the Present Age an optimistic view is expressed. Vital Energy and Construction are key words here, representing Industrial Revolution and man's insight that war and massacre stand in the way of produc- tion and may be replaced by peaceful settlement of disputes. The second panel stands for Finance and Labour, the brain and the body that determine the issue of war and thereby man's progress. Finance is depicted scrutiniz- ing the globe and keeping his finger on the telegraph machine; Labour holds Bellona enchained. The third panel illustrates the Enlightenment through Science. By conceiving dreadful war engines of destruction science is the best deterrent of war, as by providing medical care it alleviates suffering. The fourth panel represents the Philosopher and the Arts as Peacemakers. The beauty of life they reveal is expressed in the crystal, ivory and silver fountain and the crystal image of Peace they have fashioned. The minor upper panels represent the four quarters of the earth seeking mutual understanding, though balancing between a peaceful spirit (on the left) and distrust (on the right). The fourth window, Peace Achieved, announces a new age of human development. In the upper panels the

Order, Harmony and Immensity of the Universe are depicted hiding the mystery of man's destiny. The main panels tell a story on three levels from left to right. Below, the Peoples of the Earth, guided by the Phoenix, migrate from the ruined fortress on the left to the New City on the right under the aegis of the Hippogriff. In the middle section figure the Swordbreaker and Plenty on the left, Destiny weaving a tapestry of increasingly white and candid patterns in the middle, and leading Statesmen, Scientists and Philosophers on the right. In the upper portion of the second panel Arbitration can be discerned with the Four Quar- ters of the Earth, North and South hold- ing the balance, East and West abiding by the verdict. In the third panel Bellona dies in the arms of Peace.

The windows indeed represent the best of cultural traditions. The symbols and allegories are topical from classical to modern times, in the literary and plastic arts alike. It is only in recent decades that we have forgotten to understand, if not appreciate them. Typical of the atmosphere are, too, the latin legends which run along the windows in banderoles: "Non galeae, non enses erant: sine militis usu / mollia securae peragebant otia gentes" read the hexameters on the first window: "Helmet nor sword were found; man lived in peace without any need of the military". The words echo the nostalgia for the pristine ages when lamb and lion lived in perfect harmony. The idea is repeated in the legends of the fourth window which are, significantly, taken from Virgil's Fourth Eclogue: "Redeunt Saturnia Regna", "The Golden Age Returns". But in between, no doubt about it, the laws of the Iron Age rule. The second panel, again taken from Virgil, echoes Juno's address to Allecto in *Aeneid* VII 335–338: "Tu potes unanimos armare in proelia fratres / atque odiis versare domos, tu verbera tectis / funereasque inferre faces, tibi nomina mille / mille nocendi artes..." ("You know well how to set brothers, united in love, at armed conflict one against the other. You can wreck homes by hate and bring scourges and fire- brands of death within their walls. You have a thousand types of mischief, a thousand artful ways of doing harm." – W. F. Jackson Knight). The legends of the third panel, which have a Lucretian ring, are: "Sensim vis efficit ipsa vivida naturae, ut cessent fera moenera Martis..." ("Unnoticed, Nature by her vital force herself puts an end to the grim works of Mars").

The panelling and furniture of the Hall were produced by Pander & Sons after a design of W. Retera from timber shipped in from the Dutch Indies. The ceiling was designed by K. Sluyterman. The sculptured figures representing *Veritas* (Truth) and *Justitia* were sculp- tured by Toon Dupuis. The six chande- liers were designed by B. Ingenhousz and produced by Braat of Delft.

At each triennial election five judges are elected, one-third of the Court. This does not imply that the whole Court is replaced within three elections or nine years: as said before, judges may be re-elected. Should a judge die or resign during his term, a special election is held.

Once installed, the new Court proceeds to elect, by secret ballot and absolute majority, its president and vice-president for the new term of three years. The president must reside at The Hague at all times, the other members of the bench have to be on stand-by at first summons.

In the election of judges two aspects mainly are borne in mind. First, of course, the moral qualifications and legal competence of the candidates. Over the years judges have been chosen from professors of law, barristers and judges mainly, most of these with ample administrative experience, varying from legal adviser to head of State. Normally they have previously been members of similar bodies such as the Permanent Court of Arbitration or the United Nations International Law Commission or have been delegates to the General Assembly, Security Council or major conferences. Experienced and consummate jurists without exception, their average age during office is about sixty-five, the average length of their term something over nine years. The all-time record of twenty-one years which was long held by Judge Winiarski, has only this year been broken by another Polish member of the bench, Judge Lachs.

The second consideration in the elections is the fair representation in the Court of the world's principal legal systems and civilizations. Today this distribution, which is made corresponding to that in the Security Council, is: Africa three, Latin America two, Asia three, Western Europe and others, including the United States, five, Eastern Europe two. Candidates must obtain an absolute majority in both electing bodies, Assembly and Council. In case of disagreement a joint committee is to deal with any remaining vacancies, whereas in the last resort judges are chosen by co-optation of the elected members of the Court. In practice no complications of the kind have ever arisen.

Although members do not represent their nations or governments and enjoy perfect independence as to their voting, of which they have, indeed, given ample evidence over the years, the Court is unable to have two members of the same nationality. No chances are thus taken in preserving the Court's impartiality. Entanglements are also precluded by the suppression of possibly incompatible offices.

Members of the Court enjoy the immunities and privileges of diplomats. Indeed, at The Hague, the president takes precedence over the doyen of the diplomatic corps, after which there is an alternation of precedence as between judges and ambassadors.

The previous survey does not tell the full story of the Court's composition. When their nationality is not represented in the Court, parties are

His Holiness Pope John Paul II, visiting the Court on 13 May 1985, is welcomed by the Court's President H. E. Judge Nagendra Singh of India.

permitted, if not obliged, each to submit a judge *ad hoc*. As far as figures go, the value of this provision has proven itself over the years. From 1946 onwards no less than forty judges have sat *ad hoc* and several of these have become regular judges in later years. On the other hand, it shows from the records that over the decades judges have felt perfectly free to vote even against the stricter interests of the State of their nationality.

Apart from the *ad hoc* judges the Statute of the International Court also makes provisions for technical assessors, four in number, who are appointed by secret ballot, to attend meetings but without the right to vote. In practice no assessor has ever been elected.

THE REGISTRY

All administrative work and communications, either with the United Nations or with governments and international organizations, are entrusted to what is called the Registry. The name is somewhat misleading. Not unlike the Secretary of

*The actual registrar of the
Court, Mr. Eduardo Valencia-
Ospina of Colombia.*

the Permanent Court of Arbitration, this office has in fact the additional function of a secretariat to an international commission. It looks after contacts with universities, the press and the general public and also produces the publications, which are considerable indeed.

The office is headed by the Registrar, who in pursuance of the Statute resides at The Hague, has the rank of an Assistant Secretary-General of the United Nations and is elected by the Court, by secret ballot, for a seven-year term. In 1987, for the first time in the history of both Courts, a national of a Third World country, Mr. E. Valencia-Ospina from Colombia, was elected Registrar. The Registrar is the managing director of all departments including the budget. He is the channel for external communications, attends meetings of the Court, ensures that minutes are duly drawn up, countersigns the Court's decisions and has custody of its seal. He is assisted by a Deputy, secretaries and other officials.

Today, the staff comprises some forty permanent officials and many temporary officials, notably in the linguistic department. The Court's official languages are French and English; all the Registry members are required to be proficient in both, and most of them are native speakers in one of these languages. Expenses are borne by the United Nations to which the Member States pay their proportionate shares. At present the International Court takes about 1.5 per cent of the United Nations yearly budget – it was 2 per cent in 1946.

Noteworthy within the body of the Registry is the Court's Library. In 1922, one of the main reasons for the League of Nations to have the International Court situated in the Peace Palace, was the reputation of its book collection, which already served the Permanent Court of Arbitration. The arrangement made with the Carnegie Foundation therefore stipulated the use by the Court of this Library and storing facilities for its own small reference library. Following disagreement between the parties over the financial payment for these services, a new arrangement was drawn up in 1924, by which the Court's borrowing facilities were expanded and the Foundation also took it upon itself to make up for any shortcomings of the library in the field of national law, which threatened to seriously hamper the Court's functioning. In the annual reports of Dr. ter Meulen, the Peace Palace Librarian at the time, we find ample proof of the urgent needs of the Court in these respects, of his own lengthy negotiations with Mr. Hammarskjøld, the Court's time-honoured Registrar, and of his repeated requests to the Board of the Carnegie Foundation to have the budget raised and meet the Court's complaints.

However, in 1930, despite his frequent *caveats* by all means to preserve the unity of the collection, ter Meulen's old fears came true. The League voted a yearly credit of ten thousand florins on behalf of the Court's library and this meant the beginning of an independent collection. The Court formed a library-committee from its own ranks, contracted a staff member of ter Meulen, Douma, and from this moment on took care of all general reference works and acquisitions in the field of municipal law. Gifts from private collections, such

as by Judge Fromageot, soon helped extend the library which now comprises some 35,000 volumes (monographs, serialized works and periodicals) and a fine collection of documents issued by or relating to the United Nations and its predecessor, the League of Nations, many of these also on microfiches. Perhaps separate mention might be made of the archives of the Nuremburg war crimes tribunal, which are deposited with the Court, including the *verbatim* transcriptions of hearings.

The Court Library, the present staff of which is three, is not open to the public. It produces yearly bibliographies of books and articles by or relating to the Court and many lists, indexes and bibliographies for internal use only, most of these regarding current cases and advisory opinions. To this end research is made on behalf of the judges and the Registry.

FUNCTIONS OF THE COURT: CONTENTIOUS CASES

The International Court really has two functions: the settlement of international disputes by giving judgments in contentious cases and the rendering of advisory opinions upon requests to that end. We shall first discuss the adjudication of contentious cases.

Right: The first stamps with the imprint of the Court were issued in 1934, some bearing the dove, some the image of Queen Wilhelmina. On 18 May 1933, League of Nations Day, a special peace stamp with the star of David was issued. In 1940 a new series was issued with the erroneous imprint "International" which caused a slightly different reissue. The series bears the image of Queen Wilhelmina, as does the next series which was issued in 1947. All of these were regular Dutch stamps overprinted with a special imprint. In 1950, for the first time, a special stamp was designed and issued in a 2 and 4 cents version. These were discontinued on 18 March 1951 and successively replaced by two new series respectively bearing the image of the Peace Palace and Queen Juliana, the scales as a symbol of justice, the crown as symbol of royal dignity and the posthorn, the mark of the Post Office.

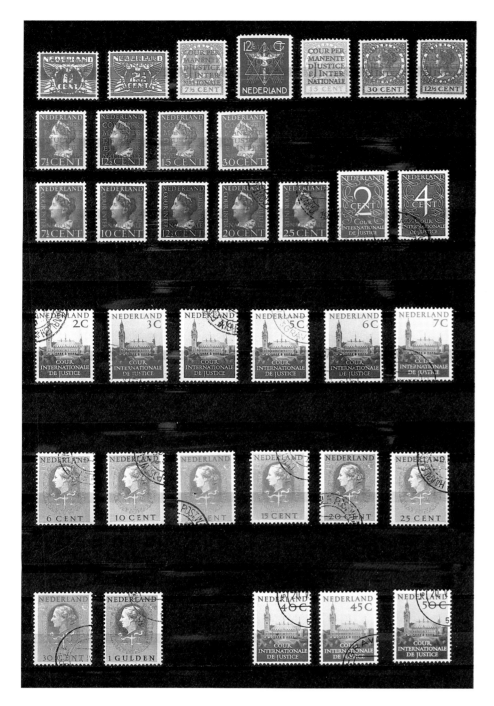

On the other hand the International Court is open to practically all States: that is, to regular members of the United Nations, to parties to the Court's Statute or to any other State that duly deposits a declaration of acceptance of the Court's jurisdiction with the Registry. For, in the last resort, the Court's jurisdiction depends on the formal consent of the parties to the particular dispute. This consent can be established in various ways: by "Special Agreement", being a compromis concluded by litigant parties to refer the dispute to the Court, or by the inclusion in an international treaty of a clause providing for the settlement of disputes by the Court or by a State declaring its acceptance of the Court's jurisdiction as compulsory, the so-called "optional clause" system.

This optional clause is much contested nowadays. On the dissolution of the League of Nations it was in force between thirty-two States out of the fifty that were parties to the Statute. At present, this number has come down to a meagre forty-six out of one hundred and fifty-nine nations. The clause is further jeopardized by all sorts of reservations found in at least thirty-four of the present forty-six declarations. These regard the term of jurisdiction, the eventual recourse to other methods of pacific settlement and the undesirability of the Court's infringement of domestic jurisdiction. The problem however is that all these reservations are reciprocal. This may result in highly frustrating experiences. Thus, the United States, having vainly tried to sue other States along these lines in seven previous cases, in recent years were a third time sued themselves, namely in the Nicaragua conflict. The incident finally led to the American withdrawal from the Court's proceedings at the time.

ADVISORY OPINIONS

The second activity of the Court concerns advisory opinions. There are two essential differences with the contentious cases here. First: the Court's opinions are indeed purely advisory and therefore have no binding force. Otherwise the full weight of the Court's prestige and authority endorses the advice which is as if sanctioned by international law. Second: the advisory procedure is available only to certain public international organizations. In the days of the Permanent Court this competence was extended to the League's Council and Assembly only. The International Court is currently open to no less than twenty-two organizations, including the United Nations agencies, ILO, FAO, IMO, WHO, IMF and Unesco. Oddly enough, though, the facility has been used less frequently in recent years than was the case with the Permanent Court: against twenty-seven instances between 1922 and 1935, are nineteen from 1946 to 1988. The most recent Advisory Opinion in April 1988, concerned the dispute between the United Nations and the United States Government in matters of the PLO- Observer Mission at the Unitid Nations Headquarters in New York.

In the province of adjudication the Hague Court is open to States only. Over the decades various proposals have been made to expand the competence of the Court to private persons, companies and international organizations. Even a treaty was drawn up providing for this kind of jurisdiction. The request was never granted, however, and unlike, for instance, the Court of Justice of the European Communities in Luxembourg and the European Court of Human Rights in Strasbourg, both applicant and respondent before the Hague Court must be States. Unfortunately, there is a persistent misunderstanding as to this competence in the world at large. Almost daily, often heart-rending and well-founded, written and oral applications from private persons come in to the Registry, which maintains, however, that it is unable to entertain them. Sadly enough, therefore, it can do little more than send the applicants a standard reply.

*The Peace Palace refectory
during the Academy-sessions.*

The Hague Academy of International Law

If the Courts that were described in the two previous chapters represent the wisdom that comes with age, the complementary institution that was founded in the Peace Palace in 1923 to round off the Hague *Trias Juridica* features the optimism of youth. Now sixty-five years in being, the Academy, as a keen observer remarked, "is as young at heart as one could wish. The spirit of innovation is part of its being". The Academy stands out in one other respect: here at last we have reached a chapter of undisputed success!

Probably the first mention ever of an "International Academy" was made in 1898 by the German Carl Ludwig von Bar (1836–1913), a later member of the Permanent Court of Arbitration. However, what von Bar had in mind was a quite different institution from the later Hague Academy. Realizing that obligatory arbitration would never fall in with the ideas of Emperor Wilhelm in matters of sovereignty, he proposed the founding of a consultative body of eminent scholars which could render services to the governments in cases of interstate conflict. Invested with high moral prestige, this Academy, through its advisory role would facilitate mediation and thus further the process of conciliation.

Two years later, in 1900, von Bar elaborated the idea in a commentary on the Russo-Finnish conflict and the Boer War. Though new, von Bar's plan was far from revolutionary. In fact, the proposal was a step backwards from the idea of the Arbitration Court. For sound reasons, therefore, protest was raised at this idea by the man who may be justly called the father of the Hague Academy, Otfried Nippold, the Bern professor (1864–1936). The role assigned to the Academy by von Bar, he argued, could as well be provided by the Court, even if no provisions to this extent were made by the 1899 Hague Convention. If, however, one wished to create a true academy of international law, in the sense of a permanent study centre and nursery for future scholars and diplomats, this institution could indeed fulfil a very welcome task complementary to the Court of Arbitration in developing an international code of law. In this way at The Hague theory and practice would go side by side.

It was this proposal, first expounded by Nippold in the *Deutsche Revue* of April 1907, which was subsequently submitted by this magazine's general editor, Richard Fleischer, to the President of the Second Hague Conference, de Nelidow. On 20 July following, de Nelidow referred to the idea in the third plenary meeting of the Conference, speaking of Nippold's "highly interesting suggestion" as of the *Asklepion* that had been founded in classical times by Hippocrates at Cos for the benefit of medical sciences. He also called on private initiative to raise the required funds.

A fortnight afterwards de Nelidow received a letter from Mr. Sturdza, Prime Minister of Romania, who pleaded "the linking of the achievement of the First Hague Conference, to wit arbitration, and the task set to the present gathering, international jurisdiction, by means of science, to be vested in an Academy". Enclosed in the letter Sturdza submitted the Statutes of such an institution, providing in seven Articles for a permanent seat at The Hague, for the appointment of ten members to be elected for a stipulated period by the Hague Conference from among prominent scholars, and for courses to be held between May and July in German, English, French and Italian. The costs, including the construction of a proper housing for this Academy, would be best met by the nations atttending the present conference. The funds were to be administered by the Administrative Council of the Hague Court and scholars remunerated from it. Nations would be permitted to send numbers of young diplomats, scholars, military men and officials to attend courses on all aspects of law in proportion to the governments' contributions.

De Nelidow communicated this proposal to the Conference in its plenary meeting of 7 September. The Conference, already overwhelmed by the burdens of its programme proper, decided to place the idea for the moment among its official papers, to be dug up "once the peacemaking institutions which the Conference was bound to create were sufficiently rooted to warrant the necessary continuity in the field of international law and a legal practice had been established which called for codifying". Despite an appeal made in the *Courrier de la Conférence* on 13 September, nothing was heard of it for the time being. Small wonder this was, though. In the midst of debate on matters of obligatory arbitration and the proposed court of jurisdiction, and faced by persistent German opposition, de Nelidow righteously anticipated that any sideline would be welcomed only too happily by the opponents of arbitration to obstruct the main issue of the Conference.

However, the idea met with instant approval at the van Lennepweg, the informal centre of International Pacifism arranged by Eykman and Horrix and serving among others as Stead's headquarters. From this International Bureau a project originated, providing for an international university of legal and political sciences at The Hague. Three years later, Eykman dispatched a brochure to all standard-bearers of Internationalism. The idea met with general acclaim – and amendment. Nippold himself submitted a plan for a two-year course covering a wide range of subjects to be taught by ten scholars of standing assisted by a competent staff. Internationalists such as Oppenheim of Cambridge and Bisshop of London in their turn enlarged on this idea, raising the number of scholars to thirteen. Prominent men such as Barclay, Fiore, von Bar and Huber expressed their approval of the ambitious enterprise. From America, Elihu Root insisted on scholarly independence whereas from France Léon Bourgeois suggested submitting the idea to the *Institut de Droit International* for further examination.

In August 1910, at its twenty-sixth meeting in London, the International Law Association supported the idea in a resolution which was reaffirmed in Paris the following year. Oddly enough, from then on the plan collapsed. Though highly meritorious in clearing the ground and furthering thinking, the project itself proved far too ambitious.

The Materializing of the Plan

Again the torch was seized. And this time it was put into the hands of no less a man than Tobias Asser, the grey eminence of Dutch legal science, co-founder of the *Institut de Droit International* in 1873, stimulating patron of four Hague Conferences of Private Law (1893–1904) and veteran of two Peace Conferences. In 1910 he took the lead of an impressive Dutch "Provisional Committee" for the furtherance of an academy of international law, featuring scholars and officials such as de Beaufort, van Karnebeek, Loder, Meyers, Oppenheim, van Vollenhoven, Cort van der Linden, van Eysinga, de Louter and Molengraaff. When sharing the Nobel Peace Prize with Alfred Fried in 1911, Asser voted part of it to the projected Academy, upon which another private pacifist, Mr. Goekoop stepped in to double the sum. Substantial support also came from the Carnegie Foundation. On 2 December 1910 van Karnebeek delivered a convincing address in favour of the idea in the Second Chamber of the States General. However, in January 1911, Asser himself made the step which would prove decisive, in contacting the board of the newly founded Carnegie Endowment for International Peace.

Carnegie had put some dear friends of his at the head of the Endowment. Among these were Elihu Root, former Secretary of State and member of the Permanent Court of Arbitration and Joseph Choate, former American Minister in London and head of the American delegation at the 1907 Conference. Choate was a well-known advocate of drastic armament limitations, of obligatory arbitration and of reinstalling the Hague Conferences at fixed inter-

vals. Other members were Nicholas Murray Butler and James Brown Scott, founder of the *American Journal of International Law,* who was appointed secretary to the executive committee. Scott also headed the Division of International Law.

From these names it may be gathered that Asser did right in applying to the Endowment. This is not to say that the request was easy sailing. After initial exchanges with Elihu Root, Asser was in for a prolonged correspondence with Scott and for numerous meetings covering well over two years. Together, the two men (Asser and Scott) may be deemed the godfathers of the Academy. Scott sympathized with the idea from the first. During the Academy's opening ceremony in 1914 it was said of him that to advance peace one would sooner find him prepared to cross the ocean than another man to drive from Paris to Versailles. What he did insist on, however, was a strict organization and a well-balanced programme of courses. Conditions implied the raising of an international Administrative Council which oversaw the choice of lecturers and which organized courses in both public and private international law and special seminars at that. Accordingly, a scenario was drawn up.

First, at the beginning of 1912 the Dutch Committee sent requests to prominent scholars begging for their assistance to the projected courses in years to come. A total of thirty-seven affirmative replies came in, featuring the most illustrious names. Second, governments were approached through their embassies in Holland, mainly to ensure their co-operation by meeting the costs and sending students. Again, the reply was fully satisfactory. Still, Scott insisted on further support, also in drawing up the Statutes, from the *Institut de droit international.* Scott's main concern in all this was the purely scientific character of the projected Academy. Quite recently, and on his specific request, the *Institut* had from its midst launched a special Consulting Committee to serve as advisory board to his, Scott's, division of the Carnegie Endowment.

In September 1912 the said Consulting Committee lent its support to the project of an Academy. This appraisal was formally reaffirmed by the *Institut* during its twenty-sixth conference in Oxford in August 1913. Halfway through January 1914 the Committee spent three full days discussing the Statutes drawn up by Asser and Scott with the help of the Dutch Preparatory Committee. The Academy was to be founded in the Peace Palace and the Board of the Carnegie Foundation was to serve *qualitate qua* as its Administrative Council. Pursuant to the Statutes drawn up on this occasion, the Academy would consist of three organs mainly:

1 A scholarly *Curatorium* of twelve, to be chosen from different nations and supervising the courses. This college would at all events include the president (or former presidents) of the *Institut,* the director of the division of international law of the Carnegie Endowment and a Dutch member to be nominated by the Administrative Council. Together these functionaries were to complete the dozen.

One of the corridors on the bel-étage of the Palace. The floors, ceilings and stained glass windows were all designed by Herman Rosse.

T. M. C. Asser (1838–1913), one of the leading Dutch internationalists of the period. A born diplomat and an eminently practical man by nature. The clear-minded initiator of the Hague Conferences on Private International Law, who himself presided over the first four conferences (1893–1904). The bronze statue was made by Professor A. W. M. Odé (1865–1955) in 1921.

Louis Renault (1843–1918), one of the initiators of the Hague Academy. The statue was presented by admirers of Renault and unveiled on 5 August, 1932 by C. Lyon-Caen, President of the Curatorium of the Academy at that time.

2 A *Council*, which was to supervise all daily affairs. It represented the Academy in all (extra)judicial matters, appointed the Treasurer and, jointly with the Curatorium, a Financial Committee and the Secretary-General. It supervised courses and awarded certificates and diplomas, fixed allowances and scholarships, concluded contracts and drew up a yearly report which was submitted to the Endowment, the *Institut* and the Curatorium.

3 A *Financial Committee*, which supervised transactions, donations, purchases and sales of any consequence, and construction and repairs and obligations met by the Council.

Lectures were to be given from July till October – that is during university holidays. This would enable the Curatorium to contract the best lecturers. As was specified in the Statutes, courses were to imply the most important and topical issues of international jurisprudence, both from the point of theory and practice, and notably as resulting from conferences and court verdicts in matters of arbitration. Accordingly, only graduates of universities were admitted to attend the courses.

Several former presidents of the *Institut* were found prepared to sit on the Board of the Curatorium, among them Renault, Hamburger, Baron Descamps, Hagerup and Lord Reay. Scott himself joined the Board and so did Mr. Heemskerk, Dutch Minister of State, on behalf of the Carnegie Foundation.

On 28 January 1914 the Foundation Deed was issued by the Hague notary and a few days later (31 January – 2 February) the Curatorium first met in Paris. It was a memorable meeting for many reasons. As a matter of fact, there was ample room for scepticism as to the political perspective. As was noticed

gloomily by Renault during these months, great steps ahead were taken on minor points, but the overall horizon of world politics grew darker with the day: "Quelle triste spectacle!" Still, the creation of an institution as the present Academy, which was unheard of in the field, constituted a heyday of pacifism and legal internationalism. In Paris, almost symbolically, Louis Renault was elected President. He had been one of the most ardent pioneers of internationalism indeed. Professor of international law at Paris since 1873, he had attended both Hague Conferences, was a member of the Permanent Court of Arbitration, a former president of the *Institut* (1894) and had in 1907 been awarded the Nobel Prize for his indefatigable peace efforts.

It was on this occasion too that French was unanimously resolved to be the only language used in the courses; this decision would stand till 1947. The official opening was set for 1 October 1914 at the Peace Palace. Courses were to start in the summer of 1915 and the Dutch Foreign Minister would notify the nations to this extent. But then, on 28 June, deadly shots rang out in the streets of Sarajevo; another month and the Great War had started. On 14 August the Dutch Foreign Minister was compelled to notify the Academy authorities that the opening was to be postponed. Among the many international meetings that had to be cancelled those months, was the Third Hague Peace Conference, meant to convene somewhere in 1915–1916 and to which end committees all over the world had been carefully planning for months ...

The Preparatory Commission

It was a different world altogether that witnessed the first peace conference which took place after the onslaught. The stage was not The Hague, but Paris: Versailles, Saint-Germain, Trianon and Neuilly ... and among the parties were found no Romanovs, no Hohenzollerns, no Habsburgers, no Ottoman emperor. A new era had dawned, in which Socialists and Bolsheviks had replaced *Tsars* and *Kaisers*. As a matter of fact, the way back had been cut off rigorously – but no one even thought of glimpsing backwards.

Admittedly, the sarcasm and scepticism of the previous decade had proved true, but, oddly enough, in the total disillusionment they too had vanished. Indeed, one looked ahead with new-born optimism. Within months new States had been formed on the ruins of others, and a new international order was in the making. And, ironically enough, from among the ashes of the Hague Conferences arose a new and truly international organization, headed by the energetic President of the world's new leading nation, Woodrow Wilson of the United States. Among others a true Court of International Justice was now projected. A preparatory committee was formed and, small wonder, featured some well-known faces: Descamps, Hagerup, Loder, Root and Scott were among them.

From 16 June to 24 July 1920 these men were found together anew at The Hague, to draw up the Statute of the Court of Justice which was to be seated alongside the pre-war Arbitration Court within the walls of the Peace Palace. It was from this comittee that the new call came for the installation of the Academy. But even before, in 1919, voices had been raised to this end, to wit at the first post-war meeting of the *Institut* in Paris. In September 1921 in Rome, at its twenty-eighth meeting, the *Institut* proceeded to replace the board of the Curatorium that had lost four out of twelve members. The president elected was Charles Lyon-Caen of Paris, to be assisted by Walter Schücking of Marburg, Catallani of Padoua and Knut Hammarskjøld of Upsala, the former Swedish Prime Minister. The new Curatorium first met in September 1922 in Grenoble at the next plenary meeting of the *Institut.*

For six months the preparatory commission formed from the Curatorium worked hard to arrange the opening in the shortest possible term. In 1973, on the occasion of the Academy's tenth lustrum, van Kleffens, the former Dutch Foreign Minister, vividly remembered these preparatory meetings of the Curatorium in Paris in the early months of 1923, which he attended in his capacity of secretary to the Administrative Council. It was "a formidable, immensely capable, unbiased and also likeable trio": here the "transparent and subtle lucidity" of the Greek, Mr. Politis, met the brilliance of Professor Gilbert Gidel. The latter was to become a great friend of van Kleffens: "together in harness … we were like two oxen under a single yoke, carefully but firmly treading our way, and walking in step."

Van Kleffens was most impressed by the Curatorium's President, the venerable Charles Lyon-Caen: extremely competent, but somewhat choleric at times, somewhat deaf too – a combination which asked for trouble. Once, having misunderstood van

Kleffens in the midst of discussions on the Law of Peace, Caen threw the ebony stick which never left him at the stunned Dutchman.

The Curatorium met twice a year in those early days, in spring in The Hague, in autumn in Paris: "Thinking of them, I still see successive members clearly before me, and I seem to hear their voices. Invariably we met in Professor Lyon-Caen's apartment in the Rue Soufflet, the heart of the Latin Quarter. It was in a building then perhaps sixty or seventy years old. There we sat, in a wide circle, in a drawing room whose ceiling was painted all over, showing a blue, sunny sky with little puffs of white cloud, more often than not in striking contrast with the weather outside, though in complete harmony with the serene, yet alert atmosphere prevailing within. Few, if any members of the Curatorium ever smoked; whether through force of habit or out of a sense of self-preservation in view of the room's size was not clear. There reigned an excellent spirit of mutual appreciation, while the very high standard of the Bureau's preparatory work acted as a gentle lubricant to the discussions. I still feel that I learnt a great deal there, in many respects. … It was not mere politeness when the President spoke of his 'chers collègues'. … Alas, of that early panel, all, all are gone, the old familiar faces."

In the spring of 1923 a brochure in six languages was sent all over the world. In it was stated that from the "immense bouleversement" the world had gone through, international law had emerged for the better, going from strength to strength. Due to four years of bestiality, fictions had been burst by now. If ever, man had learned to understand the urgency for an international legal code and for a new set of obligatory rules. To this end the Academy set out, armed with practical thinking and scholarly scrutiny. Combining in its academic personnel the particularities of national law traditions, it claimed,

Charles Lyon-Caen (1843–1935). An expert on private international law and comparative law. The bust was made by M. L. Cladel in 1935.

The central hall of the Palace, featuring two of the six gilt candelabra which were presented by Austria, the marble floors and Paonazzo-marble columms, the national gift of Italy, and the bronze entrance doors, which were presented by the Belgian Government. In the floors a radiant sun is to be seen, bearing the inscription "Sol Justitiae Illustra Nos" (Sun of Justice Enlightes Us).

The auditorium of the Academy in the main building, before the new building was opened in 1929.

through unbiased research, to help lift standards of law and international relations towards morally unprecedented levels and into a doctrine of universal validity. After another preparatory meeting in May in Paris the Curatorium felt well equipped and ready for the opening session. Was it to be on the American or the French national holiday?

The Opening of the Academy

The solemn inauguration took place on 14 July 1923 in the large Court Room of the Peace Palace. Following a luncheon offered by the French Ambassador, at three o'clock judges, ministers, diplomats, representatives of the League of Nations, and many students – no fewer than 146 from abroad – listened to an address by Mr. Cort van der Linden, the former Dutch Prime Minister and successor to Mr. van Karnebeek. Unfortunately, his health did not allow the Foundation's first President, who had resigned in the previous March to attend. It was comforting for him, however, that his son, the present Foreign Minister, presided over the meeting, which his wife also attended.

Primitive instincts, passions and egotism, Cort van der Linden taught his audience, had carried man away, making him plunge into war for centuries. Lofty labels that were invariably put on it, such as "the Lord's call", "justice that had to be done" or "the defence of the national honour" could not conceal this. Still, whatever one might think of this, as nations grew closer the era of peace based on justice that was prophesied by Isaiah seemed imminent – if only the torch of law could be kept burning till the dawning of that glorious day.

Then rose Mr. Caen, President of the Curatorium, to remember the pioneers of the Academy, Renault and Asser and to thank Mr. Scott. The Palace, he ventured to say, would soon prove too small to harbour its students and scholarly staff. Their major goal would be to spread the respect of law around: "un jour le Droit sera le souverain du monde!"

Speeches were made, too, and in the same optimistic tenor, by the younger Mr. van Karnebeek, who briefly recalled the names of von Bar, Fleischer and Sturdza; by the Hague Burgomaster Patijn who called to memory the early 18th-century Peace Treaty of Rijswijk (1713), that had been negotiated on the very soil of the Palace; and by Mr. James Brown Scott who perused the genesis of the Academy and called on France, from this, its public holiday onwards to take the intellectual lead in guiding mankind to a better world.

The session was closed at a quarter past four and high tea served in the entrance corridor. That night a banquet was offered at Scheveningen by the Dutch Government during which more speeches lavished more hope to the hearts' content of all ... Two days afterwards the first course opened. The seating accommodation in the lecture room, inadequate to harbour all students, had been adapted by the construction of a gallery. Few observers anticipated that within six years, in 1929, the help of van der Steur had to be implored once again, this time to build a brand new seat for the Academy on the grounds adjoining the Palace.

The Interbellum Years: 1923–1938

As mentioned above, of all the institutions to be found on the premises of the Palace, the Academy has doubtlessly been the most successful so far. From the first day scholars, diplomats, attorneys and officials have felt privileged to lecture at The Hague. Likewise, from the beginning generations of students have eagerly crowded the lecture rooms, strolled through the gardens in everlasting debate, made life-long friendships, met future colleagues and envied the possessors of attendance certificates. The success of the Hague Academy is the more remarkable as in those early days the initiators had no institution anywhere in the world which could serve them as an example. All they had to go by was a phrase: "to constitute a centre of advanced studies facilitating the thorough and impartial examination of problems concerning juridical relations". As van Kleffens once put it: it was an uncharted sea they sailed: "Mares nunca dantes navegados" in Luiz de Camões' words, and reefs and shoals were looming in many places.

The success of the Academy is mainly due to the formula chosen by the initiators. A basic rule throughout has been the discarding of all politics and of "hot issues" which might give rise to discord. This is not to say that lecturers do not bring up topical affairs or shrink from debating crucial differences. The impressive series of the *Recueil des cours* or *Collected Courses,* the prestigious green volumes which over the years have reached a number of well over two hundred, testify to this.

Since a long time the *Recueil* has been acclaimed as probably the most rewarding treasure-trove of contemporary international law. As Professor, now Judge Sir Robert Jennings wrote in the 1973

Jubilee Book : "The *Recueil* was the first and is still the major international work on international law." The series is, still in Professor Jennings' appraisal, "not only a unique record of the development of international law during the last half-century; it has also itself made a formidable contribution towards that development".

Naturally, one has to make allowances for the first years. One should bear in mind that with the *Recueil* at the start it was as with the Academy itself: authors had almost nothing to rely on; the field was barren. Writers therefore "painted with a large brush" those days, generalizing considerably; detailed research was to be filled in later. Somewhat surprising to modern ears for instance is the apparent lack of interest in the sources of law or for that matter the laws of war and neutrality. But, whatever may be thought of this, the authors kept true to their main target, which was commenting on basic problems and disputable, "touchy" issues. And in this at least they were often much more outspoken than any modern author.

Perusing the volumes one feels like tracing the fears and expectations, in short the preoccupations of generations of lawyers. From the detailed courses on international finance of the twenties we are drawn to matters of air law, communications and the multilateral treaty in the thirties. After lectures reflecting the initial optimism of the twenties as regards the League of Nations and the Hague Courts, one feels, from 1933 onwards, the ring of disillusionment in the lecturers' concern for "collective security" and their call for an "international police force" on account of German and Japanese menaces. In the late thirties the successive invitations to The Hague of outcasts of Nazism like Strupp, Kaufmann, Lewald and Nussbaum tell their tale. Themes like neutrality featured high during those years. As Hitler overran the Netherlands in May 1940, forcing the closing down of the Temple of Peace, international law of the interbellum-period had meanwhile found monumental expression in sixty-six volumes, harbouring four hundred and twelve lectures and sub-

scribed to by all major libraries in the world. The thirties had indeed been heydays for the Academy, its list of lecturers a true "catalogue of celebrities", as Professor Jennings puts it. By now, due to authors such as Lauterpacht, law had found its place in international society – in fact, most international lawyers themselves were positively stunned by the fundamental changes that had been brought about.

The housing of the Hague Academy since 1929. The building is connected with the library in the Palace by a covered passage.

1947 and Onwards

"It was a different world which saw a pale and unpropitious-looking sun rise at war's end", as van Kleffens observes in the *Jubilee Book*. The Academy had not been spared. Having lost Cort van der Linden and Lyon-Caen in 1935 already, the war years saw the death of no less than eight members of the Curatorium: among them its able President, Politis, and renowned internationalists such as Anzilotti, Hammarskjøld, Max Huber, Sir Cecil Hurst and James Brown Scott. However, competent young men took their places (Aghnides, Finch, McNair) and were presided over for a decade to come by Professor Gilbert Gidel.

Something else had changed too: finances. The resources of the Academy, some minor investments, had always been very modest. From the beginning though, private and public help was given generously. The Dutch Government, for one, offered yearly allowances to foreign students, other governments often supported their own participants. In 1935 and 1950 the Academy was awarded the Wateler Peace Fund Prize for its efforts. The main resource, however, had always come from overseas. Up to 1939 the Academy had, through Mr. Scott, enjoyed generous financial support by the Carnegie Endowment. Now, under new management, the Endowment struck out in new directions. Funds were soon running out at The Hague and like "a troika of mendicants in a deserving cause", Aghnides, McNair and van Kleffens approached philanthropists.

The Italian Judge D. Anzilotti who was President of the Permanent from 1928–1930.

Left: The series of the "Recueil des Cours" ("Collected Courses"), amounting to some two hundred volumes to date.

Fortunately enough, new backing was obtained from other American Foundations. Ford and Rockefeller stepped into the breach ... and some years afterwards, under Joseph Johnson, the Carnegie Endowment resumed former ties. Others stepped in as well, such as the *Krupp-Stiftung* and the Gulbenkian Foundation. Fortunately, from the late sixties onwards contributions from governments came in on a more regular base.

After a preliminary session in October 1946, courses were restarted in the summer of 1947, with English and French now on equal terms. The early programmes included courses expounding on the 1945 Charter and the future role of the United Nations. As early as 1947 Lauterpacht delivered a course on "The International Protection of Human Rights", whereas Krylov, the International Court Judge, was the first to enlarge on "The Soviet Doctrine of International Law". Likewise, the future role of international organizations and institutions was announced here in courses on the European Council and the European Communities, the Organization of American States and the Arab League. With the years, too, the decline of colonialism and the rise of the *tiers monde* are reflected in seminars.

With the institution, by the General Assembly of the United Nations, of the International Law Commission codification of international law made great progress. What resulted were the Geneva Conventions on the Law of the Sea (1958–1959), the Vienna Conventions on Diplomacy (1961–1963) and on Treaties (1968–1969). Several members of the Commission lectured at the Academy and discussed the continental shelf, seabed resources and polar regions.

The courses on the history of law likewise reflect the gradual shift of interests. In the pre-war period it was exclusively aspects of western law traditions that were dealt with: Greek and Roman times, the Middle Ages and Byzantine codification – and notably the "classical period" of the 16th and 17th centuries. From 1955 onwards the perspective widens as scholars become aware rapidly of the distinct parallel between European legal codes and non-Western traditions. Gradually, and reluctantly at first, Euro-centrist conceptions give way to a multi-cultural approach echoing the belief in the essential unity of human history. In 1949 and 1966 Milliot and Mahmanassi read on Islamic law, in 1960 and 1964 Alexandrowicz and Verosta on Asian legal traditions, in 1958 Chacko on Indian law, in 1966 Sastri on Hindu concepts. Likewise China and Japan are covered in these years. The quest for a truly universal law of nations is opened ... and its "sociological substratum" tackled at the same time.

Change announced itself in a new range of topics as well: outer-space law and celestial bodies, disarmament matters, but also pollution and acid rain, overpopulation, energy crises – "and the rest of the dialectical armoury of learned Jeremiahs whose baleful prophesies add a shrill note of impending doom to the close of the *Recueil's* first fifty years", as a bellicose Jennings put it at the time. Change made

itself felt too in the approach to "classics", such as the question of State succession. In this area, as Jennings puts it, "the sheer weight of the new material has threatened almost to sink the subject". Again, old issues gained new prominence, such as in matters of the sources of law or the adjudication of disputes and the position of the Hague Courts. With it, editors experimented with issues on thematical subject-matter. Still, despite all this, it is continuity which prevails: in the quality and dedication of lecturers and in that there remains so much to be done yet. Indeed, the most striking gap Professor Jennings noted fifteen years ago, in 1973, has not been filled: the astonishing absence of a proportionate number of women among the lecturers – and this after a first course by Sara Wambaugh as early as 1927.

Flexibility and Expansion

The preceding survey attests, if anything, to the flexibility of the courses. The same holds true, basically, for the outer history of the Academy. One may conveniently divide its history in a pre-war and post-war period for, to be sure, in many respects a great deal changed in the eight years' interval. What remained throughout, though, is the Board's innovative spirit. Through the years the Academy has always proved eager to modernize, adjust and reconsider its former achievements. Thus it grew into something which by its impact on the teaching and research of law surpassed by far anything that a Nippold or Sturdza might have possibly conceived.

If the expansion of an undertaking may be taken for a token of its success, the Academy fulfilled any man's expectations. The basic programme as started in 1923 provided for courses in public and private international law indiscriminately and on themes which were left to the discretion of the lecturers. But soon the programme was adjusted to also include seminar-sessions, so to further dialogue between teacher and pupil. As early as 1929 the Curatorium decided to insert a course of sixteen lectures yearly on the more specific issue of "principles of international law". In the public field this course was referred to as "General Rules of the Law of Peace" (mind you: not war – still the classical division!), in the private course as "General Rules of the Conflicts of Laws". The sheer confrontation of scholars from various countries and widely differing legal systems did much to point out analogies and parallels between current systems and thus notably furthered mutual understanding.

Another extension – the first post-war change if one does not count the extension of languages by adding English in 1947–, meant to further a student's excellency, was the awarding of a diploma on top of the *certificat d'assiduité* which as a rule most competent students managed to obtain. The diploma was to be obtained after a severe examination to which only the best qualified students were admitted. Thus, in 1950, out of 513 students 214 obtained the certificate, but only 44 applied for the exams, to

Hersch Lauterpacht (1897– 1960) was Professor at the Hague Academy four times between 1930 and 1947. He was a member of the International Court of Justice in 1955–1960 and of the Court of Arbitration in 1957–1960. Well-known from his revised editions of Oppenheim's handbook on "International Law". He was an expert on the law of human rights.

which finally 24 were admitted. Of these, five retired, nine failed and ten obtained the diploma. These figures have remained relatively the same throughout the years and led to the diploma becoming one of the most enviable testimonials in the field. Logically enough, some years later, in 1956, the certificate was formally abolished.

In 1954 a practical change was put through, due to the blessings of modern technology. Booths were installed with interpreters providing simultaneous interpretations of courses for the sake of students. Another major expansion was the founding in 1956 of the *Centre d'étude et de recherche de droit international et de relations internationales de l'Académie de droit international de la Haye (Le Centre)*. The idea originated with Philip C. Jessup, the renowned Columbia Professor and later Judge at the International Court and was brought up by Professor Bart Landheer, at the time director of the Peace Palace Library. The *Centre* concerns a·six-week course, immediately following the other courses and is meant for highly qualified scholars only who have given proof of "vast learning and intellectual maturity". As a rule some thirty members are admitted, fifteen for the French, and another fifteen for the English section, both headed by a Director of Studies. Entrance is free and participants even obtain a modest indemnity. Costs are met by an annual allowance from the Rockefeller Foundation. From the beginning, in 1957, the *Centre* has been highly successful. That year was marked too, incidentally, by the entrance of the first East-European participants: a dozen Polish, Czech and Russian students attended courses.

The year 1958 marked a major formal transition in the Academy's history. The courses in private and public international law, which traditionally had covered three weeks indiscriminately (only to be extended to four or five weeks from 1948 onwards), were now split into two separate, successive courses of three weeks. Thus, new ways were found all the time. During 1963–1966 seminars were organized in memory of Dag Hammarskjöld, which from 1967 on were continued in Sweden.

In 1969, following the expansion of the Curatorium to a board of fifteen, yet another ambitious project was launched, the "External Programme". This was another effort, worked out by a study group, to offer special facilities to Third World scholars. To this end, once or twice yearly a group of professors embarks for Africa, Latin America or Asia to give a three-week course on issues of specific relevance to the area. Primarily designed for the better instruction of young local scholars and government officials, the courses in effect bear a wider, regional character, involving participants from various adjoining nations. Again the programme came about thanks to a substantial donation by an American trust, being the Carnegie Endowment itself this time. It is carried through with the administrative help of "Unitar". Apart from all this, conferences on special, often commercial or economic themes have been held through the years.

The lounge of the Academy building.

As mentioned above, the outstanding feature of the Academy, as compared to university courses, is not so much the wide range of subjects dealt with yearly, however deserving this may be in itself, but rather its functioning as a meeting point of cultures. Already in July 1923 twenty-eight professors, representing fifteen nationalities, were found teaching. They were confronted by three hundred and fifty-three students, thirty-five among them female, and belonging to thirty-one nations. Nowadays, the average number of students amounts yearly to some four to five hundred, the field of public law accounting for the larger part. As before, they cover a wide range of professions, involving graduate students, young scholars, barristers, diplomats and military men.

If anything, it is the wide variety in nationality, profession and age to be met here, both among teaching staff and students, that accounts for this curious and actually unique atmosphere which through the years has proved so extremely fertile in the exchange of views. Probably the more so as, precisely due to this variety, conformity of thinking was never really aimed at – indeed far from it.

In 1973, as the Academy had its *Jubilee Book* edited by Professor R.-J. Dupuy, the former Dutch Foreign Minister van Kleffens, who served the organization of the Academy for forty-five years (1923–1968) and was at the centre of business at The Hague throughout the pre-war period, noted down some personal experiences. Among others, he tells of the positive shock Europeans, with their marked leanings toward codified law, suffered on being confronted with scholars steeped in the Anglo-Saxon conception of unwritten, customary law and the virtual sanctity of judicial decisions. Van Kleffens' notes are interesting to us, too, for their personal touch. It always struck him as almost comical the way in which unorthodox ways were used to solve problems at the Academy. It was his experience from the beginning that seemingly complicated matters, such as immunity from income-tax, were promptly solved, whereas matters of lesser order, such as permission for the sale of alcoholic beverages on the premises "required an offensive on a broad front of almost heroic proportions".

A striking example from the first years is the following. When the Permanent Court of International Justice needed more room in the Peace Palace, a new building was constructed for the use of the Academy (its present location). The refectory planned here lacked all grace, warmth and atmosphere, indeed resembled an "empty cigar box", as Louis Mazel, the inventive and unselfish worker of the early days (and later Assistant Secretary-General of the Curatorium) did not fail to notice. Van Kleffens addressed the architect, who stubbornly refused to change his plans, for vague "aesthetic" reasons. Then van Kleffens demanded at least a fire-place "as a minimum condition for peace". To this the architect replied that such an apparatus would protrude too much into the room. Van Kleffens then promised to produce a "non-protruding" fireplace within a fortnight. To this end Mazel and he packed their golf-clubs and left the same night for England "where there are more fire-places per square mile than in the whole of Holland". They found an "absolute beauty"

the very first day at Addington Palace, made a sketch and measurements, played golf to their hearts' content and returned to The Hague in triumph, "at no expense to the Academy". The fire-place still has its place in the lounge.

Van Kleffens never stopped being fascinated by the different personalities he met at the Academy. He recalled as a young secretary being warned by colleagues in advance of an elderly lecturer who was not above throwing a few darts at a neighbouring country he did not particularly like. He anticipated this by putting the man in charge of a one-man committee to prevent anyone from saying disobliging things about other nations. The man took his appointment as a great compliment and, diligently taking his colleagues aside, whispered in their ears something like "You would not believe it, but apparently there are sometimes professors ... I am sure, of course, that you would never dream of ... but you might care to warn others." No incidents occurred that year: "le braconnier devenu garde-champêtre", as van Kleffens moralizes.

To conclude, we may fall in with van Kleffens' final observation regarding the institution: the Academy is "what one might call a very healthy 'public utility' of a high order, and deserves to be nurtured as such".

THE ASSOCIATION OF ATTENDERS AND ALUMNI (AAA)

The registration desk of the pre-war "Association".

It may attest to the special atmosphere which from the beginning marked the courses at the Hague Academy, that in the very first year (1924) an internal organization was set up to maintain the friendships that were made by students and teachers during their stay. It was called the AAA: "Association des auditeurs et anciens auditeurs de l'Académie de droit international de La Haye", aiming (naturally) at the maintaining or resuming of personal ties made at The Hague, but also at the financial support of successive "levies" and at the joint effort to further international law. It is therefore meant for both attenders and alumni. James Brown Scott willingly accepted to become its honorary president. The association has statutes of its own, a general assembly, a council and bureau and many national subdivisions. It also publishes a yearbook, the *Annuaire.*

The original function of the AAA was of course that of the *amicale* and over the years its bureau has done tremendous work in helping to accommodate attenders during their stay. Dutifully it has held excursions and parties and has been an intermediary to arrange tennis and golf facilities. The second aspect was to keep in touch with the alumni. In doing so it has experienced that time and distance can easily come in the way of good intentions. Besides, the tangible result of the Bureau's efforts in this field in fact often escapes its sight. It consists mainly in the network of contacts between the alumni themselves, many of whom have with time risen to prestigious functions in their own countries. It goes without saying that their relationships with fellow members, initiated in the truly international and friendly atmosphere of the Palace garden chat, have often proved extremely valuable both in social and professional matters. However, in The Hague too the idea has taken root. Many national groups are flourishing, in recent years notably the *Deutsche Gruppe*, which publishes a scholarly *Schriftenreihe* of its own, as for that matter so do the French. However, next to its social functions, the Association's main target through the years has concerned the field of international law strictly spoken. True internationalism, it teaches, by far surpasses the simple addition of national groups. From 1949 onwards the Association proceeded to organize yearly conferences on issues of notable interest to the host country. These propagate international law and

promote dialogue – and over the years they span three continents. Speakers are drawn quite naturally from among the Association's members, a tremendous reservoir of learning and practical experience.

As time went by, themes were increasingly chosen for the sake of their topical relevance. This also happened at the 1971 Rabat Congress on environmental issues. From this conference another tradition emerged spontaneously, as after its conclusion a draft set of principles on the specific issue was elaborated by a study group. These were then published alongside the proceedings of the conference in the Association's *Yearbook* and subsequently submitted to the 1972 United Nations conference on human environment at Stockholm.

As for the *Yearbook*, this French-English scientific journal was developed in 1951 from a newsletter, the *Bulletin*, that had for decades served both the Association and the Academy. Interestingly enough, in 1966 the Association restarted a newsletter of its own alongside the journal, called *Echo of The Hague*. Meanwhile the journal, in the past thirty years, served AAA members well in offering many authors who have since risen to fame a first opportunity to contribute in the field. As the Association's honorary secretary-general Fritz Hondius put it in the 1973 *Jubilee Book:* depending entirely on voluntary work as concerns men, ideas and money, the Association has successfully sought to galvanize the younger generation and thus reinforced and supplemented the work of its *alma mater.*

The Peace Palace Library

A panoramic view of the reading room of the Peace Palace Library.

There was a time, and not too long ago indeed, when the Peace Palace Library was considered the best-equipped in the fields of both public and private international law. There have been days when its library system was unrivalled in Europe, when its printed catalogue, the impressive wine red volumes, were called a "vollständige Bibliographie des Völkerrechts" ("complete bibliography of the Law of Nations") and when also its acquisition lists, posted weekly at the entrance gates of the Palace, drew the keen attention of passing scholars; when, finally, in Rolin and ter Meulen it had librarians of world-wide scholarly fame. Those days have gone – and they have gone forever, it would seem.

There is nothing dramatic in this. Despite all the tendencies for economy of recent years, the staff of the Peace Palace Library may still justly boast a partly unique and at all times representative collection. Though no longer the world's centre for research, the library still serves many ends. The two Courts, the Hague Academy, numbers of scholars from home and abroad, men of law and university students invariably obtain all they require from the cosy reading room. In fact, and here is the irony of fate, the library has only expanded. Its domain, its collection, its staff, its facilities, all have considerably grown over the decades – but to find themselves easily outgrown by the formidable expansion in the field. Is anyone to blame for it? We don't think so; that would be too easy. No one among the first advocates of the library in the early decades of this century really anticipated the tremendous growth of international life. Indeed, the rather conservative appraisal at the time in this respect contrasts oddly with the outspoken, but falsified optimism of these pioneers with regard to the expected growth of a true international legal order.

If, in later years, anything had hampered the optimal functioning of the library while maintaining the highest thinkable level in the field, it was the very idea of universality its founders cherished. In fact, the most vexing problem for the successive librarians over the years was precisely how to adapt these ideals to the available funds and space. Interestingly enough, it is this dilemma as to the proper aims of the institution and consequently its size which had also puzzled the first Board of the Carnegie Foundation. It was this issue which notably gave rise to lengthy quarrels between Carnegie and van Karnebeek. And if anything, it has been the incompatibility of the lofty ideals on the one hand and the availability of finance and storage space on the other which pervades the history of the institution. To better understand this, we would do well to go back once again to those early years of the founding fathers.

The Founding

From our fourth chapter, the reader will recall that it was precisely the idea to set up a library on behalf of the Court of Arbitration which, in 1900, led Carnegie to intervene. Indeed, it was the millionaire's disposition towards libraries that had induced his friends Holls and White to approach him in the first place. At the time the idea of a "Temple" to house the Court, another suggestion made to him by friends, was deemed "premature" and "presumptuous" by Carnegie as he felt that too lofty quarters would jeopardize the moral authority of the new institution. What he envisaged was to simply present the Court with a "Standard Library of International Law". It was only thanks to White's persuasiveness that, towards the end of 1902, Carnegie at length became fascinated by the latter more prestigious idea of the "Temple of Peace" – but then indeed to a degree as to virtually obliterate his first option. That much at least emanates from a rather painful interview in 1906 when Carnegie was again approached by van Karnebeek with the request for an additional endowment as it appeared that Cordonnier's grand design of the Court House left no funds for the projected library.

As one will recall, Cordonnier's original building plan of the Temple provided for the so-called split design, featuring a separate library building which was linked to the Court House proper by means of a covered passage. This large scheme perfectly suited the Board's intentions to erect a true "World Library" along the lines developed in previous years by international lawyers such as de Martens, Hill, White and Holls and to create at The Hague a leading library of the civilized world with regards to international law. Accordingly, the Board intended to spend one-third of Carnegie's gift, being half a million dollars, on the library. At this point, however, in 1906, Carnegie himself interfered, rejecting both the idea of a prestigious book collection and a grand-scale library building. What he thought of then, he declared, was "simply a fine room in the Temple" to be furnished with books and amounting to the sum of $50,000 at the most. This, incidentally, though he never realized it, was contrary to his previous views and more precisely to the text of the Foundation Deed.

The outcome of it all has been told in detail in previous chapters: Carnegie adamantly refused to add to his original gift. At length, however, he did drop his opposition as to the expenditure of part of his gift on the equipment of the library, provided always that this procedure would not jeopardize the Court House itself. As for Cordonnier's design, this was drastically modified. In van der Steur's final drawings the library was integrated in the main building so as to occupy the full rear side of the Palace and with an entrance of its own in the centre of the back façade. However, the idea of a world library was maintained, as witness the projected bookshelf capacity of 10,000 metres which would accommodate some 300,000 volumes. Thus, at the opening of the Palace in August 1913 the working conditions of Baron Rolin, the first Director-General and his deputy Molhuysen seemed fully satisfying in all respects – and for a number of years to follow.

However, within ten years this perspective changed radically by the arrival, first in 1922, of the Permanent Court of International Justice, followed in 1923 by the Hague Academy. Obviously, neither the architects nor the Board had anticipated such a rapid extension of the functions of the Palace. However welcome in itself, it did assume acute problems of space. Thus, ironically, the Palace, which in 1913 had been criticized by many as preposterously large, actually proved to be too small within a decade. We have already discussed these problems as far as they regarded the Court of Arbitration. The impact on the library was far worse. In the building plans seven large rooms had been set apart to house the book treasure. Most of these were held in reserve and it was therefore only natural that the library was the first to give in to the new demands. But, at the pace maintained then, courtesy became suicidal. As early as 1922 Molhuysen had yielded six out of seven rooms, representing three-quarters of the library's total storage space and leaving room for some 75,000 volumes only. In view of the rapid growth of its collection, from over 30,000 volumes in 1920 to more than 50,000 in 1925, the situation soon became critical.

Again, in 1927, and in order to accommodate the judges of the Court of Justice who with the growing frequency of cases found themselves increasingly bound to The Hague, the Carnegie Foundation had van der Steur construct fifteen more rooms, most of them private studies, on behalf of this Court. These were again partly taken from what was left of the library storage. This time though an alternative was offered. At the cost of about Dfl. 270,000 (being fourteen times the yearly budget of the library at the time and paid from an increase in the annual contribution of the League of Nations), a new building was erected to store the book treasure. This building, adjoining the south façade of the Palace and connected to it by a covered passage, was opened in June 1929. A year later a similar procedure

was pressed on the Academy. With the increase of the number of regular judges in the Court of Justice (from eleven to fifteen) and the considerable work load, a further extension of staff and consequently of rooms could no longer be postponed. Again van der Steur set to work, this time in the area up to then occupied by the administration of the Academy. Once again, a new building was designed for the latter institute, linked to the 1929 bookstacks – and this has been the Academy's quarters ever since.

However, the new book storage amounted to some 3,600 metres of shelving, providing room for some 110,000 books – which was a third larger than the few rooms left in 1922, but still only little more than a third of the original planning, which anticipated 300,000 volumes. Interestingly enough though, the 1929 book storage was the last extension to the Palace ever undertaken on behalf of the library. To date the collection amounts to some 700,000 volumes, piled up in the 1929 storage and scattered over attics and cellars, those huge caves of the main building. Even as recently as the mid-seventies van Hall, the librarian at the time arranged a highly intricate deal between the Foundation and the International Court of Justice to have new cellars dug out and create additional storage room. Little wonder it is, therefore, if lack of space has given a headache to all successive librarians and complaints of mildew and moisture are heard incessantly!

Now, what is it that caused the enormous increase of books and what indeed is the library's province properly speaking?

The Library's Province

How often the views of the initiators may have clashed with regards to the outer limits of the library's province, they were invariably in accord as to its main target. The primary aim of the library was, in 1913 and is today, to supply a service to the institutions which reside in the Palace. Initially meant for the Permanent Court of Arbitration only,

The entrance to the library at the rear of the Palace with the pre-war porter standing by.

*Right: Title page of the
1519 edition of Erasmus'
"Querela Pacis".*

*Below: Jean de Bloch, author
of "The Future War", six
sturdy volumes and the
authoritative, first scientific
approach to pacifism.*

*Above: Alfred H. Fried
(1864–1921), founder of the
"Annuaire de la vie internationale" (1905) and
member of the Bern Peace
Bureau. He was a disciple of
Bertha von Suttner and was
awarded the Nobel Peace
Prize in 1911.*

Presumably the first book entirely devoted to pacifism, though a short tract really, is Erasmus' *Querela Pacis* ("The Complaint of Peace") of 1517. In the decades after the First World War, with the modern Peace Movement rapidly gaining political impetus and the bulk of studies on the subject increasing by the day, quite naturally the need was felt to retrace the roots of this movement and to make a proper inventory of the literature of four centuries on the subject. Hence, for instance, Aldous Huxley's sketchy outline *An Encyclopedia of Pacifism* (1937) and, from later years, Boris Gourevitch's exhaustive study *The Road to Peace and to Moral Democracy: An Encyclopedia of Peace* (1955). The idea itself was not brand new. A full century before, Upham and Beckwith had published "Peace Manuals" as they called it, designed to store the history and ideals of the peace movement in encyclopedic compass. Scientific peace research, though, only started at the turn of the last century with two men we have met in the context of the Hague Peace Conferences: Jean de Bloch and Alfred H. Fried.

De Bloch's six sturdy volumes on future war constitute the first empirical research of modern war techniques. Here, for the first time, the considerations to ban war which had up to then been stressed by peace advocates, and which were of an ethical and religious nature basically, were replaced by statistics and quantitative data and by photographic proof illustrating the devastating effects of military clashes. Mere anti-war propaganda was now effectively turned into the science of polemology. Due to modern technology, de Bloch held, future war was as senseless at it was suicidal. In his International Museum of War and Peace in Lucerne his ingenious theses were illuminated by gruesome display. Modern warfare was here shown to be not just "the continuation of diplomacy by other means" as Clausewitz had maintained, but the virtual breakdown of society.

Alfred Fried was an Austrian journalist and peace activist – in short he was the German counterpart of the Anglo-Saxon William Stead. Among other things he shared with Stead was a great admiration for de Bloch. Just as Stead published a one-volume English summary of de Bloch's six volume work, Fried introduced de Bloch's thought to Central Europe. In this he stressed the latter's scientific approach to the war problem and his focussing on the national and economic rather than the ethical elements. Fried laid down his views in his authoritative *Handbuch der Friedensbewegung*, which was first published in 1905, three years after de Bloch's death. It was an exhaustive reference work, perfectly accessible to outsiders and the best *vademecum* for peace advocates. In it he dismissed all moralizing and in fact went so far as to denounce the christian and "romantic" Tolstoyan criticism of war as utopian and unpractical. If anything it was the very materialism of the modern age, prompted by industrialism and economic internationalization which would bring about lasting peace, Fried maintained. In the second edition of his work, published ten years later, Fried illustrated this by cataloguing the innumerable international peace organizations which had been founded in recent years. No longer could pacifism be dismissed as a transitory phenomenon: it was indeed the gist of the new age.

In his optimism as regards the capitalists' blessings on society Fried was distinctly encouraged by the phenomenon of the "enlightened entrepreneurs", these philanthropic industrialists such as Nobel, Carnegie, Rockefeller and Ford. The more so as it was their support which enhanced both the finances and the professionalism of the Peace Movement – and consequently the regard in which it was held. The interesting thing to us is that it is precisely from the Nobel Institute in Oslo and Carnegie's creations such as

the Endowment in Washington and the Peace Palace at The Hague that were to originate some of the major research and documentary projects in the field. Indeed, in this they were only rivalled by a single centre of similar background, the International Institute of Peace in Monaco, which was instigated by Prince Albert in 1903. This latter research centre was the base both of Fried's *Annuaire de la vie internationale* and La Fontaine's *Bibliographie de la paix et de l'arbitrage international*, which was the first major bibliography in the field.

Still, in 1912 the Nobel Institute's Catalogue was on just grounds subtitled "Bibliography of the Peace Movement". In fact, in the years under consideration there is only one institution and a single issue which ranked next to and in a way supplemented the Monaco and Oslo bibliographical efforts – and this is the Peace Palace Library, thanks to ter Meulen catalogues on international law and bibliographies of the peace movement.

these services within ten years came to encompass the Court of the League of Nations and the Hague Academy. Since these institutions are all operative in the same fields, the extensions did not really affect the library's province proper which was and is mainly international law, both in the public and private domains. Nonetheless, it soon became manifest that in practice international differences submitted to the Courts emanated, as often as not, from the conflict of national laws. Consequently, the cases often involved the interpretation and application of municipal laws – and this in a bewildering variety of legal traditions. Indeed, it became apparent that it was precisely the clashing of these time-honoured regional traditions which, if anything, hampered the expansion and acceptance of a universal code.

Accordingly, whereas the strict province of the library was the scarce and meagre literature of a discipline-in-the-making, oddly enough the practi-

cal urge made itself felt for the acquisition of the enormous bulk of the world's municipal laws. For budgetary reasons alone, all sorts of arrangements had to be made with foreign nations to obtain statutes, codes and the kind. The outcome, won from strenuous labour on the part of the library's staff, was most gratifying indeed in terms of acquisitions. But, this in itself created the subsequent problem of organizing and storing an avalanche of books and periodicals.

Soon another expansion became imminent. Since the Courts were kept busy not so much in applying "international law" – which still was a relatively virgin field – but rather in creating this new discipline and jurisprudence, the judges had to establish their verdicts on such varying disciplines as sociology and polemology, diplomatic history and the traditions of the peace movement. This again invited a library for the Court alone.

Two capital consequences emanated from this. First, the core of the collection, the tiny body of international law proper, became embedded in, if not obscured by, enormous quantities of marginal literature from adjacent fields. Literature which, though over-abundant in certain areas, could hardly boast a representative, far less complete, coverage of the whole field. The more so as, on the one hand, literature from non-Western cultures proved difficult to obtain however hard one tried, whereas on the other hand generous donations of whole libraries in specific areas by private persons were gratefully incorporated. These circumstances further disturbed the evenly balanced growth of the collection. Indeed, it is the pioneering – if not essentially experimental – character of both the Courts and the library which accounts for many of these proceedings and later problems.

The Catalogue System

A second consequence again followed quite logically. Nowhere was any ready catalogue programme to be found which in any way claimed to systematically and hierarchically arrange the literature of so barren a field which, at that, was embedded in loads of often purely incidental works from well-trodden adjacent fields. It was up to Rolin, Molhuysen and soon their successors, ter Meulen and Lysen, to create a system out of total disorder. Considering the circumstances, they did a perfect job. As a base they took one of the very few adequate manuals on international law at their disposal, written by the English Professor Oppenheim, and applied to this the requirements of current library sciences as represented in the works of prominent authors such as Tiele. In this way they managed to cover the whole collection in a flexible system of 514 headings, starting from reference works (1–8) and sociology and economy (9–10) to law in general (11–18), over public, criminal and private international law (22–245; 246–257; 258–323) to municipal and comparative law (324–436) and case law (437–443) and finishing with political sciences, international relations and diplomacy (444–457), history (458–501) and varia (502–514). However flexible in the eyes of the first beholders, seventy-five years later expert readers of international law have little trouble in pointing out the unbalancing elements of the system. Obviously, in 1913 proceedings could not possibly anticipate items such as air and space law, environmental problematics, third world assets or the growth of international organizations. Besides, however outstanding at the time, the library's cataloguing system has since long been outdated by the post-war Universal Decimal Catalogue system.

Another handicap revealed itself from 1945 onwards, which could hardly have been anticipated thirty years before, to wit the gradual replacement of French as the current language of diplomacy by English. Now, whereas in the late twenties and early thirties the world of international law looked to the

Peace Palace Library for the innovation of catalogue systems, a field in which Lysen and ter Meulen justly gained a worldwide reputation, from about 1950 onwards the library staff in its turn went abroad in search of a definite system to replace the outdated house catalogue. Oddly enough such a system hasn't yet been found. This is mainly due to the fact that, for varying reasons, no operative overall system is to be found which has obtained undisputed prevalence and universal application. Thus, the current system of the American Library of Congress, though offering distinct advantages in many aspects, has never been generally accepted even by American law libraries. Likewise, the outstanding titling in the public sphere initiated by the German *Max Planck Institut für ausländisches öffentliches Recht und Völkerrecht* in Heidelberg has not yet found international appliance, as little for that matter as its counterpart in Hamburg, the *Institut für ausländisches und internationales Privatrecht.* And at home, the *T. M. C. Asser Instituut of International Law* at The Hague (for otherwise excellent reasons) applies home rules which are peculiarly distinct from any system used by university libraries.

To date, generally speaking, two considerations prevail with the present library staff at the Palace in these respects. First, that the switch to any new system will involve a major tour de force in matters of finance and labour. The past decade, which saw a sharp decline in the budget and a similar increase of activities, has not precisely been inviting for such an operation. Indeed, without having satisfied oneself of the long-term international prevalence of any new system to be adopted, such an interference with the current system must for obvious reasons be out of the question. The second consideration is that the rapid march of library automation and the sharp increase of legal databanks and inter-institutionary communication networks make any tampering with other than on-line catalogue systems extremely questionable. It takes little visionary power to predict that within two decades the library world will have experienced a metamorphosis beyond compare. It will cause enough headaches in future years to keep pace with current developments and adequately select the appropriate catalogue system.

The Librarians

What has been the course that the successive librarians have steered to reach the present state of affairs? Admittedly, the staff policy within the Peace Palace Library did show some distinct switches over the decades. Circumstances and matters of finance quite naturally accounted for major and minor adjustments in many departments. Still a high degree of consistency was maintained throughout. That is, personal leanings and idiosyncrasies of librarians, though numerous, never led to cross-purposes. The same holds good for the library's internal structure and outer appearance, which did

The so-called "Leidse boekjes", the now antiquated alphabetical catalogue system of numbered booklets which served the library for over sixty years.

not really undergo drastic changes. Indeed, it is safe to say that the collaborator of the early twenties would still have felt pretty much at home in the early sixties. It is only the computerizing and automation which – in recent years – changed the overall impression of the institution.

No doubt helpful in maintaining a consistent policy, has been the relatively small number of chief librarians – amounting to seven only over the full span of seventy-five years. The overall impression one gains from the work of these men, from Rolin to Schalekamp, is the gradual predominance of the management aspect over the scholarly element. In the early years it was experts in international law and library sciences who alternately functioned as chief and deputy librarians. In recent years the institute has gained a distinctly more business-like character, which in itself is hardly surprising. Meanwhile, there can be little doubt as to what were the palmy days of the library. These cover the long span of ter Meulen's librarianship (1924–1952). It was there that, in retrospect, a unique balance of management competence, scholarly research and financial facilities was maintained.

The Early Years (1913–1923): Rolin and Molhuysen, van Hamel and Lysen

On 15 August 1913, a fortnight before the opening of the Palace, the Belgian Professor Albéric Baron Rolin was appointed Director-General. Rolin was secretary to the Institute of International Law and in this capacity was involved in the preparations of the Hague Academy, the opening of which, foreseen in 1915, was sadly postponed due to the outbreak of war. Even before Rolin, on 1 July 1913, the

Board had appointed a Deputy-Director in the person of P. C. Molhuysen, then conservator at the Leiden University Library. In later years, Molhuysen was to become chief librarian at the *Koninklijke Bibliotheek* (Royal Library), also in The Hague, and besides gained himself a scholarly name by his volumes of documents relating to the origins of Leiden University and Hugo Grotius' correspondence among others.

Whereas Rolin busied himself with the management proper, Molhuysen, assisted by his conservator Miss Oppenheim (the daughter of a Groningen international lawyer), directed his attention to the cataloguing. Their major feats were the famous printed catalogue, the first bulky volume of which appeared as early as 1916, and the systematic catalogue put on index-cards, in which they improved on the *Leidse boekjes* – a system of catalogue booklets first adopted by Tiele in the 1860s. Among the first users of the reading room, opened to the public in October 1915, were the British officers who were interned at The Hague.

On 30 April 1920 Rolin departed without being replaced: a first thrifty measure, which left Molhuysen as managing director. However, on 1 September 1920 Miss Oppenheim was released from her position – to marry Molhuysen. A year later, on 1 October 1921, Molhuysen himself took his leave, to become Director of the Royal Library. Their departure was a severe loss to the library and virtually meant the end of the first generation. In came A. G. van Hamel, former librarian of the Rotterdam Economic (now Erasmus) University (where he was replaced by Jacob ter Meulen), who was to be assisted by A. Lysen. Within two years van Hamel in his turn left to become a professor at Utrecht University. It was at this point, on 1 January 1924, that ter Meulen entered the Palace. Ter Meulen and Lysen initiated the flowering days of the institution.

The first Librarians: left: Albéric Baron Rolin (1913–1920); middle: P. C. Molhuysen (1920–1921); above right: A. G. van Hamel (1921–1923); below right: A. Lysen.

Lysen is known mainly for two reasons. First, he was the author of a still authoritative study on the *History of the Carnegie Foundation and of the Peace Palace at The Hague* (1934). Second, he was the *auctor intellectualis* of, at the time, a rather contested new type of catalogue, the alphabetical subject catalogue which served as a supplement to the systematic catalogue. This comprehensive card-system, the so-called "Improved Index" was the nucleus of the later *Stichwörter-*catalogue. In the early sixties, one of Lysen's successors, Korevaar, gave a fairly negative appraisal of this innovation, and not entirely without grounds. However, despite all eventual shortcomings, the innovation again bore witness to the pioneering and resourcefulness of the Palace's early librarians. Another proof is the "never ageing encyclopedia" as Lysen called it, a reference-library of principal sources in the field put together in the reading-room as a quick reference medium.

Jacob ter Meulen (1924–1952)

Even today, a quarter-century after his departure, the name of Jacob ter Meulen still lingers in the ears of staff-members. Actually, his life and works would make the subject of a most interesting thesis or monograph. Virtually every field of the library seems permeated by his labour. Not only did he expand and reorganize the catalogues, continue the printed catalogue, assemble a mass of rare books (over three-quarters of this department, amounting to some 6,000 precious volumes, came in under his administration) and publish monographs and scholarly articles in a wide range of disciplines, he also broke fresh ground for the library in many fields. Thus, he started a portrait catalogue, which was a register featuring in endless files the alphabetically arranged names of men and women whose portraits are shown in the books collected in the library.

Ter Meulen's librarianship covers nearly three decades, rich in anecdotes and interesting notes on matters of internal affairs. His term, incidentally, was almost cut short within two years when in 1926 he tried seriously to be appointed as director of the library of the League of Nations in Geneva. The term also spans an active period of social legislation and technical innovation. In 1926 children's allowances were introduced, in 1927 the first telephone line was installed to link reading room and book storage area, in 1930 national health insurance was launched, in 1950 the first neonlights, Retocé and photocopiers came in. As for salaries, they make a sad story, though here again ter Meulen, being a man of ample means himself, showed himself an eloquent advocate for his employees. In 1931, having just won a fight over the adaptation of the national regulations on library salaries by the Carnegie Foundation, these salaries were curtailed the next year in view of the world-wide crisis. In 1946 the salaries were still below those of the Royal Library. It would take another decade before any effective change was to be introduced in these respects.

Ter Meulen was a consummate librarian, and versed as well in matters of management as in finance. His lasting repute in the library world though rests on two projects in the scholarly domain regarding the Peace Movement and Grotian studies.

To be sure, the cataloguing of Peace Studies was instigated by Molhuysen and Oppenheim as an integral part of the library's domain. It was ter Meulen though, who took the expansion of the collection into the sphere of pacifism as a matter of his personal concern. Large collections were purchased, others were offered, such as parts of Fried's private collection in 1931 and in 1951 the collection of the former *Vredeshuis*, compiled by G. J. de Voogd. Witness to Ter Meulen's personal interest is also his *Bibliography of the Peace Movement before 1899*. These concerned two lists of peace publications: the first one published in 1934 and recording the period 1776–1899 in some 3,500 items, the second published in 1936, covering the period 1490–1776 in some 500 items. The idea was initiated in 1932 by the International Historical Commission and by men such as Lange, Wehberg, Curti and Altamira. It was financed partly by the Oslo Nobel Committee and partly by ter Meulen himself. Together the lists are a most helpful instrument even to modern research.

However, ter Meulen did not content himself with bibliographical research only. Indeed by far his best-known and most penetrating study in the field is the massive three-volume *Der Gedanke der Internationalen Organisation in seiner Entwicklung* ("The Development of the Idea of International Organization") published between 1917 and 1940. The work originated from his Zurich thesis, the result of his studies with Max Huber who had greatly impressed him during the Hague Conference of 1907. In the first volume of this *magnum opus,* which saw highly appreciative reviews in such varying media as the *Times Literary Supplement* and Hans Wehberg's *Friedenswarte,* ter Meulen discussed the period 1300–1800, including all peace projects from Pierre Dubois to Immanuel Kant. The second volume runs from the French Revolution to the French-German War of 1870, featuring the Anglo-American peace societies and French Socialism among others. The third bulky volume runs to 1889, presenting an out-

Jacob ter Meulen, librarian from 1924 to 1952, in his early years.

Ter Meulen surrounded by his staff in the thirties.

The poster of the 1983 Grotius Exhibition.

line of "legal internationalism" and the arbitration movement. Together with the works of Christian Lange, the director of the Nobel Institute (*Histoire de l'internationalisme;* 1919–) and of Ruyssen, the president of the French peace society *La Paix par le Droit* (*Les Sources doctrinales de l'internationalisme*, 3 vols., 1954–1961), ter Meulen's work helped form the thoughts of generations of international lawyers.

It is positively astounding that all this work, done alongside the day to day cares of library management, is in fact only half of the scholarly work accomplished by ter Meulen during his twenty-eight years of librarianship. The second half of his term, that is from 1940 onwards, was increasingly devoted to quite another field – though as innate to the library's tradition as was pacifism! – namely the life and works of Hugo Grotius. Since the figure of Grotius permeates the library's activities throughout, we may well consider ter Meulen's efforts within this wider context.

HUGO GROTIUS IN THE PEACE PALACE LIBRARY

It goes without saying that, personal leanings set aside, the work of Holland's most renowned international lawyer, at the time almost universally looked upon as the "Father of International Law", had to be of special concern to any Peace Palace Librarian. Still, instrumental in the library's focussing on Grotius was the gift made by the Hague publisher Martinus Nijhoff in 1913 of 55 editions of Grotius' precious book of 1625, *De Jure Belli ac Pacis* ("On War and Peace"), long held to be the most influential work in world literature except the Bible. Nijhoff's donation became the nucleus of what, particularly thanks to the efforts of ter Meulen and in later years of his collaborator Diermanse, has become the world's best-equipped Grotius collection. Of the thirteen hundred editions of works by Grotius, and these include all the reprints of scattered poetry and the kind, the Peace Palace Library has more than a thousand, covering all major editions in any field.

However, again ter Meulen did not content himself with just collecting rare book editions. As early as 1925, on the tercentenary of Grotius'

masterwork, he arranged a very successful exhibition in the Hague municipal reception rooms at the Javastraat which then was continued on the premises on behalf of the Hague Academy and the *Institut de Droit International.* From these emanated a *Concise Bibliography of Hugo Grotius*, a bibliographical list of 76 editions and translations of *De Jure Belli ac Pacis* and a fine collection of letters by Grotius in a bibliophile edition. On this occasion, too, a rich collection of Grotius' manuscripts from the famous Nijhoff auction of 1864 was donated by Snelleman to the library. It was indeed in this bibliographical area that the most gratifying work awaited him. During the war years and anticipating the tercentenary of Grotius' death in 1645, along with his colleague Diermanse, ter Meulen set himself to the compilation of an exhaustive bibliography of Grotius' works. The commemoration itself, due to war conditions, was restricted to the laying of a wreath by Foreign Minister van Kleffens and the Swedish ambassador. The projected exhibition on the enlightened and free-thinking surroundings of Hugo Grotius was cancelled. However, the *Bibliographie des écrits imprimés de Hugo Grotius* which appeared with Nijhoff's imprint in 1950, is definite and will remain forever authoritative in the field, thanks to the authors' painstaking research, the work's completeness and its virtual faultlessness. The book was supplemented in 1961 by the *Bibliographie des écrits sur Hugo Grotius*, recording the vast 17th-century secondary literature on Grotius in a volume that covered 490 items.

Instrumental to ter Meulen's Grotian studies was also his founding of a *Stichting tot Bevordering van de Studie van het Leven en de Werken van Grotius* (Foundation to Promote the Study of the Life and Works of Grotius) initiated in 1949. This was actually the second Grotius Foundation to become operative in the Netherlands during those decades. As early as 1917, on the initiative of Professor C. van Vollenhoven, the Grotius expert, the *Stichting voor de Uitgave van de Werken van Grotius* (Foundation for the Publication of the Works of Grotius) was founded. It was this Foundation which, between 1917 and 1947, published ten volumes of the popular *Grotiana* series and initiated the publication of the aforementioned volumes of correspondence by Molhuysen (*Briefwisseling*, 1928–) and the preparation of a full edition of Grotius' Neo-Latin poetry. From 1966 onwards this work was continued by the *Grotius Instituut* of the Royal Netherlands Academy of Arts and Sciences, where research is currently done in the fields of letters, history, theology and legal history.

Not surprisingly, ter Meulen's continued Grotian research took definite roots at the Peace Palace and, if anyone, it is the figure of Grotius who links ter Meulen to his successor Bart Landheer. Landheer's outlook was certainly not the historical one, as soon became evident from the yearly reports. Grotius, however, did feature in his province as well. To him the 17th-century scholar was the inspiring force in the everlasting quest for the solution of international disputes. To promote research in this field Landheer, in 1954, launched the "Grotius Seminarium" which revealed itself via conferences, reports and bibliographies. Thus, in 1958 and 1961 international symposia were held in the Peace Palace on the themes of, respectively, "Ethical Values in International Decision Making" and "Limits and Problems of European Integration".

With the departure of Landheer and Diermanse, around 1970, the expertise on Grotius soon broke down in the Palace. Neither ter Meulen's *Stichting* nor Landheer's "Seminarium" were ever formally abolished but, from the late sixties onwards, both lay dormant for years. However, in the spring of 1979 a revival was announced in the launching of the Grotiana Foundation on the initiative of, again, Landheer (a septuagenarian now), Professor A. M. Stuyt (Nijmegen, International Law), Langemeijer (former Attorney-General of the Netherlands Supreme Court) and Mrs. de Kanter-van Hettinga Tromp, LL.D, the editor of the 1939 Leiden edition of *De Jure Belli* and the energetic secretary of nearly all previous Grotius Foundations in Holland. The three former foundations now merged into a new one and the *Grotiana* journal was revived in a new series, the objective of which is the furtherance of the Grotian tradition in the broadest sense. On the one hand it welcomes any contribution to a better understanding of Grotius' life and works, on the other, it more specifically intends to be a forum for exchanges concerning the philosophical, ethical and legal fundamentals of the search for an international order. To date the journal has already been issued in seven yearly volumes, also featuring sequels to ter Meulen's bibliographies. Formally independent, but operating in close touch with both the *Grotius Instituut* and the *Asser Instituut,* it now has its base in the Peace Palace Library.

It was indeed in co-operation with the *Asser Instituut of International Law* and the Grotiana Foundation that in 1983, on the occasion of the quarter-centenary of Grotius' birth, a two-day symposium on "The Grotian Heritage" was arranged at the Peace Palace. On this occasion the present Librarian, Schalekamp, arranged a fine Grotius exhibition in the reading room of the library and had a new *Concise Catalogue of the Grotius Collection at the Peace Palace* published. Thus, once again, one may conclude, the Peace Palace Library has developed into an international centre of Grotian research and documentation.

TER MEULEN'S OTHER ACTIVITIES

We have already spoken of ter Meulen's Grotius exhibitions. Ter Meulen, it seems, had a special leaning towards exhibitions and displays and was never at a loss to find an excuse for them. In February-March 1930 he helped organize a display of books and objects regarding the Peace Movement and the League of Nations at the Binnenhof in The Hague. In 1931, the First Congress of Comparative Law was supported with an exhibition and the

following year the First International Conference on the Teaching of History, headed by Rafael Altamira invited a large display. Still the same year, with the departure of B. C. J. Loder, the first president of the Permanent Court of International Justice, the latter's room (No. 20) was reshaped into a permanent exhibition room and equipped with show-cases featuring Grotius' works, former projects of international leagues, the history of the Laws of the Seas and documents relating to the Peace Palace and the League of Nations. The room, incidentally, was unsuitable for this purpose and soon the idea was given up – and in later years the exhibitions were continued in the corridors.

Typically, over the years, ter Meulen kept questioning the Board about a permanent exhibition room. To this end he also contacted van der Steur, who actually made some designs. Nothing came of it, however, as for that matter of another dream of his, namely to have a documentary film produced on Carnegie and the Palace. Still, on 25 November 1935, Carnegie's hundredth birthday was commemorated by a wreath-laying ceremony and another successful exhibition on Carnegie and Arbitration, held in four rooms of the Academy, attracting 1,600 visitors during four weeks. On this occasion a reader's guide was produced, informing the visitors of the library's goals and treasures, which in subsequent years was published in four languages. With the winds of war abating, unrelentingly, a new series of exhibitions was started. Thus, in 1947, the fortieth anniversary of the stone-laying ceremony was commemorated; in 1948 the fiftieth anniversary of Czar Nicholas' Manifest; in 1949 (ter Meulen's twenty-fifth year), the golden jubilee of the First Hague Conference; in 1950 the coming into effect of the Indian Constitution; finally, in 1951 an exhibition was put on by the International Baha'i Congress and the Conference of International Private Law.

Ter Meulen was a man of formidable energy and extreme willpower. Numerous are the projects he launched, the contacts he made and the tokens of insight of which he gave proof. He initiated Lysen's historiography of the Peace Palace, Lysen being actually the third author commissioned to the project by ter Meulen. In 1936, during the Spanish Civil War, he helped continue the Barcelona PATXOT

A meeting on 26 January, 1950 occasioned by the coming into force of the Indian Constitution. A copy of the text is handed over to ter Meulen by a representative of the Indian Government in recognition of the exhibition arranged by the Peace Palace library to highlight the Indian independence.

The core of the Grotius collection of the library, featuring the 17th-century editions of "De Jure Belli ac Pacis".

HUGO GROTIUS

Grotius by Michiel van Miere-velt (1567–1641), 1631. The best-known portrait of the internationalist, which has become canonical. This fine copy hangs in the refectory of the Academy and is on loan from the collection Gevers-van Marquette.

Hugo Grotius was born in Delft in 1583, the eldest son of an upper middle class regent. Matriculating in Leiden at twelve he soon proved himself a child prodigy. Taking general courses, which were philology and history mainly, he drew the attention of the eminent Justus Scaliger, reputedly the most learned man of his time in Europe. Though Hugo himself preferably indulged in his outspoken scholarly and literary leanings, Scaliger soon perceived the public officer and lawyer in him. Enrolled in the embassy of the States General to France, which vainly sought to prevent Henry IV's peace of Vervins with the Spanish in 1598, Grotius obtained a doctoral degree of law in Orleans.

Meanwhile the head of the embassy, the grand old man of Dutch politics, Johan van Oldenbarnevelt, had not failed to perceive the many gifts of the young "miracle de la Hollande". From then on Grotius – willy nilly at first, but soon captured by his own ambition – embarked on a career along distinct political lines under the aegis of Olden-barnevelt and with astonishing success at first. Some fifteen years later, however, from about 1613, and with Grotius generally appraised as the most feasible successor to Oldenbarnevelt as Grand Pensionary, his career was gradually wrecked by the religious quarrels which, having smouldered among theologians at Leiden for more than a decade, erupted as a social conflict with political overtones. Grotius long claimed an intermediary role in the conflict – with fatal results. At length, in the summer of 1618, Prince Maurice of

Orange, captain general of the Union's army, and backed by the uncompromising ministry and the social substratum, obtained the upperhand of the more broad-minded regent class headed by Oldenbarnevelt and Grotius. The first went to the scaffold and Grotius was only too fortunate to get away with a life-term imprisonment in the State prison, the grim Loevestein Castle. Within two years, after a spectacular escape by means of a book chest and with the help of his wife's intriguing genius, he found himself safe in Paris and on the King's pay-roll. With Maurice of Nassau succeeded by Grotius' university colleague Prince Frederik Henry in 1625, the exile gained new hope. At length, in 1631, ill-advised by well-meaning but politically naive friends he returned to Holland – only to find himself proscribed some months later. Broke und utterly depressed he fled to Germany, where he spent some gloomy years till, a true gift from heaven, the Swedish chancellor Oxenstierna offered him the embassy on behalf of Queen Christina in Paris. Here, however, in the centre of world politics and representing a military nation of the first order, for all his intellect and learning, he proved himself at a loss against the chicaneries of the Richelieus and Mazarins. Predictably, his moral code and legal genius rendered meagre results on this Macchiavellian stage. Ten years later, and anticipating his release, he resigned. On the eve of the Westphalian Conference which would take his masterwork of 1625, *De Jure Belli ac Pacis* as its guide, travelling back from Sweden with destination unknown, he was shipwrecked on the Pommeranian coast where he died from pneumonia, aged 62. It was a stormy life indeed – and not precisely a happy one either. There is plenty of tragedy and dis-illusion in both Grotius' public and private lives. Despite it all, however, his intellectual legacy has successfully withstood time. What are its main characteristics?

Grotius took his province very widely. In the course of fifty years he studied most of the *artes liberales* of his day. He is indeed the most consummate product of the "old learning", based on philology and including letters and rhetoric, philosophy and dialectics, history and law. Though his activities and publi-cations covered these fields throughout his life, a distinct rupture and switch of outlook is distinguishable in his years of imprisonment. Before, his literary and scholarly projects had no internal link except for their being prompted, in one way or another, by national feelings and being invited – if not biased – by official assignments. After Loevestein, an auto-nomous scholar is seen at work, engaged in the fulfilment of a well-set programme, operating in a truly inter-disciplinary manner and from a really international outlook. In this social programme, which presents itself in an

avalanche of books three elements are discernible, each meant to sublimate the others. These are the cultural, the religious and the political elements. Grotius' major concern, naturally, was matters of war: he lived in an age of war. However, Grotius' chief aims in launching his magnum opus *De Jure Belli ac Pacis* were not so much to banish war, which seemed preposterous at the time, as rather to regulate warfare and to establish a set of moral values and very practical rules to which the outbreak of hostilities, the waging of war itself and, finally, the concluding of peace had to be conditioned. Thus he discerned a "just war" – undertaken to defend one's territory and independence or applied as just an-other, though the ultimate means to en-force the opening of negotiations from one's foes – from a war of aggression. His second aim was to remove the most feasible causes of war – which in his day were the ecclesiastic schism and religious strife. He thereto initiated a scheme to reconcile the churches along Erasmian lines. These so-called "unionistic" efforts contained the drawing up of a credo on the base of early Patristic traditions which would be effectively acceptable to all Christian denominations and from which a new, truly "catholic", that is universal, church structure would emerge. The church system he had in mind closely resembled the Anglican High Church and, accordingly, it is from his works in this field (*De Veritate Religionis Christiana*, 1627; *Via ad Pacem*, 1642 and *Votum pro pace*, 1642), that Grotius was best known in Britain.

The third element, again closely related, was the harmonizing of the classical and Christian cultural traditions. Although many Hellenistic traditions and notions had been christianized, through the Middle Ages an undeniable tension if not conflict was maintained between the two worlds. The reapprais-al of the cultural ideals of the antique world by early humanists reactivated these slumbering issues. It was the ideal of men like Erasmus, Budé and Melanchton to reconcile these worlds and Grotius work was in accord with these ideas. They have been the main-stream of European culture till the second half of the 19th century, when romanticism gave short shrift to all former ideals and patterns. And this brings us to the reception of Grotius' works and tenets. Until then, Grotius was essentially known as a humanist. His correspondence and poetry, now virtually obsolete, were widely read for literary purposes. His now forgotten historical works – from which, inciden-tally, Grotius himself anticipated his everlasting fame! – were still authorita-tive and his theological works invar-iably invited sharp polemics.

All in all, the Grotian tradition is a complex area indeed which in fact has not been fully unearthed by modern scholarship.

prize competition by taking care of administrative affairs from The Hague. In the early forties, with typical foresight, he had his Grotius-bibliographies microfilmed and the library's treasures stored away in the basements underneath the front façade. And another proof of his clear-mindedness: in the war years he collected masses of duplicates which afterwards served the less fortunate librarians of bombed-out collections. The collection was liquidated in 1951 when vans could be seen leaving the gates, transporting piles of books to Germany.

Ter Meulen invariably displayed a marked resourcefulness. In the months immediately following the liberation in 1945 he was the first to solve the problem of obtaining foreign currency through the *Deviezen Instituut,* and tax and custom officials. Meanwhile, he managed to contact the Carnegie Endowment and secure a loan of $2,000, thus to procure recent American literature. Consequently, on 17 January 1946, the 100,000th publication was entered in the library's journal and in September of that year, again mainly thanks to ter Meulen, an exhibition of the American and British book production over 1939–1945 was opened in the Binnenhof. In that very month ter Meulen also concluded a contract with the Rockefeller Foundation stipulating a $30,000 donation over 1947–1951. When this contract had expired he successfully approached the Board of British Petroleum, Unilever and Philips for small donations.

Ter Meulen's resourcefulness must in fact have been inspiring, as witnessed by the following war-time incident. In the early days of May 1940, Miss Ada Belinfante, LLD, who had worked in the reading room since 1936, had disappeared without any previous notice. Not a word was heard of her until, shortly after the liberation in 1945, news of her whereabouts came in from London, where she proved to have been on the staff of the Department of Justice all those years ... meanwhile contacting librarians and antiquarians and collecting stores of books on behalf of ter Meulen. On hearing this, the latter ordered her to stay in England till the end of the year and purchase whatever was available of recent literature. There she proved extremely helpful indeed, if only in convincing the government official, Ir. Blaauw, whose duty it was to assemble books and periodicals for governmental institutions back in Holland, to put the Peace Palace Library on the distribution lists. Thus, in 1946, through the Royal Academy in Amsterdam, precious shipments of new acquisitions came in side by side with the many hundreds of books Miss Belinfante had collected of her own accord ... It was one of the few encouraging experiences from the war years, as may be gathered from our survey of the period in the chapter on the history of the Carnegie Foundation.

Apart from being competent, hard working and resourceful though, ter Meulen was an idealist with a warm heart for his employees. Several of his major works on the Peace Palace collection, among these the 1950 *Bibliographie,* were financed from his private means and the same holds good for the library's collection of maps, pictures and engravings. Even the book-case in which this collection was kept till 1987, came from his belongings. In Chapter X we have already had occasion to record his helping his colleagues with wheat and beans in the hunger winter of 1944–1945 when he himself lost most of his possessions in the RAF bombardments of the Bezuidenhout area. Less well-known, but recorded by Landheer and Diermanse in their "in memoriam" on ter Meulen's death in August 1962, is that this son of the landscape painter Fr. P. ter Meulen (who himself was married to a niece of the church painter Bosboom) left in the library, and its director's room in particular, some works of art. Among these are a flower still life by H. J. van der Weele, *Solomon's Judgment* after Rubens, a *Virgin and Child* after Tintoretto, a drawing of sheep by his father and a copy made after the portrait of Grotius that was at the time unearthed in a British collection and on display in the Palace for a year. Small wonder it is that after twenty-eight years the advertisements for the succession of such an authority failed to evoke a satisfying response. First announced on 24 March 1951, it would take a full year and a half before the proper man was found to reply.

Landheer (1952–1969)

A more complete change in style and outlook than that which occurred in the Peace Palace Librarianship in 1952 with the replacement of ter Meulen by Landheer is hardly thinkable. Interestingly enough, both men were as talented as they were versatile. Both were gifted with incredible energy and trained in consummate scholarship. But then, how totally different their characters and outlook were! Whereas to ter Meulen, in a way, the very premises were the limit of his horizon, Landheer's province was the world. Had ter Meulen focussed on internal structures, Landheer was if anything the expansionist. Never was the institution better organized than with ter Meulen, but never was the name of the library better known abroad, be it Europe, Asia or America, than during Landheer's term of office. Meanwhile, in 1952, to those men and women who had worked with ter Meulen for so many years, it must have been as if a hurricane were visiting the Palace.

A sociologist by education and a pupil of Othmar Spann (1878–1950) of Vienna, Bart Landheer, after a prolonged stay in the United States, had become one of the leading advocates of European integration. From this resulted a proposal submitted to the Council of Europe on 30 April 1953 that led to the founding of the *European Yearbook.* Headed by men like Pisanelli, Léon Marchal, Sørensen and Lord Layton it had Landheer and his friend Robinson as joint editors and Landheer's own Peace Palace Library as secretary and documentation centre for many years to come. Landheer enjoyed every minute of it and never got weary initiating new projects.

The *T. M. C. Asser Instituut* was founded in 1965 by the Dutch universities offering courses in international law. The aim of the Institute is to promote education and research in the fields of Private International Law, Public International Law, including the Law of International Organizations, Law of the European Communities, and International Commercial Arbitration.

Professor Bart Landheer (librarian 1952–1969) attending the opening of the exhibition commemorating the fiftieth birthday of the Palace in 1963. To his left Professor François, the long serving Secretary to the Board of the Carnegie Foundation.

J. B. van Hall (1969–1980).

He was an active member of the *Société Européenne de Culture,* contacted the Schumann Court at Luxembourg in matters of library research, and was kept permanently occupied either discussing a "Sociology of War"-project with Unesco or raising funds from the United Nations to relaunch the Peace Palace printed catalogues. He created a series of *Selective Bibliographies of the Peace Palace Library* in which topical issues in the international field were covered, and through his successive deputies van Essen and Korevaar launched the well-known "Selective Surveys of Literature on Public and Private International Law" in the Dutch leading journal in the field (NILR).

Again, in January 1954 he organized a meeting with leading Dutch internationalists such as van Asbeck, Röling, Tammes, Mrs. van der Molen, Verzijl and François to found the Netherlands International Law Research Committee (which was soon taken over by the Hague Academy). He was a master in fund raising, and actually was the only one ever to talk the Carnegie Foundation into drastically increasing the yearly budgets. Meanwhile, through the years, he published scores of books (*Mind and Society,* 1952; *Pause for Transition,* 1957; *Social Functions of Libraries,* 1957), his latest work being *Europa, noodlot en identiteit,* 1984. He also published a novel (*The Pawn,* 1947) and numerous articles in leading journals and magazines.

He lectured repeatedly at the Hague Academy, and in 1962 became a Groningen Professor of Sociology of International Relations. And imagine, alongside all this the retired ter Meulen kept frequenting the Palace for a full decade, labouring on his Grotian studies till the end. And even then Diermanse continued, with Landheer's full support, to rubricate new acquisitions and organize Grotius conferences and exhibitions such as the ones in Paris in 1963 and 1965. Landheer's many interests invited lengthy journeys. He always showed keen interest in India's society and cultural traditions. In 1959, on Nehru's personal invitation he went over to lecture on integration and international relations at Delhi. Here he met Radhakrishnan. He was on the Pugwash Commission and lectured extensively on Gandhi. Other journeys included visiting professorships at Polish and American universities.

Halfway through his term, in 1961–1962, Landheer evaluated the state of his library. His major conclusion was, sadly enough, that for all its treasures and the publicity made there was still a disquieting discrepancy between the quality of the collection and the frequency of consultation. Services were too meagre to serve the outside world. As he saw it, what was badly needed were more funds and (ironically) more outside contacts, such as with the German *Max Planck Institut* and the London Institute of Advanced Legal Studies. He also insisted on the expansion in the field of foreign municipal law. These conclusions of Landheer are noteworthy here because as we saw they concern one of the fundamental problems of the institution through the decades and because it was on this problem that Landheer's successor van Hall would focus as he took over in 1969 ... to reach very different conclusions indeed.

Van Hall (1969–1980)

Drs. J. B. van Hall was a librarian in the strictest sense. If, by way of speaking, for Landheer the universe itself at times seemed too tiny a stage, van Hall's entire world was the catalogue room. Consequently, with him all activities and most of the contacts of the library staff in the scholarly world of international law, sociology and polemology broke down abruptly. In their place, however, came the renewed attention to inner structures, the service apparatus, managing efficiency and accessibility of the collection. It was indeed time to reconsider the internal organization of the library. As successful Landheer may have been in his outer contacts, towards the end of his term it had become increasingly manifest that his main interest and competence lay not in the strict sphere of library management. Complaints about the acquisition policy invited the Board to the installation, in 1954, of a supervisory board for the library, which has been operative ever since. There was another thing which soon struck the new librarian, van Hall. Within a year it became obvious to him that the very ambition, the aiming for perfection and universality within the library had with the years become its major handicap, which in the end would lead to utter ruin. What he found were ten separate catalogues, many personal idiosyncrasies of staff members and innumerable shady house rules maintained for the sake of tradition only, though increasingly hampering the system and the institution's compatibility with current library thought. Lending statistics proved that, for all the seeming expansion, nothing much had changed in over twenty years: the number was invariably 6,500 in 1948 and 1968. The library staff, he felt, were spending a lot of time on discharging outdated and none too relevant duties that went at the cost of public service. The results were 120 shelf metres of gifts as yet uncatalogued, a perfectly impenetrable catalogue room and a most intricate administration.

The task van Hall set himself was pretty obvious: reorganization. His ideas were sound and he certainly did not lack the energy. However, major obstacles soon presented themselves. First and foremost the funds. Although the requests of the librarian were neither extravagant nor unreasonable, the Carnegie Foundation simply was in no position to provide the means. Neither the ones requested to create new storage rooms and get rid of the damp cellars and frosty ceilings – in which storehouse clerks had created a true *Geheimwissenschaft,* as he put it once with typical jest –, nor the ones to modernize catalogues and reading rooms. And if for once funds were available, all sorts of practical obstacles presented themselves, often resulting from the shortage of room all over the Palace. Whereas the sharp increase of library loans in the early seventies made mechanization of the apparatus imperative, already the initial costs of such an operation were absolutely prohibitive. There was indeed much to complain of in the librarian's yearly reports.

However frustrating, in the longer perspective these obstacles proved a blessing in disguise. They postponed the introduction of systems that would have been outdated the very year of their introduction. For fundamentally new problems came to the fore in the later seventies with the entrance of the information technology, featuring fully automated administration systems, on-line catalogue networks and databanks. One may safely say that, ironically, van Hall's term was a success both for what was done and what was left undone.

Major feats were the reorganization of the systematic and keyword catalogues, the streamlining of the overall system from acquisition to classification and storing, and the replacing of rare book collections in climatized storage rooms. Major innovations, indeed substantial at the time though probably not in the long run, were the introduction of steel drawers of catalogue cards, the introduction of microfiche-collections and readers, of "flexowriters" and of copying machines. The atmosphere of these years was characterized with a perfect blend of warmth and irony in the short stories of the writer Maarten Biesheuvel, who was a one-time reading room assistant. When in 1980 van Hall handed over the torch to Schalekamp, coffee machines hung in rooms illuminated by tubelights and the Palace gardeners had gratefully accepted as seedboxes the dozens of wooden drawers that had for over fifty years sheltered the illustrious names of thousands of international lawyers.

Schalekamp (1980–)

As we have observed before, a change of librarian cannot fail to result in a switch of outlook and priorities. The same occurred, predictably, with the arrival of Drs. J. C. Schalekamp in 1980. With his business and management background, the new director could not help being struck by the somewhat bizarre financial and management structures of the non-profit organization. It was a distressing report in many respects that he submitted to the Board in 1981. The absence both of proper internal communications and of external relations, be these in the academic or library world, seemed alarming. Many years of isolation, however understandable from shortage of funds and personnel, had not exactly improved the library's position in the field. Otherwise, Schalekamp fell in with van Hall's observation that the former librarians' ambitions to cover the whole area of national and international law had been perfectly utopian in view of the financial structure. If the library were to survive as a first rank documentary centre, it must need to concentrate on the nucleus of its collection and its primary aims, to wit international law proper. Analysing budgets and statistics and faced with ever more drastic governmental curtailing of funds on the one hand and rapid increase of costs on the other, he therefore gave short shrift to some time-honoured traditions.

But even so, acquiescence would be fatal, Schalekamp felt. What was badly needed was the active publicizing of the library's treasures and its unique status, the adjusting of the library's policy to current social developments, and the tapping of alternative sources of income. Thus, the expansion of international commercial law and the extension of contacts abroad of the major Dutch law offices opened new fields, he perceived. These, however, called for changes in the library's orientation.

The first major result of Schalekamp's efforts in this area came in 1982 with the establishing of the *Stichting tot Steun aan de Bibliotheek van het Vredespaleis* (Foundation in Support of the Peace Palace Library), initiated by the time-honoured Board member of the Carnegie Foundation, Mr. C. R. C. Wijckerheld Bisdom and Professor Sanders of Rotterdam University. Yearly financial injections on the part of these firms now enable the library to procure literature in the field of foreign municipal law which these firms need. Meanwhile, new contacts were laid by the staff's acceptance of functions in the academic and library worlds, and by its coordination of Dutch juridical collections. Similarly, exhibitions such as the one on Grotius helped propagate the library's name and so did a series of minor publications. Meanwhile, the staff was spoonfed with modern art decorating the walls.

Two other noteworthy processes were initiated in the past lustrum. First automation of the library and the adapting of the national Pica-project to facilitate the consulting and lending operations between academic libraries. In the best of Carnegian traditions, through the Board of the Carnegie Foundation, financial means were secured from private funds to realize this process. Consequently, from 1984 onwards new acquisitions can be consulted on-line. Automation also helped the library to publish a four-monthly series of Acquisitions, the first to appear in over twenty years.

The second achievement, and a capital one indeed in view of the continuing economizing tendencies, is the newly acquired status of the library as

The author Maarten Biesheuvel (born 1939) consulting the catalogue. Distemper by Charlotte Mutsaers, 1980. Biesheuvel was on the staff of the Peace Palace Library for a couple of years.

the nation's main centre and pivotal collection in the field of international and foreign municipal law. It is to be hoped that at length this otherwise fully justified qualification of the collection as the principal one in the land will help provide the substantial means that are required to maintain the library's traditional high standards.

Perspective

The story of the Peace Palace Library, as transpires from the above, is one of continuous struggle by librarians desperately trying to adjust the lofty ideals of the founding fathers to the modest means they were confronted with in reality. The yearly reports over the past sixty years invariably cry for storage room, personnel and technical facilities. Given the widely differing qualifications of these men, these cries for help obviously are no mere phrases. The very resourcefulness they applied in coping with backward conditions and shortage of means only testifies to their deep concern. One wonders, indeed, what achievements might have been accomplished by these men had they not been preoccupied with the all too basic issues of mere survival. In as far as they were of the optimistic or rather pessimistic kind, they alternatively looked upon expansion or concentration as the final solution to their dilemma. Curtailing of services would render any further exertions superfluous, extension of services would end up in wrecking the internal organization. At length, after endless nights of turning and tossing, on their final leave they all took home with them those distressing thoughts of ideals near at hand but never materialized.

So much for sure, the idea of the "World Library of International Law" in which men such as de Martens, White and Holls indulged, has remained a dream forever. But even so, and setting its sails to the winds, the Peace Palace Library has, for many decades, successfully faced the challenge to be a beacon to man in the area of international life.

In 1986 the Dalai Lama visited the Peace Palace Library and was shown around by the current librarian J. C. Schalekamp (1980–).

Unfortunately, however, the tide is falling and it is this process which invites a final critical remark on our part. Of recent years, an alarming tendency is to be noted, which in the end might well endanger any reputation the library has made for itself in past decades. The disquieting thing to the present staff – signalled repeatedly by the present chief librarian in his yearly reports – is that, owing to the lack of finances, the library is rapidly losing ground, and is now on the brink of definitely relinquishing its pivotal function in the field.

Ironically enough, this development has become increasingly manifest because of the extraordinary increase in the activities in the past years. Since 1980 lending services have tripled and the overall outside activities have seen a comparable increase. One may say that the library is performing presently in accordance with the wishes of the previous librarians. It seems also that the challenge met by the staff and the reputation of the collection have finally borne fruit in inviting scholars and students to benefit from Carnegie's Temple.

However, and here the shoe pinches, these gladdening facts sharply contrast with the current budget. It is somehow embarrassing that a collection which features eight times more serial works, six times more books and twice as many specialized periodicals in the field as any other similar collection in the Netherlands, is at present surviving with a far lower budget than that of many university centres of international law. It takes little clairvoyance to realize that we find ourselves at a crossroad whereby, if nothing is done to correct this anomaly, we shall witness in the near future a gradual process of obsoleteness which will nullify all previous efforts.

Since 1904, the Dutch State has undertaken the careful updating of the library on behalf of the Court of Arbitration – a formal pledge which was solemnly renewed in 1946 for the benefit of both Hague Courts. As late as 1987, the quality of the collection was such that the Dutch Ministry of Education acknowledged the Peace Palace Library as the National Collection of International Law.

Every year, hundreds of students from abroad proceed to the Hague Academy in order to enrich their already acquired knowledge, update their records, and interchange ideas in their daily contacts with both tutors and colleagues. They return home with an enriched experience. Many of these Academy students come from the Third World and the knowledge they gain here can be an important asset for the future of their own countries. Thus, the Peace Palace Library makes a not inconsiderable contribution to the development process.

The present position of both Courts in the Peace Palace is not under threat. Their smooth and efficient working, however, will also depend a great deal on the functioning of one of their main tools – the library. It is therefore essential that the quality and efficiency of the work of the library is maintained at a high level so that the Peace Palace remains not only a Residence for Justice but also a Domicile of Learning.

Bibliographical Note

The gist of the tale told in this book is based on archive material and unofficial sources. First of all on the files of the Carnegie Foundation, the minutes of Board meetings and the yearly reports of librarians. I have also drawn extensively on the files of the Dutch Foreign Office regarding the Hague Peace Conferences and the early years of the Carnegie Foundation, on the Cabinet's minutes protocols, on the private archives of W. H. de Beaufort and T. M. C. Asser; these are all kept in the *Algemeen Rijksarchief* at The Hague. Minor private archives, journals and illustrated weeklies from home and abroad have proven a valuable additional source. The only printed comprehensive history of the Peace Palace up till now is A. Lysen, *History of the Carnegie Foundation and of the Peace Palace at The Hague,* Leiden, 1934 [*Bibliotheca Visseriana* XI (vol. 28)], a competent report which was extracted and continued in a short mimeographic survey by J. Scherpenhuyzen in 1943. A succinct list of additional literature on the separate chapters is given below. An exhaustive bibliography is to be prepared by the Peace Palace Library this year. In view of the limited space I have here discarded all references to literature on the overall socio-political context of the era in question. An attractive survey for the general reader is given by Barbara W. Tuchman in *The Proud Tower* (1966).

Chapter I: On the history of the peace movement see for instance Q. Wright, *A Study of War,* Chicago (1965) and the extensive bibliography in the *Peace Encyclopedia* (ed. Linus Pauling), 4 vols., Oxford *etc.* 1986, in particular the *Introduction* by P. v.d. Dungen.
Chapters II and VII: The official texts in English of the Hague Peace Conferences of 1899 and 1907 are to be found in *The Proceedings of the Hague Peace Conferences,* edited by James Brown Scott (2 vols., New York 1920–1921). Scott also compiled a competent survey of the Hague proceedings in *The Hague Peace Conferences of 1899 and 1907,* 2 vols., Baltimore 1909 and *The Reports of the Hague Conferences of 1899 and 1907,* Oxfort 1917. See also the official documents of the British Foreign Office, the German "Auswärtigen Amt", the French "Ministère des affaires étrangères" and the like. Several delegates recorded their impressions in comprehensive monographs and biographical notes. See *e.g.* J. H. Choate, *The Two Hague Conferences,* Princeton-Oxford 1913; John Hay / Elihu Root, *Instructions to the American Delegates to the Hague Conferences 1899 and 1907,* Boston 1913; W. I. Hull, *The Two Hague Conferences,* Boston 1908; A. Pearce Higgins, *The Hague Peace Conferences,* Cambridge 1909, Louis Renault, *L'Oeuvre de la Haye en 1899 et en 1907,* Stockholm 1908 and id., *Les Deux Conférences de la Paix, 1899 et 1907,* Paris 1909; Bertha von Suttner, *Memoirs,* 2 vols., Boston 1910; Hans Wehberg, *Die Abkommen der Haager Friedenzkonferenzen,* Berlin 1910; A . D. White, *Autobiography,* 2 vols., New York 1905; Philipp Zorn, *Deutschland und die beiden Haager Friedenskonferenzen,* Stuttgart-Berlin 1920; finally, B. von Bülow, *Memoirs,* 4 vols., Boston 1913–1932.
Noteworthy reports of the 1899 Conference alone were made by Alfred H. Fried, *Die Haager Conferenz, ihre Bedeutung und ihre Ergebnisse,* Berlin 1900; Frederick W. Holls, *The Peace Conference at The Hague,* New York 1914; M. Riza Khan [Daniche], *Echos de la Conférence de La Haye,* Constantinople 1903; R. Lüthi, *Die Europäischen Kleinstaten und die Haager Friedenskonferenz von 1899,* Winterthur 1954; F. de Martens, *La Conférence de la Paix à La Haye,* Paris 1900; A Mérignhac, *La Conférence International de la Paix,* Paris 1900; Chr. Meurer, *Des Friedensrecht der Haager Konferenz,* München 1905; id., *Das Kriegsrecht der Haager Konferenz,* München 1907; G. H. Perris, W. T. Stead a.o., *A History of the Peace Conference at The Hague,* Londen 1899; W. T. Stead, *The Parliament of Peace and its Members,* London 1899; id., *La Chronique de la Conférence de La Haye 1899,* The Hague 1901; Bertha Suttner, *Die Haager Friedensconferenz, Tagebuchblätter von –,* Dresden-Leipzig 1901.
Competent surveys of the 1907 Conference are Sir Thomas Barclay, *The Second Hague Conference,* London 1906; *La Segunda Conferenzia de la Paz,* A. S. de Bustamante y Sirvén, Madrid 1908; Alfred H. Fried, *Die Zweite Haager Konferenz,* Leipzig 1907, H. La Fontaine, *La conférence de la paix,* Bruxelles 1908; Ernest Lémonon, *La seconde conférence de la paix,* Paris 1912; Otfried Nippold, *Die zweite Haager Friedenskonferenz,* 2 vols., Leipzig 1908; W. Stead (ed.), *Le courrier de la conférence de la paix,* Amsterdam-Leipzig 1907; *Le Parlement de l'Humanité* (biographies and photographs), Amsterdam-Leipzig 1907. On the planned third conference see: Emile Arnaud, *La troisième conférence de la paix,* Berne 1913; F. Herbert Stead, *To Abolish War at the Third Hague Conference,* Letchworth 1916.
Chapter III: Most of the text on Andrew Carnegie is drawn from his *Authobiography,* New York 1932 and collected works (10 vols., New York 1933). I have also drawn on the authoritative Burton J. Hendrick, *The Life of Andrew Carnegie,* 2 vols, New York 1932, on W. Stead, *Mr. Carnegie's Conundrum; £ 40,000,000: what shall I do with it?,* London 1900 (*Review of Reviews*) and the colourful pastiche in Ian Campbell Bradley, *Enlightened Entrepreneurs,* London 1987. A competent survey of the history and present state of the various Carnegie Foundations and Institutions is found in Simon Goodenough, *The Greatest Good Fortune, Andrew Carnegie's Gift for Today,* Edinburgh 1985. See also Larry L. Fabian, *Andrew Carnegie's Peace Endowment, The Tycoon, The President, and Their Bargain of 1910,* Washington 1985.
Chapters IV–VI: On de Martens, Holls, Stead and White, the main characters instrumental in the founding of the Peace Palace, see E. de Melville [– H. C. G. J. van der Mandere], *Frederic von Martens,* Haarlem 1912; A. D. White, *Autobiography,* 2 vols., New York 1914, id. "Zur Vorgeschichte des Haager Friedenspalastes", in *Die Friedens-Warte XV* (1913), p. 281 ff.; Stead's sketches in *The Review of Reviews* of May and June 1912; Frederic White, *Life of W. T. Stead,* London 1925. The text of the Foundation Deed is found in Lysen. On the selection of the site see *Judgments of the Dutch experts on the location of the Peace Palace in "Zorgvliet",* 1905. On the prize-competiton see the *Programme du concours,* The Hague 1905; the catalogue *Concours pour le projet du Palais de la Paix,* The Hague 1906; the lavishly illustrated *Internationale prijsvraag der Carnegie-Stichting – Concours international de la Fondation-Carnegie,* The Hague-Paris 1906; on the comments see [De Bazel, Berlage a.o.], *Adres aan de Tweede Kamer...,* Amsterdam 1907 On de Bazel see A. W. Reinink, *K. P. C. de Bazel-Architect,* Amsterdam 1965.
Chapter VIII–X: Over the years the Carnegie Foundation has issued numerous brochures and pamphlets on the history of the Palace and Institutions (M. J. van der Flier, 1913; A. C. Jager, 1914, C. H. de Boer 1948, 1952, 1954, and anonymous ones from 1962 onwards). The first comprehensive work was J. Jurriaan Kok, *Het Vredespaleis,* The Hague 1909. In 1913, on the occasion of the opening, a volume of pastiches was published in French and Dutch by the society "Vrede door Recht"; *Het Vredespaleis: gedenkboek / Le Palais de la Paix: mémoire,* The Hague 1913. In 1920 a lavishly illustrated issue of great documentary value was published by the architect J. A. G. van der Steur: *Het Vredespaleis,* Rotterdan 1920. It seems no monograph on the French architect Louis M. Cordonnier was ever written. On the layout of the gardens see T. A. Mawson's autobiography, London 1927.
Chapter XI: On the history of arbitration see J. H. Ralston, *International Arbitration from Athens to Locarno,* London 1929; H. J. Schlochauer, *Die Idee des ewigen Friedens,* Bonn 1953; M. de Taube, "Les orgines", in *Recueil des cours,* vol. 42 (1932.4). A survey of cases is found in A. M. Stuyt, *Survey of International Arbitration 1794–1970,* Leiden 1972. On the proceedings of the Court see the annual reports of the Administrative Council (*Rapport du Conseil* 1901–); J. W. Foster, *Arbitration and the Hague Court,* New York 1904; J. P. A. François, "La Cour Permanente d'Arbitrage", in *Recueil des cours,* 87 (1955.1); M. O. Hudson, "The Permanent Court of Arbitration", in *American Journal of International Law* 27 (1933); E. de Melville, *L'oeuvre de la Haye (1871–1921),* Leiden 1924.
Chapter XII: On the Permanent Court of International Justice see Manley O. Hudson, *The PCIJ 1920–1942, A Treatise,* New York-London 1972 (reprint of the 1943 edition) and H. Ch. G. J. van der Mandere, *Het PHIJ te 's-Gravenhage,* Leiden 1922. On the Ferdinand Bol Room see Albert Blankert, *Ferdinant Bol 1615–1680,* Utrecht 1976; J. J. M. Timmers, *Gérard Lairesse,* Amsterdam 1942; D. P. Snoep, "G. Lairesse als plafond- en kamerschilder", in *Bulletin Rijksmuseum* 18 (1970). On the International Court of Justice see Sir Gerald Fitzmaurice, *The Law and Procedure of the ICJ,* Cambridge 1986; Leo Gross (ed.), *The Future of the ICJ,* New York 1976; Geneviève Guyomar, *Commentaire du règlement de la CIJ adopté le 14 Avril 1978, interprétation et pratique,* Paris 1983; Hersch Lauterpacht, *The Development of Interational Law by the ICJ,* Cambridge 1982; Shabtai Rosenna, *The World Court; what it is and how it works,* Leiden-Dobbs Ferry 1973; id., *The Law and Practice of the International Court,* Leiden 1965; J. H. W. Verzijl, *The Jurisprudence of the World Court, vol. 1: the PCIJ, 1922–1940,* Leiden 1965; H. Wehberg / H. W. Goldschmidt, *Der IGH, Entstehungsgeschichte, Analyse, Dokumentation,* Leiden 1973.
Chapter XIII: On the idea of the Academy see Franz Kemény, *Entwurf einer Internationalen Gesammt-Academie: Weltacademie,* Dresden-Leipzig-Wien 1901. A comprehensive survey of the Hague Academy is found in the *Livre Jubilaire / Jubilee Book 1923–1973,* edited by R. J. Dupuy (Leiden 1973). Recent data are best found in the yearly reports (*Annuaires*). All lectures and seminars are found in the *Recueil des cours / Collected Courses* (206 vols., Leiden 1923–1987). On the *Association* see Frits W. Hondius, *The A.A.A., A Forty Years' History, 1923–1963,* The Hague 1964.
Chapter XIV: A survey of the early years (1913–1933) is found in the reports of P. C. Molhuysen and J. ter Meulen in the yearbook *Grotius: annuaire international* over the years 1918, 1925–1927, 1930, 1933. In 1938 a brochure was issued *Bibliothèque du palais de la paix, centre de documentation / Library of the Peace Palace, Documentation Centre,* Leiden 1938. On the catalogues see P. J. J. Diermanse, "De platencatalogus", in *Bibliotheekleven,* October 1942 and J. D. Korevaar, "De trefwoorden-catalogus", in *Bibliotheekleven,* November 1964.

Acknowledgments

This book was written by one author and therefore is his responsibility alone. But whoever has tried his hand at an undertaking of the kind will appreciate the indebtedness of the present author to the many who in differing qualities and varying degrees have been instrumental in its accomplishment. In preparing this book I availed myself of the willingness of numerous institutions and the warm support and extensive learning of many friends and colleagues.
First of all I acknowlegde my indebtedness to the Board and Director of the Dutch *Carnegie Stichting* for commissioning me to prepare this history of its Foundation. To the Registrar of the International Court of Justice, Mr. Valencia-Ospina, and the Director of the Peace Palace Library, Mr. Schalekamp, I feel obliged for their readiness in allowing part of the research being carried out during working hours. The book was written mainly at home though, near to those on whose unvarying indulgence I had to make yet another call.
A very special word of thanks also goes to Mr. Geoff Anderson, formerly of the Registry of the International Court of Justice, who helped with the text. Making short shrift of numerous idiosyncrasies he saved the book from many a *non liquet.* Co-operating with him was a pleasure. This book contains as much of a legal and international character as it draws from the spheres of the arts, letters and history. One cannot be a master of all weapons.
I therefore feel relieved that my manuscript was scrutinized by three good friends, each in her or his own competence: Mrs. F. Bouricius, Dr. J. van der Hoeven and Drs. Chr. van Koppen. In the course of my quest for primary sources I was at times baffled by the inaccessibility of the collections. In those moments I felt blessed with the competent and stimulating help of Miss Neline Koornneef and Mr. D. Lugthart, who were also instrumental in the collecting of the illustrations.
In the archives, libraries and institutions which I have consulted, I often met with warm response from officials whose intimate knowledge of collections was essential to the success of my research. Thus I feel grateful to Mr. Derek Barclay of the Carnegie Dunfermline Trust in Scotland, Mr. S. Plantinga of the Hague *Rijksarchief,* Mrs. Dekkers of the *Koninklijk Huisarchief* and Mrs. Hilberts and Mr. van Etten of the *Rijksvoorlichtingsdienst.* Likewise I feel indebted to the Dutch Foreign Office, the Hague and Delft Municipal Archives and the Hague Royal Library.
The production of a luxury edition as the present one is a feast in itself. In the past year I have felt privileged being surrounded by such skilled experts as Chris van Koppen and Dorine Mobron, Loek de Leeuw, Joop de Nijs and Peter Sasburg and above all Jan den Hengst, the brilliant photographer who gave me the opportunity to look at the Peace Palace in a complete new perspective.

ARTHUR EYFFINGER

Index

Italicized numbers only refer to captions